MANUFACTURING TECHNOLOGY

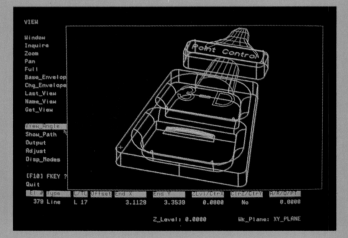

MANUFACTURING TECHNOLOGY

STANLEY A. KOMACEK
Department of Industry and Technology
California University of Pennsylvania

ANN E. LAWSON

ANDREW C. HORTON
Department of Industrial Studies
St. Cloud State University

Glencoe
McGraw-Hill

New York, New York   Columbus, Ohio   Woodland Hills, California   Peoria, Illinois

Formerly published by Delmar Publishers Inc.®

NOTICE TO THE READER

COVER CREDITS: Top left, copyright Comstock Inc.; bottom left, courtesy of Cincinnati Milacron Inc. (safety equipment may have been removed or opened to clearly illustrate the product and must be in place prior to operation); top right and bottom right, courtesy of Point Control Co.

Glencoe/McGraw-Hill

A Division of The McGraw-Hill Companies

Copyright © 1990 by Delmar Publishers Inc. **Copyright transferred in 1997 to Glencoe/McGraw-Hill.** All rights reserved. Except as permitted under the United States Copyright Act, no part of this publication may be reproduced or distributed in any form or by any means, or stored in a database or retrieval system, without prior written permission from the publisher.

Send all inquiries to:
Glencoe/McGraw-Hill
3008 W. Willow Knolls Drive
Peoria, IL 61614

ISBN 0-8273-3462-1

Printed in the United States of America

3 4 5 6 7 8 9 10   003/055   01 00

89–38857
CIP

CONTENTS

Courtesy of Allegheny Ludlum Corporation

SECTION THREE ————
MANUFACTURING PROCESSES 201

Courtesy of Aluminum Company of America

SECTION FOUR
MANUFACTURING OUTPUTS   313

*Courtesy of Sears, Roebuck and Co., 1987
Annual Report*

SECTION FIVE
MANUFACTURING IMPACTS   343

Courtesy of NASA

PREFACE

Manufacturing technology is central to the way we live. Without manufactured goods, our lifestyles would be radically different. Modern manufacturing technology makes possible the buses, cars, and bicycles we use everyday to go to school or to work. Telephones, televisions, radios, computers, even the paper that this book is printed on, would not exist without manufacturing technology. The electricity that lights our homes, as well as most of the materials used to construct our homes, would not be available without the products made by manufacturing. Manufacturing technology affects almost every aspect of our lives and of people's lives around the world.

Manufacturing: A Systems Approach

Manufacturing technology is a system of technology. One way to study technological systems is with the systems approach. This approach involves studying the inputs, processes, and outputs that are part of the system.

The systems approach is used in this book to study manufacturing technology. The main sections of the book focus on the following:

- **inputs** people, materials, tools and machines, energy, information, safety, finances, and time;
- **processes** design engineering, production engineering, organization and management, materials processing, marketing, and accounting;
and
- **outputs** manufactured goods, scrap, waste, and pollution.

Even though this text uses the systems approach to study manufacturing, you should keep in mind that manufacturing does not always happen in a perfect input-process-output order. Your teacher may ask you to read chapters out of order, and with a good reason. Manufacturing is a complex system and can be studied in many ways. The chapters in this book can be used in almost any order your teacher chooses.

Manufacturing is Making Products

Manufacturing technology is using tools, materials, and processes to make products. For this reason, the study of manufacturing technology should take a hands-on approach. This text will help you learn how to use tools and machines safely and efficiently to manufacture products.

The chapters in this book that discuss the actual "doing" of manufacturing are the chapters in Section Three on processes. Most of your studying will focus on these chapters.

Of course, in order to fully understand manufacturing technology, you must also study the inputs and outputs of manufacturing. Some of these chapters also include hands-on activities in which you will use tools and machines to process materials. But in several other chapters, you will study manufacturing by using minds-on activities.

Technology is changing the way people work in manufacturing. Today and in the future, more manufacturing jobs will call for workers with both mental skills (using mental tools and your mind) and technical skills (using technical tools and your hands).

Manufacturing Technology includes a balance of hands-on and minds-on learning activities.

The Impacts/Feedback of Manufacturing

Your study of manufacturing using the systems approach will not be complete if you do not learn about the impacts and feedback of manufacturing. We struggle with some very serious social and environmental problems today, and many of these problems have resulted in part from manufacturing technology. Unemployment, job dissatisfaction, and dangerous work situations are some of the problems that workers face. Overpriced and low-quality products and poor product safety are issues we all face as consumers. The environmental problems of air, water, and soil pollution, the greenhouse effect, and ozone depletion can all be traced in some way to manufacturing. The importance of understanding the technologies of manufacturing systems and their impacts can not be over-stressed. Many chapters in this book discuss the impacts of manufacturing on people and our natural environment.

Special Features

Manufacturing Technology uses a number of special features, including:

Key Terms. Listed at the beginning of each chapter, these important terms and phrases are highlighted within the text.

Boxed Articles. These are short stories of interesting or unusual information related to the chapter's subject.

Photographs and Illustrations. There are hundreds of color photos, illustrations, and line drawings that will help you understand the important parts of manufacturing.

Summary. The key points of each chapter are summarized.

Discussion Questions. These questions stress critical thinking and problem-solving skills.

Chapter Activities. Hands-on and/or minds-on activities are included in all chapters.

Your Classroom Manufacturing Experience. This section summarizes some of the more important chapters and includes several plans for products that you and your classmates can manufacture.

Glossary. A complete glossary of terms with definitions is included as an appendix to help you study.

Technology Student Association. A special section describes the Technology Student Association and its manufacturing-related activities.

Acknowledgments

The authors wish to express their deep appreciation to Dr. Leonard A. Colelli of Fairmont State College, Fairmont, West Virginia, for his contribution of Chapter 15, Processing Materials.

The authors also wish to thank Sonya Stang and Brent Miller of St. Cloud University, St. Cloud, Minnesota, for their assistance in gathering and taking many of the pictures appearing in the book.

The following individuals reviewed the manuscript and offered their suggestions for improvement. Their assistance is appreciated.

Steven H. McBride
Martin High School
Arlington, Texas

Terry Salmans
Pittsburg High School
Pittsburg, Kansas

Peter Tucker
Highland High School
Highland, Illinois

Kathleen Barrows
Clinton High School
Clinton, North Carolina

James E. LaPorte
Virginia Polytechnic
   Institute
Blacksburg, Virginia

Thomas Curtis
Glenoak West High School
Canton, Ohio

Raymond Romblom
Edgerton Senior High School
Edgerton, Wisconsin

Michael G. Mattson
Minneapolis Public Schools
Minneapolis, Minnesota

David Carl
Minot High School
Minot, North Dakota

Chapter Activities

Leonard A. Colelli
Fairmont State College
Fairmont, West Virginia

Automating Processes with Fluid Power Systems

Henry Harms
Great Hollow Jr. High School
Nesconset, New York

Hydraulically Controlled Robotic Arm; Package Design; Acid Rain

George McCartney
Westfield High School
Westfield, Wisconsin

Expandable Bead Molding; Cold Casting

Jerry Murphy
Gardiner, Montana

Surveying the Market

Fred Posthuma
Westfield High School
Westfield, Wisconsin

Re-Use It

Neal Swernofsky
Lincoln-Orens Jr. High School
Island Park, New York

Manufacturing Health Care Products

Product Plans

Leonard A. Colelli
Fairmont State College
Fairmont, West Virginia

Drafting Table

Larry Davis
Morgantown High School
Morgantown, West Virginia

Mantel Clock; School Clock

Mike Hardy
Oil City High School
Oil City, Pennsylvania

Lap Desk

Albert Komacek
Brownsville High School
Brownsville, Pennsylvania

Small Tool Box; Planter Box; Plant Stand; Scroll Name Sign; Name Sign Post; Sheet Metal Box and Top

Mark Nowak
California University of Pennsylvania
California, Pennsylvania

Memo Minder; Lounge Chair; Off-road Truck; Sleigh Centerpiece; Folding Table; Filing Box; Kitchen Canister; Bread Box

About the Authors

Dr. Stanley Komacek is a veteran of six years teaching technology education, including three years serving as a technology education curriculum assistant. He currently teaches technology education at California University of Pennsylvania. Dr. Komacek holds an Ed.D. degree from West Virginia University, an M.Ed. from Miami University, and a B.S. degree from California University of Pennsylvania.

Ann E. Lawson has been involved in the technology education field as a student, research assistant, and teacher. She received her B.S. degree from the State University of New York at Oswego, her M.S. degree from Eastern Illinois University, and completed additional graduate work at West Virginia University. After teaching technology education for three years in public school, she spent a year teaching in the Republic of China at the National Kaohsiung Institute of Technology. In addition to this text, Ms. Lawson has contributed to and co-authored several other texts, books, and technology resource materials.

Andrew Horton received his B.S. degree in the Department of Industrial Arts and Technology at the State University of New York at Oswego, an M.S. degree in the Technology Education Department at Eastern Illinois University, and a Ph.D. in the Technology Education Program at West Virginia University. He has contributed to and co-authored numerous publications in the technology field and presented papers at various conferences related mostly to design education, appropriate technology, and environmental issues. Since returning from a year teaching design-related courses in the Department of Mechanical Engineering at the National Kaohsiung Institute of Technology, Republic of China, he has assumed a faculty position at St. Cloud State University in the Department of Industrial Studies.

SECTION ONE

INTRODUCTION

In this section, you will learn about the study of manufacturing. First, you will learn what manufacturing technology means, and how to use the systems approach to study it. Chapter 2 describes the history of manufacturing, from cottage industries to mass production. In chapter 3, you will study different types of manufacturing systems, including custom, intermittent, and continuous manufacturing. Finally, chapter 4 will help you understand how people in different departments work together in a manufacturing company.

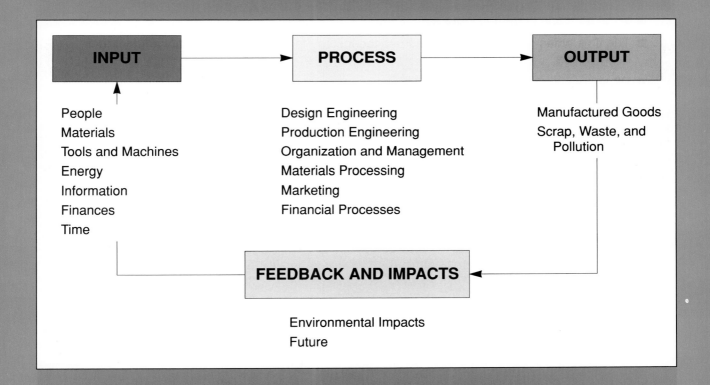

INPUT

People
Materials
Tools and Machines
Energy
Information
Finances
Time

PROCESS

Design Engineering
Production Engineering
Organization and Management
Materials Processing
Marketing
Financial Processes

OUTPUT

Manufactured Goods
Scrap, Waste, and
    Pollution

FEEDBACK AND IMPACTS

Environmental Impacts
Future

CHAPTER 1

Introduction to Manufacturing

OBJECTIVES

After completing this chapter, you will know about

- What technology is and how it relates to manufacturing.
- What it means to manufacture something.
- The time when people first began to use technology to manufacture objects to meet their basic needs.
- What a systems approach is.
- Why the systems approach is used throughout this book.
- The four components of the systems model.
- The concept that large systems are usually made of subsystems.

KEY TERMS

Basic needs
Communication
Construction
Energy
Feedback

Input
Manufacturing
Output
Power
Processes

Production
Subsystems
System
Technology
Transportation

What Is Technology?

Technology is all around us. It is part of our everyday lives. Without it our lives would be very different. Manufacturing is based on technology. What, then, is technology? Simply defined, **technology** is the tools, materials, and processes people use to extend their power to make or do something. The food we eat has been produced, packaged, and transported through technology. Your home was planned and built by people using tools, materials, and processes. Cars and gas are examples of technologies that meet people's needs and wants.

Without people, technology would not exist. Technology depends on human knowledge. People apply their knowledge through tools, materials, and processes, Figure 1-1.

Figure 1-1. Technology, including the computers shown here, depends on human knowledge. Technology includes tools that make certain tasks easier. *(Courtesy of LTV Aircraft Products Group, Dallas, TX)*

They make daily decisions about technology that shape their lives. These decisions include whether to write or call on the telephone; whether to walk, ride a bike, or drive a car; and whether to buy a product or try to make it. Decisions are based on need, cost, time, fashion, individual values, and many other factors.

Technology always results in change. Think of the changes from technology since your grandparents' youth. Your parents have also seen many advances in technology during their lifetimes. Changes in technology can affect people's life-styles, their health, and how they understand the world around them, Figure 1-2. Technology also changes the natural environment, which can affect our lives. Because humans make the decisions about the use of technology, they can control the changes caused by technology. To make the best choices, we must be informed decision-makers.

Figure 1-2. Children learn about their world from technology. *(Courtesy of Eaton Corporation)*

Technology and Manufacturing

To study technology as it relates to manufacturing, four major areas are used. These include **communication**, **transportation**, **production**, and **energy** and **power**. Communication technology is the study of sending and receiving information through visual, audio, electronic, or other means. Radios, telephones, televisions, and computers are all communication technologies. Transportation technology moves people and things using vehicles like buses, trucks, cars, bicycles, airplanes, and even the space shuttle.

Production technology is the study of how the goods and services that we use every day are made. Production is further broken into **construction** and **manufacturing**. Construction projects are usually fixed to the ground and built where they will be used. Roads, buildings, pipelines, and bridges are examples of construction technology. Manufactured products meet human needs and wants and are often transported to stores where they are sold, Figure 1-3.

Energy and power are the base of all the technical systems described above. Without energy and power, most of the communication, transportation, and production systems as we know them would not exist.

All of these areas are related. The space shuttle, Figure 1-4, transports people and equipment. It has complex communication devices and requires the construction of a launch pad. Such devices and construction need a huge number of manufactured products. Even a simple product like a package of chewing gum has been manufactured, transported to the store, and packaged with a label to tell you what it is. Manufacturing technology produces all the necessary parts of communication and transportation projects.

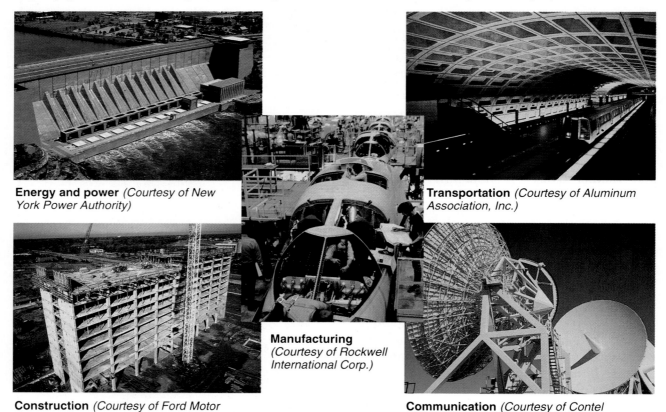

Energy and power (Courtesy of New York Power Authority)

Transportation (Courtesy of Aluminum Association, Inc.)

Manufacturing (Courtesy of Rockwell International Corp.)

Construction (Courtesy of Ford Motor Company)

Communication (Courtesy of Contel Corporation)

Figure 1-3. These systems are used to study technology.

Figure 1-4. Launching of the space shuttle requires all of the technical systems. *(Courtesy of NASA)*

This text will look at manufacturing as a technological system people use to make goods that meet our needs and wants. In addition, some impacts of manufacturing will be discussed. Our world is becoming more interconnected politically, culturally, and economically. Therefore, the impacts of manufacturing on people locally and worldwide are becoming more important. Just as important is the impact of technology on our natural environment and the overall health of our planet.

Manufacturing Entrepreneurs

Do you have an idea for a product that you feel is unique, but you're not sure how to manufacture and market it, or whether it would even be worth the try? Starting a business can be risky, especially if you have not worked in the business world. However, many good businesses have been launched with little more than an idea and a desire to make it fly. Here is the story of Donna Epp, president of Creative Fabric Design, Ltd.

Already a wife and mother, Donna began by taking business and design courses at a local college. There she met Diane Wulf, whose interest in design and fashion matched her own. Their business started as a small sewing business in the basement, where Creative Fabric Design, Ltd. was born. By investing a little money and working at home, they could balance family and work responsibilities. After a while, they felt sure enough about their business to rent space and move the operation out of the home. Their business has become a full-scale factory employing ten full-time workers and many subcontractors.

Donna and Diane feel they were maverick in their approach because they were not afraid to express and create designs that had not been tried before. They added many details and their reputation grew as people saw that they stood behind their work. Today they are ready to become one of the largest comprehensive workrooms in the trade, and were recently recognized by the International Society of Interior Designers. These entrepreneurs offer some tips for success:

- Make a list of realistic goals.
- Set the time frame within which you will reach these goals.
- Interview banks and do business with the bank that will meet your needs as your company grows.
- Use any free space at home before you take on overhead expenses.
- Research your business needs, including geographic area, market potential, income, and competitors.
- Reconcile your financial needs. Be honest about your personal financial needs and those of your business.
- Know about business etiquette. Quality of service counts.
- Avoid stereotyping images based on gender, race, and so forth.

Manufacturing and Basic Human Needs

Humans have **basic needs** that must be met for them to survive in their natural environment. Some of these include food, clothing, and shelter. These needs can vary based on climate or region. Basic needs were met by even the earliest people. At that time, the materials used were the most easily found and the tools and processes were simple, Figure 1-5. To manufacture something is to change a naturally occurring material to make it more useful or valuable. Ancient people who used fire to cook their food and scraped animal skins for robes and shelter were using technology to make products. These first manufactured items met basic needs for survival. Manufacturing is making products.

Figure 1-5. Early people used simple technology to meet their basic needs.

The Choice of Champions

In recent years, bicycle designers have tried to build the best bicycle frame by using very light, strong materials like advanced composites and titanium. They have made excellent frames, but not without difficulty. Composites and titanium need special tools and careful handling. They are also hard to bond. The performance of such frames has not necessarily justified their cost.

Manufacturers have traditionally used steel or aluminum to make bicycles. Recently a technique for varying the diameter of steel and aluminum tubing was developed. This now makes it possible to decrease the weight but keep the strength of these materials. One end can be enlarged to fit a bracket while the other end can be made to fit the hardware at that position. Changing tube diameter does not create stress, or a local area weakened by pressure. It was developed using a computer-aided design (CAD) system.

The frame offers a rider good stiffness for control, but enough flexibility to absorb road-generated shocks.

The variable diameter tubing was originally developed to make golf club shafts. It offers many advantages. Steel can be brazed, sawed, pinned, drilled, bolted, and glued in a normal manufacturing area. The cost of steel tubing is far less than composites or titanium.

Because of the advantages of variable diameter aluminum tubing, it was used for the bicycles ridden by the U.S. cycling team in the last Olympics.

Photo by Kenneth A. Deitcher, M.D.

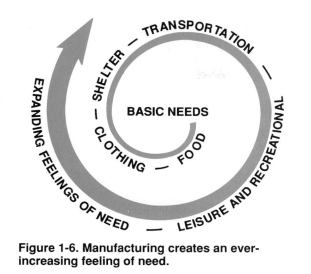

Figure 1-6. Manufacturing creates an ever-increasing feeling of need.

Beyond Basic Needs

Today manufacturing technology provides for much more than basic needs. Once the basics have been met, our feeling of need grows to include items for leisure and luxury, Figure 1-6. Advanced technology has increased the leisure time of many people. Recreational items like skis, tennis rackets, and camping equipment are things we buy to satisfy our growing feeling of need. Televisions, recreational vehicles, and vacation homes are not necessary to sustain life. These may, however, become needs based on a life-style change resulting from technology, Figure 1-7.

Almost everything you see that is not part of the natural environment has been manufactured. In fact, it is a challenge to find something that has not been manufactured. Plywood, Figure 1-8, is made of wood, a natural material, but has been manufactured into a laminated (glued together) 4' × 8' sheet. The piece of chalk your teacher may use is also a natural material (soft limestone), but it has been made into an easy shape for writing. Indeed, it is hard to find even one item that has not been changed in some way.

Figure 1-7. Life-styles, including leisure time activities, change with technology. *(Courtesy of Sony Corporation of America)*

Figure 1-8. Plywood and chipboard materials are made from wood, a natural material, but are manufactured into a more usable form. *(Courtesy of Weyerhaeuser Company Inc.)*

A Systematic Approach

Our world is complex—a wide web of systems and subsystems that can confuse us. We are part of a school system, we might travel on a public bus or subway system, and we all have our own systems for studying or for organizing our rooms. We need a way to organize our thoughts about the events we see happening around us. We need a systematic way to view our world if we are to understand how it works. Likewise, we will use a **system** to study manufacturing technology. Figure 1-9 shows a model for this system.

Input

The **input** for a manufacturing system is everything needed to start and maintain a manufacturing enterprise. The most obvious example of input is the money needed to get the tools, machines, materials, buildings, and energy for production. Wages and benefits for human workers are other considerations. However, the first sources of input include an idea for a product; development of the idea, Figure 1-10; and market research showing a demand for the product. Goals of both the company and the consumers (buyers) are also parts of input. The goals of the manufacturer might be to earn the most money possible. To reach this goal, the product must be both affordable and attractive to the buyer. The consumer's primary goal may be to buy a safe, reliable, attractive product for the least amount of money, Figure 1-11. These inputs influence the product and the type of manufacturing technology used to make it. Input will be discussed in detail in Section Two of this book.

Figure 1-10. Developing an idea often takes input from people with different experience and expertise. *(Courtesy of Allen-Bradley Company, Milwaukee, WI)*

Process

The **processes** of manufacturing relate to the jobs and tasks associated with the design, production, and selling of a product. Manufacturing processes can be grouped in the following categories:

- Design engineering
- Production planning
- Ownership and management
- Processing materials
- Marketing
- Accounting

Each person in a manufacturing company does certain jobs that relate to one of these cat-

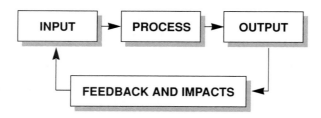

Figure 1-9. This systems model is used to study manufacturing technology.

Figure 1-11. The consumer wants a safe, reliable product at an affordable price. *(Photo by Ted Horowitz, courtesy of Schering-Plough Corporation)*

processing refers to using tools and machines to change natural or prefabricated materials into finished products, Figure 1-13. Marketing processes include deciding which products consumers want and then advertising and selling them. Finance and accounting processes relate to gaining and keeping track of the company's money. All of these processes are needed for a company to successfully make the goods we use every day. Processes will be discussed in Section Three of this book.

Output

The **output** of most manufacturing companies includes everything that exists after, and as a result of, manufacturing processes. The most obvious output is the product itself, Figure 1-14. Less apparent are the by-products of manufacturing like scrap, waste, and pollution. Scrap includes excess materials that can be recycled or reused for a different product.

Figure 1-12. Research and development of new products is just one managed area of activity in manufacturing. *(Reprinted courtesy of Eastman Kodak Company)*

egories. Some of the tasks in the engineering department include research and development, Figure 1-12; product design; machine set-up; and formulation of quality control methods. It is management's role to make sure everyone is doing his or her job and is working together as efficiently as possible. Materials

Figure 1-13. This natural material is usually changed into more convenient and usable forms before reaching the store. *(Courtesy of Weyerhaeuser Company Inc.)*

(Courtesy of Dow Chemical)   *(Courtesy of Fleet/Norstar Financial Group)*

Figure 1-14. Products are the most obvious output of manufacturing.

Waste is not easily recycled and must be properly disposed of. Pollution is visible in the form of emissions from smoke stacks and discoloration of water. It can also be less visible, like heat discharged into water (thermal pollution) or colorless chemicals discharged into the air, soil, or water, Figure 1-15. Outputs will be discussed in greater detail in Section Four of this book.

Feedback and Impacts

Feedback happens throughout the model. It is a method of monitoring and adjusting inputs, processes, and outputs in manufacturing. Much feedback is based on the company's impact on people, both workers and consumers, Figure 1-16. Just as important are the impacts of manufacturing processes on the environment. Feedback is important in deciding which products are manufactured and how to do it.

Feedback can also occur on a small (micro) scale. An example of microfeedback is quality control in materials processing. For example, a hole must be drilled exactly two inches deep. A worker might drill the hole and then mea-

Figure 1-15. Although not always obvious, pollution is also an output from manufacturing. *(Copyright © Wayne Michael Lottinville)*

Figure 1-16. A satisfied consumer provides positive feedback for this product. *(Reprinted courtesy of Eastman Kodak Company)*

Figure 1-17. The systems approach can be used to think about the manufacture of bicycles.

sure it. If it is less than two inches deep, the worker can adjust the drill to make the hole a little deeper. If the hole is more than two inches deep, the worker can adjust the drill for less depth. Feedback of this sort happens constantly on a production line. On a microscale, feedback is a basic part of all manufacturing processes.

Feedback is used to keep manufacturing systems working safely and efficiently. Because both feedback and impacts are critical in making decisions about manufacturing, Section Five of this book deals with these in greater detail.

Applying the Model

We can look at a typical manufacturing company using the systems model. Let's consider producing a bicycle, Figure 1-17.

Inputs include such things as the ideas and knowledge needed to make bicycles as well as a perceived market (people who want to buy the product). In addition, money is needed to invest in the necessary energy, tools, machines, materials, transportation, building(s), wages, and benefits for workers.

Materials processes used to make a bicycle may include casting, forming, welding, assembling, finishing, and transporting. Other processes may be managing workers; studying consumer needs; researching, developing, and improving products; maintaining productivity;

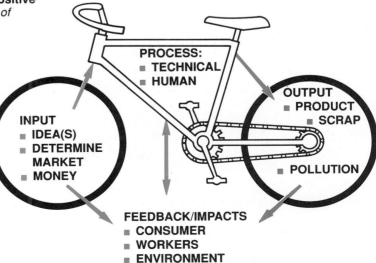

INPUT
■ IDEA(S)
■ DETERMINE MARKET
■ MONEY

PROCESS:
■ TECHNICAL
■ HUMAN

OUTPUT
■ PRODUCT
■ SCRAP
■ POLLUTION

FEEDBACK/IMPACTS
■ CONSUMER
■ WORKERS
■ ENVIRONMENT

controlling quality; financial accounting; advertising; and selling.

Outputs include the product itself, scrap, waste, and other by-products like pollution from the manufacturing processes.

Feedback is based on sales; what consumers think of the product, Figure 1-18; design flaws and changes; availability of new materials; product safety concerns and regulations; pollution control regulations; and workers' satisfaction, efficiency, or safety. All of these factors, and others, can change the overall system. Feedback is based on the impact of the product and its manufacture on individuals, society, and the environment. It occurs throughout the model, even during the first stages of research and design. Workers receive and react to feedback on a microscale daily. It is important to receive and react to both positive and negative feedback.

Subsystems

Large systems often contain **subsystems.** Subsystems are smaller systems within larger systems. A bicycle is a subsystem within the general transportation system. It may be described using the systems model as follows:

- Input—human energy from food needed to pedal.
- Process—the action of pedaling burns calories, a chemical change.
- Output—transportation; heat from the human body that results from rapid burning of calories.
- Feedback—comfort, speed, mechanical adjustments. Impacts include exercise and good health, no reliance on gasoline or other fuels, less overall expense, more easily understood and repaired product, and a feeling of independence.

We can look at even smaller subsystems using the systems model. The pedal/chain drive, Figure 1-19, and gears are subsystems of the bicycle. Your laboratory where you will work on a manufacturing project is a system that contains many subsystems. Each machine is a subsystem that contains even smaller subsystems like motor-powered belt drives or gears.

By using the systems approach, we can more easily understand and make decisions about technology, manufacturing, and the importance of their impacts on us as individuals and as a society. These informed decisions will affect the quality of life for generations to come, Figure 1-20.

Figure 1-18. Product performance is an important source of feedback for manufacturers. *(Courtesy of L.L. Bean, Inc.)*

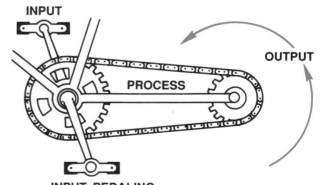

INPUT: PEDALING
PROCESS: PEDALING—CHAIN DRIVE
OUTPUT: REAR TIRE ROTATES

Figure 1-19. The pedal/chain drive is a subsystem of a bicycle.

Figure 1-20. The quality of life for future generations depends on our decisions about technology today. *(Photo by Ruby Gold)*

Summary

Technology has been defined simply as the tools, materials, and processes used by people to extend their potential to make or do something. Manufacturing is a technological system that provides goods to meet needs and wants. Manufacturing can be traced back in time to ancient people who changed a material in their environment to meet their basic needs. Once basic needs have been met, feelings of need can expand to include much more. To help us organize and study manufacturing technology, we use a systems model. This model is made up of four components. These include input, processes, output, and feedback and impacts. Feedback is often based on the impacts of the product and the processes used to make it as well as on people and the natural environment. Within a system, various subsystems can usually be identified.

The study of manufacturing technology is important because almost everything we use in our daily lives has been manufactured. An understanding of the changes affecting our lives that occur from manufacturing technology is needed in order to become informed decision-makers. The decisions we make about technology will affect the quality of life for many generations to come.

This book is organized into major sections that include, input, processes, output, and feedback and impacts. In addition, each unit will use the systems approach to discuss manufacturing and how it affects you, society, the world, and the environment.

DISCUSSION QUESTIONS

1. It was stated that advancing technology always results in change. Describe at least three examples of how recent advances in technology have changed your life.

2. In order to study manufacturing, it has been divided into four major areas. List the four areas and give an example of each that you use every day.

3. What are your basic needs? Would you be happy with just your basic needs? Explain.

4. Describe the systems model. Apply this model to a television, a motorcycle, and another item of your choice in your classroom.

5. Why is it important to become an informed decision-maker? How will studying manufacturing technology help you become better informed?

6. List some unexpected impacts of technology and how they have affected people, the environment, and further developments or uses of technology.

CHAPTER ACTIVITIES

⚙ A SYSTEMATIC VIEW

OBJECTIVE

This activity will help you think about technology with the systems model found in this chapter. You must understand this model and how it works to gain the critical thinking skills you need to make responsible decisions.

MATERIALS AND SUPPLIES

1. Handout "Technology: The Systems Approach"
2. Handout "The Systems Model: Social and Environmental Considerations"

PROCEDURE

1. As a class, discuss the systems model found in chapter one.
2. Alone or in small groups, complete the handout "Technology: The Systems Approach."
3. Alone or in small groups, complete the handout "The Systems Model: Social and Environmental Considerations."
4. As a class, discuss the handouts.

Mathematicians use literally hundreds of systems, called formulae, in which a set of symbols represents mathematical rules.

RELATED QUESTIONS

1. Name and describe the parts of a system.
2. How can you use feedback to help improve a system?
3. Why is it important to consider the impacts created by a system?

 MANUFACTURED NEEDS

OBJECTIVE

In this activity, you will use group brainstorming to solve a manufacturing problem. The activity focuses on meeting basic human needs in the future when conditions on earth will be quite different.

MATERIALS AND SUPPLIES

1. Handout "Manufactured Needs Scenario"
2. Handout "Brainstorming Rules"
3. Paper
4. Pencils

PROCEDURE

1. As a class, discuss the rules of brainstorming.
2. Practice brainstorming (ways to use a quarter, uses for a brick, for example) and follow the brainstorming rules.
3. Work in small groups of four to five students.
4. Review handout "Manufactured Needs Scenario."
5. Brainstorm products to be made based on the information in the handout. (Hint: remember that plastics are oil-based.)
6. As a class, compare and discuss lists and vote on the twelve best products.

MATH/SCIENCE CONNECTION

Scientists often use scenarios to help them prepare for the future. Computers help scientists determine trends by putting together information fed into them. The study of the future and forecasting techniques have proven very valuable in planning for the wise use of natural resources.

RELATED QUESTIONS

1. Do basic needs change? Explain.
2. How did available natural resources affect your list of products?
3. In your opinion, is the information about the year 2090 realistic? Explain.

CHAPTER 2

The History of Manufacturing

OBJECTIVES

After completing this chapter, you will know about

- The importance of early manufacturing before and after the start of agriculture.
- The development of specialization and cottage industries.
- The three innovations that brought about the Industrial Revolution in England.
- The reasons why factory workers organized to form labor unions.
- The development of division of labor and assembly lines that became known as the American system of manufacturing.
- The five characteristics of mass production.
- Automation and its impact on manufacturing and on people.
- The future trends of manufacturing.

KEY TERMS

Age of Automation	Entrepreneurs	Multinationalizing
Assembly lines	Factory system	Natural resources
Bartering	Industrial Revolution	Nonrenewable
Computer	Innovation	Precision measurement
Continuity	Interchangeability	Productivity
Continuous flow	Inventory	Refining
Conveyor systems	Job planning	Specialization
Cottage industries	Labor laws	Standardization
Developing countries	Labor unions	Synchronization
Division of labor	Mass production	Time and motion

Early History and Manufacturing

Humans have been making items to meet their needs for centuries. As mentioned in Chapter 1, even the first recorded people used simple tools and natural materials from their surroundings to make things. An early example is weapons for hunting and protection. Although these early people probably didn't make anything more than what they needed for survival, they were manufacturing nonetheless. It is suggested that these early humans first lived as a single family unit. That unit slowly grew to include several families who found survival to be easier together. These groups were hunters and gatherers. They often moved to follow food sources and seasons.

Eventually, between 10,000 and 9000 B.C., people discovered how to grow food. It was then that the first permanent villages appeared. Farming tools, like the hand plow, greatly changed the people's lives, Figure 2-1. Because of agriculture, people began to have more time to manufacture more things. New items included better homes, clothes, and cooking and eating utensils. Each person or family had to make everything needed to live. They used local materials and simple hand tools. The processes for manufacturing were often very slow. There were no shops or stores in which to buy things. Cooperation in the field and in defending the village did not extend to sharing homemade clothes, tools, weapons, and other necessities. Trading did sometimes take place, but a money system did not yet exist.

Although the items being made during this period met basic needs, these needs had changed since the days of hunting and gathering. Permanent shelters, clothing, food preparation, and other needs changed as societies and cultures evolved. Basic needs were, however, still the main consideration.

The population steadily grew during this period, yet the number of people on the planet was small and spread out by our modern standards. Their impact on the environment was also small. However, as the sizes of villages increased, so did the problems. People living

Figure 2-1. Early agriculture became more efficient with simple plowing devices. *(Photo by Edith Raviola)*

in larger groups put far more pressure on the surrounding land than mobile (moving) hunters and gatherers. Along with agriculture and larger villages came the related problems of soil erosion, human waste disposal, and greater competition for local manufacturing materials.

Specialization

The next important stage in the development of manufacturing was **specialization**. Specialization means that people become experts in a particular trade, rather than making everything themselves. These specialized activities, when carried out in the home, became known as **cottage industries**, Figure 2-2. Cottage industries still exist today and are becoming more popular as small, home-based manufacturers use computerized mail order systems. Mail order lets consumers shop and buy products without leaving home. It also lets a cottage industry sell items without using expensive store space and marketing methods.

A system of **bartering** developed. This allowed someone who specialized in candle-making, for example, to trade candles for shoes from a shoemaker. Although bartering still exists informally in many places, money quickly replaced it as the most common way to exchange goods.

Figure 2-2. This cloth-dying cottage industry probably used the specialized skills of a single family. *(Courtesy of the Museum of American Textile History)*

The Industrial Revolution

The **Industrial Revolution** refers to the vast change in industry that happened in England around 1750 to 1850. These changes affected almost all aspects of people's lives in England. Later, the Industrial Revolution spread to the United States and other parts of the world. The changes did not happen overnight. They resulted from an accumulation and application of many centuries of discoveries and information.

The main changes credited to this time period in England were in the areas of manufacturing and distribution of goods. Central to the Industrial Revolution was the discovery of new inventions (technology) that made the manufacture of products easier and less time-consuming than handmade cottage crafts. The process of improving on existing ideas or the combining of several ideas is called innovation. Without **innovation,** there would have been no Industrial Revolution.

The three basic innovations that brought about the Industrial Revolution were

1. the replacement of hand tools with power tools and machines,
2. the introduction of new power sources, and

3. the operation of factories as a new form of organizing for production (manufacture) of goods.

Work once done with tools was replaced by machines. The main difference between tools and machines is the power source. Hand tools need a person to supply the power and control the operation, Figure 2-3. Power tools and machines use a power source other than a person. They are often self-controlling, but a person is still needed to turn on and set up the machine.

Certain labor-saving machines increased the amount of goods made in a set amount of time. This is called **productivity**. Increased productivity made more goods available to more people, often at less cost.

The most famous industry in England changed by innovation during the Industrial Revolution was the textile (cloth-making) industry, Figure 2-4. Some of the inventions that contributed to this industry were the spinning machine (John Wyatt, 1733), the carding machine (Lewis Paul, 1738), and the power loom (Edmund Cartwright, 1785). These machines needed a source of power other than human to run.

Up to this point in history, wind and water were the most common sources of nonhuman power. Because wind and water depended on

Figure 2-4. Early textile mills employed mostly women. *(Courtesy of the Museum of American Textile History)*

local weather conditions and the seasons, a more reliable source was needed. The development of the steam engine by James Watt around 1770 is thought of as the most important innovation of the period. It was the backbone of the Industrial Revolution, Figure 2-5. Without the steam engine, the change from hand tools to power machines would not have been possible. Another advantage of the steam engine was that it was mobile (movable). This made it possible for areas without water or wind resources to industrialize.

The **factory system** of manufacturing developed because the new machines were too expensive for individuals to own and operate in the home. As a result, it became common

Figure 2-3. The evolution of simple tools to more sophisticated machines helped bring about the Industrial Revolution. *(Copyright © Wayne Michael Lottinville)*

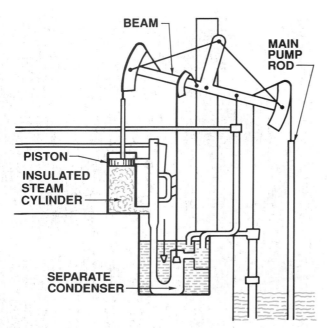

BEAM

MAIN PUMP ROD

PISTON

INSULATED STEAM CYLINDER

SEPARATE CONDENSER

Figure 2-5. James Watt's version of the steam engine included a condenser to cool the steam.

for several people to combine their money and form manufacturing companies. These people were called **entrepreneurs**. They built special buildings that would hold many machines and the workers needed to operate them, Figure 2-6. The result was a movement of most manufacturing from the home to these buildings, called factories.

Working conditions in early factories were often not very good. There were no laws to protect the rights of workers. They often worked twelve or more hours each day, six to seven days a week. Women and young children made up most of the factory work force. Other bad working conditions in factories included poor lighting, no heating or cooling, no windows or ventilation, and no breaks, Figure 2-7. As a result, workers organized groups to demand better working conditions. These groups became known as **labor unions**. Labor unions helped improve the lives of factory workers and made working conditions more bearable. **Labor laws** resulted from labor union activities. These laws protected the

Figure 2-6. This farm tools plant was typical of early factories that used new machines in the early twentieth century. *(Courtesy of Deere & Company)*

Figure 2-7. Poor working conditions were common during the Industrial Revolution. *(Courtesy of the Museum of American Textile History)*

workers' rights and guaranteed certain working conditions in factories. When management resisted the efforts of labor unions, strikes and work stoppages sometimes took place.

Another impact of the Industrial Revolution in England was a movement of people from the country to the cities, where most factories were located. As a result, problems like overcrowding and pollution became more serious. There were no environmental protection laws yet.

The factory system is still in use today in most parts of the world. There are many varia-

tions of the original system developed in England, but the original goal of increased productivity remains the same.

Changes took place as the factory system moved from England to the United States. It became known as the American system of mass production. Generally, **mass production** is a way of organizing people to work together. This organization, called **division of labor**, meant that much of the work was divided into simple tasks that required very little skill. Each worker did the same task all day and became very efficient at it. Workers standing

Rosie the Riveter

For millions of women, consciousness-raising didn't start in the 1960s. It started when they helped win World War II. During the first three years of the war, five million women covered their hair, put on pants, and went to work. The government urged them to help the war effort by working, because most of the men were off fighting. Women did every kind of job; but the largest single need was for riveters, mostly in the defense industry.

Rivets are metal pins used to permanently assemble (hold together) parts. They are one-piece fasteners that have a body and a head. The rivet is placed in a hole until the two layers of material are forced tightly together. A force applied to the rivet enlarges its diameter, tightly filling the hole. The same force clinches the head of the rivet, enlarging it to about one and a half times the diameter of the hole. The riveting process used can be done either manually or automatically. Among other things, rivets were used to assemble the wings of airplanes and the bodies of tanks.

Most of the women had never before worked outside the home. It was traditional for women to remain at home to raise the children and keep the house. The call to work during the war got them out of the house to earn wages. The jobs were often physically demanding and dangerous. For many women, the experience was one that would affect their lives and their perception of themselves forever. As one woman later described,

I loved working at Convair. I loved the challenge of getting dirty and getting into the work. I did one special riveting job, hand riveting that could not be done by machine. I worked on that job for three months, ten hours a day, six days a week, and slapped three-eighths or three-quarter-inch rivets by hand that no one else would do. I didn't have that kind of confidence as a kid growing up because I didn't have that opportunity. Convair was the first time in my life that I had a chance to prove that I could do something, and I did. They finally made me a group leader, although they didn't pay me the wages that went with the job, because I was a woman.

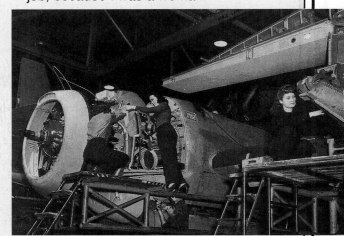

Courtesy of Grumman Corporation

The experiences of all of the "Rosies," as they were collectively called, set the stage for the entry of women into the world of employment and opportunity. Today, women make up about half of the work force. Equality in the proportion of management-level positions held by women and comparable wages are still issues. But the experiences of these wartime workers demonstrated the capabilities and boosted the confidence of all women, then and now.

SOURCE: From *American Heritage*, February/March 1984, pp. 94–103.

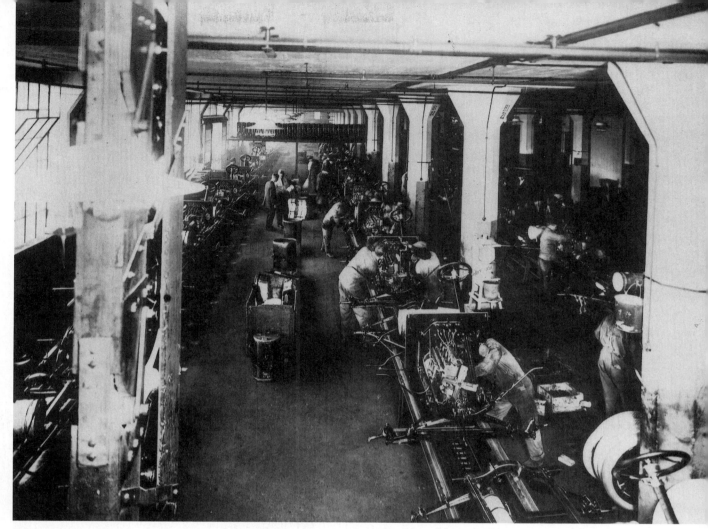

Figure 2-8. This early auto plant shows assembly lines where each worker did a simple task in the manufacture of the final product (1914). *(Courtesy of Ford Motor Company)*

side by side in long lines, each doing their task, became known as **assembly lines**, Figure 2-8. Henry Ford is often credited with using the first assembly line to mass produce early automobiles. Characteristics of mass production include

1. precision measurement,
2. standardization,
3. interchangeability,
4. synchronization, and
5. continuity.

Precision measurement was especially important in clock-making and the measurement of time. This, in effect, brought about precision measurement in other areas. Precision mea-

surements are usually made to at least thousandths ($1/1,000$) of an inch.

Standardization is closely related to precision measurement. The accuracy of a measurement depended on where the measurement was made and who made it. Therefore, it became necessary to make sure everyone measured the same so that standardized (identical) parts could be made.

Interchangeability of standardized parts became a central part of mass production. Ely Whitney manufactured the first interchangeable parts for his invention, the cotton gin. Through the use of jigs and fixtures, Whitney eliminated the time-consuming need for measuring by hand. Jigs and fixtures are devices used to hold a workpiece in place while it is being worked on. You will use simple jigs and fixtures during your class manufacturing experience.

Synchronization is defined as occurring at the same time. In manufacturing, synchronization requires planning so that tools, machines, materials, workers, and actions are at the right place at the right time. The innovation of **conveyor systems** to move materials and parts at a constant rate of speed is an important part of synchronization, Figure 2-9. This is known as **continuous flow**.

Continuity means repeating something over and over in an identical way. Continuity depends on the four characteristics listed above. It is a basic part of mass production manufacturing.

The study of making mass production as efficient as possible became an important part of manufacturing. **Job planning** and **time and motion** studies are methods to find the most efficient way to do a job.

Automation

Ways to increase the efficiency of manufacturing products continued to unfold from the early days of Henry Ford and his assembly line. As information increased, innovative ideas and inventions continued to affect mass production. As a result, we entered what became known as the **Age of Automation**.

Automation is a manufacturing system in which most or all of the machines and processes run with little or no human control. Electronic devices, which are designed and set up by people, do many of the jobs once done by assembly line workers. Automation is often more efficient because machines don't need breaks, healthy or comfortable working conditions, or wages, and they can work twenty-four hours a day. However, some people are still needed to set up, operate, and repair the machines.

The benefits of automation can be outweighed by the additional costs of implementing and maintaining automated machines. Before automation takes place, a careful cost analysis is done to see if it will be cost-efficient. Keeping human workers, or a combination of human workers and automation, may turn out to be most efficient.

The most important electronic machine used in automated manufacturing today is the

Figure 2-9. Conveyor systems automatically move parts, greatly increasing the efficiency of manufacturing. *(Courtesy of Ford Motor Company)*

Figure 2-10. A chemical manufacturer uses a computerized process control program. *(Courtesy of the Dow Chemical Company)*

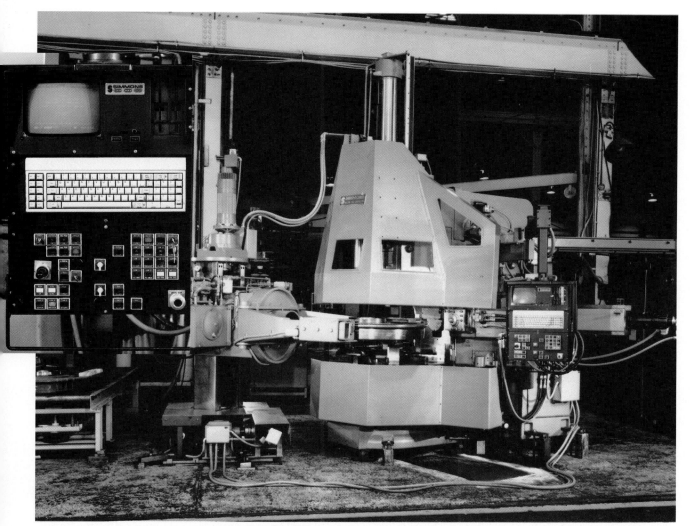

Figure 2-11. A computer-numerical control (CNC) diesel wheel machining center. *(Courtesy of Simmons Machine Tool Corp.)*

computer. A **computer** is a programmable machine that accepts, processes, and displays data (information). A common use for computers in manufacturing is to control machines used to make parts and products, Figure 2-10. Businesses also use them to keep track of all the materials needed for production and to order more when they run low. This is called **inventory**.

Manufacturing that is automated with computers is called computer-integrated manufacturing (CIM), computer-aided manufacturing (CAM), or computer numerical control (CNC), Figure 2-11.

Reliance on Machine Technology

It is important to remember that computers can quickly process information, but they make decisions based only on what has been programmed into them by people. Computers and the machines they control are not perfect. For example, in 1965 a single mechanism that controlled the flow of electricity in northeastern United States and Canada failed. As a result, a total of 80,000 square miles experienced a blackout that had scientists and engineers puzzled for many days, Figure 2-12. The failure knocked out a huge network that was supposed to shift electric power from areas

Figure 2-12. A blackout darkened New York City in 1965. Only one building—a hospital with a generator—has lights. Such a loss of power makes people realize how much they rely on technology. *(Courtesy of UPI/Bettmann Newsphotos)*

with extra power to those in need of more. That night, in 1965, the system worked as it had been programmed, but the result was something completely unexpected. Instead of simply stopping a local power failure, it spread the trouble until the entire system was out of control. Millions of people were affected.

The result for many who experienced the blackout was a new awareness of technology and our reliance on it. Automation can free creative, problem-solving people from mundane tasks and let them put their skills to better use. Automation technology in manufacturing does increase productivity (efficiency), but it cannot be expected to operate flawlessly.

Manufacturing in the Future

The trend of automated manufacturing is expected to continue as we learn more about it

and use it more. Increased automation may result in more products produced less expensively. Currently many companies are moving to **developing countries** (less industrialized) where labor is cheaper. Local governments offer incentives to these companies. The trend toward **multinationalizing** (locating in more than one country) will be discussed in more detail in Section Five of this book.

Another important future trend is toward manufacturing in space, Figure 2-13. The advantages of space manufacturing include weightlessness (zero gravity) and a sterile vacuum (perfectly clean and pressureless) environment. These conditions suit certain combinations of materials and processes that might otherwise be unavailable to us, Figure 2-14. These include the following:

1. Growing crystal chips used in some electronic products including watches,

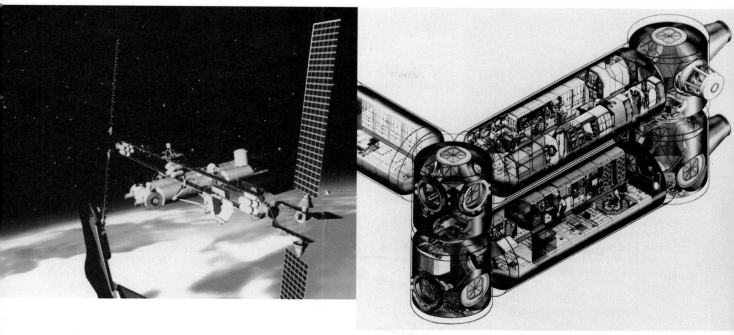

Figure 2-13. Manufacturing in space is expected to be an important part of future manufacturing. Here are an artist's drawings of (left) the outside of a space station, and (right) the inside of a space station, showing the lab and living quarters. *(Courtesy of Boeing Aerospace)*

Figure 2-14. To increase the thrust of liquid fuel rockets, NASA developed the technology to boost the flow rate of rocket fuel pumps. A pump manufacturer used NASA technology to increase the speed of a pump used to recirculate wood molasses. *(Courtesy of NASA)*

calculators, and other small devices. Crystals are the "brains" of these products, similar in purpose to the silicon chips used in computers.

2. Making pure metals by processing in the sterile vacuum environment. This process is called **refining**. It is almost impossible to refine pure metals in laboratories on earth because dust and even air can contaminate (pollute and ruin) the product. Metals that benefit from zero gravity processing include gold and silver.

3. Mixing liquids that don't easily mix together (for example, oil and water). Because of gravity on earth, differing weights of some liquids allow one to float to the top when mixed with another. In space, everything is weightless, so different liquids can be easily mixed.

4. Making perfect spheres (round ball-like objects) used for bearings. Spheres

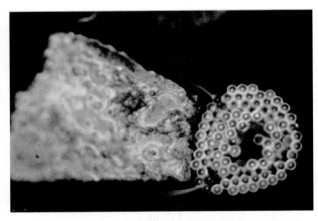

Figure 2-15. It is nearly impossible to make perfectly spherical ball bearings on Earth because of the forces of gravity. The zero gravity of space provides a perfect environment for this manufacturing process. *(Courtesy of NASA)*

made on earth are never truly round because of the earth's gravitational pull, Figure 2-15.

Manufacturers are concerned about the wise use of natural resources and will be even more so in the future. **Natural resources** are the raw materials used to make all products. Many of these resources are **nonrenewable**. This means that there is a limited amount available for use. The supply will eventually run out. It is very important that we stretch out the use of these resources for as long as possible and that we search for other resources.

Summary

There is evidence that the earliest recorded humans manufactured simple tools for hunting and protection. Later people learned to grow food and began manufacturing other items including clothes, shelter, and cooking and eating utensils. Villages appeared, and specialization took place in certain trades that became known as cottage industries.

Technological innovations led to many innovations that brought about the Industrial Revolution in England. The most important invention during this period was the steam engine. The steam engine provided a mobile power source. This led to the replacement of hand tools by machines. The factory system of manufacturing then emerged. Unbearable working conditions in factories forced the workers to form labor unions.

The American system of mass production was based on the ideas of the division of labor and the assembly line. Characteristics of this system include precision measurement, standardization, interchangeability, synchronization, and continuity.

The Age of Automation is a manufacturing system in which most of the machines and processes run with little or no human power. The computer is the most important machine in automated manufacturing. Although automated machine technology makes our lives easier, we cannot expect it always to run perfectly.

The future of manufacturing will see more multinational corporations, space manufacturing of certain materials and processes, and a growing concern for the wise use of our limited natural resources.

Figure 2-16. Complex tools, machines, materials, and processes make manufacturing technology more automated and efficient. *(Courtesy of Miller Electric Manufacturing Co. of Appleton, WI)*

DISCUSSION QUESTIONS

1. Using your knowledge of the history of manufacturing and your imagination, describe the following about the tools made by early humans:

   ▪ From what material might they have been made?
   ▪ How might they have been made (by what processes)?
   ▪ For what purpose(s) were they made?
   ▪ How have they evolved?

2. Describe at least three cottage industries. Which would you choose if you had lived during that time period? Why?

3. What brought about the Industrial Revolution in England? What role did the invention of the steam engine play?

4. Labor unions are still active today. What are some of the advantages and disadvantages of belonging to a union? Would you belong to one? Why or why not?

5. In what ways did the American system of manufacturing differ from England's? How does present-day American manufacturing differ from that of Japan?

6. What is automated manufacturing? How has the Age of Automation affected people (positively and negatively)?

7. Describe an incident where automation and/or technology has failed. What can we learn from these examples?

8. Describe how the explosion of the space shuttle Challenger affected space manufacturing.

9. Why is the wise use of natural resources going to become critical in the future of manufacturing? How might artificially made materials impact the future of manufacturing?

CHAPTER ACTIVITIES

 TOOLMAKER

OBJECTIVE

This activity will help you understand how the earliest people made the simple tools they needed to survive. They used only easily found natural materials, human power, and creative thinking.

MATERIALS AND SUPPLIES

1. Handout "Biography of a Toolmaker"
2. Any materials found locally (rocks and stones, sticks and branches, vines and other rope-like materials, mud, clay, shells)

PROCEDURE

1. As a class, discuss early toolmaking methods and uses for types of tools. Refer to the toolmaking handout or overhead transparency.
2. Complete Part I of handout "Biography of a Toolmaker."
3. Find the right toolmaking materials.
4. Carefully shape and put together (manufacture) your tool.
   Note: Be sure to wear eye protection for this activity. Remember, early people did not have work benches, vices, or other conveniences found in your laboratory.

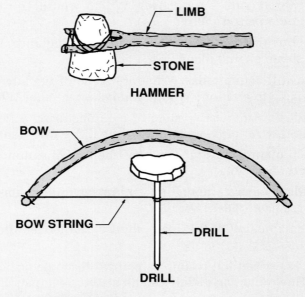

Some toolmaking ideas

5. Report the biographical data about your toolmaker and share your toolmaking experience with the class. If possible, demonstrate the use of your tool.

MATH/SCIENCE CONNECTION

Scientists commonly use two systems for dating archeological finds such as early tools and bones from early humans. *Relative dating* is based on the fact that layers of rock and other materials in the ground get older as one digs deeper. So, a find made in an upper layer is younger than one in a lower layer. *Absolute dating* (age in actual years) is done with chemical or radioactive methods, such as carbon-14.

RELATED QUESTIONS

1. Good toolmaking skills often made the difference between life and death for early humans. Now that you have tried to make a simple tool, what would you do differently next time, if your life depended on it?
2. The earliest examples of manufactured tools were used for hunting and defense. What might have been manufactured next as experience, tools, materials, and processes progressed? Explain what materials and processes might have been used.

3. What impact do you think controlled fire-making had on early people, especially in terms of processes used to make things?
4. How are the materials and processes used in this activity still used today? What new materials and processes have replaced them?
5. Naturally occurring materials are still popular today. What natural materials are most commonly used today?

Types of Manufacturing Systems

OBJECTIVES

After completing this chapter, you will know about

■ Factors to consider when choosing a type of manufacturing.

■ The continuous system of manufacturing.

■ The intermittent system of manufacturing.

■ The custom system of manufacturing.

■ The just-in-time (JIT) system of manufacturing

KEY TERMS

Batch manufacturing
Buffer inventory
Carrying charges
Continuous
  manufacturing
Custom manufacturing
Depreciate
Economic order quantity
  (EOQ)
Flexible manufacturing

Intermittent
  manufacturing
Jobbing manufacturing
Job lot manufacturing
Job rotation
Just-in-time
  manufacturing (JIT)
Kanban
Lots
Mass production

Material requirements
  planning (MRP)
One-touch set-up
Repetitive manufacturing
Self-developed machines
Set-up
Single set-up
Stockless production
Tooling

Is All Manufacturing the Same?

When most people think of manufacturing, they automatically think of mass production and assembly lines. But are there other types of manufacturing systems? Is the type of manufacturing system used to produce cars the same as that used to make designer clothes? Is a pencil made in the same manner as the cus-tom cabinets in your kitchen? Do other countries and cultures use the same systems? Because of the diversity of items that are produced, several types of manufacturing systems have evolved. Each meets the unique demands and characteristics of the product and its projected market.

Choosing an Appropriate Type of Manufacturing

There are several types of manufacturing systems used by industry today. They include continuous, intermittent, custom, and just-in-time (JIT). Choosing which type fits a certain industry is based on the following factors:

1. Volume (quantity) to be produced
2. Availability of necessary inputs
3. Type(s) of products to be made
4. The life cycle or durability of a product
5. Production philosophy of the organization

The combination of these factors along with market forecasts makes choosing a manufacturing system rather difficult. Studying the types of manufacturing systems will help us see why this is a tough process. The difficulty lies in producing the highest quality product at an affordable price while providing meaningful work for people.

Volume to Be Produced. The volume to be produced is an important factor in choosing a type of manufacturing system, Figure 3-1. For example, an automobile may be produced using any one of the methods of manufacturing mentioned above. If, however, an order is placed for 50,000 automobiles of one model, custom manufacturing is eliminated from the list of possibilities. Fifty thousand washers using an automated punch press may take as little as one hour to make. Using hand tools this process may take a work force of 100, at the rate of fifty per hour, ten hours. One system is highly machine intensive; the other is highly labor intensive. The automated machine, however, may cost more than twenty times the cost of one year's labor. Regional high unemployment may also play a part in which type of production process is chosen. Knowing the quantity of products needed is just one of the factors to be considered.

Availability of Inputs. Highly capital-intensive (expensive) equipment may not be available to certain regions. It may also not be affordable because of its high investment cost. Imported

Figure 3-1. The volume of products to be manufactured is just one consideration when choosing an appropriate manufacturing system. *(Courtesy of Rockwell International Corporation)*

materials, although often more expensive, are commonly substituted for locally available materials. Highly skilled technicians needed for production set-up may not be found locally. Labor is a key input that often helps decide which type of manufacturing is most appropriate, Figure 3-2. Availability of inputs must, however, be weighed with other factors.

Type of Product. The type of product often helps the manufacturer to determine the right manufacturing system. Some technical systems are inappropriate by the very nature of the product. For example, a regular automobile may require a different type of manufacturing system than a racing dragster, Figure 3-3. One

Machine and Nature, Industry and Art

Here is the story of an Israeli manufacturer, who saved a failing company by combining computer technology with the needs and strengths of its workers. Iscar Ltd., a thirty-year-old company, decided to shut the doors of its saw blade division. With sales of less than $100,000 per year, Iscar sold blades to the local and regional market only. A man named Ben Dov was given permission to try to save the company. His first move was to rent space in a small, simple building. He landed foreign contracts with Delta International (Pittsburgh, PA). Production jumped from about 1,000 blades per month to 10,000 blades per month.

In April of 1987, an automated facility was finished. It could handle the increased production levels created by new foreign contracts. The building was designed based on the philosophy of Stef Wertheimer, the founder and president of Iscar. Wertheimer believed that there should be a union between machine and nature and industry and art. This union would allow humans to have dignity and pride in their work.

A number of projects were completed based on the philosophy of industry and art. An art museum, an entrepreneurial training center, and a modern housing community were built for workers of Iscar. This was an attempt to change the image of industry and to balance machines with beauty. The octagon plant design is rather unique. The outer ring of the structure is the manufacturing processes area, while the inner ring of the structure is a courtyard-styled ancient Arab garden. Within the garden is a display of old farm and manufacturing tools. In good weather the roof over the garden may be retracted to allow fresh air and light into the courtyard area.

Giant windows allow workers to be in touch with nature even during production runs. Windows also are inside the manufacturing area to allow worker eye contact. This is especially important at night when there are fewer workers. Eye contact reassures workers with a feeling of security and comradery.

Wertheimer, citing E.F. Schumacher's work *Small Is Beautiful*, believes in small-scale operations with a small but dedicated work force. The entire work force is forty-five people. Thirty are production workers; fifteen are in administration, maintenance, and the warehouse. A new computer-integrated manufacturing (CIM) system, usually found in larger companies, allows the small work force a high degree of job security. Similar companies must employ 150 workers who are often laid off from time to time. With CIM, Ben Dov believes he "will always be able to find enough work for forty-five people."

---

may be mass produced continuously and the other would most likely be custom produced.

Life Cycle. The life cycle of a product also aids in the decision-making. Manufacturers who make products that may **depreciate** (wear out or become outdated) very quickly would choose a different manufacturing system than those who make products that are in demand for many years. For example, the style of clothing often changes. This is a form of depreciation. What you buy six months from now may differ from what you buy today. Because most clothing has a short life cycle, labor-intensive intermittent manufacturing may be more

Figure 3-2. Manufacture and maintenance of this aircraft requires both human and machine labor. *(Courtesy of Grumman Corporation)*

Figure 3-3. This racing dragster was probably custom manufactured. *(Courtesy of Schiefer Sports Marketing)*

Figure 3-4. The variety seen in these styles may make labor-intensive intermittent manufacturing the most appropriate system. *(Courtesy of Burlington Industries, Inc.)*

appropriate than continuous manufacturing, Figure 3-4.

Production Philosophy. Finally, production philosophy plays an important role. Some manufacturers choose to stay small to ensure a high-quality product and a high-quality work life for their employees regardless of consumer demand and profitability. Others choose capital-intensive methods that produce items more quickly but at a lower cost to the consumer. Philosophy of employment is part of the production philosophy. While the quality of work life for one work force may be high, the cost of the product may also be high. As a result, only select income groups can afford the product. While the quality of a product of another company may be lower, the price to the consumer may also be low. However, it is often possible to produce high-quality products at affordable prices, Figure 3-5.

Figure 3-5. Great care is taken in the manufacture of this truck body, resulting in a quality product. *(Courtesy of Grumman Corporation)*

The combination of all these factors helps choose the best type of manufacturing system. Production volume, availability of inputs, type of product, life cycle of a product, and production philosophy make this a complex decision for prospective manufacturers.

Types of Manufacturing Systems

Continuous Manufacturing. Continuous manufacturing is also known as **repetitive manufacturing** or **mass production**. The product is moved continuously throughout the manufacturing process, almost like water flowing in a river. In continuous manufacturing, moving conveyors transport materials as well as the product throughout its various stages of manufacture, Figure 3-6. In many cases, a continuous manufacturing system runs twenty-four hours a day. Continuous manufacturing produces a large number of identical products. Companies that make only a single product or only very closely related items have a narrow product line.

Figure 3-7. These popular food items are examples of products in constant high demand and continuously manufactured. *(Courtesy of The Pillsbury Company)*

Examples of products that are made in a continuous manufacturing system may include items commonly found in most homes. Televisions, radios, refrigerators, food, and utensils are some examples. In other regions of the world, the items produced might vary based on cultural differences. In China, chopsticks are continuously produced from bamboo. In western Africa, the Bantu people continually make beds, furniture, and roofs from a raw material called raffia palm. Products that depreciate quickly or that are in high demand are often continuously produced, Figure 3-7.

Continuous manufacturing often requires that workers become specialized at their job. This means that they are trained to do one job quickly and efficiently. Generally, work on a continuous manufacturing line is of an unskilled or semiskilled nature. There can be problems of boredom, inattention, injuries, and worker dissatisfaction at these jobs.

Perhaps the greatest complaint of the continuous manufacturing system is that the workers are often not mentally challenged. Most production line workers have little decision-making power or control over the out-

Figure 3-6. Conveyor systems move the product continuously throughout the manufacturing process. *(Courtesy of Johnson Controls)*

come of the final product. In an effort to overcome some of the problems of repetitive tasks, **job rotation** is sometimes used. Line workers may rotate on an hourly, daily, or monthly basis to increase the quality of work life by making the work more interesting.

Mechanization and automation have greatly affected continuous manufacturing. Just as production line workers have become specialized, so too have tools and machines. Specialized equipment intended for a particular task is often used when a large quantity is to be produced with little product variation.

The increasing use of computers in the design and manufacture of products is known as computer-aided design (CAD) and computer-aided manufacturing (CAM). CAD involves the use of computers in creating and modifying product designs. CAM involves the monitoring or controlling of manufacturing operations.

Computer-integrated manufacturing (CIM) enterprises use programmable automation systems such as computer numerical control (CNC). The computer in a CNC unit stores an application program in its memory that makes it "think" like a lathe or a milling machine. Robots actually carry out the manual part of the programmed operation, Figure 3-8.

The most advanced programmable automated manufacturing systems contain the following features:

- Automatic machine control
- Automatic tool changing
- Automatic material handling

Figure 3-8. Extensive use of robots for welding and other assembly line tasks helps Toyota maintain its high efficiency and quality standards. (*Courtesy of Toyota Motor Manufacturing, U.S.A., Inc.*)

These features help make the "factory of the future" a reality in today's world.

Increases in unemployment can be the result of an industrial shift from labor-intensive to capital-intensive manufacturing techniques. While not always the case, continuous manufacturing systems have a reputation for producing medium-quality products at very low prices while employing people in repetitive work.

Intermittent Manufacturing. Intermittent manufacturing is also known as **flexible**, **job lot**, **jobbing**, or **batch** manufacturing. This type of manufacturing produces products in **lots** (specified number of products). A lot is typically made up of 500 or less products. A company that uses intermittent manufacturing usually has a large inventory, Figure 3-9. Inventory is the amount of materials stored at the site. This requires more storage space than a company using the continuous manufacturing system.

Intermittent manufacturing is usually chosen for medium-length production runs of a wide variety of products. The intermittent manufacturer must react quickly to a hard-to-predict mix of necessary materials. A technique known as **material requirements planning** (MRP) aids in the ordering of raw materials, parts, and subassemblies. MRP is an inventory management and control tool. Emphasis is placed not only on having the right quantity of an item, but also on having it at the right place at the right time as needed in the production cycle.

Set-up and **tooling** are changed often in intermittent manufacturing because modifications in the model or product line require that flexible general purpose equipment be used. The available tools, machines, and processes determine the method of production. Set-up for a production may take longer than the production run itself.

An advantage of this type of production is that the same production line may be used to make different products without investing in new tools, machines, materials, and buildings. If one product is not a good seller, the production line can be redesigned to produce another product that might sell better. Without investing much, the job lot manufacturer can quickly adapt to changing consumer buying patterns.

Products that are common to the job lot technique are those that are seasonal or that appeal to a smaller group of people, Figure 3-10. Holiday candy, musical instruments, and house paint may be manufactured in batches as opposed to the continuous system.

Figure 3-9. This paper company keeps a large inventory that requires a large amount of storage space.
(Courtesy of Hammermill Papers)

Figure 3-10. A Rohr Aero Services mechanic assembles a McDonnell Douglas DC-9 thrust reverser.
(Courtesy of Rohr Industries, Inc.)

Figure 3-11. Sailboats, like those raced in the America's Cup, are custom designed and manufactured. *(Courtesy of Miller Electric Manufacturing Co., Appleton, WI)*

Because products and processes are always changing, workers in this kind of manufacturing have more flexible work and are often semiskilled or skilled. As a result, boredom and inattention are less common. In most cases, automation does not replace many human workers because people are more adaptable to change.

Custom Manufacturing. Custom manufacturing produces one or just a few products at a time. Each product is unique. One person or several people may work on a product from beginning to end. Workers usually have a variety of skills. Problem-solving and troubleshooting are necessary because each product presents new challenges. In some cases a single product may take several months to make.

For example, large yachts, airplanes, and custom tools may take a long time to manufacture, Figure 3-11. Other products that are often custom manufactured are traditional crafts including jewelry, pottery, custom furniture, and signs.

Boredom and inattention are uncommon in custom manufacturing. Products that are custom made are often of the highest quality because of the time, care, and pride taken by workers. As a result, the price of custom goods is usually quite high. Custom manufacturers often have a buyer for their product before production even begins. This person is called a guaranteed buyer. Guaranteed buyers reduce the risk of custom manufacturing.

Just-in-Time Manufacturing. Just-in-time (JIT) manufacturing is a system that can be applied to continuous, intermittent, and custom manufacturing. The JIT concept is simple. Its goal is to make and deliver products just in time to be sold. Subassemblies are completed just in time to be made into finished products. Fabricated parts are finished just in time to be used in subassemblies. And raw materials are purchased just in time to be made into fabricated parts. One key goal in the JIT approach is to

Figure 3-12. Kanban is one type of inventory replenishment system. The removal of an item from inventory is kept track of by these cards. *(Courtesy of New United Motor)*

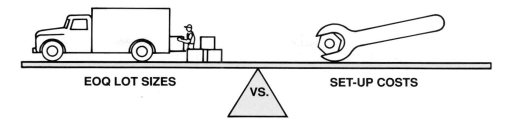

EOQ LOT SIZES   VS.   SET-UP COSTS

Figure 3-13. Determining appropriate EOQ lot sizes in accordance with manageable set-up cost is often a difficult balance to maintain.

reduce inactive inventory. JIT is sometimes referred to as **stockless production** or **kanban**, which is the name for a specific Japanese inventory replenishment system developed by Toyota, Figure 3-12.

The key characteristic in JIT manufacturing is to have all materials in an active stage of processing, never at rest collecting **carrying charges**. Carrying charges are the interest cost on material that is in inventory, warehouse costs, and warehouse workers' wages.

Another important goal in JIT is to cut lot sizes. Large lot sizes make it harder to identify defective parts. With smaller lot sizes, defective parts are not hidden in a pile. If a worker makes only fifty parts compared to 5,000, it is much easier to notice fifteen defective parts. Workers find it easier to identify and care about solving defect problems. Committed and motivated workers can troubleshoot defects, problem areas, slowdowns, and breakdowns.

When a manufacturer orders smaller material lot sizes, the inventory is smaller. This reduces carrying costs. But there is a conflict in the use of smaller lot sizes. The purchasing component of a manufacturing plant wants to hold down carrying costs, but the production component wants purchasing to order large lot sizes in order to reduce set-up times. JIT requires a compromise between purchasing and production. The appropriate lot size is known as **economic order quantity (EOQ)**. The EOQ varies from company to company, but it should be kept small enough so that carrying charges are not excessive and large enough so that set-up costs are not excessive, Figure 3-13.

Single set-up is a tooling change that takes one minute or less. This very quick retooling is also known as **one-touch set-up**. Machines used by automobile manufacturers are sometimes modified using this technique, Figure 3-14.

In some companies toolmaking workers make their own **self-developed machines** in order to decrease set-up times. Self-developed machines are lightweight, special purpose, low-cost machines made and used as opposed to expensive general purpose machines.

Cutting purchase order costs is another important feature of JIT manufacturing. Many companies that use JIT have found ways to reduce the usual red tape associated with the

Figure 3-14. The Flexible Body Line enables the efficient manufacture of several different models on the same line. (Courtesy of New United Motors)

Just-in-Time Manufacturing

Richard J. Schonberger studied the just-in-time techniques used by manufacturers around the world. He discovered eight hidden lessons in simplicity related to the just-in-time manufacturing technique.

Lesson One. Management technology is a highly transportable commodity. This means that ideas used by Japanese manufacturers can be adopted by American counterparts. In fact, management techniques are not necessarily culturally dependent. We are seeing more and more Japanese-owned and -managed companies in the United States that are very successful using an American labor force.

Lesson Two. Just-in-time production exposes problems otherwise hidden by excess inventories and staff. Excess inventories or buffer stock can hide problems that should be exposed immediately. Once quality problems are exposed, they may be solved before too many poor quality parts have been made. Rework is also reduced when problems are exposed quickly.

Lesson Three. Quality begins with production and requires a company-wide habit of improvement. Increased quality is the responsibility of all workers, especially production line workers who are closest to quality problems. A company-wide "habit of improvement" means that everyone is working to improve the product in some manner. This continues as long as the company is in business.

Lesson Four. Simplify plant configurations and goods will flow like water. Just-in-time manufacturing requires simple plant configurations that allow simple flows of materials throughout the manufacturing process. Conveyors are often replaced by work stations where workers can hand materials to each other.

Lesson Five. Flexibility opens doors in production line management. Production line flexibility is more important than the Western approach to production line balancing. Worker flexibility is matched with small machine flexibility. Smaller self-developed machines cost less and allow a company a degree of flexibility.

Lesson Six. Travel light and make numerous trips in just-in-time purchasing. Rather than buying large lots from vendors once a month, it is better to purchase material as it is needed and have it delivered often. This requires vendors to be located near the "mother plant." It reduces warehouse costs and frees up large capital expenditures for other things.

Lesson Seven. Support more self-improvement, decrease programs, and have less specialist intervention. Rather than spend a lot of time and money implementing programs to increase worker productivity, a manufacturer should give more responsibility to production line workers. Increased responsibility often leads to an increased feeling of self-worth. This then leads to increased productivity, increased quality, and a high work life quality. Simply respect production workers by allowing them a high degree of decision-making responsibility.

Lesson Eight. Simplicity is a natural state. It is actually easier and less costly to simplify. Simplification of complex processes is usually criticized by manufacturing engineers who were trained to increase complexity. Simplifying all aspects of production increases production, problem troubleshooting, and quality.

purchasing of materials. Suppliers may even make deliveries of small lots more than once every day. This can be accomplished with as little as a phone call from the purchaser to the supplier. This is in contrast to the large monthly shipments by train or truckload lots. Suppliers to JIT manufacturers are local, if possible, in order to reduce time and transportation costs.

Also common in JIT manufacturing is the withdrawal of **buffer inventory**. Buffer inventory, sometimes called safety stock, is intentionally removed so that any problems are immediately discovered by production workers. Buffer inventories operate on the principle that the more irregularity in the production process, the more buffer stock needed to smooth out product output. When quality control problems occur, it is very difficult to iden-

tify the root of the problem when buffer inventories are used. Workers without buffer inventories must continually troubleshoot problems as they surface, Figure 3-15.

The benefits of just-in-time manufacturing include increased worker motivation and increased product quality. It is because of these benefits that continuous, intermittent, and custom manufacturers are adopting elements of JIT manufacturing. Accountability of the worker is increased as the quality of any part in the process becomes the responsibility of the worker who made it. Quality responsibility shifts away from the traditional quality control department to the workers themselves. With this increased responsibility, workers often feel a greater sense of self-worth. This carries over to increased levels of pride and workmanship, which, by the end of the process, affects

Figure 3-15. Workers are involved in troubleshooting problems with quality, which makes their jobs more interesting and challenging. *(Courtesy of Toyota Motor Manufacturing, U.S.A., Inc.)*

Figure 3-16. The quality of work life affects the final quality of manufactured products. *(Courtesy of Scott Paper Company)*

product quality. The quality of work life directly impacts the final quality of manufactured products, Figure 3-16.

Summary

The type of manufacturing best suited to make a product is determined by the volume of products needed, the availability of inputs (equipment, capital, labor), the desired quality of the product, the life cycle of the product, and the production philosophy. Four major types of manufacturing include continuous, intermittent, custom, and just-in-time.

Continuous manufacturing is characterized by high-volume production of a narrow product line and specialized equipment. Mechanization and automation have greatly affected continuous manufacturing. Increasingly, the computer has become part of the manufacturing process with the use of computer-aided design (CAD), computer-aided manufacturing (CAM), computer-integrated manufacturing (CIM), and computer numerical control (CNC).

Intermittent manufacturing is characterized by medium-volume production, wide product line, generalized equipment, work flexibility, and large inventory. Retooling and continual set-up with generalized equipment allow this system to react quickly to varying consumer buying patterns.

Custom manufacturing is characterized by low-volume production of a wide product line. It is often associated with high quality because of the pride and high level of technical skill of the workers. Problem-solving and troubleshooting are necessary because each new product presents new challenges.

Just-in-time manufacturing is characterized by low-, medium-, or high-volume production; high quality; and high worker satisfaction. Through reduction of inventory and buffer stock, quality problems are identified and solved quickly. An increased level of worker responsibility directly affects product quality. Currently, many traditional manufacturers are adopting just-in-time manufacturing.

DISCUSSION QUESTIONS

1. Why is choosing a type of manufacturing system a difficult and complex process?
2. What role does production philosophy play in determining which type of manufacturing system is used?
3. Describe and discuss the advantages and disadvantages of the various types of manufacturing systems introduced in the chapter (continuous, intermittent, custom, and JIT).
4. Why is the just-in-time manufacturing system gaining wide-spread appeal in all types of manufacturing systems?
5. Quality of work life is an important issue in manufacturing. Explain why this is an important factor in determining the quality of products.
6. What are the effects of reducing inventory in JIT manufacturing?
7. Depreciation of products may occur naturally or it may be forced by creating style changes. Explain the difference between these two types of depreciation, and give examples.
8. Identify local manufacturing companies, and identify the type of manufacturing system they use.

CHAPTER ACTIVITIES

 COMPARING CUSTOM AND CONTINUOUS MANUFACTURING

OBJECTIVE

Manufacturers use three common methods: custom, intermittent, and continuous manufacturing. This activity focuses on custom and continuous manufacturing.

Custom manufacturing produces low-volume, high-quality, one-of-a-kind products. This type of manufacturing employs highly skilled craftspeople. Continuous manufacturing produces high-volume, medium-quality, identical products, and employs semiskilled or unskilled workers.

In this activity, you will make a product twice; first with custom manufacturing, and then with continuous manufacturing. You will compare the products made and the manufacturing systems used using four criteria: 1) consistency of product quality, 2) interchangeability of parts, 3) production times, and 4) product appeal. The product is a yo-yo, Figure 1.

MATERIALS AND SUPPLIES

For Custom Manufacturing

1. Two precut squares of hardwood per student, size .563" thick by 2.5" square
2. One dowel rod per student, size .25" diameter by 1 inch long

Figure 1. Yo-yo

3. 36" kite string per student
4. Wood glue
5. 100 and 150 grit sandpaper
6. Assorted hand tools: saws, files, rasps, drills, vises, rulers
7. Finishes and brushes
8. Safety glasses
9. Stop watch
10. Yo-yo product drawing, Figure 2

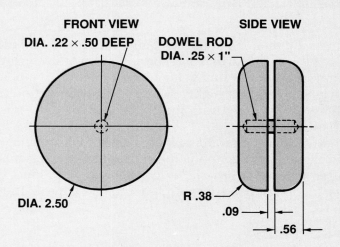

Figure 2. Yo-yo product drawing

For Continuous Manufacturing

1. Precut hardwood boards, .563" thick by 2.5" wide by any length (you will need two pieces per student at 2.5" long)
2. One dowel rod per student, size .25" diameter by 1 inch long
3. 36" kite string per student
4. Wood glue
5. 100 and 150 grit sandpaper
6. Power tools and machines: radial saw, bandsaw, router, drill press, finish sander
7. Spray finish
8. Safety glasses
9. Stop watch
10. Operation sheets (from your teacher)
11. Jigs and fixtures (from your teacher)

PROCEDURE

Custom Manufacturing

1. Obtain the yo-yo product drawing, necessary materials, and hand tools from your teacher.
2. Custom manufacture one yo-yo using handtools and following the plans in the yo-yo product drawing. Each student will make a yo-yo. You will perform all the steps needed to make the yo-yo, from cutting the wood to make it round, to drilling the hole, to finishing and assembling the yo-yo.

    NOTE: Be sure to follow all safety rules when using hand tools and to wear your safety glasses.
3. Each student should keep track of the time it takes to make the yo-yo using the custom manufacturing system.

Continuous Manufacturing

1. Help your teacher set up a continuous yo-yo manufacturing line. Special aids called jigs and fixtures will be attached to certain machines or used with power tools. These jigs and fixtures will help you manufacture the yo-yo using the continuous manufacturing system.
2. Your teacher will select one student to specialize in each of the processes on the continuous manufacturing line. At each machine or bench will be a sheet that explains the steps to be done. Your teacher will also train each student in his or her specialized job on the continuous manufacturing line.
3. After your teacher is sure all students understand their jobs, continuous manufacturing of the yo-yo can begin.
4. Use the stop watch to keep track of the time it takes to make one yo-yo for each student in the class using the continuous manufacturing system.

DISCUSSION

When yo-yos have been made by both systems, the class will discuss the products. Compare the yo-yos using the following criteria:

	YO-YO EVALUATION CRITERIA					
	CONSISTENT QUALITY	**INTERCHANGEABLE PARTS**	**PRODUCTION TIMES**		**PRODUCT APPEAL**	
SYSTEM	YO-YO YO-YO DRAWING RULER	YO-YO PARTS	YO-YO STOP WATCH		YO-YO YES NO	
			TOTAL	**1 YO-YO**		
CUSTOM						
CONTINUOUS						

Figure 3. Yo-yo evaluation sheet

1. **Consistency of product quality.** Collect all the yo-yos made by custom and continuous manufacturing. Measure each yo-yo and compare the dimensions with those on the yo-yo product drawing. Keep track of the number of products that match and do not match the dimensions in the drawing.

2. **Interchangeability of parts.** Randomly select three yo-yos each from the custom and continuous manufacturing groups. Interchange parts among the three yo-yos in each group. Again, compare the yo-yos for consistency of size and quality after parts have been interchanged.

3. **Production times.** Calculate and compare the total production time to the one-product production time for yo-yos made with custom and continuous manufacturing.

4. **Product appeal.** Finally, take a poll of the students in your class. Ask them to rate the custom and the continuous manufactured yo-yos on product appeal. Which product would you be more willing to buy if you saw it in a store?

MATH/SCIENCE CONNECTION

Total Production Time: Custom Manufacturing

To calculate total production time (TPT) for custom manufacturing, multiply the time each student took to make a yo-yo by the number of students in the class.

$$\text{Custom TPT} = \text{Time to make each yo-yo} \times \text{Number of Students}$$

One-Product Production Time: Custom Manufacturing

To calculate one-product production time (OPPT) for custom manufacturing, divide Custom TPT by the number of students in the class. This will give you the average custom manufacturing time for each student to produce one yo-yo.

$$\text{Custom OPPT} = \text{Custom TPT} \div \text{Number of Students}$$

Total Production Time: Continuous Manufacturing

The total production time for continuous manufacturing will be measured directly by the stop watch.

One-Product Production Time: Continuous Manufacturing

Divide total production time for continuous manufacturing by the number of products made. This will give you the average time needed to make one product.

$$\text{Continuous OPPT} = \text{Continuous TPT} \div \text{Number of Products}$$

RELATED QUESTIONS

1. What are the characteristics of custom manufacturing and continuous manufacturing?
2. Which manufacturing system produced the products with the best consistency of quality? Why?
3. Which manufacturing system produced the products with the best interchangeability of parts? Why?
4. Which manufacturing system produced the products with the best production times? What makes a production time "best"?
5. Which manufacturing system produced the products your classmates found most appealing? What were their reasons?

CHAPTER 4

Careers in Manufacturing

OBJECTIVES

After completing this chapter, you will know about:

- The career opportunities you can find in manufacturing.

- Why people with many skills and talents are important to the efficient operation of a manufacturing company.

- The types of departments found in a manufacturing company and how they work together toward one goal.

- The effect technology will have on the future of manufacturing careers.

KEY TERMS

CEO
Department
Distribution worker
Engineer
Engineering department
Finance department
Hierarchical order
Human resources
  department
Knowledge-intensive
  technology

Labor-intensive
  technology
Management
  department
Marketing department
Production department
Prototype
Research and
  development
Salespeople
Semiskilled

Shipping worker
Skilled
Statistician
Supervisor
Technician
Technologist
Unemployment
Unskilled

Careers in Manufacturing

Manufacturing gives jobs to people and makes the products consumers need. Manufacturing companies hire people with many types of skills and talents to help the companies compete well in the world of business, Figure 4-1.

In this chapter, you will learn about the different types of jobs and careers in manufacturing. You will also read about how new technologies can change manufacturing jobs in the future.

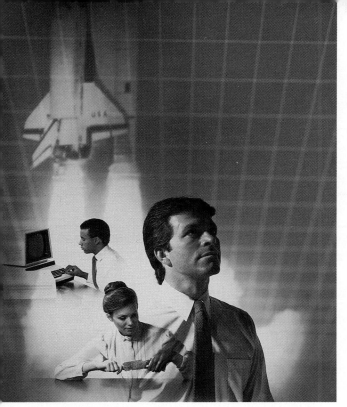

Figure 4-1. Manufacturing companies employ many people with different work interests. *(Courtesy of Du Pont Co.)*

Several Departments, One Goal

Manufacturing companies often divide themselves into several departments. A **department** is a small part of the company. We can think of the departments in a manufacturing company as subsystems of the entire manufacturing company system. Just as in all systems, the subsystems work together to help the larger system meet an overall goal. In manufacturing, the departments work together to meet the overall goal of producing and selling a product.

Your school has different departments too; the English Department, Math Department, History Department, and Industrial Arts/Technology Department are examples. In your school, the departments work together to meet the goal of the school system; that is, to educate the students. To achieve this goal, each department hires people with special skills that allow the division of labor your school needs to make the entire organization work efficiently.

Manufacturing works in the same way, Figure 4-2. Some of the more common departments found in large manufacturing companies include **management, engineering, production, marketing, finances,** and **human resources**. People with different talents, skills, and educational training can find many different types of jobs and careers in each of these departments.

Management Department. For a manufacturing company to be successful, all of the departments must work together toward one goal. Management's job is to make sure all the departments work together. Workers in management, called managers, make company policies and then make sure the other depart-

SYSTEM	SCHOOL	MANUFACTURING COMPANY
GOAL	Educate students	Manufacture products and make a profit
SUBSYSTEMS	Art Department English Department History Department Indust. Arts/Tech. Dept. Physical Education Department Science Department	Engineering Department Finance Department Human Resources Department Management Department Marketing Department Production Department

Figure 4-2. Large organizations, like your school and like manufacturing companies, are often broken into departments. All the departments and the people in them work together toward one goal.

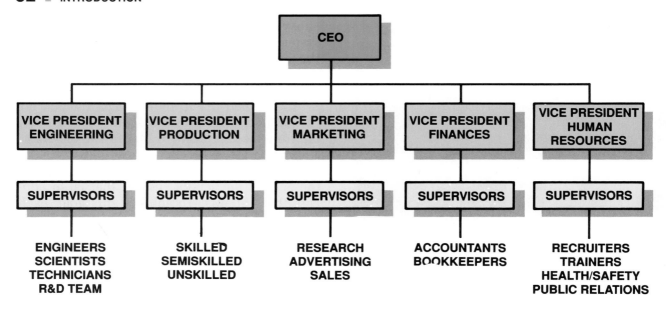

Figure 4-3. One form of manufacturing management structure is the hierarchical order.

ments follow these policies. One type of management system is the **hierarchical order**. Figure 4-3 shows a simple hierarchical order for a manufacturing company. At the top of the hierarchy, a chief executive officer, or **CEO**, is in charge of the whole company. Below the CEO are the vice presidents, who manage different departments in the company. These vice presidents communicate company policies to the supervisors, Figure 4-4.

Supervisors make sure that workers in their departments follow the policies made by the upper-level managers.

Engineering Department. The engineering department designs, produces, and tests the first model of a new product. These first mod-

Figure 4-4. These managers create company policies and make sure all the departments work together. *(Courtesy of Hexcel Corporation)*

Figure 4-5. Scientists work in the engineering department in manufacturing. This scientist is testing different plastics materials for bottles. *(Courtesy of Amoco Corporation)*

ing a new product or the system for making that product. In the automobile manufacturing industry, automotive engineers study the ways new materials or different systems, such as a new suspension system, can change the performance of the car, Figure 4-7. Electronics engineers work for companies that manufacture products that have electronic components. Today, that group includes almost everything from the automobiles we ride in to the radios we listen to. Some of the types of engineers found more often in manufacturing are listed in Table 4-1.

Many engineering departments have a **research and development** team, Figure 4-8. This team is made up of the best engineers, technicians, and production workers. Their job is to create and test new product ideas.

Figure 4-6. Technicians often work with computer-controlled tools, equipment, and machines. *(Courtesy of Cincinnati Milacron Inc.)*

els are called **prototypes**. In the engineering department, scientists conduct tests and experiments on new materials like plastics, ceramics, and metal alloys, Figure 4-5. Scientists also conduct experiments with the chemistry of new paints and finishes. Technicians also work in the engineering department, Figure 4-6. A **technician** is usually a skilled and experienced design or production worker. Only the most experienced and skilled technicians can work in the engineering department as drafters, designers, and machinists. We also use the term **technologist** today to mean technician. Finally, many different types of engineers work in manufacturing depending on what product is being produced. **Engineers** are the problem-solvers when it comes to design-

Figure 4-7. This engineer is testing a new automotive suspension system. Often, engineers and technicians work together on this type of job. *(Photo courtesy of EG&G, Wellesley, MA)*

COMMON ENGINEERING JOBS IN MANUFACTURING
aerospace engineer
ceramic engineer
chemical engineer
electrical engineer
electronic engineer
facilities design engineer
industrial engineer
manufacturing engineer
mechanical engineer
metallurgical engineer
product design engineer
product safety engineer
time-study engineer

Table 4-1. These are some of the engineers who work in manufacturing.

Production Department. The production department sets up and uses the tools and machines to make the product. A management worker, the supervisor, is normally in charge of this department. The supervisor tells the production workers what to do and then makes sure they do it. Supervisors also train new workers and encourage safe work habits. Frequently, supervisors begin as production workers.

Production jobs use skilled, semiskilled, and unskilled labor. **Skilled** workers design and make specialized tools, jigs, fixtures, and quality control devices used to manufacture the product. They also adjust and maintain equipment, fixtures, or quality control devices when they break down. Skilled workers include tool and die makers, pattern makers, millwrights, and mechanics. Because their jobs require precision skills, these workers usually have years of manufacturing experience and training. Skilled workers also set up and operate a variety of machines, including computer-controlled devices such as lathes, mills, and even robots, Figure 4-9. **Semiskilled** workers run machines and use the special tools, jigs, and fixtures that are made and set up by skilled workers, Figure 4-10. Semiskilled workers include machinists, machine tool operators, and welders. These workers get their training on the job and do not have the experience of the skilled worker to set up a

Figure 4-8. This member of a research and development team is a highly skilled technician. He is producing a prototype for a toy manufacturing company. *(Courtesy of Fisher-Price, a Division of The Quaker Oats Company)*

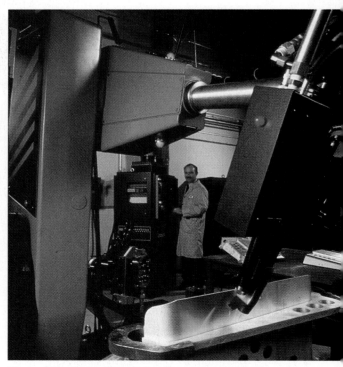

Figure 4-9. Skilled production workers get automated equipment, like this robotic welder, ready for a production run. This takes years of experience and training. *(Courtesy of FMC Corporation)*

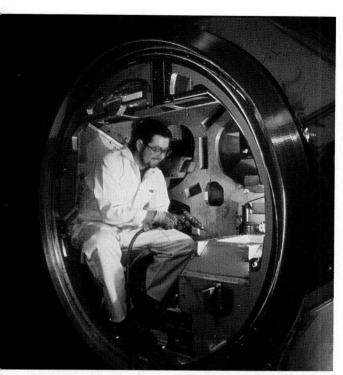

Figure 4-10. Semiskilled production workers develop skills using hand tools and other machines to make a product. *(Courtesy of FMC Corporation)*

production line. **Unskilled** workers perform physically demanding, routine jobs. They include material handlers, finishers, helpers, and assemblers. Unskilled workers do not have the skills to run machinery.

Marketing Department. The marketing department conducts market research and advertises, packages, sells, and distributes the product. Market researchers do surveys to see what consumers want, if they like their product, and what price they will pay, Figure 4-11. They also compare their products to those of competitors. The "taste tests" shown on television by soda companies are examples of market research in action. Market research employs survey designers and **statisticians**.

Advertisers decide which media will be used to publicize the new product. Artists, photographers, and writers prepare advertising campaigns for print media like newspapers, magazines, and direct mailing or for broadcast media like radio and television. The advertising department decides on a name and a trade-

mark for the product as well as a theme or motto for the campaign.

Package designers and artists match the product to the best packaging system. A good package is easy to make, adds little to the product cost, displays the best product features, and attracts consumer attention. Package designers want to make their product stand out from the crowd. They use bright colors as well as unusual package shapes, sizes, and trademarks.

Salespeople identify ways to get the manufactured product into consumers' hands. The consumer could be either an individual or another industry. When an individual buys a manufactured product in a store, it is called a retail sale. When another industry buys a manufactured product, it is called an industrial sale. Several good examples of industrial sales take place in the automobile manufacturing industry. For example, tire manufacturers make tires to sell to automobile manufacturers for use on new cars. Also, steel manufacturers form steel into sheets to sell to automobile manufacturers who transform the sheets into door panels, hoods, and fenders. The job of salespeople, whether in retail or industrial sales, is to point out the product's best features

Figure 4-11. Marketing workers determine consumer interest in new products. These workers are evaluating the response of children to a new game. *(Courtesy of Fisher-Price, a Division of The Quaker Oats Company)*

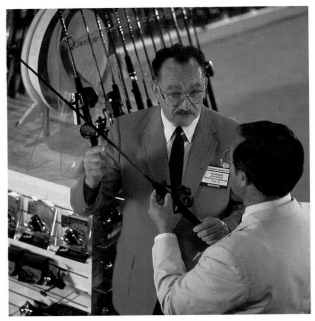

Figure 4-12. One function of marketing is sales. This salesperson is telling a retailer about a new line of fishing equipment. *(Courtesy of Zebco Division of Brunswick Corporation)*

as well as how it can be sold or used, Figure 4-12.

Getting the product from the production facility to the consumer is the job of distribution or shipping workers. **Distribution** or **shipping workers** identify the most economical and efficient way to transport the product to the retail store. Comparisons of truck, train, boat, or plane transportation are made based on the cost of delivery, speed of delivery needed, and location of the retail store. Some large manufacturing companies have their own distribution division consisting of dozens of trucks.

Finance Department. Financial record-keeping is very important to manufacturing companies. The main objective of a manufacturing company is to make a profit on the product they produce and sell. The finance department keeps track of all income and expenditures. Expenditures include payroll; materials costs; utility costs for lighting, heating, air conditioning, and machines; and the costs of buying and maintaining tools, equipment, and machines.

Accountants, bookkeepers, and other record-keepers work in the finance department to make sure the company develops and follows a budget, Figure 4-13.

Human Resources Department. The human resources department is responsible for the following:

1. Recruitment—Recruiters identify new workers to fill vacant positions in the manufacturing company. They must match workers to the jobs by examining job applications and by conducting interviews and performance testing.

Figure 4-13. Most manufacturing companies keep their financial records on computers. This woman is an accountant for a large manufacturing company; she works in the finance department. *(Courtesy of Fleetwood Enterprises)*

2. Negotiation—Negotiators work with labor or unions to agree on a contract that specifies wages, fringe benefits, and insurances.

3. Training—Trainers are teachers in industry. They prepare new workers for their jobs or teach experienced workers how to use new equipment, Figure 4-14.

Figure 4-14. One function of the human resources department is to train new employees. The man on the left is a trainer for a manufacturing company. He is getting the man on the right ready for his new job. *(Courtesy of Du Pont Co.)*

4. Health and Safety—Safety officers maintain a safe work environment by following standards set by the Occupational Safety and Health Administration (OSHA).

5. Public Relations—Public relations people keep the general public aware of the most recent developments in the company.

It is important that human resources workers get along well with other people. Their job is working with people to make the manufacturing company run smoothly and efficiently.

White Collar—Blue Collar

Manufacturing jobs are divided between white collar and blue collar workers. These terms refer to the shirt color traditionally work by each class of worker. White collar workers do not usually perform manual labor. They work with other people in management positions or with data, such as drawings, charts, and financial records, to plan and direct the manufacturing enterprise. White collar workers are in the management, engineering, marketing, finance, and human resources departments.

Blue collar workers are the laborers in manufacturing. They usually work with tools, machines, and equipment to produce the product. Blue collar workers are mainly in the production department, but many technicians in the engineering department are also blue collar workers.

In manufacturing companies today, there are about seventy-five percent blue collar workers and twenty-five percent white collar workers. In other industries, the number of blue and white collar workers is very different. For example, the insurance industry employs almost ninety percent white collar workers (clerical, sales, etc.) and only ten percent blue collar workers (technicians and laborers).

Job Considerations

There are many considerations when thinking about a career in manufacturing. One of the most important is the impact new technologies will have on manufacturing jobs in the future. Other important factors to consider include educational requirements, the nature of the work, and the salary.

Technological Impact on Manufacturing Jobs

In the past, one person could have had the same job for thirty years before retiring. Today, the average worker could have twelve different jobs throughout life. One reason for this is the rapid change caused by new technology. Does this mean that technology destroys jobs? Some new technologies, like robotics, are replacing thousands of workers on today's manufacturing lines. Many of yesterday's jobs, such as the blacksmith, milkman, harness maker, and ice man, no longer exist because of technological changes. But technology also creates new jobs that never existed before. Compare the backhoe with the robot. When the backhoe was first used, it did the work of ten workers, it could run without taking a break, and it needed only one operator, Figure 4-15. Many ditch diggers were replaced by the backhoe, but new jobs were created in the fields of hydraulics, mechanics, control systems, and backhoe maintenance. Jobs were also created for workers who manufactured backhoes. Today, workers are afraid of losing their jobs because one robot can replace seven workers. Robots can also work without taking breaks or vacations, they do not go on strike, and usually only one operator is required. But just as the

Figure 4-16. The new jobs that will be created by technology, like these robotics technicians, require a strong technology, math, and science education. *(Courtesy of NASA)*

backhoe created new jobs, new jobs will also grow around robotic technology.

The Impact of Robots. Robots are a labor-saving technology designed to raise productivity and lower production costs. They will displace 100,000 to 200,000 jobs by the year 2000. Most of the resulting **unemployment** will affect unskilled and semiskilled jobs, such as material feeding, product assembly, welding, and painting.

On the other hand, robotics will create many jobs. The biggest growth is expected at the technician level, with up to 64,000 robotic technicians needed by the year 2000 to test, program, install, troubleshoot, and maintain industrial robots. More engineers will also be required. Robots are made of electrical, electronic, mechanical, and fluid power systems. Companies will need engineers in each of these fields to design and produce new robots, Figure 4-16.

Most of the jobs lost will be semiskilled or unskilled positions that require little education beyond high school. Many of the new jobs will require a high degree of technical, scientific, and mathematical background. Robotic technicians must have two or more years of college training, and engineers need a four-year college degree or more.

Figure 4-15. The backhoe is a labor-saving device that gave jobs to semiskilled workers. *(Courtesy of Deere and Company, Moline, IL)*

Yesterday, our society went through the industrial age. During that time, physical skills were important to the efficient operation of manufacturing. This was **labor-intensive technology**. We are now in the information age. Mental skills are now important to improving our society. **Knowledge-intensive technology** will be the buzz term for the twenty-first century.

Educational Requirements

Each job in a manufacturing company requires different skills and talents. Everyone together, from artists and writers to engineers and machinists, makes a company work. The educational requirements are as varied as the jobs themselves, Figure 4-17. Some of the different educational training grounds follow.

College. Many jobs require a four-year college degree, called a bachelor's degree. Workers in management, finances, and marketing often have college degrees in fields like management, industrial relations, business, account-

ing, and computer science. Some even have a master's or a doctor's degree. Engineers and scientists have college degrees that require extensive math and science training. Many technicians can receive a two-year college degree called an associate's degree. Because technicians carry out the ideas of engineers, their two years of education are filled with hands-on technical courses and the math and science courses needed to understand the basics of engineering.

Technical School. Many skilled and semi-skilled workers receive their first educational training through a high school or a postsecondary vocational or technical school. The program length varies with the school and the technical area. Programs can run from several months to several years.

Apprenticeship Training. Skilled workers usually complete an apprenticeship training program. As apprentices, they work with skilled craftspeople on the job to learn specific skills,

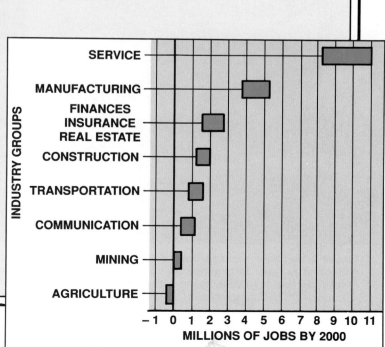

Changes in Employment by the Year 2000

Which fields will have the best growth by the year 2000? The following bar chart identifies the number of jobs expected in different industries.

This chart illustrates the changes in employment expected in different fields into the year 2000. Notice the number of new manufacturing jobs expected.

INDUSTRY GROUPS

SERVICE
MANUFACTURING
FINANCES INSURANCE REAL ESTATE
CONSTRUCTION
TRANSPORTATION
COMMUNICATION
MINING
AGRICULTURE

−1 0 1 2 3 4 5 6 7 8 9 10 11
MILLIONS OF JOBS BY 2000

Figure 4-17. Education is the key to the development of new technologies for manufacturing. The ability to use computers may become a basic skill requirement. *(Courtesy of NASA)*

and they take classes that supply the knowledge base they need.

On-the-Job Training. Semiskilled workers get their training on the job. This can be done because these jobs do not require a high degree of skill that would take years to learn.

Future Educational Requirements

With the increased use of new complex computer, robotic, and automation technologies, many more jobs in manufacturing will require some sort of education beyond high school. In the past, a high school education was required as a minimum for getting a good job. In the future, the minimum requirement will be some sort of postsecondary education.

Nature of the Work

All jobs can be described by the amount of interaction workers have with other people, data, or things. The *Dictionary of Occupational Titles* ranks jobs by these three factors. Jobs that require the most interaction with people include management, human resources, and marketing positions, Figure 4-18. Workers in these jobs must get along with others, give and take instructions, and supervise. Workers in financial affairs, marketing, and engineering spend most of their time

Figure 4-18. These managers work very closely with other people. Jobs in marketing and human resources also involve working with people. *(Courtesy of The Stanley Works)*

Figure 4-19. This technician is checking the number of screwdriver handles being produced. He works with data, counting products and solving calculations. *(Courtesy of FMC Corporation)*

Fastest Growing Occupations by 2000

The job market is changing faster today than at any other time in history. This makes it more difficult for students to make decisions about the education and training they need for a good job. Staying informed can help. The *Dictionary of Occupational Titles* and the *Occupational Outlook Handbook* are good sources. These books describe various occupations, educational requirements, working conditions, future outlooks and salary levels. They provide good information on the best jobs for the future. The U.S. Department of Labor is also a good source. A recent report listed some manufacturing-related jobs among the fastest growing occupations into the year 2000. Not all of the growth listed will be in manufacturing companies; some will be in other industries. The job titles are shown with the growth percentage expected through the end of the century. Use the *Dictionary of Occupational Titles* or the *Occupational Outlook Handbook* to learn more about each of these jobs.

OCCUPATION	PERCENTAGE OF GROWTH
Computer service technicians	97%
Computer systems analysts	85%
Computer programmers	77%
Electrical engineers	65%
Electrical/electronics technicians	61%
Mechanical engineers	52%
Mechanical engineering technicians	52%
Plastics compression mold operator	50%
Plastics injection mold operator	50%
Industrial engineers	47%
Metallurgical engineers	47%

By the year 2000, these manufacturing-related fields are expected to grow in the number of workers hired.

working with data, Figure 4-19. They like to handle numbers, perform calculations, and compile information. Those who spend most of their time working with things, such as tools, machines, and equipment, include the unskilled, semiskilled, and skilled production and research and development workers, Figure 4-20.

Most people find they are more comfortable working with people, data, *or* things. Manufacturing today needs a new type of worker; one who can work easily with people, data, *and* things. These well-rounded workers, the technologists or technicians, work with data by reading drawings and making precise calculations. They work with people by talking with engineers and other technicians to decide the best way to do a job. They work with things by turning ideas on paper into products by using tools, materials, processes, and equipment.

Everyone has unique talents and interests. When considering any career, first decide how much you like to work with people, data, and things. Then identify careers that seem to match your interests. To help decide what might attract you, consider the terms Table 4-2 uses in job descriptions.

Figure 4-20. Production workers, like this machinist, enjoy working with things, such as tools and machines, to create new objects. *(Courtesy of Simpson Industries)*

Salaries

Everyone wants to know how much money certain jobs pay. The *Occupational Outlook Handbook* provides some idea of the salary range for most jobs. In general, it seems that those who receive the highest wages are the same people who have the most education, work the longest hours, or have the most responsibility.

Summary

Manufacturing companies hire many workers with different types of education, training, and job skills. People are hired to work in the management, production, finance, engineering, marketing, and human resources departments. The people in each department believe that their jobs are critical to a successful company. The truth is that all departments must work together for the manufacturing company to compete well in the business world. A variety of people are needed with different skills and talents. One way to categorize these skills and talents is by the amount of time employees will spend working with people, data, or things.

If you are considering a career in manufacturing, you should examine four factors: 1) possible future impacts of technology; 2) educational requirements for particular jobs; 3) nature of the work; and 4) salaries. There is a job suited to almost everyone in a large manufacturing company.

TERM	DESCRIPTION
Competition	Compete with others for advancement
Confined space	Work in a small, crowded area
Creativity	Use your creative abilities
Details	Follow specifications, exact work
Hazardous	Involves danger
Help others	Train or teach other people
Influence others	Stimulate or inspire others to work
Initiative	See what needs to be done and do it
Outdoors	Work in all weather conditions
Physical stamina	Takes muscle power
Precision	Work to accurate standards
Public contact	Work with the general public
Repetitious	Do the same thing over and over again
Results seen	End result is a physical product
Solving problems	See problems, make/carry out decisions
Teamwork	Work with others
Use tools/machines	Use your hands to operate machines

Table 4-2. These terms can be used to describe the nature of work in any job.

DISCUSSION QUESTIONS

1. The management structure discussed was that of large manufacturing companies. What would the management structure for smaller companies look like?

2. Several impacts of technological development were mentioned. Do you agree or disagree with the idea that new technology will create new jobs in the future? If so, will these jobs be better than the ones that will be replaced?

3. What are the differences between blue collar and white collar jobs in manufacturing?

4. Compare the kind of work, educational requirements, and job outlook for skilled, semiskilled, and unskilled manufacturing workers.

5. Which department do you think is most important to the successful operation of a manufacturing company? Why?

6. Working together to achieve one goal was identified as a major task for the various departments of a manufacturing company. What could cause the biggest problems for departments trying to work together?

CHAPTER ACTIVITIES

✿ CONSIDERING A CAREER IN MANUFACTURING

OBJECTIVE

The *Dictionary of Occupational Titles* (called the *DOT*) and the *Occupational Outlook Handbook* are fine resources for finding the educational requirements, working conditions, job description, and future employment trends in various careers.

In this activity, you will use the *DOT* and the *Occupational Outlook Handbook* to learn more about some manufacturing jobs.

When you think about a career in manufacturing, you need to gather information about the job. Some of the more important questions to ask yourself include:

■ What kind of work will I do?

■ How much will I work with data, things, and people?

■ What kind of education do I need?

■ What are the future employment trends?

The *Dictionary of Occupational Titles* (*DOT*) and the *Occupational Outlook Handbook*, which can be found in many large libraries, are good starting points for gathering this information. The manufacturing company you will create with your classmates will need to write job descriptions for many positions, and the *DOT* is a good reference book for that purpose. Here are some of the jobs commonly found in a manufacturing company:

Accountant	Handmolder	Quality control director
Advertising director	Helper	Research engineer
Assembler	Job/die setter	Sales person
CAD operator	Machine operator	Sales representative
CAM operator	Machine tool operator	Supervisor
CEO	Machinist	Technical illustrator
Designer	NC mill operator	Technician
Drafter	Packager	Toolmaker
Facilities design engineer	Pattern maker	Union leader
Finisher	Product design engineer	Welder

MATERIALS AND SUPPLIES

1. *Dictionary of Occupational Titles*
2. *Occupational Outlook Handbook*
3. Other references that describe manufacturing jobs

PROCEDURE

1. As a class, make a complete list of the workers you will need for your manufacturing company. Your teacher may help you identify specialized jobs that are not on the list above.
2. Research the jobs using the *DOT* and the *Occupational Outlook Handbook*.
3. Write a short description for each job to include the following:
   a. Nature of the Work—what kind of work is done?
   b. Involvement with Data, Things, and People—how much work is done with data, things, or people?
   c. Educational Requirements—what degree or training is required?
   d. Future Employment Trends—what is the outlook for jobs in this field in the future?

RELATED QUESTIONS

1. Why do some manufacturing careers require four years of college, while others only require a high school or technical school education? What is the difference in these jobs?
2. Which manufacturing careers spend the most time working with people? With data? With things?
3. What are the differences among skilled, semiskilled, and unskilled production careers? Consider kind of work, education, training, and pay.
4. What impact do you think changing technology will have on the job outlook for certain careers in manufacturing?

⚙ DEVELOPING A MANAGEMENT STRUCTURE

OBJECTIVE

One of the most important decisions that must be made early in the life of a manufacturing company is what type of management structure to use. Managers will make most of the decisions throughout the life of a company; choosing the right people for management positions is critical.

In this activity, you will make a chart that shows the management structure and managers for your company.

In this chapter, you read about one type of management structure that is commonly used in manufacturing—the hierarchical order. At the top of the hierarchy is the CEO. When your class develops a manufacturing enterprise, your teacher will probably act as the CEO and make the final decision on tough problems. You will need several other managers—the vice presidents and supervisors for the departments. Managers should be leaders and should be responsible enough to make the right decisions when needed.

MATERIALS AND SUPPLIES

1. Hierarchical order found in Figure 4-3 in this chapter
2. Poster board
3. Drafting tools or computer graphics program

PROCEDURE

1. Using drafting tools or a computer graphics program, draw the hierarchical management structure on a large piece of poster board.
2. Make the blocks on the chart big enough to include the job title and the name of a student.
3. Write the name of your teacher in as CEO. (Your teacher might decide to let someone else act as CEO.)
4. Hold an election to identify those people who would make good vice presidents and supervisors for the engineering, production, marketing, finance, and human resources departments.
5. Place the names of the elected managers on the poster board in the proper places.
6. The names of the workers for each department will be filled in later, after you read more about the hiring process in Chapter 5.
7. Hang the management structure chart on the wall in your lab.

RELATED QUESTIONS

1. What personal qualities or characteristics do you think a good manager needs in manufacturing?
2. What are the disadvantages of the hierarchical management structure? Can you think of any other structures that would work?
3. Why is the work in manufacturing divided among a number of different departments?
4. What are the major responsibilities and tasks of management?

SECTION TWO
MANUFACTURING INPUTS

Inputs are the resources needed to start and operate a manufacturing system. This section will show you the broad array of inputs that manufacturing uses. The most important input is people and the skills, knowledge, and attitudes they bring to their companies. You will learn about the materials used in manufacturing and the tools and machines that process them, from hammers and saws to computers, robots, and lasers. Chapter 8 describes the energy sources that manufacturers use to run tools and machines. Chapter 9 discusses the importance of knowing about safety and knowing the market. In Chapter 10, you will read about the costs of making a product and how manufacturers raise that money. And in chapter 11, you will learn about how manufacturers use time measurement studies to improve their operations.

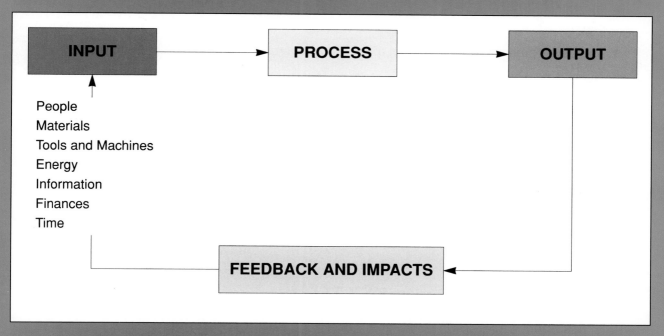

| INPUT | | PROCESS | | OUTPUT |

People
Materials
Tools and Machines
Energy
Information
Finances
Time

FEEDBACK AND IMPACTS

CHAPTER 5

People: The Most Important Resource

After completing this chapter, you will know about:

■ Several important people who contributed to the development of manufacturing technology.

■ The development, and importance, of the Occupational Safety and Health Administration (OSHA).

■ The importance of designing manufacturing systems ergonomically; that is, keeping workers safe and productive.

■ The environmental and personal factors included in the use of ergonomics in the workplace.

■ Various efforts made to humanize the workplace.

■ The importance of worker involvement in safety and production in manufacturing.

KEY TERMS

Ambition	Ergonomics	Persistence
Basic literacy	Hire	Promptness
Communication skills	Humanize	Quality awareness
Cooperation	Innovator	Reliability
Creativity	Inventor	Safety awareness
Entrepreneur	Job application	Technical skills
Equal Employment	Job description	Technological literacy
Opportunity Act	Patience	Worker involvement

The Most Important Resource

"Technology makes it possible; people make it happen" is more than just an old saying. People are the most important input in manufacturing. A few famous people have had dramatic impacts on manufacturing as inventors, innovators, and entrepreneurs. For every famous person, there have been thousands of others hired as managers, designers, producers, and salespeople. Workers are very valuable resources, and manufacturing companies have a responsibility to keep them safe, happy, and healthy.

Inventors, Innovators, and Entrepreneurs

Throughout history, inventors, innovators, and entrepreneurs have made some of the most important contributions to manufacturing and society. **Inventors** create or discover new ideas or products, called inventions. Thomas Edison and Alexander Graham Bell are names you probably know, Figure 5-1. Each invented new products that were very important to manufacturing and society. **Innovators** improve an existing product or combine several ideas to create a new and different product. **Entrepreneurs** take an idea and turn it into a new business. Many inventors do not successfully sell their inventions; they are not good entrepreneurs. Entrepreneurs create jobs for our society. When an entrepreneur finds a product people want, he or she creates a manufacturing company to produce and sell it. Steve Jobs and Steve Wozniak are two entrepreneurs who revolutionized the computer manufacturing industry, Figure 5-2. They formed Apple Computer. It was one of the first companies to produce and sell personal computers—small, inexpensive computers for home use. Before this, business and industry used only large, expensive computers.

(Courtesy of General Electric)

(Courtesy of AT&T Archives)

Figure 5-1. Thomas Edison (left) and Alexander Graham Bell (right) are two inventors who made valuable contributions to manufacturing and society. Can you name their inventions?

(Courtesy of NEXT)

(Courtesy of Unisom)

Figure 5-2. Steve Jobs (left) and Steve Wozniak (right) were entrepreneurs. The company they formed, Apple Computer, was one of the first to manufacture and sell computers for home use.

Every day, people invent new products, improve existing products with innovations, or create new entrepreneurial businesses. Their creative efforts are very important to the continued growth and development of manufacturing and our society.

Hiring People for Manufacturing

Very few people get the chance to be inventors, innovators, or entrepreneurs. There is a need, however, for thousands of good workers in manufacturing. As discussed in Chapter 4, a manufacturing company needs people with varied skills and talents to allow it to run smoothly and efficiently. Manufacturing companies **hire** employees they feel will make positive contributions to their productivity and efficiency. The human resources department locates and prepares people to work in the manufacturing company. When the company needs a person with certain skills, a **job description** is written, Figure 5-3, p. 72. Job descriptions identify the experience, skills, education, and training needed for a specific job. When job descriptions are advertised, people can show their interest by filling out a **job application**, Figure 5-4, p. 73. Recruiters review job applications to see which people most closely match the requirements listed in the job description. The best qualified candidates get an interview to talk to company officials about their qualifications. Interviewers decide whom to hire for the new job, Figure 5-5, p. 74.

Reasons for Hiring

There are many reasons why certain people are hired and others are not. The human resources department considers three areas—knowledge, skills, and attitudes, Figure 5-6, p. 74.

Henry Ford, Manufacturing Innovator

Henry Ford is well known for his contributions to the automobile manufacturing industry. During Ford's time, cars were only for the rich. They were very expensive because of how they were made. Before 1913, they built cars like houses. Workers stood the car frame in one place in the shop and took all the parts to it for assembly, just like building a house. This process, called custom manufacturing, took much time and money. Ford wanted to lower automobile prices so workers who built cars could afford to buy them. He reduced production time by using continuous mass production.

Ford is an excellent example of an innovator. He took ideas developed by others and combined them in a new way to create continuous mass production. The time line below traces the history of just a few of the important ideas from others that Ford tied together in 1913.

Ford combined these ideas to create continuously mass-produced automobiles. For the first time in history, automobile production workers stood in one spot next to a moving assembly line conveyor (Oliver Evans, 1783) and did one task (Sam Slater, 1790), such as putting lug nuts on a wheel. Ford controlled quality with a division of labor (Elisha Root, 1849), interchangeability of parts (Eli Whitney, 1798), precision, and synchronization (Frederick Taylor, 1910). Bringing these ideas together had a dramatic impact on the price of cars. It greatly decreased the time needed to produce one car. Finished cars rolled off the assembly line every few minutes. This shorter production time allowed car prices to drop to the point where most workers could afford to buy one. Mass

Henry Ford was a great innovator in the automobile manufacturing industry. Ford's innovations reduced car prices so workers who made cars could afford to buy them. *(Courtesy of Ford Motor Company)*

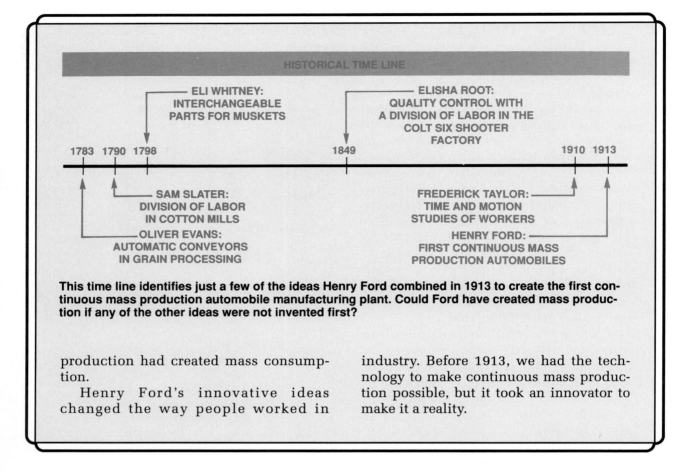

This time line identifies just a few of the ideas Henry Ford combined in 1913 to create the first continuous mass production automobile manufacturing plant. Could Ford have created mass production if any of the other ideas were not invented first?

production had created mass consumption.

Henry Ford's innovative ideas changed the way people worked in industry. Before 1913, we had the technology to make continuous mass production possible, but it took an innovator to make it a reality.

Knowledge. Companies want people who can perform the job for which they are applying. That is why people with work experience or related educational training often have a good chance of getting the job. Table 5-1, p. 74, lists some general points manufacturing companies want people to know. These are very important qualities in a successful worker.

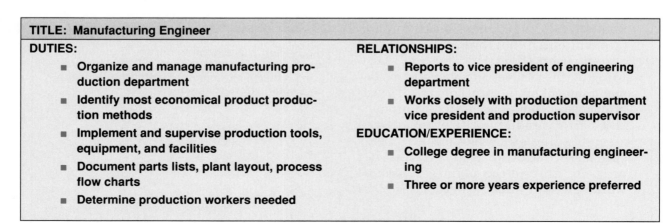

Figure 5-3. Job descriptions are created for each position in a manufacturing company.

APPLICATION FOR EMPLOYMENT

(Please Print Plainly)

NAME _____   Social Security No. _____

      Last   First   Middle Initial

Present Address _____   Telephone No. _____

        No.   Street   City   State

How long have you lived at above address? _____   Are you a citizen? _____

Position applied for _____   Rate of pay expected $_____ per week

Have you been previously employed by us? _____   If so, when? _____

Do you have any friends or relatives employed by us? _____

                                      Name   Address

      Name   Address   Name   Address

If application is considered favorably, when will you be available for work? _____

Any special skills or qualifications which you feel would especially fit you for work with the Company? _____

EDUCATION RECORD

             Years Attended

High School _____ to _____   Did you graduate? _____   If not, highest grade _____

College _____ to _____   Did you graduate? _____   If not, highest grade _____

MILITARY SERVICE RECORD

Are you a veteran? _____   Any job-related experience? _____   If so, please state type _____

EMPLOYMENT RECORD

List your most recent, all present and past employment for past five years

Name of Company	from/to	Type of Work	Salary

PERSONAL REFERENCES

(not relatives)

Name	Address	Phone Number

Person to be notified in event of accident or emergency

Name _____   Address _____   Phone Number_____

Figure 5-4. Manufacturing companies gather information about potential employees with job applications.

Figure 5-5. This person is interviewing a potential employee. What questions do you think he will ask? *(Photo courtesy of UNISYS Corporation)*

- The value of going to work regularly
- The value of getting to work on time
- How to take and follow directions
- How to work hard and get the job done
- How to communicate (read, write, speak, and compute)
- How to adapt to changes created by technology

Table 5-1. Having these qualities can make a person a valuable worker for a manufacturing company.

job. For machinists in the production department, this means being able to set up, operate, adjust, and maintain the tools and machines used to produce the product. In the finance department, accountants must be able to run adding machines, calculators, and computers to keep track of the company's money. In manufacturing, dozens of different jobs call for people with specific technical skills.

Attitudes. Worker attitudes are very important to the safe and efficient operation of a manufacturing enterprise. Without the proper atti-

Skills. Two types of skills important in manufacturing are communication skills and technical skills, Figure 5-7. **Communication skills** include reading, writing, listening, taking instructions, and learning new techniques and processes when technology changes. **Technical skills** relate to the tools and processes of the

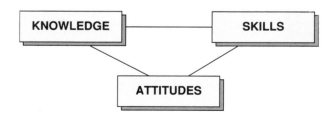

Figure 5-6. Recruiters are interested in learning more about the knowledge, skills, and attitudes of a person considering a job in manufacturing.

Figure 5-7. Manufacturing workers need technical skills to do their job. They also need communication skills because of their constant interaction with supervisors and other workers. What specific technical and communication skills do you think these workers need? *(Photo courtesy of Ford Motor Company)*

Equal Employment Opportunity Act

Employers must, by law, treat all job applicants and workers fairly. The **Equal Employment Opportunity Act** includes federal and state laws that require all employees and applicants to be treated fairly without regard to race, color, sex, age, marital status, religious belief, or national origin. This law protects workers and people looking for jobs from any type of discrimination.

tudes, people with all the necessary knowledge and skills can have a negative impact on the company. Table 5-2 lists some of the more important attitudes employers look for in potential employees, Figure 5-8.

The Problems of Illiteracy

There is some concern that our country might not have the human resources needed to operate future manufacturing technology. Industrial leaders say people lack basic literacy and technological literacy. Literacy involves having certain knowledge, skills, and attitudes. **Basic literacy** includes reading, writing, communicating, computing, and learning. **Technological literacy** involves understanding how technology works, adapting to changes

Figure 5-8. One of the most important attitudes a manufacturing worker can have is a concern for the quality of the product being made. Product quality is very important to the success of a manufacturing enterprise. *(Reproduced with permission of AT&T)*

- **Ambition: a desire to be the best**
- **Cooperation: the ability to work with others**
- **Creativity: problem-solving with good ideas**
- **Patience: remaining calm and in control**
- **Persistence: being determined; finishing a job**
- **Promptness: being on time to work or to do a job**
- **Quality awareness: concern for product quality**
- **Reliability: showing people they can count on you**
- **Safety awareness: concern for safety**

Table 5-2. These attitudes are very important to manufacturing workers. Which of these do you think is most important?

NEGATIVE IMPACTS OF BASIC AND TECHNOLOGICAL ILLITERACY

SHORT-RANGE IMPACTS
- **Increased costs:** Illiterate workers cost companies money by breaking tools, ruining products, or getting hurt.
- **Adapt to change:** When technology changes a job, workers can't read or learn new processes or equipment.
- **Product quality:** When a worker can't learn to use a new piece of equipment, product quality suffers.
- **Hiring new workers:** When a worker is fired, new workers are expensive to find and train.
- **Health hazards:** Illiterate workers can't read safety signs or operating manuals.

LONG-RANGE IMPACTS
- **Lower productivity:** Production goes down.
- **Competitiveness:** Japan, Korea, Taiwan, and other developing countries take our manufacturing business.
- **Unemployment:** When companies lose their business, people lose their jobs.
- **Standard of living:** Widespread unemployment will cause the standard of living in America to go down.

Table 5-3. Workers who lack basic and technological literacy might have a dramatic impact on manufacturing and the American economy.

created by new technologies, and understanding the impacts of using new manufacturing technologies on people, society, and the environment. People who lack basic and technological literacy could have a dramatic impact on the future of manufacturing and America's place in the world economy. Table 5-3 lists some short-range and long-range negative impacts of workers limited in basic and technological literacy. Notice how the short-range impacts may eventually affect the standard of

living in our country. The standard of living includes the money we have to spend, the luxuries we can afford, and the quality of our lives. People who lack basic and technological literacy pose important problems for manufacturing and our technological society.

Worker Involvement in Manufacturing

In the past, managers used manufacturing workers for their muscle power but not to help make decisions. Today, managers see the im-

Figure 5-9. This worker involvement team includes production workers, supervisors, and other managers. They are reviewing product plans to determine the best production processes to be used. In the past, production workers were not involved in decision-making. *(Courtesy of The Stanley Works)*

portance of worker involvement in making decisions, policies, and work procedures. Workers are more involved in the day-to-day business and know best how things should be done.

The Japanese and Swedish automobile manufacturers were the first to involve workers in decision-making. Recently, American manufacturers have started **worker involvement** programs, Figure 5-9. Usually, small groups of workers help make decisions about their workplace, the product design, and the manufacturing processes. Companies using worker involvement believe the positive psychological impacts include more pride in workmanship, more self-respect, and a feeling of contributing more to the company. In the end, worker involvement programs result in a heightened sense of responsibility, better product quality, and more worker and plant productivity.

Protecting People in the Workplace

People are not only valuable resources to their company, but they are also very important to their families and communities. People are fragile biological systems that must be protected from an often dangerous manufacturing environment, Figure 5-10. Every year thousands of people contract diseases or are killed or hurt in accidents as the result of working in industry. Obviously, the most tragic accidents involve the loss of human life. However, many more people get hurt or contract disease than are killed.

Accidents and Diseases

At the start of the industrial age, working conditions were often dangerous and difficult. People could work twelve to fourteen hours a day, six to seven days per week, in buildings with poor heating, lighting, ventilation, and machine safety. Many deaths and injuries resulted. One study made in 1906 in Allegheny County, Pennsylvania, where steel was the leading manufactured product, found 526 deaths and 500 permanent disabilities for

Figure 5-10. A manufacturing plant can be a very dangerous place to work. Companies have a responsibility to keep their employees safe, happy, and healthy in the workplace. *(Courtesy of Allegheny Ludlum Corporation)*

the year from on-the-job accidents. That is more than one person killed every day.

Workers also contracted many diseases on the job. In the match manufacturing industries, for example, people who worked with phosphorous-containing chemicals developed a disease called "phossy-jaw." This was a painful inflammation of the jaw that made it impossible for the worker to function.

OSHA—Setting Safety Standards

Since the days of America's early industrial age, many steps have been taken to humanize the workplace. To **humanize** means to make the workplace safe and comfortable for humans. Two people who made valuable contributions to these efforts were Lillian Gilbreth and Alice Hamilton.

One of the most important actions was the development of the Occupational Safety and Health Administration (OSHA). OSHA is a part of the federal government responsible for ensuring safe and healthful working conditions, Figure 5-11. It protects workers by setting the standards for safety in American industry. OSHA says that workers have the right to a safe workplace, and that both the company and the workers must comply with the development, implementation, and fol-

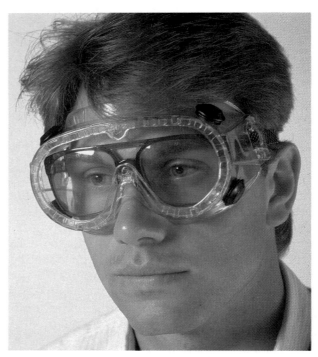

Figure 5-12. The combination of safety goggles and safety glasses will give this worker extra protection from flying debris and dust on the job. *(Courtesy of 1989 Lab Safety Supply Catalog)*

lowing of the regulations. It sets guidelines on machine safety, electrical hazards, personal protection equipment, and many other areas. Failure to follow OSHA regulations could result in company fines.

Ergonomics

Manufacturers must design the workplace and work practices for the people who do the job. Designing systems for people is called **ergonomics**. The aim of ergonomics in the workplace is to improve the efficiency, safety, and well-being of the worker by reducing the chance of accidents and diseases. Manufacturing companies have a responsibility to design systems ergonomically to protect their workers. The following factors should be considered.

Eye Protection

Manufacturing workers should always wear proper personal eye protection and use

Figure 5-11. In accordance with OSHA regulations, this safety officer is wearing a hard hat and safety glasses. *(Photo reprinted with permission of Waste Management, Inc.)*

Gilbreth and Hamilton, Humanizing the Workplace

Two Americans who were pioneers in improving the working conditions in industry were Lillian Gilbreth and Alice Hamilton.

In 1878, Lillian Gilbreth went to work in her husband's company as an engineering apprentice. She was amazed at the working conditions. The engineers in the company saw workers as machines, not people. Gilbreth was the first to see that this attitude had a terrible psychological effect on the workers and made them less productive. She thought of the workers as the most important part of a productive company. Her approach was to humanize industrial work by trying to make the workers happy. She convinced her husband that happy workers would be more productive. With his help, Gilbreth was the first person to give fifteen-minute work breaks, bonuses for the most productive workers, and vacations.

Alice Hamilton was a medical doctor in Chicago during the early 1900s. Dr. Hamilton was the first American to study the health effects of dangerous and toxic materials on industrial workers. She became an expert in the ailments caused by exposure to lead. Her work resulted in state laws requiring the use of safety devices, medical examinations for workers, and worker's compensation for diseases caused by exposure to toxic industrial materials.

Dr. Alice Hamilton was the first American to investigate the effects of dangerous materials on industrial workers. *(Courtesy of the National Portrait Gallery, Smithsonian Institution)*

Both these Americans stressed the importance of the worker as a valuable resource for industry. Through their efforts, working conditions and safety were greatly improved.

machine guards, Figure 5-12. There is a variety of eye protection devices for each job and machine. Welders, for example, wear special tinted lenses to block out harmful ultraviolet rays when welding. They also wear clear lenses when cleaning a weld to keep flying metal from entering their eyes. In general, personal eye protection and machine guards should meet approved standards and be suited to the process being performed, Figure 5-13.

Proper Lighting. Studies have shown that too much or too little light can cause eyestrain and lead to bodily fatigue and accidents. More light is needed in areas where a great amount

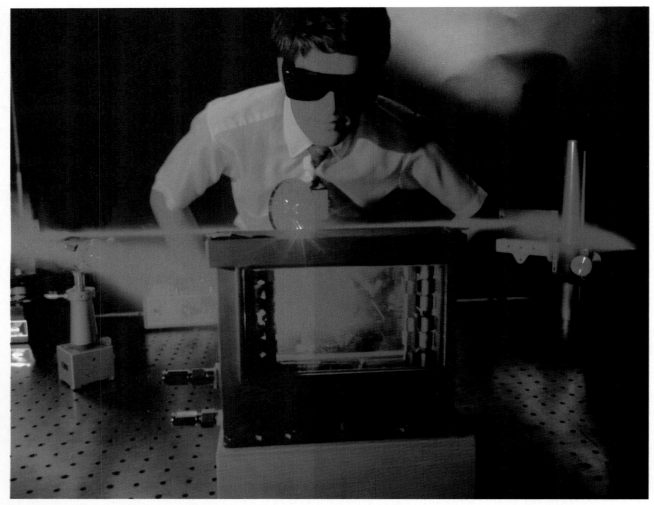

Figure 5-13. Many types of specialized protective eyewear are worn in manufacturing. The tinted lenses worn by this laser technician would not be suitable for welding or running a cutting machine. Choose the right eye protection for the job. *(Courtesy of Caterpillar Inc.)*

of detail or accuracy is required. Drafting areas, for example, need more lighting than machining or welding areas.

Skin Protection

The most obvious danger to the skin results from tool and machine accidents that cause cuts, pinches, abrasions, and punctures. To prevent these, machine guards should always be used. Less obvious dangers include skin diseases. OSHA has identified over 2,000 primary irritants that can cause skin redness, inflammation, or blisters. Individuals might have an initial reaction to a substance or develop an allergy after prolonged contact. Chemicals in glues and finishes, dusts from certain woods, and treated lumber are just a few examples of skin irritants found in manufacturing, Figure 5-14.

Hearing Protection

Excess noise can annoy a worker or disrupt communication between workers and lead to costly accidents or mistakes. Very loud noises or exposure to loud noise over a long time period can cause temporary or permanent hearing loss. Noise is measured in decibels (dB). Figure 5-15 lists decibel levels for vari-

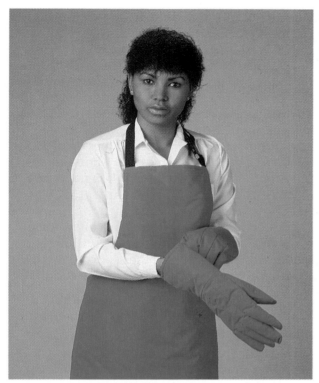

Figure 5-14. Gloves should be worn when working with chemicals or substances to prevent skin irritations or allergies. *(Courtesy of 1989 Lab Safety Catalog)*

DECIBEL LEVELS FOR VARIOUS SOUNDS

DECIBELS

140—
| —50 hp siren (100 ft)
130—
| —jet takeoff (200 ft)
120— —rock concert
| —OSHA standard (15 minutes)
110— —riveter
|
100— —pneumatic hammer
| —heavy city traffic
90— —OSHA standard (8 hours)
| —printing press plant
80— —subway train (20 ft)
| —average factory
70— —vacuum cleaner (10 ft)
| —average conversation (1 ft)
60— —business accounting office
|
50— —quiet automobile
| —running refrigerator
40— —inside an average household
|
30— —soft whisper (5 ft)
|
20—
| —normal breathing
10— —average threshold of hearing

Figure 5-15. Noise is measured in decibels (dB). This chart identifies decibel levels for specific sources of noise. Compare the decibel level of a rock concert with the standard specified by OSHA for an eight-hour workday.

ous activities. OSHA has established ninety decibels per eight-hour day as the standard for the maximum level of noise exposure. Companies are required to provide means to reduce noise above that level. The first choice is to place the noisy process in an enclosure. Workers should use personal hearing protection devices, such as ear muffs or plugs, only as a second choice because they can block out other sounds the worker must hear.

Protection from Heat

In manufacturing plants where high heat is used to process materials, there is a danger of overheating the body. Often, workers in these areas wear special clothing such as gloves, hat, boots, and coats, to protect them from the high heat, Figure 5-16. However, this special clothing also tends to increase the worker's body temperature, which can lead to heat exhaustion, heat cramps, or heat stroke. Heat stroke is the most dangerous and can cause death. The company must control the climate in a manufacturing facility.

Respiratory System Protection

The respiratory system, including the nose, mouth, throat, and lungs, provides the oxygen the body needs. Normal air has twenty-one percent oxygen and seventy-nine percent nitrogen and other gases. Contaminants or pollutants can create an imbalance in these percentages. This could affect the respiratory system's ability to feed oxygen to the body. Figure 5-17 identifies the five types of contaminants.

Figure 5-16. Notice the protective clothing this person working molten metal is wearing. Although he is protected from skin burns, there is a danger of overheating his body. *(Courtesy of NASA)*

The problems possible from contaminants include nose, throat, and lung irritations; blood poisoning; and lung disease.

The use of ventilation systems or respirators can prevent contaminants from entering the respiratory system. Ventilation should always be the first choice. A good ventilation system should both remove contaminated air and supply fresh air. Respirators, which are worn over the mouth and nose, should be used only for temporary situations. It is necessary to choose the appropriate respirator. Those designed to remove dust may not remove vapors or fumes. Respirators are often uncomfortable, hot, and difficult to use. Therefore, workers often do not use them effectively. This is another reason why ventilation should be the first choice.

Worker Interaction with Tools, Machines, and Furniture

The interaction of people with tools, machines, and furniture in manufacturing can result in injuries if the equipment is not ergonomically designed.

Tools. Workers use their hands to hold tools. Holding a tool for eight hours a day can be very tiring, Figure 5-18. In fact, over time,

Figure 5-17. Contaminants found in the manufacturing plant can come from solids or liquids. The five different types of contaminants are fumes, dust, smoke, vapors, and mists. How should workers be protected from these contaminants? *(Adapted with permission from National Safety Council:* Protecting Workers' Lives: A Safety and Health Guide for Unions. *Chicago: National Safety Council, 1983.)*

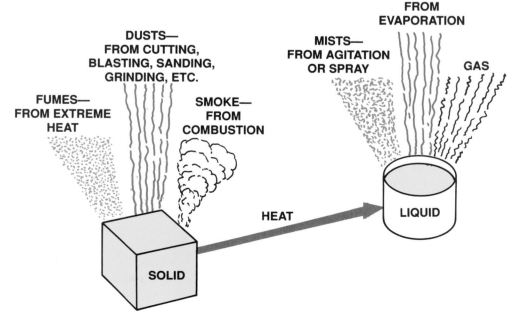

some workers develop injuries similar to tennis elbow (an inflammation of the tendons in the elbow) from using poorly designed tools. Many standard tools can be improved. Figure 5-19 shows an improved pair of needle nose pliers. Workers who used the curved-handle pliers reported fifty percent fewer cases of inflammation and pain. Tools must match the work being done as well as protect the worker from fatigue and injury.

Machines. The most important concern with machines is protection of the worker from dangerous moving parts. The best way to do this is to use commercial machine guards. These guards are designed to protect the worker from getting a hand or other body part caught in a machine. Various machine controls are a second area of concern. Switches and warning labels should be large enough for a worker to read. They should also use color to attract attention. The on/off switch should be in an area that will not allow the machine to be activated by accident. Switches that can be kicked or bumped when a worker is in a danger zone are not ergonomically designed. Every year people lose body parts while operating machines.

Furniture. Employers should provide chairs, workbenches, and tables designed to protect the worker from fatigue and injury. Working at a bench for eight hours a day can be very tiring. When possible, employers should give workers the chance to vary between sitting and standing. Whether sitting or standing, there are optimum work-surface heights. They are based on the height of the worker, the type of work being done, and personal preferences, Figure 5-20. The first concern is to protect the back. There are more back injuries in industry every year than any other injury.

In general, remember that everyone is different. The key words to use in the selection of tools, machines, and furniture are "appropriate" (best for the job) and "adjustable." The appropriate tool or machine should be used in an appropriate manner. Also, adjustable equipment can easily be modified to meet individual needs.

Figure 5-18. Tools must be designed to do the job. They should also protect the worker from fatigue and the possibility of developing permanent damage to the muscles and tendons. *(Courtesy of Chevrolet-Pontiac-Canada Group, General Motors)*

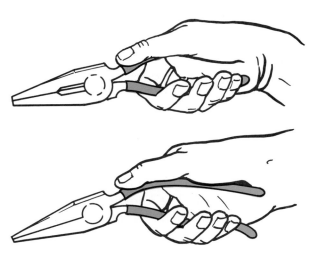

Figure 5-19. The needle nose pliers on the bottom have been ergonomically designed to reduce fatigue and injury. *(Adapted with permission from National Safety Council:* Protecting Workers' Lives: A Safety and Health Guide for Unions. *Chicago: National Safety Council, 1983.)*

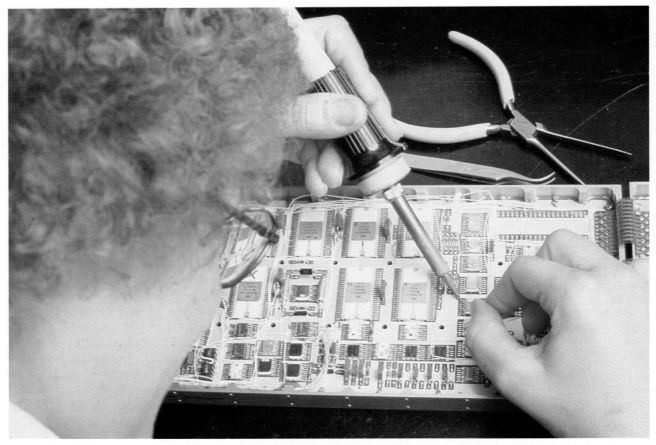

Figure 5-20. This woman is working at an ergonomically designed workbench. There is adequate lighting for the accuracy required in her work; the bench top keeps the small, detailed electronic component close to her eyes; and the soldering pen is lightweight for extended use. *(Courtesy of Motorola Government Electronics Group)*

Summary

Technology is increasingly important in manufacturing. The use of robots and other computer-controlled equipment requires people who can understand, operate, and manage this technology. For this reason and others, people are the most important input in manufacturing. Manufacturing companies have recently realized the importance of their workers.

Efforts to humanize the workplace, such as safety standards, worker involvement programs, and ergonomics, have been implemented. However, companies still believe there is a shortage of potential employees who can use future technology. The knowledge, skills, and attitudes of tomorrow's workers will determine the success or failure of manufacturing.

DISCUSSION QUESTIONS

1. Inventors, innovators, and entrepreneurs begin by wanting to do something in a better way. Is there something you think could be done better, safer, more economically, or more ergonomically? How about your school lockers, desks, pencils, computers? Do you have what it takes to be an inventor, innovator, or entrepreneur?

2. This chapter described communication and technical skills. Which of these do you think is more important in management, production, and finances? Why? Could the amount of interaction with people, data, or things have anything to do with your answer?

3. This chapter identified several attitudes, from ambition to safety awareness, as important qualities in a manufacturing worker. Which of these attitudes do you think is most important? Why?

4. This chapter described the Equal Employment Opportunity Act as a means of protecting workers and job applicants from discrimination. Why do you think this law was created? Is it still needed? Will it be needed in the future?

5. This chapter described worker involvement programs as a means of improving working conditions. Could student involvement programs be used in schools to improve the learning conditions of students?

CHAPTER ACTIVITIES

 BIOGRAPHIES OF IMPORTANT PEOPLE

OBJECTIVE

People make valuable contributions to manufacturing in many ways. As you read in Chapter 4, people with different skills and talents can help a manufacturing company as workers. Another important way that people have contributed to manufacturing is through invention, innovation, or entrepreneurship.

In this activity, you will learn more about an important inventor, innovator, or entrepreneur whose work contributed to manufacturing.

The history of manufacturing was shaped by hundreds of important inventors, innovators, and entrepreneurs. In this unit you read about several important people, including Henry Ford, Eli Whitney, and Alice Hamilton. Reading their life stories can be an inspiration. Many inventors faced very difficult times throughout their lives, but they worked hard, persisted, and sometimes they found an important idea that helped make life easier or better.

MATERIALS AND SUPPLIES

1. Library Resources (encyclopedias and reference books)

PROCEDURE

1. Pick an important inventor, innovator, or entrepreneur.
2. Go to the library and ask the librarian to help you find some information on that person.
3. Write a short paper on the person that describes:
   a. the years when they lived;
   b. where they lived and worked;
   c. their invention, innovation, or idea; and
   d. how this invention, innovation, or idea changed manufacturing technology and our way of life.
4. Make a small poster that describes the person you investigated and his or her contribution. You might even photocopy a photograph out of a book to paste on your poster.
5. Make a bulletin board with other members of your class. You might use this title: "Technology Makes it Possible, People Make it Happen"

RELATED QUESTIONS

1. What are the differences between innovation and invention?
2. What is an entrepreneur?
3. While researching inventors, innovators, and entrepreneurs, did you notice any similarities in their personalities, backgrounds, educations, or other factors?
4. For the specific person you studied, what were the events that lead up to the development of their invention or innovation?

⚙ IDENTIFYING AND HIRING EMPLOYEES

OBJECTIVE

The manufacturing company you are creating with your classmates will need to hire employees that can do their jobs well and safely so that the company will make profits.

In this activity, you will get first-hand experience in filling out job applications and interviewing for a job.

Filling out a job application correctly is very important for the applicant and for the company. Personnel managers use job applications to reduce a list of dozens or hundreds of applicants to several workers who will get a job interview. In addition to interviewing, some companies will test workers to determine what special abilities they might have. Your manufacturing company will want to hire the best people for each position. Hiring people for positions where they can work best will help the manufacturing company work best. This is the job of the human resources department.

MATERIALS AND SUPPLIES

1. Sample job applications
2. Video camera or audio cassette recorder (optional)
3. Problem-solving abilities tester, Figure 1
4. Stop watch
5. Safety glasses

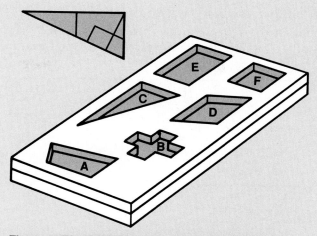

Figure 1. The problem-solving abilities tester

PROCEDURE

1. Custom manufacture the problem-solving abilities tester following all safety rules.

   ■ Lay out the puzzle pattern accurately on ³/₈"- or ¹/₂"-thick wood or plexiglass, Figure 2.

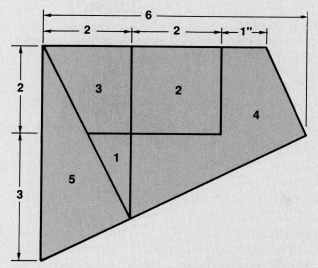

Figure 2. Lay out the pattern for these pieces accurately on a piece of wood or plexiglass.

■ Cut out the pieces using the finest saw blade possible. Try to split the lines when cutting.

■ Sand the edges of the shapes using a disk sander. Try to leave just a bit of the line showing. Do not sand away the line.

■ The pieces do not have to be numbered; this will make it more difficult to complete the puzzles later.

- Sand the pieces to finish them and apply a coating of wax.
- Lay out the pieces in the five patterns shown in Figure 3. Trace around the patterns on a sheet of 1/4" plywood. Do not use fragile, open-grained plywood.

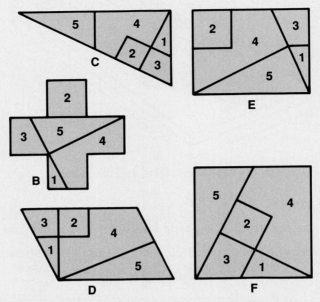

Figure 3. Five possible patterns for the pieces. These are also the solutions to the problem-solving abilities tester.

- Use a jigsaw to cut out the various patterns.
- Attach the cut-out pattern to another sheet of plywood as shown in Figure 1.

2. Make a list of the workers you will need for management, finances, production, engineering, and marketing jobs. Ask your teacher for help.

3. Write short job descriptions for each worker needed. Use your readings in this chapter or the DOT for help.

4. Post the job descriptions on the bulletin board in your classroom and invite interested students to apply for the positions.

5. The vice president and supervisor in the human resources department should narrow the applications down to several people for each position. These people will get an interview.

6. Conduct interviews of the job applicants. You many want to videotape or make an audio tape of the interview.

7. Use the problem-solving abilities tester to test workers' problem-solving skills.

   - Take the individual puzzle pieces and mix them up.
   - Use a stop watch to determine how long it takes each job applicant to complete all five puzzles.

8. Use the results of the problem-solving abilities test, along with the job application and interview, to make hiring decisions for workers.

RELATED QUESTIONS

1. What types of questions would you ask a prospective employee if you were an employer?
2. What manufacturing department is responsible for hiring employees?
3. What qualities do you think employers look for in their workers?
4. During the interviews you conducted, what factors or events would make you not want to hire a person?

CHAPTER 6

Manufacturing Materials

OBJECTIVES

After completing this chapter, you will know about:

- The renewable and exhaustible resources used as raw materials for manufacturing.
- The primary manufacturing processes that change raw materials into standard forms of manufacturing materials.
- The science of materials, including their properties.
- A variety of manufacturing materials in the metallics, polymerics, ceramics, and composites categories.

KEY TERMS

Alloy
Board foot
Brittleness
Ceramic
Chemical refining
Composite
Compression strength
Ductility
Elasticity
Fatigue strength
Ferrous

Fiber-reinforced
   composite
Hardwood
Impact strength
Layered composite
Malleability
Mechanical refining
Metallic
Monomers
Nonferrous
Particle composite

Plasticity
Polymeric
Polymerization
Primary manufacturing
Recycling
Softwood
Tensile strength
Thermal refining
Thermoplastics
Thermosets
Toughness

Manufacturing Materials

The materials that make the finished products we use are manufactured products themselves. For example, before a finished product like a bicycle can be made, the metal for the frame, rubber for the tires, plastics for the seat and reflectors, and even the paint for the frame must be manufactured first. Then these individual materials can be combined to produce a bicycle.

The process of converting raw materials into standard manufacturing materials is called **primary manufacturing**. Using standard materials to make bicycles and other products is called secondary manufacturing. This chapter discusses primary manufacturing. It also identifies some of the most important manufacturing materials. Secondary manufacturing processes will be discussed in Chapter 15.

Renewable and Exhaustible Materials Resources

The source of all materials is the earth. The natural resources in the land, water, and air provide the raw materials that are the basis for all manufacturing materials. Raw materials resources are either renewable or exhaustible, Figure 6-1.

Renewable Raw Materials Resources. Renewable raw materials resources are living, growing organisms. Examples include trees, plants, and animals. Trees are a resource for wood. Some plants provide materials like cotton and rubber. An example of a material from an animal is the wool provided by sheep.

Renewable materials resources can be renewed. When one tree, plant, or animal is harvested for raw materials, a new living organism can begin growing to renew the available supply of raw materials.

Exhaustible Raw Materials Resources. Exhaustible raw materials resources are inorganic (not living) substances found in the earth. Examples include iron and other mineral ores, petroleum, and natural gas. There are limited amounts of these materials available on earth. Once people have extracted or removed all the available resources, the raw materials will no longer exist. In other words, exhaustible materials resources cannot be renewed.

Recycling: Additional Materials Resources. Many materials that come from renewable and exhaustible resources can be recycled. **Recycling** is the process of gathering and reusing discarded or waste materials. Every year, we throw away hundreds of millions of tons of scrap or waste material. Many of these materials can be recycled. They include metals, plastics, glass, and paper. Figure 6-2 lists some yearly averages for recycled materials. Despite these impressive numbers, estimates by the Institute of Scrap Recycling Industries show more than 800 million tons of scrap iron and steel in the United States alone waiting to be recycled. Recycling gives manufacturers another valuable resource for raw materials.

In addition to providing a resource for raw materials, recycling also offers many other advantages to manufacturers and society in general. For example, recycled waste can be processed using less energy than required to process new raw materials. Processing new aluminum consumes large amounts of electrical energy. Recycling aluminum cans and other products can save about ninety-six

RAW MATERIALS RESOURCES	
RENEWABLE	**EXHAUSTIBLE**
TREES, PLANTS, ANIMALS	PETROLEUM, MINERAL ORES, NATURAL GAS

Figure 6-1. Raw materials resources can be renewable or exhaustible.

RECYCLED SCRAP	TONS
Iron and Steel	56,000,000
Paper	24,000,000
Aluminum	2,500,000
Copper	1,500,000
Lead	1,300,000
Stainless Steel	800,000
Zinc	300,000

Figure 6-2. These figures represent only a small fraction of the scrap materials available for recycling.

Figure 6-3. Recycling waste and scrap is an important way to preserve our valuable raw materials resources. *(Courtesy of Aluminum Association, Inc.)*

percent of this electricity. Saving energy also means lower costs for primary manufacturers. In addition to energy and financial savings, we can save our valuable exhaustible energy resources with recycling. Finally, recycling scrap materials reduces the amount of waste placed in garbage dumps and landfills.

In today's throw-away society, recycling is a common-sense solution to saving energy, money, and our natural resources, Figure 6-3.

Primary Manufacturing Processes

All raw materials must be processed; that is, changed to make them more useful. Most materials cannot be used in their raw, natural state. Processing raw materials increases their value. It changes them into a more useful form for secondary manufacturing. The steps in primary manufacturing include obtaining raw materials, refining raw materials, and manufacturing standard materials.

Obtaining Raw Materials

Renewable raw materials are obtained from the earth by harvesting. Examples of harvesting include cutting down trees for wood, tapping rubber trees for latex rubber, picking cotton from plants, and shearing wool from sheep.

Exhaustible raw materials are obtained from the earth by mining and drilling, Figure 6-4. Mineral ores, such as iron, coal, and gold, must be mined. Miners dig shafts or large open pits in the ground and remove the raw ore with heavy equipment. Liquid and gaseous raw materials are removed from the earth by drilling holes deep into the ground. Drilling is used to obtain petroleum and natural gas, which are important raw materials for plastics. Often, workers must drill holes several miles deep to locate petroleum and gas deposits.

Refining Raw Materials

Once obtained, raw materials must be refined. Refining separates the useful part of the raw

Harvesting *(Courtesy of Weyerhaeuser Co.)*

Mining *(Courtesy of the Office of Surface Mining Reclamation, United States Department of the Interior)*

Drilling *(Courtesy of Conoco Inc.)*

Figure 6-4. Raw materials are obtained from the earth by harvesting, mining, and drilling.

material from unwanted and less useful materials. Refining is a way of purifying the raw material.

Logs cut from trees have limited usefulness. They can be used to build log homes or as firewood. Refining logs makes them more useful. At a sawmill the bark is removed, and the logs are cut into different sizes of lumber and boards. Also, thin strips of wood can be shaved off a log for use in making plywood. Workers can then use these refined wood materials to make or build a number of useful products. Examples include furniture, baseball

bats, and structural lumber and wooden molding for homes.

Exhaustible resources must also be refined. Mineral ores usually come from the earth mixed with dirt, rocks, and other less useful mineral ores. Petroleum and natural gas are also contaminated with many impurities that must be removed.

Three major types of processes are used to refine both renewable and exhaustible raw materials. These include mechanical, chemical, and thermal processes, Figure 6-5.

Thermal *(Courtesy of U.S. Iron and Steel Institute)*

Figure 6-5. Thermal and mechanical processes are two of the ways that primary manufacturing refines raw materials.

Mechanical *(Courtesy of Weyerhaeuser Co.)*

Mechanical refining processes use a mechanical force to change the raw materials. Cutting logs into lumber or boards at a sawmill is an example of a mechanical refining process. The sawblade applies the mechanical force. Mechanical forces are applied to mineral ores for crushing. Crushing separates the wanted mineral ore from dirt, rocks, and other unwanted minerals.

Chemical refining processes use chemicals to change the raw material into a more useful form. Plastics are created by chemical reactions using petroleum or natural gas as raw materials. Lumber cut from a log can be treated with chemicals to make it resist decay in outside construction projects. Bauxite, the raw material used to make aluminum, is treated with several chemicals during the refining processes.

Thermal refining processes use heat. Ores, like iron, are often melted in a furnace. When melted, the iron ore separates from unwanted minerals and other impurities. The thermal process that refines petroleum is called distillation. Distillation involves heating petroleum until it vaporizes. When cooled, the petroleum vapor is refined into various products, such as motor oil, gasoline, and kerosene. Wood is also treated thermally. Excess moisture content in lumber is removed by heating and drying wood in kilns.

Manufacturing Standard Materials

First raw materials are obtained from the earth and refined. Then they are manufactured into standard forms of materials called standard stock. Metals and plastics are produced in many of the same forms, such as plates, sheets, rolls, tubes, pipes, bars, rods, and other structural shapes. Wood is prepared in standard sizes, such as two-inch by four-inch lumber and four-foot by eight-foot plywood sheets. Manufacturing materials into standard forms makes them easier to use by secondary manufacturing companies, construction companies, and private consumers. With standardized forms, consumers can be sure they will always get the same shapes and sizes in a product.

Materials Science

Understanding the basic science and properties of materials will help you understand why certain materials are used in certain products or applications.

To a materials scientist, materials are made of atoms and molecules. Atoms are the basic building blocks of all materials. They cannot be broken down into smaller particles. Molecules are combinations of two or more individual atoms, Figure 6-6.

Materials are classified as elements or compounds. Elements are materials that are made up of only one type of atom. We know of 106 elements. Many of these elements are metals. Most materials are compounds. Compounds are materials made by combining two or more elements. Water, a compound, is a combination of the elements oxygen and hydrogen.

Molecular Structure of Materials

Molecular structure is the attractions and connections between molecules and atoms in a material. Materials elements and compounds can be in the form of gas, liquid, or solid, Figure 6-7. Gases have no connections among molecules. Liquids have only slight attractions and connections among molecules. Solid materials have varying degrees of connection among molecules.

The molecules in certain solids, such as wood and plastics, link together to form long chains. These long chains make wood easy to split and certain plastics easy to melt.

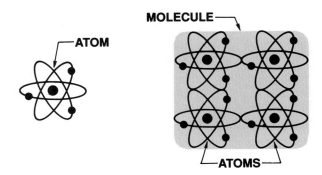

Figure 6-6. Atoms are the building blocks of all materials. Molecules are combinations of two or more atoms.

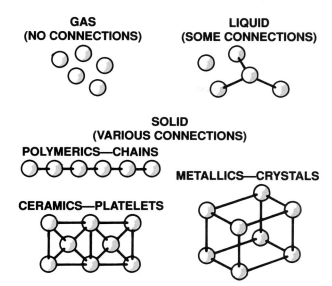

GAS (NO CONNECTIONS)

LIQUID (SOME CONNECTIONS)

SOLID (VARIOUS CONNECTIONS)

POLYMERICS—CHAINS

METALLICS—CRYSTALS

CERAMICS—PLATELETS

Figure 6-7. Elements and compounds can be found in the molecular structures of gas, liquid, or solid forms.

The molecules in ceramic materials link together in flat grids called platelets. There is very little attraction among platelets. In fact, platelets slip against one another. This permits clay to be formed and shaped easily when wet. However, once clay materials are fired (heated in an oven), the platelets melt together and fuse into solid masses. This process cannot be reversed.

Molecules in metals form three-dimensional shapes called crystalline structures. The cross-linking among molecules makes metals strong materials.

Changing the Form of Materials

The form of many materials can often be changed. Water (a liquid) can be frozen to form ice (a solid). Water can also be heated to create steam (a gas). The form of manufacturing materials can also be changed. Metals and certain plastics can be heated and made into liquid or semiliquid forms.

Being able to change the form of a manufacturing material is useful in making products. For example, metals, plastics, and ceramics can be shaped much more easily when they are in a molten or liquid form. When liquid materials are forced into a container, they take

on the shape of that container. More detailed information on forming materials appears in Chapter 15.

Properties of Materials

Properties of materials relate to the characteristics, or nature, of the materials in certain applications. The most common materials properties are mechanical, chemical, thermal, and electrical. The properties of a material depend on its molecular structure. The attraction or connection between molecules and atoms determines how a material reacts when used in a product.

Mechanical Properties

Mechanical properties relate to the reaction of a material to mechanical forces and loads, such as pressing, pulling, and pounding. Mechanical properties described here include several measures of strength, elasticity and plasticity, malleability, ductility, and hardness.

Strength. There are several measures of strength. The most common are tensile, compression, fatigue, and impact, Figure 6-8.

Tensile strength allows a material to resist being pulled apart. It is easily measured and frequently used as a measure of strength. A fishing line being pulled by a fish is an example of tensile strength.

Compression strength allows a material to resist crushing or compressive forces. It is the opposite of tensile strength. Concrete blocks in a foundation resisting the crushing forces of the house are an example of compression strength.

Fatigue strength keeps a material from breaking after it is forced many times in opposite directions. You can see fatigue by bending a paper clip back and forth several times until it breaks. The repeated forces cause the metal in the clip to harden. This is called "work hardening." Once hardened, the metal becomes brittle and fails. The material gets tired or fatigued. Fatigue is the most common cause of failure in metals.

Impact strength allows a material to absorb energy during impacts. Another name for

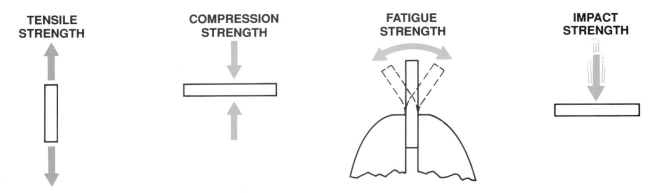

Figure 6-8. Four important measures of strength in materials are tensile, compression, fatigue, and impact.

impact strength is **toughness**. Tough materials absorb energy during impact by changing their shape. We call this ability "deforming plastically." Metals are tough materials. When a piece of sheet metal is hit with a hammer, the metal indents, or deforms plastically. The opposite of toughness is **brittleness**. Brittle materials do not absorb energy well during impact, and they usually shatter. Glass and ceramic are brittle materials.

Elasticity and Plasticity. Elasticity allows a material to return to its original shape after being changed. Springs and rubber bands are examples of elastic materials.

Clay and putty are the opposite of elastic materials. They display plasticity. **Plasticity** allows a material to be easily formed into various shapes that the material retains, Figure 6-9.

Malleability. Malleability lets a material be pounded, rolled, and formed into sheets. Many metals, such as copper, aluminum, and mild steels, are malleable. Aluminum foil is an example of a malleable material.

Ductility. Ductility allows a material to be elongated or drawn down into a wire shape. Materials used in wiring, such as copper, are ductile.

Hardness. Hardness allows a material to resist scratching. Diamonds are the hardest of all materials. Carborundum, a commonly used synthetic (human-made) abrasive material, is almost as hard as diamonds. Usually, hard

materials are also strong. In general, metal and ceramic materials are harder and stronger than plastics and wood materials.

Hardness is an important property when a product is likely to be rubbed or scratched, such as floor tiles. However, hard materials are difficult to machine and form. They also tend to wear out cutting tools.

Chemical Properties

Chemical properties relate to the reaction of materials to certain chemicals. This reaction is called corrosion. One of the most common forms of corrosion is oxidation. The iron in most metals reacts with oxygen in the air to

Figure 6-9. The plasticity of clay makes it useful for making models. *(Courtesy of Ford Motor Company)*

The Importance of Strength-to-Weight Ratios

Strength is an important factor in seeing how well a material will work in a product. In some products, especially vehicles, weight is also important. Airplanes, boats, bicycles, and automobiles must be lightweight. They use energy to move. The heavier they are, the more energy they use.

Designers and engineers are always looking for materials that are lightweight yet strong. They run tests to find materials with high strength-to-weight ratios. These materials are both strong and light.

Strength-to-weight ratios can be improved by changing the shape of a material, reinforcing, making composites, or changing the molecular structure. You can demonstrate these improvements with a sheet of paper.

One reason why plastics, particularly fiber-reinforced plastics composites, are used in so many products is their strength-to-weight ratios. Some of these plastics can have strength-to-weight ratios greater than steel.

When testing the suitability of a material for an application, consider the strength-to-weight ratio and not just strength alone.

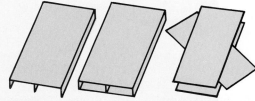

SHEET OF PAPER **FOLDED PAPER STANDS UP** **OTHER FORMS ARE EVEN STRONGER** **REINFORCED PAPER COMPOSITES** **LAYERED PAPER COMPOSITES**

Improving the strength-to-weight ratio of a material can be demonstrated by folding a sheet of paper into various forms or by making reinforced composites.

The fiber-reinforced plastics composites used in this kayak have excellent strength-to-weight ratios. *(Photo by Rob Lesser. Courtesy of Perception Inc.)*

form iron oxides or rust. Tin is, however, one metal that is resistant to corrosion, Figure 6-10. In general, glass, ceramic, and plastic also resist corrosion.

Thermal Properties

The thermal properties of materials describe how the materials react to heat. The important thermal properties relate to conductivity, fire, melting, and expansion. Conductivity allows a material to conduct heat. If you hold the end of a metal bar that is heated on the other end, the heat will be conducted through the metal to your hand. Wood, on the other hand, is not a good conductor of heat. Certain materials, especially wood and plastics, will catch fire when exposed to high temperatures. Metals, glass, and certain plastics can melt when exposed to heat. Generally, plastics have a much lower melting point than glass and metals. Metals also expand when heated.

Electrical Properties

Electrical properties relate to the reaction of materials to the flow of electricity. Materials with a low resistance to the flow of electricity are conductors. Materials with a high resistance to the flow of electricity are insulators. Generally, metals are conductors; while plastics, ceramics, and woods are insulators.

Classification of Manufacturing Materials

Most manufacturing materials can be classified into four broad groups: metallics, polymerics, ceramics, and composites. These classifications do not include every material used in manufacturing, but they do include a vast majority of the most important ones.

Metallic materials are metals, such as iron, steel, and aluminum. **Polymeric** materials include natural polymers like wood and rubber, as well as synthetic polymers like plastics. Pottery, china, porcelain, and glass are examples of **ceramic** materials. **Composite** materials are actually combinations of two or more materials bonded together. Plywood is an example of a wood-based composite material. Fiberglass, a composite also, is a combination of glass fibers embedded in plastic.

Metallic Materials

Metals are one of the most important of all manufacturing materials. Think of all the products made from the many metals available today. Automobiles, airplanes, bicycles, piping, eating utensils, and tools are just a few examples.

In general, metals are good conductors of electricity and heat. They are strong and can be formed and machined without breaking. They also can be melted for casting. There is a

Figure 6-10. Tin is used to plate steel cans because of its resistance to corrosion from food. *(Courtesy of the Canned Food Information Council)*

wide variety of metal types. More than seventy of the chemical elements are metals, and there are more than 70,000 metallic alloys. An **alloy** is a combination of two or more metals. A wide range of properties also exists. The melting points of mercury (–38 degrees Fahrenheit) and tungsten (6,170 degrees Fahrenheit) point out just one example of the diversity. Primary metal manufacturing also gives a wide variety of standard metal shapes, Figure 6-11.

Metals are grouped in two broad categories, ferrous and nonferrous. The basis for these categories is the amount of iron present. Iron is the primary element in **ferrous** metals, while **nonferrous** metals contain little or no iron.

Ferrous Metals. The two major groups of ferrous metals are cast iron and steel. Cast iron is an alloy of iron, carbon, silicon, and other materials. It is a heavy, brittle metal that is often used to make engine blocks and the bases for machine tools.

Steel is by far the most important ferrous metal. Like cast iron, steel is an alloy of iron, carbon, and other materials. The 25,000 different steels can be grouped into two categories—carbon steel and alloy steel.

Carbon steels are rated by the amount of carbon they contain. Low-carbon steels contain less than 0.30 percent carbon. Often called mild steel, low-carbon steel is relatively soft. It cannot be hardened by heat treating. Low-carbon steel is for screws, pipe, bridges, and skyscrapers, Figure 6-12. Medium-carbon steel

Figure 6-12. One important use for steel is for construction projects, like skyscrapers and bridges. *(Courtesy of Turner Construction Company)*

contains between 0.30 percent and 0.80 percent carbon. It can be heat treated. Medium-carbon steel is commonly used in shafts and axles. High-carbon steel contains more than 0.80 percent carbon. It is difficult to machine. High-carbon steel is heat treated and used to make springs and cutting tools, such as drill bits and taps.

Steel can be alloyed with a number of different materials to give it special qualities. When chromium is the main alloy ingredient, the result is stainless steel or chromium alloy steel. Chromium makes steel more resistant to corrosion. Some steel alloys with carbon contents greater than 1.00 percent are called tool steels. The additional carbon gives these steels

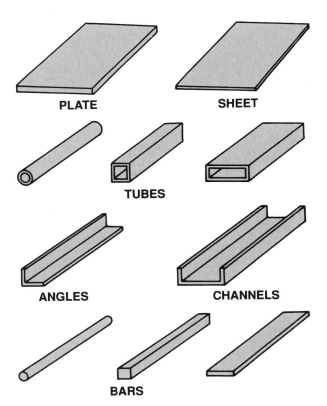

PLATE   SHEET

TUBES

ANGLES   CHANNELS

BARS

Figure 6-11. Metal and other materials are made in a variety of standard forms.

more strength and resistance to wear. Tool steels are used to make special, high-quality cutting tools.

Nonferrous Metals. Nonferrous metals contain little or no iron. Those most commonly used include aluminum, copper, zinc, and lead.

Aluminum is found in a mineral ore called bauxite. Aluminum is lightweight and strong, is an excellent conductor, and resists corrosion. Automobile manufacturers use aluminum as a replacement for cast iron in engine blocks. This maintains strength but reduces weight. The outer skin on airplanes is also made from aluminum. Because aluminum resists corrosion and conducts heat and electricity well, it is useful for beverage cans, metal cooking utensils, and electrical wiring, Figure 6-13.

Silver is the best conductor of electricity. Copper is second to silver. The price of silver makes it impractical for electrical applications. Copper, therefore, is the number one material for wiring, motor windings, and other electrical parts. Copper is also highly resistant to corrosion. This makes it an excellent choice for plumbing applications as pipe and fixtures.

Two popular copper alloys you may have heard of are brass (copper and zinc alloy) and

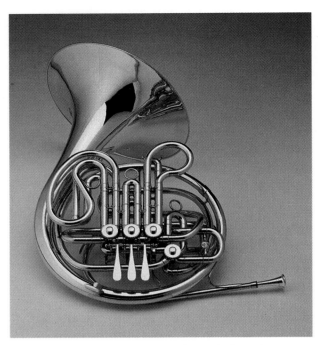

Figure 6-14. This French horn is made from brass, an alloy of copper and zinc. *(Photo courtesy of the G. Leblanc Corporation, Kenosha, WI)*

bronze (copper and tin alloy). These metals are valued for their color and beauty, Figure 6-14.

Lead is a very dense and heavy metal. Its density makes it valuable as a protective barrier when X rays are taken. Lead is also highly resistant to corrosion by acids. This makes it useful in storage batteries. The natural lubricating characteristics of lead make it useful as a material in bearings. It is also an ingredient in solder because of its low melting point.

The two properties of zinc that make it so useful are its corrosion resistance and electroplating qualities. Electroplating uses electrical current and an electrolyte solution to coat or plate one metal onto another. Zinc is plated onto sheet metal and fasteners to make galvanized sheet metal and galvanized fasteners for outdoor construction.

There are dozens of other important metals. Some of the more common ones are listed in Figure 6-15. Also included are the primary mineral ores, special properties, and some applications.

Figure 6-13. Aluminum cans keep soft drinks safe from corrosion. *(Used with permission. Copyright © PepsiCo, Inc., 1980.)*

METAL	IMPORTANT ORES	IMPORTANT PROPERTIES	IMPORTANT USES
Aluminum	Bauxite	Lightweight	Planes, foil, pots & pans
Chromium	Chromite	Corrosion resistant	Chrome plating, stainless
Copper	Chalcocite	Second best conductor	Wiring, brass, bronze
Gold	Gold	Most malleable metal	Jewelry
Iron	Hematite	Magnetic	Cast iron, steel
Lead	Galena	High density	Batteries, solder
Magnesium	Magnesite	Lightweight	Aircraft, tools
Nickel	Pentlandite	Corrosion resistant	Coins, nickel plating
Platinum	Platinum	Catalyst	Catalytic Converters
Silver	Argentite	Best conductor	Coins, jewelry, photography
Tin	Cassiterite	Corrosion resistant	Coating tin cans
Titanium	Ilmenite	Lightweight, strong	Gas turbine engines
Tungsten	Wolframite	High melting point	Light bulb filaments
Uranium	Pitchblend	Radioactive	Nuclear fuel
Zinc	Sphalerite	Corrosion resistant	Galvanized metals

Figure 6-15. This chart lists just a few of the more important metals.

Polymeric Materials

The two categories of polymer are natural polymers, such as wood, and synthetic polymers, such as plastics. Natural polymers are a renewable raw material resource. Synthetic polymers come from exhaustible raw materials.

Wood. Trees have been a valuable resource for thousands of years. They will continue to be important in the future. Wood isn't the only material to come from trees. Trees support the manufacture of thousands of products. These include paper, plywood, turpentine, and even a few resins that make plastics. Most of the lumber from trees is used to build homes and similar structures. The lumber used in manufacturing goes primarily into furniture.

Wood can be classified into softwoods and hardwoods. These classifications have nothing to do with the hardness or softness of the wood. Rather, they relate to the type of tree. **Softwoods** come from coniferous trees. Conifers are cone-bearing trees with needles. **Hardwoods** come from deciduous trees that have broad leaves. Examples of softwoods and hardwoods are listed in Figure 6-16.

There are hundreds of different species of trees. Each produces wood with unique properties. Some woods, like balsa, are extremely light and soft. Others, like oak, are very heavy and hard. Because of the wide variety available, there are woods to match almost any needs. In general wood has been admired for years as a material that is easy to work, strong and durable, and shows beautiful grain patterns.

One property of wood of special concern for manufacturing is moisture content. Wood

HARDWOODS	SOFTWOODS
ash	cedar
basswood	fir
birch	pine
cherry	redwood
mahogany	spruce
maple	
oak	
poplar	
walnut	

Figure 6-16. This list shows the common hardwoods and softwoods.

SOFTWOODS		HARDWOODS		SOFTWOODS	HARDWOODS
THICKNESS AND WIDTH		THICKNESS		GRADES	GRADES
NOMINAL	ACTUAL	GREEN Rgh*	DRIED S2S**	*Select*—good appearance and finish quality	*FAS*—first and seconds, highest quality, clear
1"	3/4"	3/8"	3/16"	Grade A—clear, no knots	
2"	1 1/2"	1/2"	5/16"	Grade B—high quality	*No. 1 Common* and
3"	2 1/2"	5/8"	7/16"	Grade C—for painting	Select, some defects
4"	3 1/2"	3/4"	9/16"	Grade D—lowest select	
5"	4 1/2"	(4/4) 1"	13/16"	*Common*—general use, not	*No. 2 Common*, for
6"	5 1/2"	(5/4) 1 1/4"	1 1/16"	finish quality	smaller cuttings
7"	6 1/2"	(6/4) 1 1/2"	1 1/4"	Construction/No. 1—best	
8"	7 1/2"	(8/4) 2"	1 3/4"	Standard/No. 2—good	
9"	8 1/2"	(12/4) 3"	2 1/2"	Utility/No. 3—fair	
10"	9 1/2"			Economy/No. 4—poor	

*Rgh = Rough (directly from sawmill)
**S2S = Surfaced on two sides

Figure 6-17. Lumber is sold in standard sizes and grades.

is made up of tiny cellulose fibers held together by a substance called lignin. There are many pores and gaps between the wood fibers. When a tree is growing, moisture is contained within the cell structure of the wood. Before wood can be used, it must be dried to remove this moisture. As the moisture content decreases, wood shrinks. This shrinking would be disastrous for homes or products made from wood with a high moisture content.

Acceptable moisture content for construction lumber is approximately 19 percent. For furniture manufacturing, the moisture content must be held to 6 to 10 percent. Furniture made with a higher moisture content will shrink, warp, and crack when the wood dries in a home.

Two methods of drying wood are air and kiln drying. In air drying, wood is stacked outdoors under shelter and left to dry naturally. In kiln drying, the wood is forced dry by treating it in a kiln (oven). Kiln drying is a much faster method.

Lumber is sold in standard sizes and grades. Figure 6-17 lists sizes and grades for both hardwood and softwood lumber. Sizes are given in a nominal size and an actual size. Nominal size is the name size given. The actu-

al size is the exact measurements of the lumber. As an example, a common pine (softwood) two by four (nominal size) has an actual size of 1 1/2 by 3 1/2 inches.

Wood is also graded to uniform standards. These indicate the presence or absence of defects such as knots, checks (splits), stains, or pitch. The best lumber grades have the fewest defects.

Lumber is sold by a standard measure called a **board foot**. One board foot is equal to one inch thick, one foot wide, and one foot long, Figure 6-18. To determine the number of board feet in a piece of lumber, use the formula in Figure 6-18.

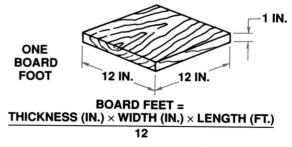

$$BOARD\ FEET = \frac{THICKNESS\ (IN.) \times WIDTH\ (IN.) \times LENGTH\ (FT.)}{12}$$

Figure 6-18. One board-foot is one inch thick, twelve inches wide, and twelve inches long. You can calculate the amount of board feet in any piece of wood with this formula.

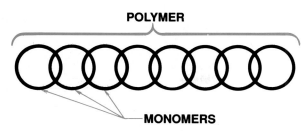

Figure 6-19. In polymerization, individual monomers are joined chemically to form long chains called polymers.

Plastics. The primary raw material used to make plastics is the carbon found in petroleum and natural gas. Plastics polymers are formed by a chemical reaction called **polymerization**. In polymerization, individual molecules called **monomers** are reacted together to form long chains of monomers called polymers, Figure 6-19.

In general, plastics are excellent thermal and electrical insulators. They are lightweight and easily formed with heat and pressure. Also, they need very little finishing such as sanding and painting. Some plastics can be corroded by certain solvents. For the most part, however, plastics have excellent corrosion resistance.

Plastics are being used in many different applications. New plastics are always being developed. In recent years, plastics have been applied where woods and metals were traditionally used. Some of the most common uses of plastics include electrical wiring insulation, vinyl flooring and house siding, polyvinyl chloride (PVC) piping, telephones, stereos, toys, utensils, and squeeze bottles, Figure 6-20.

The two basic types of plastics are **thermoplastics** and **thermosets**. Thermoplastics are made of many long polymer chains with no links between the chains, Figure 6-21. Thermoplastic materials can repeatedly be reheated and reshaped. When heated, the bonds between the polymer chains weaken. The material can then be reshaped by pressure. When the reshaped thermoplastic cools, it retains the new shape. Thermoplastics are like wax in a candle that can be remelted and reshaped over and over again.

Thermoset plastics are also made of many long polymer chains, but they have links between the chains. Once formed into shape, thermosets cannot be reheated and reshaped. This process is like hard boiling an egg; once it is hardened, the shape is permanent.

(Courtesy of Dow Chemical)

(Photo by Brent Miller and Sonya Stang)

Figure 6-20. Plastics are used for many manufactured products.

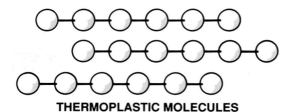

THERMOPLASTIC MOLECULES

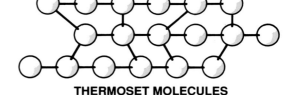

THERMOSET MOLECULES

THE SHAPE OF A
THERMOPLASTIC CAN BE
CHANGED WHEN THE
MATERIAL IS REHEATED

ONCE A THERMOSET
IS HARDENED BY HEAT,
ITS SHAPE IS PERMANENT

Figure 6-21. Notice how the molecular structure of thermoplastics differs from thermosets.

Generally, thermosets are harder and more stable at high temperatures than thermoplastics. Thermoplastics, on the other hand, are easier to work and cost less. They are used more often because of cost and the possibility of recycling wastes.

MATERIAL	USES
THERMOPLASTICS	
ABS (Acrylonitrile-butadiene-styrene)	Telephones, car grilles, sports helmets
Acetal	Small gears in toys
Acrylic	Plexiglass, skylights
Cellulose acetate	Photographic film base, eyeglass frames
Nylon	Clothing, bearings, gears
Polycarbonate	Safety eyeglasses, space helmets
Polyethylene	Packing film, plastic bottles, garbage bags
Polypropylene	Battery cases, washing machine agitators
Polystyrene	Disposable tableware, meat trays, cups
Polyurethane	Packing foam, surface finish (varnish)
Polyvinyl chloride	Plastic pipe (PVC)
Vinyl acetate	Vinyl floor tiles, phonograph records
THERMOSETS	
Amino plastics	Plastic laminates (formica)
Epoxy	Adhesives, fiberglass
Polyester	Clothes, fiberglass
Polytetrafluoroethylene	Nonstick surfaces (Teflon)
Silicone	Printed circuit boards, sealants

Figure 6-22. Here are some of the more common thermoplastics and thermosets and their uses.

Figure 6-22 lists a number of the more common thermoset and thermoplastic materials along with their uses.

Ceramic Materials

Ceramics are one of the oldest manufacturing materials. Some of the first evidence of technology were clay pots found in archaeological digs. Today, the field of ceramic materials is expanding. Many new types and applications are being found.

One reason for such growth is the abundance of raw materials for ceramics. Ceramics are compounds of oxygen and another element, usually silicon. Silicon is found in silicates, which are the most common minerals on earth. Silicates are found in sands and clays.

Ceramic materials are plastic and moldable when wet. This makes them easy to shape into finished products by a number of processes. Once the material dries, it becomes rigid and maintains its shape. After forming, ceramics are fired (heated) in a kiln or oven. Once fired, the shape is permanent. The material is then hard and strong.

Ceramics are very good insulators. Two important applications are as furnace lining for glass and metalworking and the heat shield tiles on the space shuttle. Ceramics are also hard, stiff, strong, and unaffected by weather. Common building bricks are one of the most common examples of a product that takes advantage of these properties.

Figure 6-24. Heat-resistant tiles on the space shuttle are an example of refractories. *(Courtesy of NASA)*

Many different products are made from ceramic materials, Figure 6-23. Four of the more common categories of ceramics are clay-based, refractories, glasses, and abrasives. Clay-based ceramics include dinnerware, ceramic floor tiles, structural bricks, and porcelains used to coat metals. Refractories are made for high-heat applications. Examples include furnace lining bricks, spark plug insulators, and the tiles on the space shuttle, Figure 6-24. Ceramic glasses include common window glass and the glass fibers used in fiberglass and fiber optics. Two common ceramic abrasives are silicon carbide and aluminum oxide. The trade name for silicon carbide is carborundum. Both these abrasives are used in grinding wheels and abrasive sheets.

Composite Materials

Composite materials are made of two or more materials bonded together. In a composite, each material retains its original properties; when composited (combined), a superior material results. There are three basic types of composites—layered, fiber-reinforced, and particle.

Layered Composites. In a **layered composite**, layers of materials are sandwiched together by an adhesive or other binder. Plywood is an example of a layered composite, Figure 6-25. Thin layers of wood are glued together to create a composite board. The individual wood layers are fairly strong and flexible, but they can swell and shrink because of moisture. They therefore split easily. When composited,

Figure 6-23. Floor tiles, toilets, and porcelain-lined tubs are common ceramic products. *(Courtesy of Kohler Company)*

Figure 6-25. Plywood, hardboard, waferboard, and particleboard are common composite materials. *(Courtesy of American Plywood Association)*

a material with superior strength results. It does not split easily and is more stable in different moisture conditions. Other examples of layered composites include plastic laminate countertops, wax-coated paper on milk cartons, cardboard, and the covering on textbooks.

Fiber-reinforced Composites. The most common **fiber-reinforced composite** is fiberglass. Glass fibers are used to reinforce a matrix of plastic. Two common matrix materials are epoxy and polyamide plastics. Fibers of carbon, graphite, and boron are also common. Fibers are available in the form of loose fibers, ropes, and woven mats (similar to mat insulation material).

A popular fiber-reinforced composite is Kevlar. Kevlar is a composite of epoxy matrix, boron, and graphite fibers. It has been applied to aircraft, boats, fishing poles, and other sports equipment.

Fiber-reinforced composites have properties similar to most plastics (lightweight, insulators, corrosion resistant) with strength comparable to many metals.

Particle Composites. In **particle composites**, particles, or small bits of reinforcement, are used instead of fibers. Concrete is an example. A water and cement matrix is reinforced by rock and sand particles. Several common wood-based particle composites include hardboard, waferboard, and particleboard. In each of these, wood chips or particles are suspended in an adhesive matrix and pressurized to form a board similar to plywood.

Summary

All manufacturing materials come from either renewable or exhaustible raw material resources in the earth. Primary manufacturing obtains and refines raw material resources and changes them into standard forms of manufacturing materials.

Many manufacturing materials come from exhaustible resources that are limited and scarce. Recycling is one technique being used to help us preserve these valuable limited resources. Recycling also helps manufacturers to reduce their energy use, control costs, and keep the environment free from waste and scrap piles.

The major types of manufacturing materials include metallics, polymers, ceramics, and composites. Iron, steel, aluminum, copper, lead, and zinc are the most important metallic materials. Woods are natural polymeric materials, while plastics are synthetic polymers. The two types of plastics are thermoplastics and thermosets. Pottery, china, porcelain, and glass are examples of ceramic materials. Composite materials are two or more materials bonded together, such as plywood, fiberglass, and Kevlar.

Understanding the molecular science and various properties of materials helps designers and manufacturers make appropriate choices when selecting materials for a product.

DISCUSSION QUESTIONS

1. What is the difference between primary manufacturing and secondary manufacturing?

2. What are the two types of raw materials resources? What are the differences between these two types?

3. What manufacturing materials are candidates for recycling? What are three reasons why recycling is a good idea?

4. What properties are important in a manufacturing material? Pick a product application and describe why you think a designer chose the material used.

5. What is the difference between ferrous and nonferrous metals? Can you list and describe two ferrous and two nonferrous metals?

6. What are the two main types of plastics? Can you describe the difference between them?

7. What are the differences between a softwood and a hardwood?

8. Can you give one example of each of the four types of ceramic materials?

9. What are the three different types of composite materials? Can you give one example of each?

CHAPTER ACTIVITIES

⚙ TESTING MATERIALS PROPERTIES

OBJECTIVE

Before designers choose materials for a product, they must know about the properties of materials. You can learn about the properties of materials by making a few simple tests in your manufacturing lab.

In this activity, you will test some materials for their properties.

Some of the more important materials properties include mechanical properties, such as strength, elasticity, plasticity, malleability, ductility, and hardness.

Product designers find the materials that will work best for a certain product. Every day research and development helps us learn more about which materials should be used in given situations. Much of this research is based on materials testing.

MATERIALS AND SUPPLIES

1. Materials for testing. Materials of different types (metals, polymers, ceramics, and composites) or materials of only one type (steel, aluminum, copper, lead) can be tested and compared.

2. Materials testing devices. Many tests can be done with simple tools; others will need testing devices. Figure 1 gives some ideas for various materials testing methods.

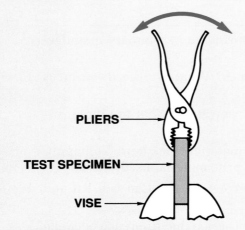

A. Fatigue strength—bend back and forth until material fails; count cycles.

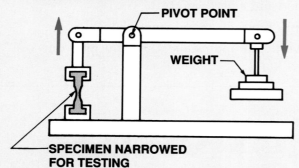

C. Tensile strength—use lever to apply load (weight).

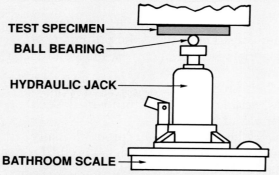

E. Hardness—measure the size of the indentation at a specific weight.

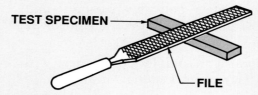

F. Hardness

- **A TOUGH MATERIAL WILL BEND AND NOT REACT**
- **A BRITTLE MATERIAL WILL CRACK OR FRACTURE**

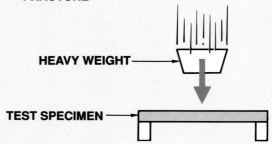

B. Impact strength

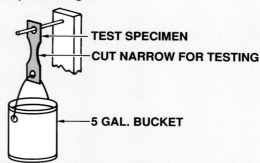

D. Tensile strength—fill bucket until specimen fails.

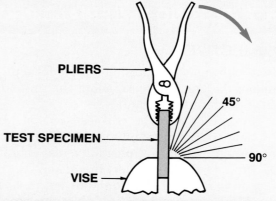

- **BEND MATERIALS TO DIFFERENT DEGREES AND SEE IF THEY RETURN TO ORIGINAL SHAPE (ELASTICITY)**
- **IF THEY DO NOT RETURN TO ORIGINAL SHAPE, THEY DISPLAY PLASTICITY**

G. Elasticity/plasticity

Figure 1. Ideas for materials testing devices.

3. Materials testing data sheet (handout). Decide which properties you will test for in each material and record the data on the handout from your instructor.

4. Product materials analysis chart (handout).

5. Safety glasses

PROCEDURE

1. Decide which materials tests you will do. Discuss materials testing with your teacher and classmates. Based on the materials and tools available in your school, decide which materials you will test and what properties you will investigate.

2. Construct any special materials testing devices you need, Figure 1.

3. Prepare samples for testing. The size of the test specimens must be identical for each test. As an example, if you test the fatigue strength of two different sized paper clips, you will find they vary even though both are made from the same material. Keep the cross-sectional area constant.

4. Test the materials. Be sure to follow all safety rules and use caution when running the tests.

5. Pick a product that you would like to manufacture. Decide which properties you think your materials should have. Any number of properties may be important, such as cost, strength, hardness, plasticity, ductility, and so on.

6. Fill out the product materials analysis chart your instructor gives you. Write the names of the materials you tested across the top and fill in the properties your product should have. Use this chart to choose the materials you will use to make your product.

MATH/SCIENCE CONNECTION

The properties a material shows come from its molecular structure. The molecular structures of solid manufacturing materials are very different, from the long chain polymers in plastics and woods, to the crystal structures in metals.

RELATED QUESTIONS

1. What are the four different measures of strength discussed in this chapter?

2. What is the difference between plasticity and elasticity?

3. What is the difference between malleability and ductility?

4. Pick any product, such as a skateboard or bicycle, and describe why you think the manufacturer chose the particular materials used.

 **RE-USE IT**

OBJECTIVE

Some people say we live in a wasteful, "throw away" society. Landfills in many communities are overflowing. Many states send thousands of tons of garbage to other states for dumping every week. Many of the things we throw away could be recycled.

In this activity, you will make fire starters from a waste product of manufacturing (sawdust) and discarded wax. You will see how easy it is to recycle a waste product into a usable product.

Recycling has much to offer society. We dump less garbage in landfills, we save natural raw materials resources, and we use less energy for materials processing. Also, products made from recycled materials can cost less.

Most recycling is done with materials that come from limited resources, such as iron, steel, aluminum, and plastic. But recycling materials that come from renewable resources, like wood and paper, also makes sense. The garbage we throw away every day gives us a new materials resource, Figure 2.

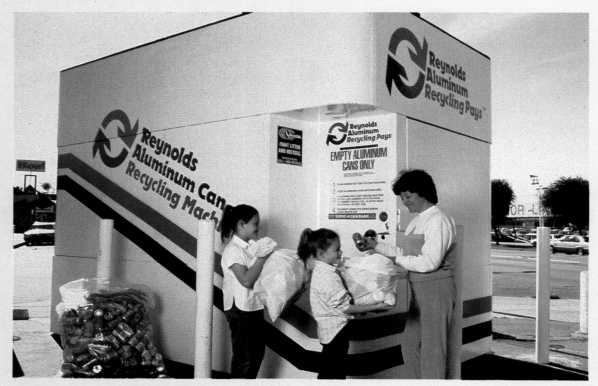

Figure 2. *Courtesy of Reynolds Aluminum Recycling Company*

MATERIALS AND SUPPLIES

1. 2 sheets of 8.5" × 11" paper, 50 to 70#
2. 1 wooden dowel, 1" diameter by 8.5" to 9.5" long
3. 1 wooden dowel, 1/2" diameter by 10" long
4. 2 sheets of tissue paper
5. 16 pieces of lightweight string (2 per starter), 6" long
6. Transparent tape or masking tape
7. 2 pints sawdust
8. Discarded wax (paraffin); 5 to 10 large old candles will do. Bring enough!
9. Tablespoon
10. Stir stick (a paint stir stick will do, or any long slender wood scrap)
11. Safety glasses and gloves

PROCEDURE

1. Using the 1" wooden dowel, roll one sheet of 8.5" × 11" paper around it so that the finished tube is 8.5" long. Tape the tube on the outside lengthwise with tape. Then slide the paper off the wooden dowel. Do this twice so that you have two paper tubes.

2. Now, set the tube in an upright position using the pre-made stand or by setting the tube on the table. We are now ready to fill the tube with the sawdust and paraffin mixture.

3. Carefully melt the old wax that you brought in using a double boiler. Do this with the supervision of your instructor. Do not do this in an ordinary pan from home: at 140° Fahrenheit, the wax will actually burn! This could be dangerous so be careful.

4. Next, carefully pour 1 pint of the melted wax into the container holding the sawdust. Using a stir stick, mix until the wax has coated all the sawdust. Do this quickly so that the mixture remains warm! You're out of luck if it cools and hardens!

5. Now using your tablespoon, carefully spoon the mixture into each of the two paper tubes, being careful not to bend them. *As you are doing this*, take the 1/2" dowel and gently but firmly ram the mixture into the tube. Fill the tubes as full as possible.

6. Allow the paraffin/sawdust mixture to cool in the tubes.

7. Remove the paper from the outside. Handle carefully as the hardened mixture can break or crumble easily.

8. Using a knife or small sawblade, cut each paraffin and sawdust mold into four equal pieces. You will now have eight pieces.

9. Next, using the tissue, wrap each of the eight fire starters. Twist each end and then tie it with some string.

10. Use the fire starters wisely!

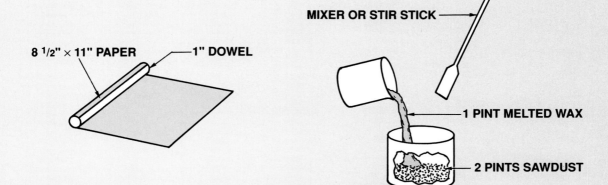

8 1/2" × 11" PAPER — 1" DOWEL

MIXER OR STIR STICK

1 PINT MELTED WAX

2 PINTS SAWDUST

MATH/SCIENCE CONNECTION

Consider making a cost comparison for the fire starter you made from recycled materials with the cost of the same product made with new materials.

RELATED QUESTIONS

1. What are the advantages of manufacturing products from recycled materials?
2. Why are most recycling efforts directed toward exhaustible raw material resources?
3. What specific materials are recycled most?
4. If recycling is not used, what will society do with all its waste?

CHAPTER 7

Tools and Machines

OBJECTIVES

After completing this chapter, you will know about:

■ The importance of tools and machines as inputs for manufacturing.

■ The importance of safety in using tools and machines.

■ The types of separating, forming, and combining tools and machines found often in manufacturing.

■ Uses of computers in manufacturing and the importance of computer software.

■ The types of robots and their uses in manufacturing.

KEY TERMS

Abrasive papers	Files	Mold
Arc welder	Fixture	Oxyacetylene torch
Bits	Flexible manufacturing	Pliers
CAD	Gage	Power hand tools
CAD/CAM	Go–No go gage	Punches
CADD	Grinding wheels	Robot
CAM	Hand tools	Rolls
CIM	Jigs	Saw blades
Chisels	JIT	Shears
Clamp	Laser	Software
Cutters	Lathe	Spot welder
Degree of freedom	Machine	Tool
Die	Mechanical advantage	Work envelope
Drills	Metal shaper	
EDM	Micrometer	

Tools and Machines

Each department in manufacturing uses tools to do its job. In general, tools and machines process (change) materials or information. Production department workers use tools to change materials into finished products. The finance department uses calculators and computers to keep track of the company's finances. Marketing workers send product information to consumers through advertisements made with video and audio recording machines. Workers in manufacturing must know how to use the tools of their trade.

Defining Tools and Machines

Tools extend human abilities in doing the work of processing (changing) materials or information. So, strictly speaking, machines are also tools. Tools extend human abilities by increasing the power, speed, efficiency, accuracy, and productivity of work. We cannot drive nails in boards with our bare hands, but we can drive nails with a tool—the hammer. We can do math problems in our head, but an electronic calculator is faster and more accurate. Both the hammer and the calculator are tools that extend our abilities.

Generally, tools can be described as hand tools, power hand tools, or machines. A **hand tool** is the simplest form. The user holds it in the hand and moves it to perform work. It is powered only by the user. Hand saws, screwdrivers, and hand planes are examples of hand tools. **Power hand tools** are improved hand tools. The user holds one in the hand and moves it to perform work, but the processing

Using Tools and Machines Safely

Using tools and machines safely is a big concern in manufacturing. Every year, thousands of workers get hurt using tools. Injuries do not happen only with big, powerful machines, but also with hand tools. More people are hurt by screwdrivers and hammers than by large industrial machines.

Accidents and injuries happen for two reasons: (1) working conditions are unsafe and (2) worker actions are unsafe. Using dull or broken tools, working in cluttered conditions, or taking poor care of machines are examples of unsafe working conditions. Not knowing how to use a tool, not knowing or following the proper safety rules, or using a tool or machine the wrong way are all unsafe worker actions. Always follow the safety guidelines listed in Table 1 when using tools. Also follow other safety rules and guidelines set by your teacher. Using tools and machines safely should be your number one concern.

TABLE 1. SAFETY GUIDELINES FOR USING TOOLS AND MACHINES

- **Get permission from your teacher before using any tool or machine.**
- **Learn the safety rules for every tool and machine you will use; learn the dangers involved.**
- **Select the right tool for the job, match the tool to the work to be done.**
- **Use tools and machines in a safe and proper manner.**
- **Use tools and machines only for the uses for which they were designed.**
- **Keep tools and machines properly maintained and adjusted.**
- **Use tool and machine safety devices such as guards.**
- **Tools are for work: Never play with tools and machines.**
- **Respect the power of tools and machines.**

Always follow these safety guidelines and other safety rules set up by your teacher. Using tools and machines can be dangerous. Think and act safety first.

power comes from an external source, such as an electric motor. Power circular saws, electric screwdrivers, and power planes are some power hand tools. **Machines** stay still during processing and use an externally powered tool that is fastened to the machine to do the actual processing. Table saws, drill presses, and planers are all machines.

Another category of manufacturing tools is equipment. Equipment covers devices that cannot be defined as machines, power hand tools, or hand tools. Equipment stays still on a structure during processing and uses human or thermal (heat) power to process materials. Examples include the human-powered squaring shears for shearing metal and ovens, kilns, and furnaces used to melt materials.

All tools, machines, and equipment extend human abilities by increasing the power, speed, efficiency, accuracy, and productivity of processing materials or information.

The Six Basic Machines

We base the principles that describe how tools work on the six basic machines—wheels, levers, pulleys, inclined planes, wedges, and screws, Figure 7-1. The purpose of these basic machines is to gain a mechanical advantage in doing work. A **mechanical advantage** is an increase in a force. Mechanical advantage of force is abbreviated MAf. A simple example is driving nails in wood. Without a hammer, you would not be able to drive the nails. By placing the hammer in your hand, you create a lever that gives you a mechanical advantage of force over the nail. The nail itself uses wedge action to cut into the wood.

For another example, look at the drill press, Figure 7-2, often found in labs. The drill bit uses a wedge for its cutting action. Inclined planes hold the drill bit in the chuck. Screw threads hold the drill press together. Pulleys transfer power from the motor to the drill bit. The handle on the drill press acts as a lever attached to a wheel and axle. Every time one of the six basic machines is used in a tool or machine, mechanical advantage is realized. Identify the six basic machines in other tools and machines in your lab.

Materials-processing Tools and Machines

We describe tools and machines that change materials into products by their processes. Chapter 15 looks more closely at materials processes; for now processes and tools will be described as separating, forming, and conditioning.

Separating Tools

Separating tools separate or remove part of the original material and leave the required size and shape. Cutting a piece of paper to size or drilling a hole are examples of separating processes. Separating tools must be made from materials that are harder than the material being separated. Separating tools are made from hard tool steel, carbide, ceramic, or industrial diamonds. There are three categories of separating tools—chip removal tools, shearing tools, and other nontraditional separating tools.

Chip Removal Tools. Chip removal tools remove small bits of waste called chips from the material being separated. Sawing is an example of chip removal. It removes sawdust chips from the material during separating. Chip removal tools usually have multiple points or single points.

Multiple-point chip removal tools include (1) drills and bits; (2) saw blades; (3) cutters; and (4) files, grinders, and abrasive papers.

Drills and **bits** make round holes by removing chips from materials. There is a wide variety of drills for different materials and types of holes, Figure 7-3.

- Twist drills are the most common drill used for wood, metal, and plastic.
- Spade bits make large holes in materials.
- Spur bits have a center point to guide the bit; they make clean, smooth holes.
- Forstner bits make flat-bottomed holes.
- Taps cut threads on the inside of a hole that has already been drilled.
- Reamers smooth out a drilled hole to specifications.

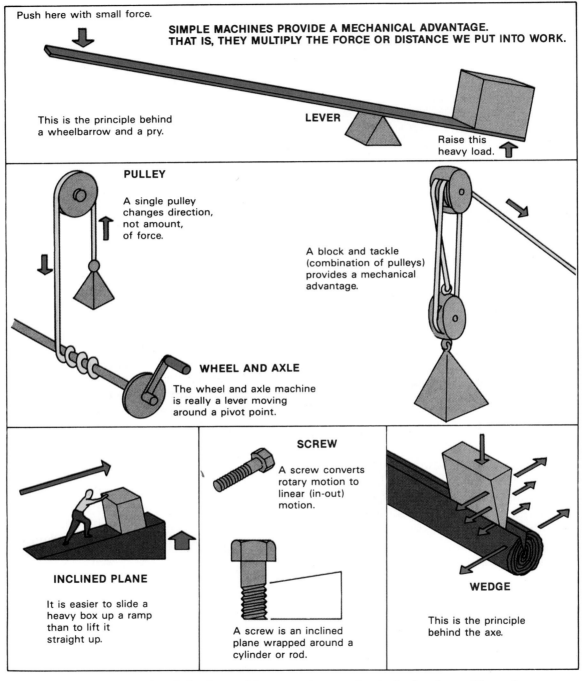

Push here with small force.

**SIMPLE MACHINES PROVIDE A MECHANICAL ADVANTAGE.
THAT IS, THEY MULTIPLY THE FORCE OR DISTANCE WE PUT INTO WORK.**

This is the principle behind
a wheelbarrow and a pry.

LEVER

Raise this
heavy load.

PULLEY

A single pulley
changes direction,
not amount,
of force.

A block and tackle
(combination of pulleys)
provides a mechanical
advantage.

WHEEL AND AXLE

The wheel and axle machine
is really a lever moving
around a pivot point.

INCLINED PLANE

It is easier to slide a
heavy box up a ramp
than to lift it
straight up.

SCREW

A screw converts
rotary motion to
linear (in-out)
motion.

A screw is an inclined
plane wrapped around a
cylinder or rod.

WEDGE

This is the principle
behind the axe.

Figure 7-1. Workers use the six basic machines to gain a mechanical advantage of force in processing materials. *(Reprinted from* LIVING WITH TECHNOLOGY *by Hacker and Barden, © 1988 by Delmar Publishers Inc.)*

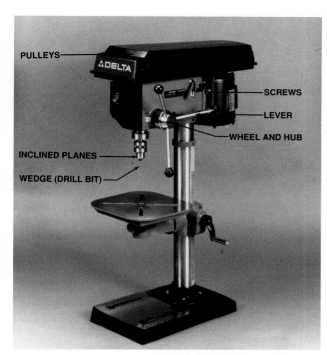

Figure 7-2. The six basic machines can be found in any machine. *(Courtesy of Delta International Machinery)*

Drills and bits can be used in hand tools, power hand tools, or machines. The drill press is one of the most important manufacturing machines.

Saw blades separate materials along straight or curved lines. They can be used in hand tools, power hand tools, and machines. Blade shapes are straight, circular, or continuous band. Steel is used for most saw blades, but some are carbide tipped. There is a wide variety of saw blades available based on the material being separated, including special blades for wood, plywood, metal, plastic, and masonry. Generally, the following categories of saw blades are used.

- Crosscut saw blades separate wood across the grain.
- Ripsaw blades separate wood along the grain, Figure 7-4.
- Hacksaw blades separate metals.
- Scroll, coping, and saber saw blades separate materials along curved lines.

Some of the more common sawing machines used in manufacturing are table saws, radial arm saws, band saws, and scroll saws, Figure 7-5.

Cutters process materials to a certain thickness, cut grooves, and make special edges. They have two, three, or more cutting points. Most cutters are made from steel; some are carbide tipped. A few of the different types of cutters used in manufacturing follow.

- A router uses router cutters. Router cutters have two cutting points that make decorative edges or grooves in wood.

Twist drill *(Courtesy of DoAll Company, Des Plaines, IL)*

Spur bits *(Courtesy of Woodworker's Supply of NM)*

Forstner bits *(Courtesy of Woodworker's Supply of NM)*

Spade bits *(Courtesy of Irwin Co.)*

Figure 7-3. Here are four different styles of drills and bits that make holes in materials.

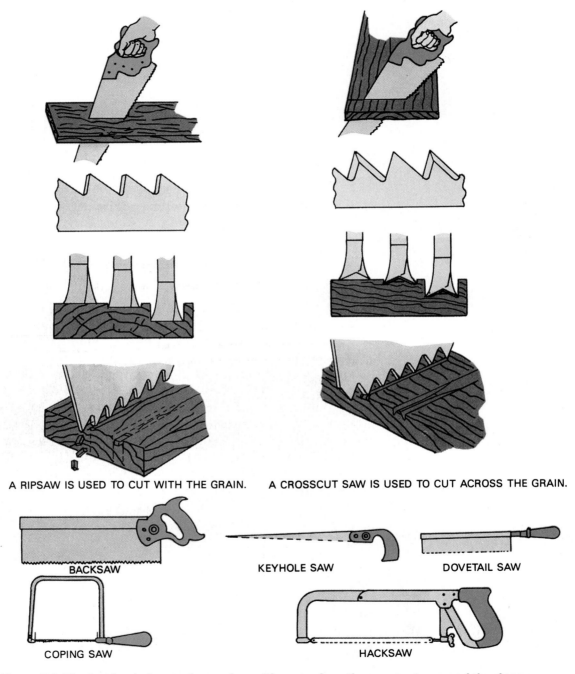

A RIPSAW IS USED TO CUT WITH THE GRAIN.   A CROSSCUT SAW IS USED TO CUT ACROSS THE GRAIN.

BACKSAW   KEYHOLE SAW   DOVETAIL SAW

COPING SAW   HACKSAW

Figure 7-4. The two basic types of saws for cutting wood are the crosscut saw and the ripsaw.
(Reprinted from LIVING WITH TECHNOLOGY by Hacker and Barden, © 1988 by Delmar Publishers Inc.)

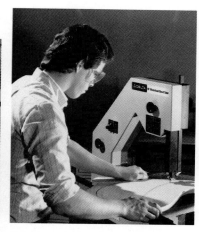

Table saw *(Courtesy of Delta International Machinery)*

Hand held saw *(Courtesy of Ryobi America)*

Band saw *(Courtesy of Delta International Machinery)*

Figure 7-5. Saw blades use chip removal to separate. Can you identify the saw blade shape used in each of these tools?

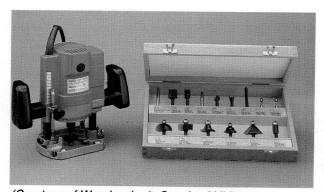

(Courtesy of Woodworker's Supply of NM)

■ A shaper uses shaper cutters. Shapers perform processes similar to the router, Figure 7-6.

■ A milling machine uses milling cutters, Figure 7-7. Milling cutters have many cutting points. Milling machines cut gears, grooves, and flat surfaces in metal.

(Courtesy of Delta International Machinery)

Figure 7-6. Router and shaper cutters make decorative edges or grooves in wood.

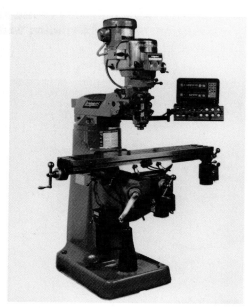

Figure 7-7. This milling machine has a multiple point cutter that cuts gears, grooves, and flat surfaces in metal. *(Courtesy of Bridgeport Machines)*

Kinds of teeth
Single-cut

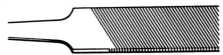

Single set of parallel, diagonal rows of teeth. Single-cut files are often used with light pressure to produce a smooth surface finish or to put a keen edge on knives, shears or saws.

Double-cut

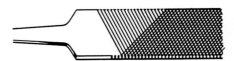

Two sets of diagonal rows of teeth. The second set of teeth is cut in the opposite diagonal direction and on top of the first set. The first set of teeth is known as the overcut while the second is called the upcut. The upcut is finer than the overcut. The double-cut file is used with heavier pressure than the single-cut and removes material faster from the workpiece.

Figure 7-8. Close-up views of single-cut and double-cut files. *(Courtesy of Cooper Tools)*

■ Planers and jointers are machines with three or four cutting points called knives. Planers and jointers are mostly used to cut flat surfaces on wood.

Files, grinding wheels, and abrasive papers remove small amounts of a material. **Files** are hand tools with rows of cutting edges that remove small amounts of metal, wood, or other materials. Single-cut files have chisel-shaped cutting edges, while double-cut files have diamond-shaped cutting edges, Figure 7-8. Files usually have flat, half round, and round cross-sectional shapes. **Grinding wheels**

are used on power hand tools or machines called grinders, Figure 7-9. The wheels are made from hard, abrasive (scraping) materials, such as aluminum oxide, silicon carbide, or

Bench top grinder

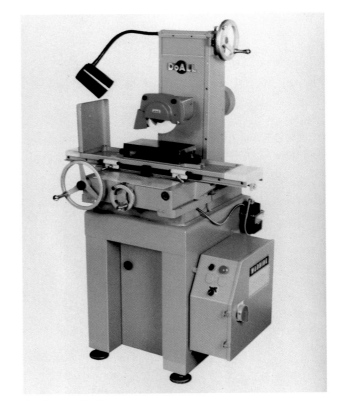

Surface grinder

Figure 7-9. Both of these grinders use abrasive grinding wheels to cut metal. *(Courtesy of DoAll Company, Des Plaines, IL)*

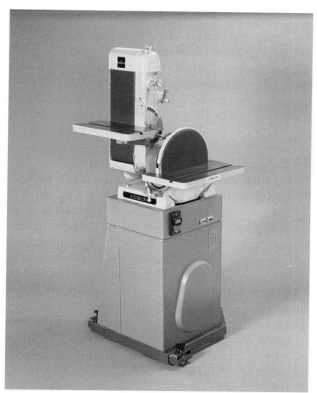

Disk/belt sanding machine *(Courtesy of Delta International Machinery)*

Belt sander *(Courtesy of Woodworker's Supply of NM)*

Orbital sander *(Courtesy of Woodworker's Supply of NM)*

Figure 7-10. Here are three different types of sanders; each uses abrasive papers to sand and finish materials.

diamond materials. Workers mostly use grinders on metals. **Abrasive papers** smooth or finish the surface of materials. They are made by gluing thousands of tiny grains of an abrasive material to paper or cloth. Some of the more common abrasive materials are aluminum oxide, garnet, and flint. The separating action of abrasive papers is rated by grit. Grit numbers describe the size and number of the tiny grains of abrasive material glued to the paper. An abrasive paper with a high grit number has smaller and fewer grits. Abrasive papers come as sheets, disks, belts, and sleeves. Sanders are power hand tools and machines used with abrasive papers. Sander styles include belt, disk, orbital, and drum sanders, Figure 7-10.

Single-point chip removal tools include lathe tools and the metal shaper. Each of these tools is usually made from steel and can be modified to cut wood, metals, plastics, and other materials.

Lathe tools are usually held in the hand when cutting wood but secured to a machine (a lathe) when cutting metal. The lathe is one of the most important machines in manufacturing, and is used to add threads or to cut cylinder-shaped objects to size, Figure 7-11.

The **metal shaper** uses a single cutting tool similar to a metal lathe tool. Shapers cut straight and angular surfaces, such as keyways and slots in metal.

Shearing Tools. Shearing is the second category of separating tools. Shearing tools separate thin sheet materials by applying a force to two opposing surfaces. Shearing tools do not make chips as they separate materials. A good example is cutting paper with scissors. The paper is sheared or cut clean without making paper chips. The most common shearing tools used in manufacturing are shears, chisels, and punches.

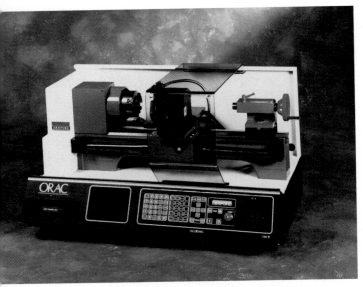

Figure 7-11. The lathe is one of the most important machines in manufacturing. This lathe is computer controlled. (*Courtesy of Brodhead Garrett/Denford Machine Tools Ltd.*)

Shears are large, heavy-duty scissors used to cut materials. Tin snips and aviation snips are two hand tools that shear thin sheet metal, Figure 7-12. Squaring shears shear thicker metal pieces. A person or some other source powers squaring shears.

Chisels have a single, straight cutting edge. The most common chisels are those used as hand tools in woodworking.

Punches are similar to cookie cutters. As with all shearing tools, a sharp edge forces through the material without making chips. Punches come in a variety of sizes based on the thickness and type of material to be sheared.

Nontraditional Separating Tools. This category includes other separating tools that do not fit into the chip-removing and shearing categories. Some of the more important nontraditional separating tools include flame cutting equipment, electrical discharge machines, and lasers.

Flame cutting uses the heat from burning gases to separate materials. The most common flame cutting tools use an **oxyacetylene torch** to burn oxygen and acetylene gas. The oxyacetylene torch can produce flames with temperatures higher than 6,000 degrees Fahrenheit, Figure 7-13.

Electrical discharge machines (**EDM**) use an electric spark for careful separation of metal materials. An electrode and the material being cut are placed in an oil bath called a **dielectric**.

Aviation snips

Straight cutting snips

Circular cutting snips

Combination snips

Figure 7-12. Here are four different styles of hand-held shears, also called snips. (*Courtesy of Stanley-Proto Industrial Tools, Covington, GA*)

tool called a mold. A **mold** is a cavity used to form liquid materials, Figure 7-14. Casting is the act of pouring the liquid material into the mold. Manufacturers use casting to form metals and plastics. Sand or metal usually form molds for casting. Sand molds are called one-shot because they are broken after use. Metal molds are called permanent because they can be used over and over again.

Compressing and Stretching Tools. Compressing and stretching are like rolling pizza dough flat with a rolling pin. The pizza maker pushes down (compresses) and pulls out (stretches) the dough to make it fit the pan. Manufacturers use tools to compress and stretch materials. In one process, called rolling, metal is forced under cylindrical tools called **rolls**. The rolls have a shape cut into their surfaces that forms the metal into shapes. Railroad rails are made by forcing metal through two matched rolls.

A second group of compressing and stretching tools is dies. A **die** has a metal surface with a shape matching the surface shape wanted on

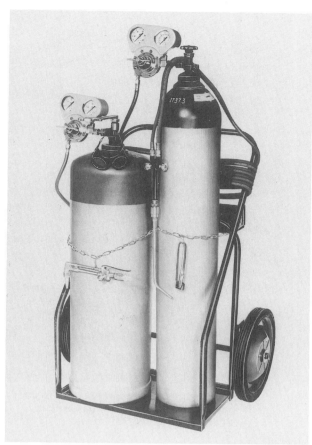

Figure 7-13. An oxyacetylene torch burns a mixture of oxygen and acetylene for flame cutting of metals. *(Courtesy of MECO—Modern Engineering Company, Inc.)*

When an electrical current feeds through the electrode, a spark is made that cuts away the unwanted metal.

Lasers use high-intensity light to cut a variety of materials.

Forming Tools

Forming tools process materials by casting, compressing and stretching, and conditioning.

Casting Tools. Casting is a process like making ice cubes in a freezer. The ice cube tray is a

Figure 7-14. The molds in this photo form molten metal into brick-shaped blocks. *(Courtesy of FMC Gold Company)*

the finished piece of material. Here is an easy-to-use example of die-forming materials. Take two identical cereal bowls that fit inside one another. Place a piece of paper between them and press down on the top bowl. This is die forming, also called stamping, and the two bowls are matched dies. Die forming makes car parts like fenders, hoods, and trunk lids. In actual manufacturing, large hydraulic presses power dies to supply the needed pressures, Figure 7-15.

Conditioning Tools. Conditioning processes change the internal properties of materials, such as hardness or softness. The manufacture of drill bits is a good example of how conditioning is used. Drill bits are made from steel and are often used to drill holes in other steel parts. If the bit must drill holes in steel, the bit must be made harder than the steel. Metal

Figure 7-16. Spray guns use compressed air to coat materials with finishes such as paint or varnish. *(Courtesy of Binks Manufacturing Company)*

products, like drill bits, can be made harder by conditioning.

One important conditioning process used to make materials harder or softer is heat treating. The equipment used in this conditioning process is an oven or forge. Metal parts, like drill bits, are placed in the oven or forge at high temperatures. After the part reaches a certain temperature, it can be cooled quickly in a bath of water or oil.

Another example of special equipment for conditioning are kilns used to dry lumber or ceramic products.

Combining Tools

Combining tools add one material to another material. The added material will protect, decorate, or improve the first material. Two common examples of combining processes are adding paint to a material and nailing two materials together. The three categories of

Figure 7-15. These metal disks are used in batteries. They were formed by a die. *(Courtesy of FMC Corporation)*

combining are coating, bonding, and mechanical fastening.

Coating Tools. The most common coatings added to materials in manufacturing are paints and other finishes. Paint brushes and spray guns are two tools that add finishes to materials, Figure 7-16. Molding plastic over tool handles or other metal surfaces is another important coating technique. Ovens are equipment (tools) that heat the metal surfaces on which the plastic is molded.

Bonding Tools. Two common bonding processes are welding and soldering or brazing. Welding bonds two pieces of metal by melting them together. Two common pieces of welding equipment are **spot welders** and **arc welders**, Figure 7-17. The tongs or points of a spot welder attach to two pieces of metal on one spot, then an electrical current passes through the tongs. The electrical flow heats the two pieces of metal until they are bonded (melted) together on the one spot. Arc welders also use electrical flow to bond metals. In arc welding, a welding rod is positioned a short distance away from two pieces of metal and an arc jumps the gap between the electrode and the metal. This electrical arc melts the two pieces of metal together. The arc welding electrode moves along in a continuous path, while the spot welder stays in one spot.

In soldering or brazing, the two pieces of metal being bonded are not melted together. Instead, a third metal, called solder or brazing rod, is melted into a small gap between two pieces of metal. When this third piece of metal hardens, it bonds (solders or brazes) the two metal pieces. Soldering usually requires an electric soldering gun, Figure 7-18. Brazing uses an oxyacetylene torch to melt the brazing rod into the gap between the two pieces of metal being bonded.

Mechanical Fastening Tools. This method uses mechanical fasteners to combine two pieces of material. Three of the more common mechanical fasteners are nails and staples, threaded fasteners, and rivets.

Combining materials with nails and staples are very similar processes. In both cases, workers combine two or more materials by forcing straight metal mechanical fasteners (nails or staples) through the materials being combined. The most common tool for forcing nails through materials is the hammer, Figure 7-19. Workers use staple guns to staple. Both of

Figure 7-17. Arc welders can bond two pieces of metal together by welding or melting. *(Courtesy of Miller Electric Manufacturing Co., Appleton, WI)*

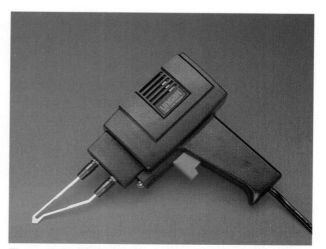

Figure 7-18. This electric soldering gun bonds metal pieces together. *(Courtesy of Ungar Division of Eldon Industries)*

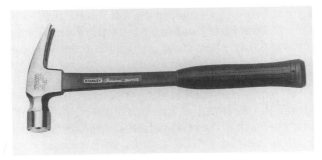

Claw hammer

Ball peen hammer

Figure 7-19. Hammers are hand tools that extend the force of the user in applying mechanical fasteners. (Courtesy of Stanley-Proto Industrial Tools, Covington, GA)

these are hand tools that use human power to force the mechanical fasteners through the materials. In recent years, hammers and staple guns have improved with the addition of an outside power source, such as electricity or pneumatic (compressed air) power. Powered nail guns and staple guns greatly speed up the job of nailing and stapling.

Combining materials with threaded fasteners usually involves screws or bolts and nuts. The two most common tools used with mechanical fasteners are screwdrivers and wrenches. Many sizes and styles of screwdrivers are available, with the most common styles being the straight slotted screwdriver and the Phillips® head screwdriver, Figure 7-20. Wrenches hold bolts and nuts so they can be threaded together to combine two materials. Once again, many sizes and styles of wrenches are available, with the most common styles being the fixed size open and box end wrench and the adjustable size wrench, Figure

7-21. As with hammers and staple guns, screwdrivers and wrenches are hand tools that have improved with the addition of an outside power source. Electric and pneumatic-powered screwdrivers and wrenches make the job of mechanical fastening with screws and bolts easier and faster.

Nails and threaded fasteners can often be removed from the materials that were combined. Combining materials with rivets, on the other hand, is permanent. A rivet is a metal pin with a head on one end and a straight shank on the other; it looks like a bolt without threads, Figure 7-22. Rivets are used to combine two or more pieces of metal. The rivet is placed in a hole drilled through the pieces, then the straight shank end is flattened or spread so the rivet will not come out of the hole. The metal skin on the outside of an airplane is fastened to the frame of the plane with rivets.

Three common riveting tools are hammers, rivet sets, and pop rivet guns. Hammers and rivet sets are used together. The rivet set pro-

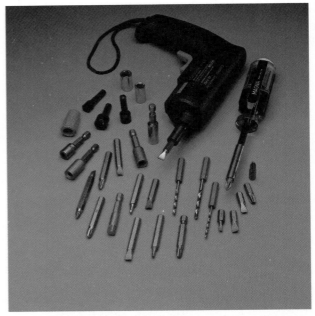

Figure 7-20. Here are an electric screwdriver and a hand tool screwdriver that adapt to a number of uses. Notice the different sizes of interchangeable straight slotted and Phillips® head screwdriver bits. (Courtesy of Vermont American Corporation)

Adjustable size

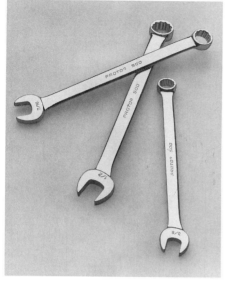

Fixed size

Figure 7-21. Here are the two basic wrench styles—the adjustable size and the fixed size. *(Courtesy of Stanley-Proto Industrial Tools, Covington, GA)*

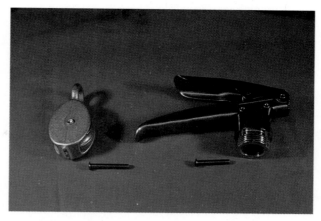

Figure 7-22. Here are some different sized rivets and the products they help make. *(Courtesy of Townsend Fastening Systems)*

tects the rivet head and holds the rivet in place. The hammer is used to spread the straight shank end of the rivet. Pop rivet guns combine the processes of holding and flattening the rivet so that workers don't need hammers and rivet sets. Pop rivets are often used on lighter pieces of metal.

The speed and efficiency of riveting has also been improved by using outside power sources like electricity and pneumatic power.

Other Important Manufacturing Tools

Separating, forming, and combining are the three types of materials processing tools used in manufacturing. Some other tools are also used for measuring, holding, positioning, and transporting materials.

Measuring Tools. Manufacturing workers use a number of measuring tools including rulers, gages, micrometers, and squares, Figure 7-23. Rulers measure lengths. **Gages** check sizes and dimensions on product parts. One of the more common gages is the **go–no go gage** used during quality control checks. When a product part is checked with this type of gage, it is either kept (a go) or rejected (a no go). **Micrometers** accurately measure to a thousandth of an inch on precision parts. Squares usually measure ninety-degree (square) angles.

Holding Tools. People are not strong enough to hold parts securely during certain processes. The two most common holding tools used in manufacturing are pliers and clamps. **Pliers** are hand tools that hold small parts. The most common plier styles are the slip joint, groove joint, locking, and needle nose, Figure 7-24. **Clamps** hold pieces of material to a machine during processes such as drilling. They also hold two pieces of material together during bonding or gluing. Some of the more common hand-held clamps are the bar clamp, C-clamp, hand screw, and toggle clamp, Figure 7-25. For increased holding power, pneumatic (compressed air) or hydraulic (compressed liquid) cylinders can power clamps.

Positioning Tools. On a consistent basis, workers must accurately hold the materials being

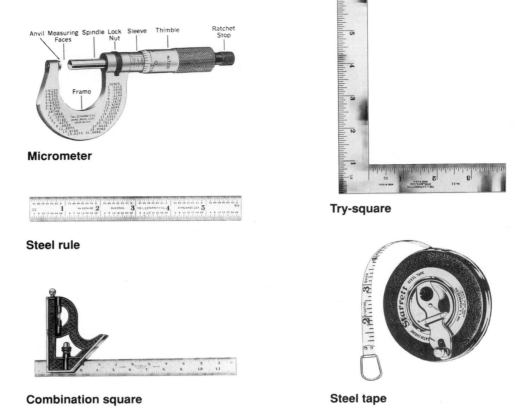

Micrometer

Steel rule

Try-square

Combination square

Steel tape

Figure 7-23. Manufacturing workers perform many measuring processes. Here are some of the more common measuring tools. *(Courtesy of L.G. Starrett Company)*

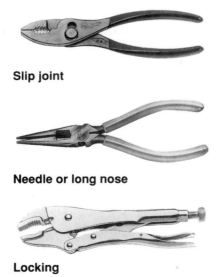

Slip joint

Needle or long nose

Locking

Figure 7-24. Pliers are hand tools that help workers hold small parts. Here are three common styles of pliers. *(Courtesy of Stanley-Proto Industrial Tools, Covington, GA)*

processed. Two common positioning tools are jigs and fixtures. **Jigs** guide the path of a tool on a part being processed. Jigs attach to the part being processed, or the part attaches to the jig. **Fixtures** attach to a machine and position parts being processed in a specific location on that machine. Both jigs and fixtures improve accuracy in processing materials by eliminating the need for the worker to measure and lay out exactly where a hole is to be drilled or a material is to be cut, Figure 7-26.

Transporting Machines. An important part of mass production manufacturing is transporting or moving materials or product parts from one machine to another. Manufacturers use a number of different transporting machines. These include conveyor belts, overhead rail conveyors, high lifts, and automatic guided vehicles (AGV), Figure 7-27.

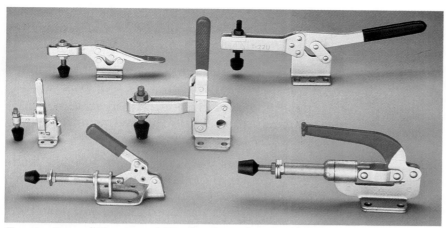

Toggle clamps *(Courtesy of Woodworker's Supply of NM)*

C-clamps *(Courtesy of Stanley-Proto Industrial Tools, Covington, GA)*

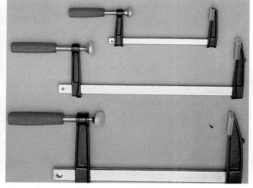

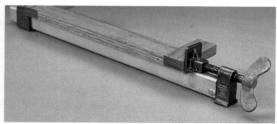

Hand screw *(Courtesy of Woodworker's Supply of NM)*

Bar clamps *(Courtesy of Woodworker's Supply of NM)*

Bar clamp *(Courtesy of Woodworker's Supply of NM)*

Figure 7-25. Clamps are very important in manufacturing for holding objects securely while processing. Here are several different clamp styles.

Figure 7-26. This device is a centering jig. A jig guides the path of a tool on the part being processed. In the right-hand photo, a drill bit is the tool being guided. *(Courtesy of Woodworker's Supply of NM)*

Figure 7-27. In manufacturing, the workers stay in one place and transportation systems, like this conveyor, move the product through the plant. *(Courtesy of American Honda Motor Co., Inc.)*

Computers—Multi-purpose Machines

Computers have been used in nearly every manufacturing job. Computers improve the efficiency, accuracy, and productivity of many manufacturing processes. Just like the other tools and machines described in this chapter, computers extend human capabilities and make some jobs easier. Every department in manufacturing has found a use for computers.

In the management department, supervisors and managers use computers to gather information about the progress of work in all the other departments. In marketing, researchers, advertisers, and sales people use computers to get data on potential buyers, to study market research, and to create advertisements. In the finance department, accountants and bookkeepers use computers to do the payroll, create cost estimate budgets, and keep track of other financial information.

The real tool when using any computer is the software. **Software** is the set of coded instructions written to control the operations of the computer, Figure 7-28. Without software, a computer would be a useless machine. The list of written instructions in software is called a *program*. Many software programs are available for every department in manufactur-ing, but the most important uses of computers have been in the engineering and production departments.

Computers in the Engineering Department

Two uses of computers in the engineering department are computer-aided drafting (CAD) and computer-aided drawing and design (CADD).

CAD. Drafters use **CAD** systems to make technical drawings of the product to be manufactured, Figure 7-29. In the past, drafters worked with T-squares, scales, triangles, and pencils to create these drawings by hand on paper. Today, more and more drafters use CAD systems to perform drafting operations. Doing drawings by hand requires a great deal of time. Each line, letter, and shape on a drawing must be created by the drafter. The drafter must have great skill to draw these features exactly the same every time.

In CAD, most of these jobs are done by the computer. CAD software programs are written so that a drafter needs only to identify the type of line, letter, or shape required; the computer then draws the feature perfectly on a computer screen. Most CAD systems also include a drawing library of commonly used symbols and shapes to allow faster drawing. As an example, the design for an electronic product

Figure 7-28. This screen is showing the computer user a "menu" of options. *(Courtesy of Hewlett Packard)*

Figure 7-29. A CAD system lets drafters produce complex drawings faster and with more precision. *(Courtesy of Hewlett Packard)*

might have hundreds of symbols to identify different electronic components. Before CAD systems, the drafter would draw each of these symbols by hand. With a CAD system, the drafter needs only to pull a copy of the needed symbol from the library and place it on the drawing.

Another advantage of CAD is ease in revising drawings. In the past, when a product was changed or improved, the drawings (on paper) had to be completely redrawn or traced. Today, CAD systems allow the drafter to redraw only those parts and features that have been revised.

As drafting tools, CAD systems reduce the amount of time it takes to make and revise product drawings. They can also reduce the number of mistakes made in drawing special symbols and features in a product.

CADD. CADD systems are used by engineers in manufacturing to design and test product plans. The difference between CAD and CADD systems is the simulation ability in CADD. While CAD is used to make two- and three-dimensional drawings of objects, CADD can be used to make those drawings plus simulate

Figure 7-30. One area in manufacturing that uses computers extensively is drafting and design. Computer-aided drawing and design (CADD) is a tool that improves the speed and efficiency of product testing. *(Courtesy of Gillette Co.)*

product testing procedures. In the past, when a product was designed by an engineer, scale models and full-sized prototypes were often made and tested for durability, strength, and performance. This process involved making dozens of different models and prototypes until the engineers found the combination of materials, parts, and design they wanted. CADD systems have simulation programs built in so that product design models can be built, tested, and changed on a computer screen in a small portion of the time needed to make real models. Engineers can change materials and parts on the product and simulate the stresses, strains, and wear the product must take when used. Drawings that look like wire models are used. The procedure of testing products this way on a computer is called *finite element analysis.*

Designing and testing products this way takes less time, saves the company money that used to be spent on models and prototypes, and improves the quality of manufactured products, Figure 7-30.

Computers in the Production Department

The use of computers in processing materials is called computer-aided manufacturing or CAM. **CAM** involves controlling tools and machines with computers, Figure 7-31. In the past, all manufacturing machines were operated and controlled directly by human operators. Then, numerical control (NC) machining was introduced. With NC, operators code the machine operations onto a punched tape. The punch tape is then used to control the machines. Recently, CAM has been replacing NC. Instead of coding operations onto a punch tape, CAM operators write software programs for computers that are used to control machines.

CAD/CAM. The next step in computerizing manufacturing operations was to tie the engineering department to the production department using CAD/CAM systems. With **CAD/CAM,** a drafter in the engineering department draws the plans for a product on a CAD system, and the design information is then sent directly to machines in the production

Figure 7-31. The machines in this CAM system are controlled by computer. *(Courtesy of Cincinnati Milacron)*

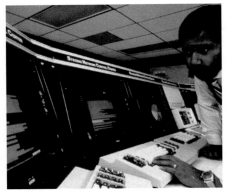

Figure 7-33. Workers using a CIM system can get a broad picture of the entire manufacturing operation by looking at a computer screen. *(Courtesy of International Business Machines Corp.)*

department where the product is made, Figure 7-32.

Computer Integrated Manufacturing (CIM). After the engineering and production depart-

ments were connected with CAD/CAM, computers were used to integrate (tie together) all the departments. In **CIM**, the management, engineering, production, finance, marketing, and human resources departments are all linked by computer, Figure 7-33. Information about the progress in any department can be seen at once in any other department. Company-wide planning can be done with CIM. The human resources department can prepare workers for specific jobs; the finance department can plan to buy materials to match the production schedule; marketing can plan advertising to match the finished-product dates, engineering and production communicate with CAD/CAM, and management can

Figure 7-32. A CAD/CAM system lets the designers store plans in the computer, and then send them to a computer-controlled machine in the production department, where the product is made. *(Courtesy of Grumman Corporation)*

direct the whole company by following the progress of each department. With CIM, six separate departments can work toward the single goal of producing and selling a quality product for a profit.

Just In Time (JIT). Once a company has started working with CIM, it is not far from JIT manufacturing. With **JIT**, a manufacturing company can save money by carefully timing the different parts of the manufacturing process so that they all fit together "just in time."

For example, manufacturing companies have always ordered materials and supplies in large quantities long before they were needed. These materials and supplies were then stored in nearby warehouses and delivered to the plant when needed. Renting a warehouse, storing supplies, and moving supplies from the warehouse can be expensive for a company. Since CIM helps a company know just when it needs certain supplies or materials, the company can have supplies delivered just in time at the manufacturing plant. This saves the company money that would have been spent to rent the warehouse. Similarly, the company

will finish the products and deliver them to the market immediately, again saving the cost to store finished items in a warehouse.

Flexible Manufacturing. Another important new use of computers is flexible manufacturing. **Flexible manufacturing** lets a company make many versions of the same product to meet specific consumer wants. The General Electric Company uses flexible manufacturing to make 2,000 versions of a basic electric meter.

In flexible manufacturing, complex combination machines, called flexible manufacturing centers, make product parts, Figure 7-34. A typical center has several machines, such as drills, mills, lathes, robots, and conveyors, that are all controlled by one computer. The center computer is programmed to make several different versions of the same basic product. As an example, an automobile manufacturer can use one flexible manufacturing center to make engines with four, six, and eight cylinders. As an engine moves toward the center on a conveyor, a laser or other tool reads a code on the engine. This code tells the computer whether

Figure 7-34. The flexible manufacturing centers in this system let the company adapt its product to buyer needs. *(Courtesy of Cincinnati Milacron Inc.)*

Lasers in Manufacturing

Lasers are important new tools in manufacturing. *Laser* stands for "light amplification by stimulated emissions of radiation." Lasers provide a perfectly straight and monochromatic light that can be focused in very tiny diameters. Have you ever concentrated the sun's rays with a magnifying glass and burned paper? This is the basic principle behind using lasers in manufacturing. High-powered laser light is concentrated down to a tiny diameter of light. This tiny light beam can reach a temperature of 4,800 degrees Fahrenheit—hot enough to melt steel. Even with this power, lasers can cut cloth, paper, and plastic without burning.

In manufacturing, lasers can cut, drill, and measure. A cutting laser melts and vaporizes the material being cut. When drilling, the holes are actually burned in the material. In measuring, lasers can accurately measure to ten-millionths of an inch. (If the Empire State Building were equal to twelve inches, ten-millionths of an inch would be equal to the thickness of a piece of paper!) Automobile manufacturers use lasers to measure car assemblies for straightness.

Several of the advantages and disadvantages of using lasers in manufacturing are listed in the following table.

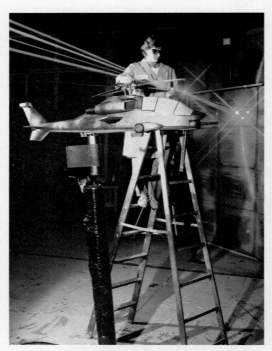

Lasers are used in many manufacturing processes, including precision measurement. *(Courtesy of NASA)*

ADVANTAGES OF LASERS
■ Cut materials are vaporized, no scrap is left over
■ Tiny light concentration during cutting, little wasted material
■ Fast cutting, which means lower production costs
■ Can cut or drill virtually any material
■ Highly accurate cutting, drilling, and measuring
■ Do not dull or wear out like drill bits or saw blades

DISADVANTAGES OF LASERS
■ Lasers are very expensive pieces of equipment
■ Trained, skilled workers are needed to set up and maintain lasers
■ Drilled holes are not straight and smooth like conventional drilled holes
■ High heat laser beam can be dangerous to workers and other equipment

Before lasers can be used in manufacturing, workers must think about their pros and cons.

Figure 7-35. Although most robots look nothing like human beings, they can perform some human tasks with speed and accuracy. *(Courtesy of AMP Incorporated)*

the engine should have four, six, or eight cylinders. The computer then sends the right instructions to each machine in the center.

Robots—Computer-controlled Machines

One computer-controlled machine we hear so much about is the robot. The Robot Institute of America defines a **robot** as a "reprogrammable multifunctional manipulator designed to move material, parts, tools, or specialized devices through variable programmed motions for the performance of a variety of tasks." Notice the words "reprogrammable" and "multifunctional." Reprogrammable means different software can be used with a robot. Different software makes the robot multifunctional (able to do several jobs). Robots are very accurate and reliable machines that can often do the job of a production worker faster and better.

Basic Parts of a Robot. Basic robot parts include sensors, a control mechanism, actuators, and drives. Robots replace human work-

ers and can be likened to humans. Robot sensors are like the human senses of sight, hearing, and touch. Robots have pressure sensors, touch sensors, limit switches, light switches, and even video camera–based vision sensors. The robot control mechanism is like the human brain. A computer and software are used to control robots. Robot actuators are like a human hand. Robots have a variety of actuators, called end affectors, including grippers, suction devices, and special attachments for welding, spray painting, and drilling. Robot drives are like human muscles. Robots have electrical, pneumatic, and hydraulic motors that drive the robot and its actuators.

Robot Classifications. The most common way to classify robots is by their degree of freedom. The most complex robot, an anthropomorphic robot, duplicates complete human arm motions. Anthropomorphic means having human characteristics. This robot has six **degrees of freedom**.

1. Arm sweep—rotation about the base axis
2. Shoulder swivel—rotation about the shoulder axis
3. Elbow extension—rotation about the elbow axis
4. Wrist pitch—up and down wrist movements
5. Wrist yaw—side-to-side wrist movements
6. Wrist roll—rotation about the wrist joint

The more degrees of arm freedom a robot has, the more complex processes it can perform. Degrees of arm freedom is important to robot work envelope. **Work envelope** is the area in which the robot can reach and work. An anthropomorphic robot has a spherical work envelope. Less complex robots with fewer degrees of arm freedom have work envelopes that are shaped like rectangles, cylinders, or other shapes, Figure 7-36.

Using Robots in Manufacturing. Robots can replace production workers in dangerous or

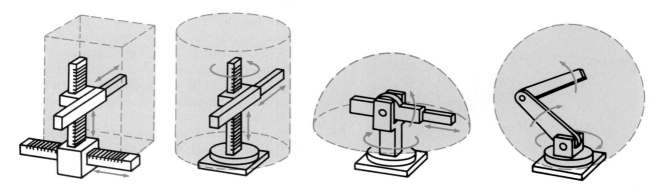

Figure 7-36. The space in which a robot can reach to do work is called a *work envelope*. The number of degrees of freedom will determine the shape of a robot's work envelope.

unhealthy work conditions or where highly accurate, consistent work is needed. Robots have a high degree of repeatability; they can do one job over and over again with consistent results.

The primary uses for robots in manufacturing are welding (spot and continuous path arc), spray painting, drilling, and pick and place operations such as feeding parts to and from other machines. In the future, robots will continue to replace production workers in manufacturing, Figure 7-37.

Figure 7-37. Robots have been used in manufacturing to do spot welding. This robot is spot welding the frame of an automobile. *(Courtesy of Ford Motor Company)*

Summary

Tools and machines are important to every department in manufacturing for processing materials and information. You can describe all tools and machines with the six basic machines—wheels, pulleys, levers, inclined planes, wedges, and screws. Using tools safely is very important to successful manufacturing. Materials processing tools separate, form, and combine materials. The most important information-processing machine in manufacturing today is the computer. One materials-processing machine controlled by computers is the robot.

DISCUSSION QUESTIONS

1. Why are materials-processing tools made from steel, carbide, ceramics, and diamonds?

2. Name six separating tools or machines. Identify them as having multiple or single cutting points and as being chip removal, shearing, or nontraditional tools. What types of products are made with these tools?

3. Name two forming tools—one for casting and one for compressing/stretching. What types of products are made with these tools?

4. Name three combining tools—one for coating, one for bonding, and one for mechanical fastening. What types of products are made with these tools?

5. The three main categories of materials processing tools identified in this chapter were separating, forming, and combining. Four other categories of tools were identified. Name these four categories and identify specific tools or machines in each category.

6. Why do you think manufacturers are using computers, robots, and lasers? Do you think these tools and machines will be used more in the future? Why?

7. This chapter described the six basic manufacturing machines. What other uses can you identify for these six basic machines?

8. Accidents and injuries in manufacturing happen because of unsafe working conditions or unsafe worker actions. Which of these do you think leads to more accidents? Why? Which of these can be more easily controlled in manufacturing?

CHAPTER ACTIVITIES

 ## LEARNING SAFETY RULES FOR TOOLS AND MACHINES

OBJECTIVE

Using manufacturing tools and machines safely is very important. First, you must learn certain safety guidelines and rules.

In this activity, you will learn these guidelines and rules for the tools and machines in your school's lab.

Many tools and machines can be used in manufacturing. The materials used in the finished product will tell you what tools and machines you will need. Your school's lab has tools and machines that you and your classmates will use to manufacture a product. Your teacher has made safety guidelines and rules that every student must know before using a tool and machine. To be a successful manufacturing student (and worker in your class enterprise), you must know these safety guidelines and rules.

MATERIALS AND SUPPLIES

1. List of tools and machines in lab
2. Safety guidelines and rules

PROCEDURE

1. Make a list of the tools and machines in your lab.
2. Obtain a list of the safety guidelines and rules for the tools and machines in your lab from your teacher.
3. Learn the following facts about tools and machines in your lab:
   a. names of the tools and machines;
   b. uses for the tools and machines;
   c. names of the important parts on tools and machines;
   d. specific safety hazards when using certain tools and machines; and
   e. specific guidelines and rules established by your teacher.
4. Take a safety quiz on the tools and machines that you will use in your manufacturing enterprise.

RELATED QUESTIONS

1. Why is it important for manufacturing workers and students to know the safety rules for tools and machines?
2. Why do you think your teacher requires students to pass a safety quiz before allowing them to work with tools and machines?
3. What tools or machines do you think are the most dangerous in your lab? Why?
4. Are there any safety guidelines or rules that apply to all, or mostly all, the tools and machines in your lab?

 HYDRAULICALLY CONTROLLED ROBOTIC ARM

OBJECTIVE

Problem solving in industry requires individuals to work as effective team members. In this activity, you will work as part of a team to design and manufacture a model robotic arm. You will also be introduced to fluid power. When complete, the robot should be able to pick up and put down small objects, move up and down, and to the left and right.

More robots are being added to factory assembly lines each year. Many companies are experimenting with new applications of robotics to reduce production costs. Robots are taking over hazardous tasks such as spray painting and handling hot materials. Not everyone is pleased with the increased use of robots. Reduced employment is one possible negative impact that concerns workers and labor unions.

MATERIALS AND SUPPLIES

1. Six 60 cc syringes and 6' of aquarium tubing
2. 12" × 12" × 3/4" plywood for base
3. Scrapwood, dowels, and assorted fasteners
4. Sink or pan to fill syringes
5. Safety glasses

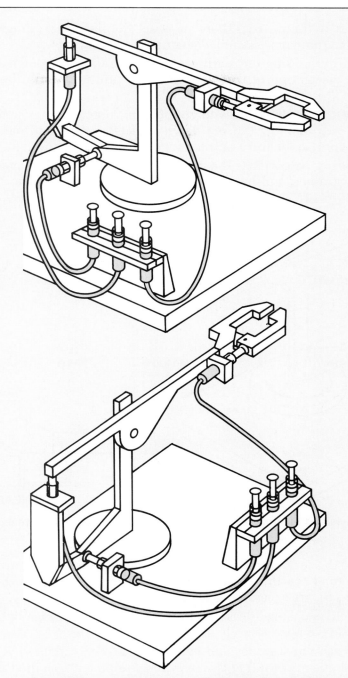

Figure 1. A hydraulically controlled robot arm, with three pairs of syringes.

PROCEDURE

1. Form groups of three students.
2. Connect a pair of syringes with twenty-four inches of tubing. Remove the plungers.

3. Fill the syringes by immersing them in water. Replace the plungers and remove them from water. You have assembled a simple hydraulic system.

4. Test the system by holding one syringe in each hand. Push down on one plunger while resisting the motion of the other one. Try pulling out on the plunger. What happens?

5. Plan to use three pairs of syringes to control the robotic arm. Use one pair for the gripper, which will pick up and put down objects. The second pair will move the arm up and down. Use the third pair to move the base right and left.

6. One syringe of each pair will be the controller. The other will move one part of the robot (the arm, gripper, and base). The drawings below give ideas to help you get started.

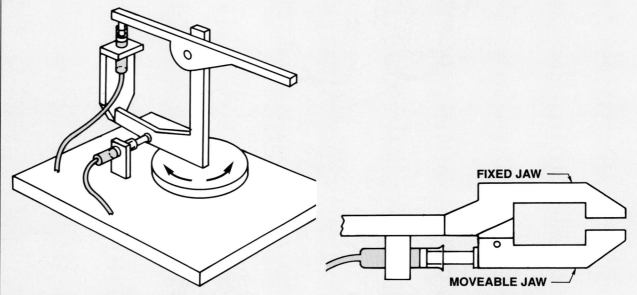

Figure 2. Ideas for the base and the arm.   **Figure 3. The gripper might look like this.**

7. One member of the team should design the gripper, another team member should design the arm, and the third person should design the movable base. Each team member should prepare several idea sketches.

8. Meet as a group to exchange ideas. Combine the best ideas and submit a final sketch to your teacher. Make necessary changes.

9. After approval, use the supplies and equipment made available by your teacher to construct the robotic arm. *NOTE:* Use only the equipment specified by your teacher. Follow safe procedures at all times.

10. Work as a team to solve problems as they occur.

11. When the robotic arm is complete, demonstrate it to your class.

MATH/SCIENCE CONNECTION

Air can be compressed, liquids can not. Connect two syringes using tubing to make a pneumatic system. Compare to the hydraulic system used for the robot. Connect a 30cc syringe to a 60cc syringe. Operate hydraulically and try to express the results mathematically.

RELATED QUESTIONS

1. Name three uses of robotics in industry.
2. How could a robot help a handicapped person?
3. Describe how teamwork helped in the design of your robot.
4. Describe one change that could be made to improve the way your team's robotic arm works.

CHAPTER 8

Energy

OBJECTIVES

After completing this chapter, you will know about:

- The four largest energy-using groups in our society.
- The different sources of energy, including limited, unlimited, and renewable types.
- The energy sources used in manufacturing and their applications.
- Energy conservation techniques used in manufacturing.

KEY TERMS

Alternative energy
  sources
Cogeneration
Efficiency rating
Electrical energy
Energy
Energy conservation
Energy-consuming
  sectors
Energy converter
Engine

Fossil fuels
Generator
Hydraulics
Hydropower
Kilowatt-hour
Kilowatts
Limited energy sources
Mechanical energy
Motor
Pneumatics
Pump

Radiant energy
Recycling
Renewable energy
  sources
Thermal energy
Turbines
Unlimited energy
  sources
Watts

Energy

Manufacturing and related industries are the largest energy consumers in our society. Every year, manufacturing companies use large amounts of energy to run machines and equipment, to provide lighting, and to process materials. Energy is an important input for manufacturing.

In simple terms, **energy** is the ability to do work. All matter has energy, but useful energy is found in materials called fuels. The three main fuels used as energy sources in our society are petroleum, natural gas, and coal.

Energy Sources

Energy sources are broken into three types: limited, unlimited, or renewable. **Limited energy sources** have a limited or fixed supply. They will someday be completely consumed, no longer available for use. **Unlimited energy sources** should be available indefinitely. **Renewable energy sources** can be replaced or renewed, given enough time, Figure 8-1.

ENERGY SOURCES		
Limited	**Unlimited**	**Renewable**
coal	solar	wood
natural gas	water	biomass
petroleum	wind	human and animal
uranium	geothermal	muscle power

Figure 8-1. Energy sources are categorized as limited, unlimited, or renewable.

Limited Energy Sources. The main limited energy sources include coal, petroleum, natural gas, and uranium. Coal, petroleum, and natural gas are **fossil fuels**, Figure 8-2. These fuels resulted from millions of years of decay and pressure exerted on plant and animal fossils. Manufacturers burn fossil fuels to produce heat. They then use this heat to generate electricity, to heat air in a building, or to perform some other process. Uranium is not a fossil fuel, but rather an ore found in the earth. It is the fuel used in nuclear electricity-generating plants. There are limited supplies of these energy sources on earth; someday they will be completely consumed. Because these energy sources are limited, people must try to use them wisely.

Unlimited Energy Sources. The sun, wind, and water are examples of unlimited energy sources, Figure 8-3. The word "unlimited" is used even though someday these energy sources will also be completely consumed. For example, the sun will eventually burn itself out. Luckily, this is not expected for a few billion years. The same is true for the other unlimited energy sources. Because of the long time frame, these energy sources are said to be unlimited.

Unlimited energy sources have not been used very much lately by any energy-consuming sector. In the past these sources of energy, especially wind and water, were very important. Historically, manufacturing industries located their plants next to a stream or river and used water wheels to run machines, Figure 8-4. At first they used belts and pulleys to transfer the motion of the water wheel directly to machines. Later, the water wheel generated electricity, which was then used to run machines. Electricity generated by water is now called **hydropower**.

Unlimited energy sources are also called **alternative energy sources**. When limited energy sources run out, people will use unlimited energy sources as an alternative or second

A. *Courtesy of Du Pont Company*

B. *Courtesy of Dominion Resources Annual Report*

C. *Courtesy of Amoco Corporation*

Figure 8-2. (A) Coal, (B) natural gas, and (C) petroleum are the three most important energy sources in the United States. There is a limited supply of these fossil fuels on earth.

Figure 8-3. Water behind a dam is an important unlimited energy source. *(Photo by Ruby S. Gold)*

choice. Wind power is showing some promise as an alternative energy source. Several experimental wind farms, which generate electricity, are already in use.

Figure 8-4. Historically, manufacturing shops were located next to a supply of water. A water wheel converted moving water into working machines. *(Photo by Barbara L. Russell. Courtesy Town of Sandwich, MA.)*

Renewable Energy Sources. Wood, biomass, and human and animal muscle power are examples of renewable energy sources. At one time, manufacturing extensively used wood and human and animal muscle power. In fact, when the industrial revolution began, the use of wood as a fuel almost lead to the total deforestation of England. Fortunately, wood is a renewable source of energy. Given enough time, trees can be grown to renew the supply of wood available for energy. In biomass, a fuel in the form of gas or alcohol is created from vegetation and animal wastes. Gasohol is an example of a biomass fuel. Biomass-generated alcohol, made from vegetables like corn, is mixed with gasoline to make gasohol. Renewable energy sources are also not often used for today's energy needs.

Three Important Energy Sources

There are several energy source options available. In the United States, however, only a few of these sources are used for most of the energy needs. Figure 8-5 shows the percentages of each of the important energy sources in our country. Notice that petroleum accounts for more than forty percent of the total. Petroleum (crude oil) is used to make heating oils, diesel fuels, gasoline, and other fuels. Natural gas

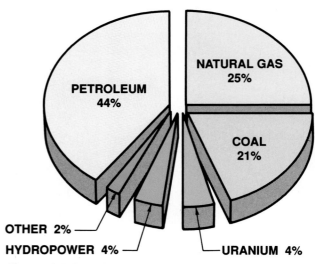

Figure 8-5. The limited fossil fuels of petroleum, natural gas, and coal are used for ninety percent of the energy applications in the United States.

accounts for twenty-five percent of the energy we use, while coal accounts for twenty-one percent. Together, uranium and hydropower account for only eight percent of our total energy. Included in the other category are solar, wind, geothermal, biomass, and other energy sources. Petroleum, natural gas, and coal are the three most important sources of energy used in the United States. These limited energy sources account for ninety percent of our energy. Someday the supplies of these fossil fuels will run out and have to be replaced with alternative sources of energy.

Forms of Energy

Energy can take on many different forms. Four important forms are mechanical, thermal, radiant, and electrical energy. **Mechanical energy** is the energy found in moving objects, such as a rotating saw blade or a turning drill bit. **Thermal energy** is heat generated by the movement of molecules in materials. Thermal energy or heat is the simplest form of energy, being generated from all other energy forms. **Radiant energy**, also called electromagnetic energy, is visible and invisible light energy. The sun is the largest supply of radiant energy on earth. **Electrical energy** is the energy of moving electrons in a conductor (usually a wire). Electrical energy is adaptable to several applications, such as operating motors (mechanical energy), creating heat (thermal energy), and providing light (radiant energy).

Energy Converters

Often, one form of energy must be changed to a more usable form. For example, electrical energy is changed into radiant (light) energy with a light bulb. The light bulb is an energy converter. **Energy converters** change energy from one form into another more usable form. Some of the more common energy converters are generators, turbines, engines, and motors. **Generators** change mechanical energy into electrical energy. Generators work on the principle that when a wire is passed through a magnetic field, an electric current is generated in that wire, Figure 8-6. Generators are usually powered by an engine or a turbine. **Engines**

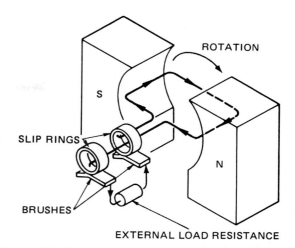

Figure 8-6. A generator is an energy converter that changes mechanical energy into electrical energy. *(Reprinted from* ALTERNATING CURRENT FUNDAMENTALS *by Duff and Herman, © 1986 Delmar Publishers Inc.)*

change the thermal energy of burning gasoline or diesel fuel into the mechanical energy of rotary motion. Manufacturing companies often have large diesel engines attached to generators as back-up systems for electrical energy in case of a blackout. Engines are more commonly used in automobiles and trucks for transportation. **Turbines** change the mechanical energy of wind, water, or steam into rotary mechanical energy. Wind mills and water wheels are examples of turbines, Figure 8-7. Most turbines today are turned by steam or moving water. Steam is generated by burning coal or by nuclear power. Turbines powered by water are usually located at the base of a large dam.

Motors are just the opposite of generators. A **motor** changes electrical energy into rotary mechanical energy. Electric motors, found on many machines and power tools, are very common energy converters in manufacturing. The rotary motion of a motor is usually transmitted to some tool by an arrangement of gears, belts, pulleys, or chains, Figure 8-8. Motors can also be used to run pumps. **Pumps** pressurize air or liquids and are important for fluid power systems.

Fluid power systems, including hydraulics and pneumatics, are very important energy

Figure 8-7. This man is standing on the blade of a giant turbine being installed in a hydroelectric dam. The turbine turns a generator, and the generator produces electricity. (Courtesy of Dominion Resources Annual Report)

Figure 8-8. The mechanical energy created by an electric motor is transmitted to a tool or machine part with pulleys, belts, gears, or chains. (Reprinted from POWER TECHNOLOGY by George E. Stephenson, © 1986 Delmar Publishers Inc.)

converters in manufacturing for clamping, positioning, and holding objects during processing. **Hydraulics** uses liquids under pressure (usually oil), while **pneumatics** uses air under pressure to do work. Figure 8-9 shows some typical applications of fluid power systems in manufacturing.

Energy-consuming Sectors of Society

Energy experts divide society into four different **energy-consuming sectors**. These include the commercial, residential, transportation, and industrial sectors. The commercial sector entails office buildings and shopping centers. Homes and apartments make up the residential sector. The transportation sector includes cars, trucks, planes, and other vehicles and systems used to move goods and people. The industrial sector entails manufacturing, construction, and related industries. Each of these sectors consumes energy. The total energy used by each is shown in Figure 8-10. Notice that the industrial sector, which includes manufacturing, is the largest energy user in our society. It consumes nearly forty percent of all energy used in the United States.

The Industrial Sector

The industrial sector of society includes manufacturing, construction, and related industries. Manufacturers who convert raw materials into standard materials are the largest energy consumers. Steel, plastics, petroleum products, clay, and glass producers are examples of standard materials manufacturers. Converting raw materials into standard materials takes large amounts of thermal energy, Figure 8-11. Manufacturers who make consumer products from standard materials also use large amounts of energy, but not as much as standard materials producers.

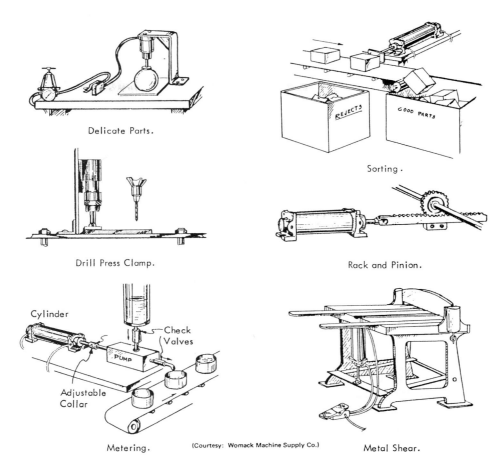

Delicate Parts.

Sorting.

Drill Press Clamp.

Rack and Pinion.

Cylinder

Check Valves

PUMP

Adjustable Collar

Metering. (Courtesy: Womack Machine Supply Co.)

Metal Shear.

Figure 8-9. Hydraulics and pneumatics have many applications in manufacturing. *(Reprinted from* POWER TECHNOLOGY *by George E. Stephenson, © 1986 Delmar Publishers Inc.)*

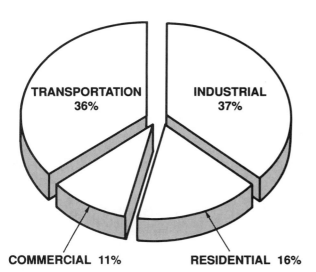

TRANSPORTATION 36%

INDUSTRIAL 37%

COMMERCIAL 11%

RESIDENTIAL 16%

Figure 8-10. The industrial sector, which includes manufacturing, is the largest energy consumer in our society; it is followed closely by transportation.

Figure 8-11. Manufacturing standard materials, such as this molten steel, uses large amounts of thermal or heat energy. *(Courtesy of Allegheny Ludlum)*

Use the manufacturing lab in your school to describe the energy needed by product manufacturers. What are the energy needs in your school lab? Probably the largest energy need is for thermal energy in the winter. Manufacturing buildings, like your school lab, have big open spaces that require large amounts of energy to heat their internal space to a comfortable level. The second important energy application in your school lab and in manufacturing is electric motors. Most power hand tools and machines have electric motors. When a product is being produced, every machine in a production area may be running for eight or more hours a day. This uses large amounts of electricity. The third most important energy user is lighting. Adequate lighting must be provided throughout the entire facility.

Energy Efficiency in Manufacturing. The energy converters used in manufacturing, and other areas of technology, are very inefficient in terms of using energy. Table 8-1 lists the efficiency ratings of furnaces, motors, and two different types of lights. **Efficiency ratings** are calculated with the following formula:

Efficiency Rating = Output Energy / Input Energy × 100

A 100 percent efficient energy converter would get one unit of output energy for every one unit of input energy.

100% Efficiency = 1 Unit Output / 1 Unit Input × 100

Very few energy converters even come close to being 100 percent efficient. As you can see

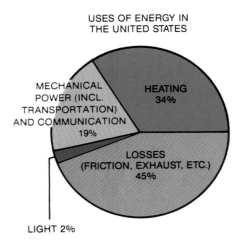

USES OF ENERGY IN THE UNITED STATES

MECHANICAL POWER (INCL. TRANSPORTATION) AND COMMUNICATION 19%

HEATING 34%

LOSSES (FRICTION, EXHAUST, ETC.) 45%

LIGHT 2%

Figure 8-12. Overall, manufacturing plants are forty-five percent inefficient. Almost half the energy used in manufacturing is wasted or lost. *(Reprinted from* LIVING WITH TECHNOLOGY *by Hacker and Barden,* © *1988 Delmar Publishers Inc.)*

from Table 8-1, electric motors get only 0.6 (⁶/₁₀) of a unit of energy output for every one unit of energy input.

60% Efficiency = 0.6 Units Output / 1 Unit Input × 100

What happens to the other 0.4 units of input energy? This energy is lost or wasted, usually as thermal or heat energy. Overall, manufacturing plants lose about forty-five percent of the energy they use. That makes them fifty-five percent efficient. Figure 8-12 shows the relationship between energy losses and the other applications of energy for manufacturing.

The Importance of Electricity

Electricity is a very important form of energy for manufacturing, Figure 8-13. Often, energy experts identify electricity generation as one of the major sectors of energy use. Figure 8-14 shows the percentages of energy used by the various energy-consuming sectors when electricity generation is considered as a sector by itself. The chart shows that the generation of electricity accounts for more than twenty-five percent of the total energy used. Of course, the industrial, residential, and commercial sectors

ELECTRICAL DEVICE	EFFICIENCY RATING
Oil/gas furnaces	65%
Small electrical motors	60%
Fluorescent lights	20%
Incandescent lights	5%

Table 8-1. Most electrical devices in manufacturing are less than sixty-five percent efficient.

Figure 8-13. Electricity is an important form of energy for manufacturing and society. *(Courtesy of Niagara-Mohawk Power Corporation)*

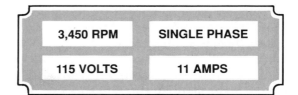

Figure 8-15. This is a simplified version of a label that appears on most electric motors. Can you find labels like this on the manufacturing machines in your school?

all use electricity to a certain degree. Manufacturing companies spend hundreds of thousands of dollars per year on electrical energy. Such companies always check the cost of electricity before opening a plant in a certain location.

The Cost of Electricity. Electrical energy is measured in volts, amps, and watts. **Watts** is a measure of the total amount of electrical energy used by a machine or other electrical

device. Multiply volts times amps to determine watts.

Watts = Volts × Amps

Figure 8-15 shows a typical label from an electric motor on a manufacturing machine. Notice that watts is not given, but volts and amps are. By multiplying volts times amps, we can determine watts.

Watts = 115 Volts × 11 Amps
Watts = 1,265

Electric utility companies charge for electricity by the kilowatt-hour. A **kilowatt** is equal to 1,000 watts. To convert watts to kilowatts, divide watts by 1,000.

Kilowatts = Watts / 1,000

The electric motor described in Figure 8-15 would use 1.265 kilowatts.

Kilowatts = 1,265 / 1,000
Kilowatts = 1.265

To find **kilowatt-hours** (kwh), multiply kilowatts times the number of hours that an electrical device is used over a period of time, such as one month.

Kwh = Kilowatts × Hours of Use

If the 1,265 watt electric motor above ran for eight hours per day for thirty days, the total kilowatt-hours would be 303.6.

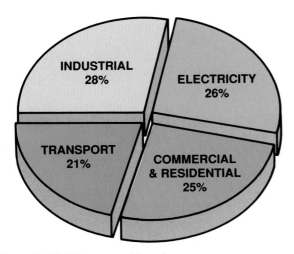

Figure 8-14. When considered as an energy-consuming sector, electricity generation consumes more than twenty-five percent of our energy sources.

Kilowatt-hours =
1.265 Kilowatts × 8 Hrs. × 30 Days
Kilowatt-hours = 303.6

To find the total number of kilowatt-hours used by a manufacturing plant, add together the kilowatt-hours of all electrical devices used, Table 8-2. Table 8-3 shows the amount of electricity, in kilowatt-hours, that a typical manufacturing plant might use for one year. The amount of money a manufacturing company pays for electricity is based on the number of kilowatt-hours of electricity used per month. Table 8-4 shows a typical electricity cost table. Cost rates vary with the amount of kilowatt-hours. As you can see, the more electricity a company uses, the less money they pay for each kilowatt-hour.

Transportation, Energy, and Manufacturing

Transportation accounts for thirty-six percent of the total energy used in the United States. Private citizens use a large part of this, but business and industry consume more than one-third of transportation energy, Figure 8-16. Manufacturers transport all goods and products from the place of manufacture to the consumer. It is very difficult to identify a product that is not transported. Transportation adds to the final cost of the product. Someone has to pay for the operator's salary, the vehicle maintenance, and the fuel. These transportation costs are usually passed along to the consumer as higher product prices.

One of the problems with transportation systems is the inefficiency of their engines. The gasoline engine used in most automobiles is only twenty-five percent efficient; the diesel engine, used in trucks, is only about thirty-three percent efficient. These vehicles, therefore, waste more energy than they use. Manufacturers use trucks more than any other vehicle to move goods from the manufacturing plant to the consumer. Almost all transportation systems use limited fossil fuels as an energy source. The relationship between manufac-

ELECTRICAL DEVICE	QTY.	WATTS	KILOWATTS
LIGHTING			
fluorescent lights	12	40	.480
incandescent lights	6	100	.600
POWER TOOLS			
drill	1	345	.345
router	1	920	.920
circular saw	1	1,150	1.150
MACHINES			
bandsaw	1	690	.690
disk sander	1	880	.880
drill press	1	1,000	1.000
lathe	1	582	.582
planer	1	1,066	1.066
radial arm saw	1	1,265	1.265
scroll saw	1	312	.312
table saw	1	1,230	1.230
TOTALS		10,520	10.520

Table 8-2. Find the total kilowatt rating of the electrical devices in a manufacturing plant by adding together each individual electrical device.

TYPICAL MANUFACTURING PLANT ELECTRICITY USE BY MONTH*											
JAN. 390	FEB. 416	MAR. 393	APR. 373	MAY 408	JUN. 408	JUL. 418	AUG. 498	SEP. 458	OCT. 418	NOV. 420	DEC. 373

*Figures given are in 1,000 kilowatt-hours.

Table 8-3. These figures show the amount of electricity (in kilowatt-hours) that a typical manufacturing plant will use from month to month.

Table 8-4. Electric utility companies charge for electricity by the kilowatt-hour. The more kilowatt-hours of electricity used, the lower the price per kilowatt-hour.

first 2,000 kwh	$.04/kwh
next 18,000 kwh	$.035/kwh
next 180,000 kwh	$.0325/kwh
next 550,000 kwh	$.03/kwh
over 550,000 kwh	$.0275/kwh

Calculating an Electric Bill

The following problem shows how to calculate an electric bill.

Problem: A manufacturing company operates sixteen hours per day for twenty-two days and uses 1,200 kilowatts of electricity. How much will their electric bill be for this month using the rate structure in Table 8-4?

Solution: First, find kilowatt-hours:

Kilowatt-hours = Kilowatts × Hours Used
Kilowatt-hours = 1,200 Kilowatts × 16 Hrs./Day
    × 22 Days
Kilowatt-hours = 422,400

Next, break down the number of kilowatt-hours to match the rate structure and multiply:

first 2,000 kwh = 2,000 × $.04 = $80
next 18,000 kwh = 18,000 × $.035 = $630
next 180,000 kwh = 180,000 × $.0325 = $5,850
remaining 222,400 kwh = 222,400 × $.03 = $6,672
         $13,232

If you multiply this number by 12, you would get some idea of how much money the company spends a year for electricity.

turing and transportation is increasing the speed with which we consume our important limited energy sources, Figure 8-17.

Conservation of Energy

As you now know, the three primary energy sources used in this country are limited fossil fuels. Energy is a very important resource for all areas of technology and society. Inefficient energy converters cause a large percentage of this precious energy to be lost. This lost energy can become an important resource if we can capture and use it. Energy conservation techniques can help manufacturers and other energy users recover some of this lost energy. **Energy conservation** means making wise use of and not wasting energy. Manufacturing industries can use many of the same energy conservation techniques that home owners use to save energy, Table 8-5. You can use some of

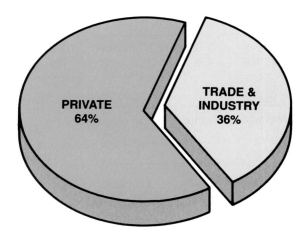

Figure 8-16. Trade and industry account for more than one-third of all the energy used in the transportation sector.

these conservation techniques to reduce the energy consumed by your school manufacturing company. By lowering the amount of energy consumed, a company can reduce the amount of money spent on energy and also the final cost of products.

Figure 8-17. Truck manufacturers are trying to reduce the energy used by their trucks with improved aerodynamics. This will reduce the transportation energy costs passed on to manufacturers and consumers. *(Courtesy of Navistar International Transportation Corporation)*

ENERGY CONSERVATION TECHNIQUES
■ lowering thermostats
■ insulating roof and walls to retain space heat
■ reducing the amount of heat that escapes through ventilation systems
■ insulating steam pipes to reduce heat loss
■ turning off lights when not in use
■ using windows and skylights for natural lighting
■ sealing cracks and leaks around doors, windows, vents
■ installing more efficient electric motors on machines
■ turning off machines when not in use
■ recycling wasted materials

Table 8-5. These are just a few of the energy conservation techniques that can be used by manufacturing companies to lower the amount of energy consumed. Lowering energy use lowers overall operating costs.

Recycling Saves Energy. Recycling is an important way of reducing energy consumption. **Recycling** takes scrap materials and reprocesses them to make new materials, Figure 8-18. Many manufacturing industries, especially the producers of standard metals, plastics, and glass, recycle to reduce energy costs.

The amount of energy saved by recycling can be very dramatic. Table 8-6 compares the number of kilowatt-hours of electricity needed to make steel from scrap and from natural ore. It takes almost four times as much electric

MAKING STEEL FROM	ELECTRICITY USED
Raw materials, ores	2,700 kilowatt-hours
Scrap steel	700 kilowatt-hours

Table 8-6. Making steel from raw materials uses almost four times as much electricity as making steel from scrap. Recycling can reduce the amount of energy a manufacturing company uses.

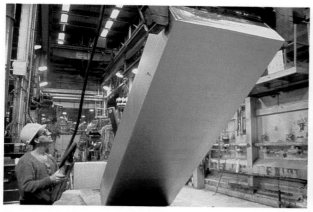

Figure 8-18. The large block (sheet ingot) of aluminum (left) was made from used beverage containers (UBC). The aluminum will be used to make new cans (right). *(Courtesy of Alcan Aluminum Ltd.)*

energy to make steel from ore as from scrap. Consider what impact this savings would have on the final cost of a product like a car, which uses hundreds of pounds of steel. Table 8-6 compares only the processing costs of using scrap and ore to make steel. If we considered

the difference in the amount of energy used to pick up and transport scrap versus the energy used to mine and transport ore, the impact would be even greater. Recycling is an important way for manufacturing companies to save energy.

Cogeneration: Improving Energy Efficiency in Manufacturing

Cogeneration is an energy-generating technique that uses one energy source to supply two or more energy applications. In a conventional manufacturing plant,

two of the largest energy uses are for steam heat and electricity. Such plants often use a boiler furnace to produce steam for materials processing and space

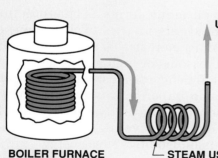

USED STEAM VENTED INTO ATMOSPHERE

ELECTRICITY PURCHASED FROM A UTILITY COMPANY

ELECTRICITY FOR MACHINES

BOILER FURNACE GENERATES STEAM

STEAM USED FOR SPACE HEATING AND MATERIAL PROCESSING

Many manufacturing companies generate steam for space heating and materials processing with their own boiler furnaces while they purchase electricity from a utility company.

heating applications, while they purchase electricity from a local utility company. Once the manufacturing company uses the steam, they often vent it into the atmosphere. This vented steam is wasted energy. With cogeneration, the manufacturing company also uses a steam-generating boiler to produce the needed steam; but instead of venting the used steam, they generate their own electricity. Cogeneration turns once-wasted steam

heat into usable energy and improves the energy efficiency of the plant. Manufacturing companies can save up to fifty percent of their electrical energy costs with cogeneration. These savings can result in lower product costs for consumers. Cogeneration also conserves our limited energy sources, such as coal, petroleum, and natural gas, that are often used by electric utility companies.

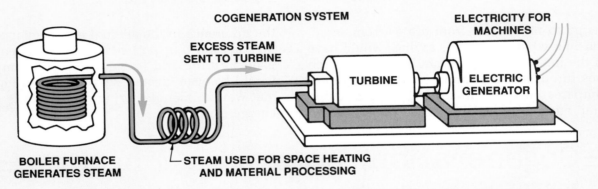

When a manufacturing company uses cogeneration, the steam generated for space heating and materials processing is also used to generate the electricity needed for machines. Cogeneration can save a company up to fifty percent on electricity bills.

Summary

The industrial sector, including manufacturing, is the largest energy consumer in our society. Although several energy options are available, the three most important energy sources are coal, petroleum, and natural gas. These sources are limited fossil fuels. Unlimited and renewable energy sources are not being used to any great extent today, but in the future they will be important alternatives when limited energy sources are totally consumed. Energy can take on many forms in manufacturing. Energy converters are used to change one energy form into a more usable energy form. One of the main reasons for high energy consumption is the inefficiency of most energy converters. Energy is an important resource that must be used wisely and efficiently. Conservation techniques, such as recycling and cogeneration, can help manufacturers save energy.

DISCUSSION QUESTIONS

1. Limited energy sources, such as petroleum, coal, and natural gas, are used more than unlimited or renewable energy sources. Why are these limited energy sources used so much more than other types? Why aren't more unlimited and renewable energy sources used?
2. What energy sources are used to supply the energy needs of your school?
3. How much does it cost for the energy used each year in your school or your home? Can you identify any ways to reduce the amount of money your school or family spends on energy?
4. Four important forms of energy are mechanical, thermal, radiant, and electrical energy. Can you identify applications of these energy forms in your school manufacturing lab?
5. Conservation techniques, such as lowering thermostats, sealing cracks around doors, or turning off electrical devices when not in use, can reduce energy costs. In your school manufacturing lab, how could you better conserve energy?
6. Why do you think the industrial sector consumes the most energy in our society? What are the three biggest uses for energy in manufacturing?

CHAPTER ACTIVITIES

CALCULATING ELECTRICAL ENERGY COSTS

OBJECTIVE

A manufacturing company can pay hundreds of thousands of dollars each year to a utility company for the electricity they use to run machines and equipment. Your manufacturing company will also need to pay for the electrical energy you use. How much will it cost to run lights, machines, and other equipment during this manufacturing class?

In this activity, you will add the total electrical energy costs for the manufacturing lab in your school.

Your manufacturing lab uses electricity for lighting, ventilation, machines, and other tools and equipment. Most of the materials processing that your production department will do to make a product will use electricity. Most electrical machines have labels on their motors that show the volts, amps, and watts used. Lighting is also labeled by the amount of energy consumed. By adding together all the electrical machines, equipment, and lights that you will use, you can find the total number of kilowatts used. Electrical energy use is measured in kilowatt hours. This is the total number of kilowatts used, times the number of hours you use each device. You will need to ask the local electricity company about the energy costs per kilowatt hour for your area. You will need to add this cost to the total cost of manufacturing the product.

MATERIALS AND SUPPLIES

1. List of all electrical power tools, machines, and equipment that will be used in the manufacturing lab
2. List of all lighting fixtures in your lab
3. Calculators

PROCEDURE

1. Break the class into groups and divide the work to be done.
2. Calculate the kilowatts of electricity used by each tool, machine, piece of equipment, and lighting fixture in your lab.
3. Find the number of hours that each piece of equipment will be used during a specific time period. You can go by the month, grading period, semester, school year, or calendar year.
4. Contact your local electricity company for information on the electricity rates for your area.
5. Find the total cost to run certain machines or other electrical devices for the time period you chose.
6. Once you know kilowatt hours and operating costs for specific electrical devices, you can total the electrical operating costs for your manufacturing lab.

MATH/SCIENCE CONNECTION

Calculating Watts. Watts are a measure of electrical power that can be found with the following formula:

$$Watts = Volts \times Amps$$

Most electrical devices have labels that show the volts, amps, and watts. If not, you will need to find these figures. Given two of these measures, you can always find the third.

Calculating Kilowatts. A kilowatt is equal to one thousand watts.

$$1 \text{ Kilowatt} = 1,000 \text{ Watts}$$

To convert watts to kilowatts, divide the watt rating of an electrical device by 1,000.

$$Kilowatts = Watts/1,000$$

Calculating Kilowatt Hours. Electricity companies charge by the kilowatt hour. One kilowatt hour equals one kilowatt used in one hour.

$$1 \text{ Kilowatt Hour} = 1 \text{ Kilowatt} \times 1 \text{ Hour}$$

RELATED QUESTIONS

1. A machine in your lab runs on 115 volts and draws twelve amps. How many watts of power does the machine generate?

2. A machine in your lab has a label with a rating of 1,200 watts. You know that the machine runs on 115 volts. How many amps does the machine draw?

3. An electric motor uses 1,575 watts. Convert this to kilowatts.

4. An electric motor using 1,150 watts is run for five hours per day, during twenty-two days this month. How many kilowatt hours will the motor use this month?

5. What are some of the uses of electrical energy in your manufacturing lab?

6. Before there were electrical utility companies to supply power, how did manufacturers operate their machines?

AUTOMATING PROCESSES WITH FLUID POWER SYSTEMS

OBJECTIVE

You will design and build a simple fluid power system to automate some manufacturing process.

Fluid power systems are commonly used by manufacturing companies to automate their production machines or processes. They provide safe, fast, smooth operation. Fluid power systems include hydraulic systems and pneumatic systems.

The operating principles of a fluid power system are very simple, as shown in Figure 1. Oil or gas is first put under pressure by a pump or compressor. The fluid is then transmitted through a hose or pipe. Finally, a cylinder moves in and out. By attaching this cylinder to a machine, such as a drill press, the operation of the machine is automated. Figure 8-9 shows several examples of how fluid power systems can be used.

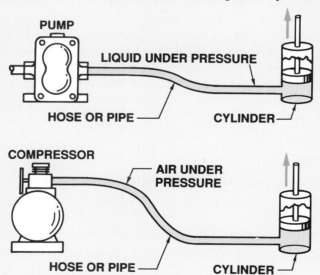

Figure 1. Operating principles of a fluid power system.

Fluid power systems have many uses in manufacturing companies and in the technology education laboratory in your school. Fluid power can be used in production tooling (jigs, fixtures, templates) to clamp or eject parts. They can also remove chips of material during separating processes.

MATERIALS AND SUPPLIES

1. Fluid (air for pneumatic/oil for hydraulic) and fluid reservoir (oil or air tank)
2. Filter
3. Oil pump or air compressor
4. Control valves (two-way rate flow valves, pressure relief regulators, three-way or four-way directional check valves)
5. Transmission lines (pipes, hoses, tubes)
6. Actuators (fluid cylinders or motors that do the actual work)
7. Fittings to connect actuators, transmission lines, control valves, and fluid reservoir
8. Mechanical fasteners to clamp fluid system components to bread-board, machines, or tooling
9. Tools and materials to build jigs, fixtures, or fabricate special-purpose machines
10. Fluid power system schematic component sheet
11. Scissors
12. Drawing paper, ruler, irregular curve, pencil
13. Rubber cement
14. Safety glasses

PROCEDURE

1. Identify a machine, materials handling process, jig, or fixture that can be automated with a fluid power system.
2. Design and sketch a fluid power system to fit the use you identified. Obtain approval from your teacher.
3. Build and test your fluid power system.
   a. Mechanically fasten individual fluid power components (regulator, valves, cylinders) to your machine.
   b. Add fluid transmission hoses or pipelines using appropriate connection fittings.
   c. Connect your fluid power system to an air compressor or hydraulic pump.
   d. Test your set-up under your teacher's supervision.
4. Include your newly automated machine in your production run.

RELATED QUESTIONS

1. What two major types of fluid are used in fluid power systems ?
2. List at least three advantages of using fluid power systems to automate production machines and processes.
3. Describe the operating principle of a typical fluid power system.
4. List at least three applications of fluid power systems in manufacturing.

CHAPTER 9

Information: The Importance of Knowledge

OBJECTIVES

After completing this chapter, you will know about:

■ The impact of exponential population growth on the amount of information we are exposed to in our lifetimes.

■ Four components of successful industrial safety programs.

■ The importance of the Occupational Safety and Health Act (OSHA) of 1970.

■ Environmental considerations for healthy and safe workplace.

■ Individual health and safety considerations.

■ Three common market research techniques important for predicting the success of products.

■ The importance of creative problem-solving skills.

KEY TERMS

Age of Information
Experimental marketing research
Exponential growth
Historical studies

Industrial safety
Market research
Problem-solving
Public relations
Representative group

Safety program
Sales analysis
Survey
Technological literacy

The Growth of Knowledge

Throughout most of history, children were trained by word of mouth and example of their parents. There was a common body of knowledge and set of customs passed from generation to generation, often with little or no change, Figure 9-1. Cultures differed from each other depending on geographic location and climate, among other things. But for thousands of years, the amount of knowledge we needed to survive, and even for life beyond survival level, remained as it had been for ages.

Recent history has seen this stability shatter in almost every conceivable way. Consider the jumps in population in just the last century and a half. It was only in 1860 that the world achieved a population of one billion people.

Figure 9-1. Throughout most of recorded history, the amount of information passed on from generation to generation remained relatively constant. *(Copyright © Wayne Michael Lottinville)*

amount of scientific work completed since Isaac Newton formed his theory of gravity has doubled every fifteen years. Some people refer to these rapid gains in knowledge as a type of exponential growth. Societies have come to depend so heavily on the constant exchange of knowledge that we call this era the **Age of Information**.

No longer can children live in the same kind of world, socially or intellectually, as their parents. Not only must the children live with radical change from the past, but they also must prepare themselves for an uncertain future. In technically advanced countries, there is a concern that all people achieve a certain degree of **technological literacy**, believed to be a necessary life skill, Figure 9-2.

Knowledge and Manufacturing: How Much Do We Need to Know?

Knowledge is a basic input necessary for any manufacturing enterprise to succeed. There are

The second billion took seventy-five years and the third billion arrived only thirty-five years later, in 1970. The fourth billion mark was reached around 1980. Today we have nearly five billion people living on our planet. To look at these doubling rates another way, it is estimated that one fifth of the people who have ever lived are alive today.

Exponential Growth

Exponential growth is growth that happens at an ever-increasing rate. The exponential growth of the world population has had many impacts on the planet and on the quality of life. One such impact has been more contact between cultures and individuals. As a result, the amount of knowledge that we share has grown more rapidly with each new generation. Much of the knowledge has been scientific and technological in nature. For example, the

Figure 9-2. Part of achieving technological literacy might include familiarity with computers. *(Courtesy of CSX Corporation)*

many kinds of knowledge. Advances in science and technology have had the greatest impact on the information base for manufacturing. Tools, machines, materials, and processes have all changed dramatically since the Industrial Revolution. They continue to do so. Workers must have some knowledge of the "tools of their trade" and of any materials and processes they use. This knowledge is gained through formal education like high school, vocational and trade schools, and college. It can also be gained informally in on-the-job training, Figure 9-3. The education necessary for workers in specific types of jobs was discussed in Chapter 4. Descriptions and specific information about tools and machines, materials, and processes can be found in Section Three of this book. This chapter will deal with two aspects of knowledge as an input for manufacturing—worker safety and market research.

Knowledge of Safety: A Must for All Workers

Industrial safety should be a primary concern for all manufacturers. It is achieved by providing the safest possible work environment and maintaining strict safety behavior of employ-ees. Both of these goals take knowledge on the part of employers and employees. The employers' job is to provide a safe working environment for employees and to encourage safe work habits. The employees' job is to work safely, Figure 9-4. Knowledge of the hazards associated with the job is an essential part of any safety training.

Most manufacturing companies have a coordinated safety effort called a **safety program**. Most successful safety programs have the following four components.

1. They educate employees to be alert to hazardous conditions. This knowledge is often specific and might not come automatically to workers.
2. They coordinate safety and engineering when designing or installing new

Figure 9-3. On-the-job training is a major part of running an efficient and profitable manufacturing enterprise. *(Courtesy of ITT Corporation)*

Figure 9-4. Protective clothing and other safety precautions are used to protect workers from various hazards. *(Courtesy of Underwriters Laboratories, Inc. [UL])*

equipment. Jobs should be designed with safety in mind.

3. They encourage workers and management to have a positive attitude about safety. Examples include safety meetings, safety posters, safety movies, bonuses, and so on, Figure 9-5.

4. Support from all levels of management. This includes a willingness to enforce safety rules and to join the program.

Employers have a duty to give workers a safe, healthy work environment. An injured worker may cost the company much more than the salary and safety training for that same worker, Figure 9-6. In addition, morale in the company may go down if there are many accidents. Low morale not only affects employees of the company, but also **public relations**. Public relations, in turn, affect the way the company is viewed by the public. This then has a bearing on product sales.

Figure 9-6. Expenses of caring for an injured worker are usually more than the cost of having an effective safety program. *(Courtesy of Empire Blue Cross and Blue Shield)*

Environmental and Individual Health and Safety

The goal of the Williams-Steiger Occupational Safety and Health Act (OSHA) of 1970 is to guarantee safety for workers. Its purpose is "to assure so far as possible every working man and woman in the nation safe and healthful working conditions and to preserve our human resources." OSHA inspectors are authorized to cite violations. The results are usually expensive penalties for employers. OSHA states specific safety standards for the work environment as well as for individual workers. Some environmental considerations include the following:

■ Lighting, which affects not only health and safety, but also efficiency and morale. Employers must think about the intensity (brightness), distribution, and color of light, Figure 9-7.

■ Ventilation, which can affect workers' health, safety, efficiency, and morale. Toxic and unpleasant fumes should be

Figure 9-5. Safety posters are often used to remind workers of hazards in the workplace. *(Photo by Brent Miller and Sonya Stang)*

Figure 9-7. Proper lighting is necessary for maintaining worker morale as well as for safety. *(Courtesy of Johnson Controls, Inc.)*

properly vented at the point of generation, Figure 9-8.

- Noise, which is a more controversial environmental factor. People react differently to various noise levels. Even so, more employers are looking at this problem. Especially damaging to human ears are high-frequency noises that can cause permanent hearing loss, Figure 9-9.

- Job-specific hazards, which each manufacturer should know about. Toxic chemicals and radioactive materials need special treatment.

In addition to the factors already mentioned, a clean, attractive work environment is an important part of a successful health and safety program, Figure 9-10.

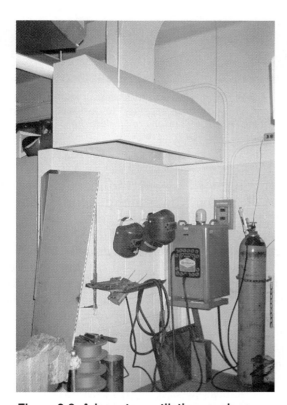

Figure 9-8. Adequate ventilation, such as that provided by this hood, is an important safety consideration in the workplace as well as in your technology laboratory. *(Photo by Brent Miller and Sonya Stang)*

Figure 9-9. Workers who wear proper ear protection ensure against possible hearing loss from dangerous work-related noise. *(Photo by Bob Takis. Courtesy of American Airlines)*

Figure 9-10. A clean, healthy work environment is especially important in food industries. *(Courtesy of CSX Corporation)*

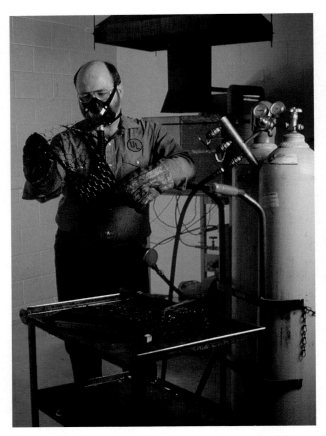

Figure 9-11. Special protective gear is required for workers who could be exposed to dangerous chemicals or radiation. *(Courtesy of Underwriters Laboratories, Inc. [UL])*

Individual Health and Safety

Just as you are required to wear proper safety gear in your technology laboratory, workers should be encouraged to guard their personal safety at the workplace. Eye and ear protection as well as hard hats and other specialized clothing are a necessity at many jobs. People who work with flammable materials must wear clothing that is fire retardant. All protective safety gear should be provided by the employer. Overall, it is of great benefit to the employer to ensure the safety of workers to the greatest extent possible, Figure 9-11.

Market Research

Information about who and where the customers are; what they need, want, and will buy; where and how they will buy it; and how much they will pay is important to know before jumping into a manufacturing operation, Figure 9-12. In addition, knowledge about other manufacturers of the same or similar products is critical. The process of gathering this information is called **market research.** Market research is actually part of marketing (see Chapter 16). But because it is important that some phases of market research be done before production begins, it is thought of as an input necessary for success of the operation. Market research continues throughout production, but input from research done before production begins is critical in predicting the success of a product.

Gathering this information is not always easy. Determining how many times a car door

DISPOSABLE PERSONAL INCOME

DISPOSABLE PERSONAL INCOME PER CAPITA
IN CURRENT DOLLARS—STATES: 1986

Region:

Northeast	$14,085
Midwest	13,085
South	14,946
West	18,946

New England **14,575**

Maine	11,106
New Hampshire	13,891
Vermont	11,354
Massachusetts	14,836
Rhode Island	12,834
Connecticut	16,672

Middle Atlantic **13,918**

New York	14,070
New Jersey	15,927
Pennsylvania	12,403

East North Central **12,468**

Ohio	12,015
Indiana	11,291
Illinois	13,518
Michigan	12,598
Wisconsin	12,055

West North Central **12,163**

Minnesota	13,117
Iowa	11,540
Missouri	11,933
North Dakota	11,100
South Dakota	10,730
Nebraska	12,051
Kansas	12,500

South Atlantic **$11,939**

Delaware	12,745
Maryland	14,091
District of Columbia	15,955
Virginia	12,993
West Virginia	9,479
North Carolina	10,543
South Carolina	9,685
Georgia	11,122
Florida	12,576

East South Central **9,722**

Kentucky	9,933
Tennessee	10,395
Alabama	9,591
Mississippi	8,395

West South Central **10,913**

Arkansas	9,857
Louisiana	9,827
Oklahoma	9,837
Texas	11,569

Mountain **11,360**

Montana	10,446
Idaho	9,873
Wyoming	10,675
Colorado	12,765
New Mexico	9,890
Arizona	11,767
Utah	9,665
Nevada	13,071

Pacific **14,058**

Washington	13,194
Oregon	10,726
California	14,553
Arizona	15,453
Hawaii	12,893

Source: U.S. Bureau of Economic Analysis, *Survey of Current Business*, August issues; and unpublished data.

Figure 9-12. Information about the potential markets is gathered before the manufacturing process begins.

OSHA: Employer Responsibilities

The Occupational Safety and Health Act was passed in 1970 "to assure so far as possible every working man and woman in the nation safe and healthful working conditions and to preserve our human resources." The purpose of the Act is to set job safety and health standards, to help employers and employees reduce workplace hazards, and to enforce the law. Under OSHA, employers must:

- Rid the workplace of recognized hazards that can harm or kill employees.
- Follow the standards, rules, and regulations of the Act.
- Know the OSHA safety and health standards.
- Tell all workers about OSHA and any standards for the workplace.

- Check workplace conditions to make sure they meet the standards and to keep any hazards small.
- Make sure employees have, use, and maintain safe tools and equipment.
- Set and update operating procedures and let employees know about them so they can follow safety and health rules.
- Keep OSHA-required records of work-related injuries and illnesses.
- Make sure employees know their rights and responsibilities under the Act and not discriminate against employees who use their rights.

---

will open and close before it falls off is easy. Determining why a person chooses one car over another is more difficult. For this reason, market researchers do a number of different kinds of studies to provide the answers they need. The three most common types of market research done before and throughout production include the following:

1. **Historical studies** include researching similar products previously made by the company and by other companies. Sales data (information) classified by territory (geographic area), customer characteristics, and other historical information can often be taken from routine records. Also, various government agencies, local chambers of commerce, and trade associations might have data about specific characteristics of consumers and potential consumers. This kind of research is called **sales analysis**. It is the most commonly used

because it is fairly fast and easy to do, Figure 9-13.

2. **Surveys** try to reach a **representative group** of people to study in order to find the information needed to predict product success. A representative group is a group of people that represents the targeted consumer group. For example, a company that makes business computers would try to survey only business people who might use the product. Data collected might include reaction to a product or an intention to buy the product within the next year, Figure 9-14.

3. **Experimental marketing research** is a process created by an investigator that will help determine additional information about the product. For example, a toy company may make prototypes (working models) of a product in several colors or sizes. Children may

7-COUNTY METROPOLITAN AREA POPULATION PROJECTIONS BY AGE

AGE	1985	1990	1995	2000
0 - 4 yrs	161,108	160,504	147,752	131,198
5 - 9 yrs	140,485	158,591	158,241	145,814
10 - 14 yrs	138,139	137,298	154,786	154,682
15 - 19 yrs	157,497	134,789	133,983	150,851
20 - 24 yrs	191,755	161,854	137,370	136,735
25 - 29 yrs	218,351	206,115	170,200	144,800
30 - 34 yrs	195,823	215,904	204,986	168,970
35 - 39 yrs	168,716	188,849	209,240	199,008
40 - 44 yrs	129,013	164,100	183,761	203,974
45 - 49 yrs	100,768	125,152	159,738	178,934
50 - 54 yrs	89,397	96,752	120,756	154,229
55 - 59 yrs	89,083	84,997	92,561	115,811
60 - 64 yrs	81,214	81,437	78,590	85,942
65 - 69 yrs	63,728	71,545	72,561	70,364
70 - 74 yrs	49,385	54,325	61,898	63,209
75 - 79 yrs	38,472	41,407	46,681	53,726
80 - + yrs	51,578	57,234	64,146	72,937

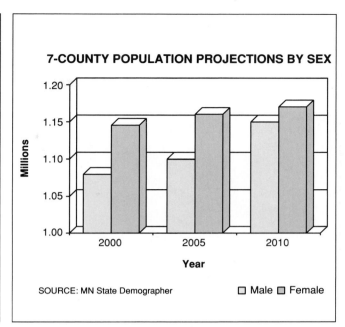

Figure 9-13. A sales analysis often contains very specific demographic information about potential customers. Based on data from the past, researchers can predict future demographic trends. *(Reprinted from the* Economic Profile, *produced by the Greater Minneapolis Chamber of Commerce. Used with permission.)*

Figure 9-14. Surveys are used to determine exactly who is likely to purchase a product and why. *(Courtesy of Field Facts)*

then be observed playing with the toys as researchers note the exact number of times each prototype is picked up, and how long it is played with. Researchers also note whether boys or girls use the toy, and what age group uses it, Figure 9-15. Manufacturers often make other sales tests by producing a few products and then keeping careful track of sales. Such experiments provide useful data that help predict customer acceptance.

Knowledge: The Art of Problem-Solving

It has been shown that knowledge is an essential input for the manufacturing system. Recently a survey of employers showed that **problem-solving** ability is the skill they want most in potential employees. Problem-solving skills involve understanding the problem itself and using creative problem-solving techniques, Figure 9-16. Problem-solving is a skill that can be learned. It is important for everyone from the assembly line worker to engineers to all levels of management.

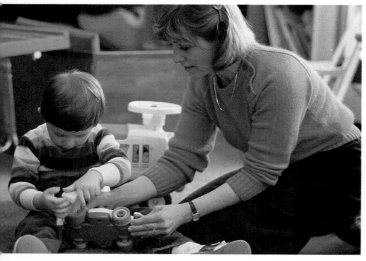

Figure 9-15. Toy manufacturers often make several prototypes of a product and observe children playing. Information about which toys are played with, for how long, and by whom is recorded to determine the best possibilities for future sales. *(Courtesy of Fisher-Price, a division of the Quaker Oats Company)*

Figure 9-17. A healthy and safe work environment, as well as a feeling of self-worth in the workplace, usually results in a satisfied worker. *(Courtesy of Hexel Corporation)*

Summary

The exponential growth of world population during the last century and a half has influenced the rapid growth of knowledge. This has brought about what is sometimes called the Age of Information. To keep pace with increas-

Figure 9-16. Problem-solving is an important skill for all workers today. *(Courtesy of Barnes Group, Inc.)*

ing information, people in industrialized countries are encouraged to become technologically literate.

Knowledge of safety in the workplace by workers and management is critical. Most companies have programs to promote industrial safety. Successful safety programs often include:

■ education of employees,
■ safety inspections,
■ coordinated safety and engineering efforts,
■ adoption of positive attitudes about safety, and
■ support from management.

OSHA is an act of Congress that was introduced in 1970 to set safety standards and enforce them. Health and safety concerns related to the work environment include lighting, ventilation, noise control, hazardous waste control, and maintenance of a clean and attractive work environment. Meeting these conditions enhances the morale of workers and helps maintain positive public relations, Figure 9-17.

Individual health and safety is an important concern of workers and management. Proper safety gear and safe behavior help ensure the safety of everyone.

Marketing research is also an important source of knowledge for a manufacturing system. Three common types of market research include historical studies, surveys, and experimentation.

Creative problem-solving skills are the most sought-after skills by employers. These skills can be learned. They involve an understanding of the problem and of specific problem-solving skills.

DISCUSSION QUESTIONS

1. List at least five things you feel are important to know to be technologically literate.

2. List the general safety rules you are expected to know in your laboratory.

3. Whose responsibility is it to prevent accidents in the manufacturing plant? In your technology laboratory?

4. What improvements (that is, lighting, ventilation, and so on) could be made in the work environment of your technology laboratory?

5. Have you ever been asked to complete a telephone survey? If so, describe it.

6. Why is market research an important input in the manufacturing system?

7. Describe a problem you were able to solve yourself. Are you a creative problem-solver? Explain.

CHAPTER ACTIVITIES

⚙ SURVEYING THE MARKET

OBJECTIVE

It has become more and more important for a manufacturer to understand the buying public and to test ideas before making large financial commitments to new or improved products. The information a market survey gives is a vital input to any manufacturing system.

When you have finished this activity, you will be able to design a market survey to answer specific product questions, and analyze results to help make informed management decisions.

MATERIALS AND SUPPLIES

1. Adequate copies of the survey form for each class member to distribute.

PROCEDURE

1. Break into small groups. Each group will develop a survey area. Later, the class will combine these areas into a final survey form.

2. Compile questions about the public that you need to ask before your product design becomes final. Typical areas to include are:
   a. How many consumers will buy the product?
   b. How much are they willing to pay?
   c. What do they want the product to look like?
   d. Who is our typical buyer?
   e. How can we reach more of these people?
   f. What would make our product more desirable?

3. For each area, write a question with multiple choice answers that will give you the exact single answer you need. For example, suppose you need to know what price people expect to pay for an automatic banana slicer. You could phrase your question a couple of different ways: you could ask "How much would you give me for this?" Or you could ask "Assuming a close friend wants a banana slicer, how much would you pay for this gift? $3–$5? $5–$10? $10–$20?" The second question does not allow the option of not buying and gives comfortable price ranges to select from. Remember—do not ask personal questions or identify your respondents. You might offend the people who are helping you by filling out the form.

4. Compile each group's work onto one form. You might want to condense your list of questions so that the form does not take more than three to five minutes to fill out.

5. Each class member should distribute a copy of the form to one person in each of the following demographic groups:
   a. People younger than twelve years old
   b. People between twelve and eighteen years old
   c. Adult males
   d. Adult females
   e. Elderly people

6. Place all returned copies in one pile and review them. If you find a survey with an inappropriate response, throw it out. That person did not take the survey seriously, and all responses on it are of questionable value.

7. Total the responses to each question in your original groups and write a statement that answers the original question. For example, you might conclude that "The majority of people who want to buy a banana slicer expect to pay $10–$20."

8. You might want to write a composite description of the person most likely to buy your product. A composite description combines the wants and preferences of the people who answered your survey.

9. Based on this analysis, design, manufacture, and market your product as though you know your customer as well as a close friend. Give them what they want.

RELATED QUESTIONS

1. How can a survey prevent costly mistakes in manufacturing?
2. Why would a sales staff want to see the results of a survey?
3. Why should someone answering a survey be guaranteed anonymity?

 **SAFETY FIRST!**

OBJECTIVE

This activity asks you to think about safety for workers in a manufacturing setting. Acting as safety experts, your team will design a safety program for a manufacturing operation in your technology laboratory.

MATERIALS AND SUPPLIES

1. Handout: *Safety First! Designing a Safety Program*
2. Your school's technology laboratory

PROCEDURE

1. Divide into groups of four. You are safety expert teams who must make a safety program for a manufacturing company.
2. As a class, choose a product and list the steps, including tools, machines, materials, and processes needed to manufacture it.
3. Working with your safety team, review the section in this chapter on safety programs.
4. Complete the handout *Safety First! Designing a Safety Program*. Hint: If you have four people on your team, assign one section of the handout to each person.
5. Present your safety program to the class. As a class, discuss the strengths and weaknesses of each program. Vote on the most practical program, and on the one that inspires workers the most.

MATH/SCIENCE CONNECTION

Safety is one of the most important concerns for scientists. Because they often work with materials and processes that are unpredictable, extreme safety precautions are a must. However, even when safety is a prime consideration, many scientists have been injured from their work. When scientists working on the Manhattan Project first divided the atom, many were exposed to dangerous amounts of radiation poisoning.

RELATED QUESTIONS

1. What do you think is the most important part of a successful safety program?
2. Describe what happens when you or someone you know does not follow safety rules.
3. What should happen to a person who breaks the safety rules in your technology laboratory?
4. Part of working in a group is learning to compromise. Did your group disagree while designing the safety program? If so, how did you resolve your conflict?
5. List the general safety rules for your technology laboratory. Using what you know about safety programs, list at least one more safety rule that would fit.

CHAPTER 10

The Finances of Manufacturing

OBJECTIVES

After completing this chapter, you will know about:

- The importance of finance or money as an input in manufacturing.

- The many expenses associated with manufacturing a product.

- The types of budget expense projections created by the manufacturing finance department to identify the total cost of making a product.

- The various means of financing a manufacturing enterprise.

- The difference between fixed and variable costs in manufacturing.

KEY TERMS

Bill of materials	General expenses budget	Profitable
Bonds	Interest	Profit
Budget projections	Labor estimates	Sales projections budget
Dividend	Loan	Selling expenses budget
Estimate range	Master budget	Stock
Finances	Production expenses budget	Unit costs
Fixed costs		Variable costs

Finances: It Takes Money to Make Money

When a manufacturing enterprise decides to go into business to produce a product, it soon learns the importance of having enough finances. **Finances** is a term business and industry use to mean the management of money, Figure 10-1. Money is an extremely important input in any system of technology. In manufacturing, money pays for all the inputs needed to design, produce, and sell a product. Money pays for workers' salaries, tool

Figure 10-1. Money is a very important input for manufacturing. *(Photo by Paul Meyers)*

Figure 10-2A. Workers must be paid a salary. *(Courtesy of NASA)*

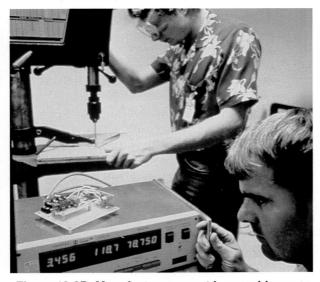

Figure 10-2B. Manufacturers must buy a wide range of tools and machines. Here are an inexpensive drill press and a very expensive piece of electronic testing equipment for manufacturing. *(Courtesy of NASA)*

and machine purchases, needed utility company energy, and information, Figure 10-2. Manufacturing companies even need money to get more money. After all, "It takes money to make money."

Figure 10-2C. Materials to make products, like these rolls of aluminum used to make cans, must be purchased. *(Courtesy of Reynolds Metals Company)*

Figure 10-2D. A manufacturing plant like this one uses large amounts of energy, such as electricity, for lighting, heating, cooling, and running machines and equipment. *(Courtesy of Toyota Motor Manufacturing, U.S.A., Inc.)*

The goal of manufacturing is to produce products and make a profit. A **profit** is the money left over after a product is sold and all the input expenses are paid. This chapter deals with the importance of money as an input for manufacturing.

The Finance Department

The finance department is responsible for four activities.

1. Determining financial needs of the company
2. Acquiring adequate financing (money)
3. Spending money to pay for needed inputs
4. Reporting on the financial condition of the company

This chapter looks at the first two activities. It also examines the costs associated with manufacturing a product, Figure 10-3.

Figure 10-3. Workers in the finance department keep track of the company's money. (Courtesy of Union Pacific Corporation)

Determining Financial Needs

One of the first things a new manufacturing company should do is conduct a study to determine its financial needs. Market research is done to answer these questions.

- What products do consumers want?
- Who are the consumers of these products?
- How many products are being purchased each year?
- How much will people pay for the products?
- What companies are already producing these products?
- Can we compete with other companies to produce and sell the products?

With this information, finance personnel will make budget projections. **Budget projections** are estimates of the expenses a company expects from making and selling the product. Finance department personnel try to get the best possible estimates by creating estimate ranges. An **estimate range** includes a high estimate, a low estimate, and a middle estimate. Estimate ranges make the job of determining financial needs a little easier. Several types of budget projections are usually made. Five different budget descriptions follow.

1. **Sales projections budget.** This budget estimates the number of products market researchers expect the company to sell. Also projected is the expected selling price and the total income expected from sales, Table 10-1.
2. **Production expenses budget.** Production expenses cover all the money spent to actually manufacture a product. Included are the bill of materials and labor estimates. A **bill of materials** lists every part of a product, the exact specifications and cost of each part, and the total cost for each product, Table 10-2. **Labor estimates** show the number of workers needed to produce the product, the total worker time spent making one product, and the total cost for production labor wages, Table 10-3.

XYZ MANUFACTURING CO.
SALES PROJECTION BUDGET

PRODUCT CODE: X125-A					19X1				UNIT PRICE: $15	
ESTIMATE RANGE	1ST QTR.		2ND QTR.		3RD QTR.		4TH QTR.		YEAR TOTALS	
	UNITS	INCOME	UNITS	INCOME	UNITS	INCOME	UNITS	INCOME	UNITS	INCOME
High	110	$1,650	121	$1,815	115	$1,725	126	$1,890	472	$7,080
Medium	100	1,500	110	1,650	105	1,575	115	1,725	430	6,450
Low	90	1,350	99	1,485	94	1,410	103	1,545	386	5,790

Table 10-1. A sales projection budget estimates the number of products that might be sold by a company during a certain time period. Also included in a sales projection is the amount of income a company can expect from sales.

XYZ MANUFACTURING CO.

PRODUCT CODE		X-125-A			MODEL	08
	QUANTITY	450		BILL OF MATERIALS	DRAWING	125
PART NO.	QTY.	PART NAME	DESCRIPTION		COST	
					UNIT	TOTAL
1	1	Base	walnut, 1 $\frac{1}{8}$ × 4 $\frac{1}{4}$ × 10 $\frac{3}{8}$		1.64	1.64
2	2	Sides	walnut, $\frac{5}{8}$ × 3 $\frac{3}{8}$ × 7 $\frac{7}{8}$		.48	.96
3	1	Case Top	walnut, $\frac{1}{2}$ × 4 × 10 $\frac{3}{8}$		.62	.62
4	1	Middle Top	walnut, $\frac{1}{2}$ × 3 $\frac{5}{8}$ × 9 $\frac{3}{8}$		.50	.50
5	1	Cap	walnut, $\frac{1}{2}$ × 3 × 8 $\frac{1}{2}$		.35	.35
6	4	Frame	walnut, $\frac{1}{2}$ × $\frac{1}{2}$ × 8		.06	.24
7	2	Retainer	pine, $\frac{1}{2}$ × $\frac{1}{2}$ × 7		.02	.04
8	1	Handle	#H-750, brass finish		.75	.75
9	1	Clock Face	#547CF, painted, Clock Co. Intl.		1.25	1.25
10	1	Movement	#629MV, battery, Clock Co. Intl.		2.50	2.50
11	1	Glass	$\frac{1}{8}$ × 8 $\frac{3}{16}$ × 7 $\frac{7}{8}$, City Glass		.28	.28
					TOTAL	$9.13

APPROVED BY:_____   DATE: _____

Table 10-2. A bill of materials is a very important part of the production expenses budget. Listed on the bill of materials are all the parts needed to manufacture one product, the cost of each part, and the total cost for one product.

3. **Selling expenses budget.** Some expenses associated with selling a product include advertising, product transportation to the consumer, and sales commissions.

4. **General expenses budget.** General expenses cover all other costs associated with manufacturing a product. Included are

a. wages for management, finance, human resources, and engineering departments;

b. utility expenses for electricity, water, heat, lights, air-conditioning, etc.;

c. payments for insurance coverage on equipment, buildings, machines, and people; and

XYZ MANUFACTURING CO.					
PRODUCT CODE X-125-A		**LABOR ESTIMATE**		**MODEL**	08
QUANTITY 450				**DRAWING**	125
PROCESS AREA	**DIVISION**	**WORKERS**	**LABOR HOURS**	**WAGE RATE**	**LABOR COST**
Machine	Planing	2	80	$9.60	$768.00
	Cutting	2	72	9.60	691.20
	Routing	3	65	9.60	624.00
	Drilling	2	58	9.60	556.80
	Rework	0	0	9.60	000.00
Assembly	Basic Case	4	75	$9.60	$720.00
	Top Assy.	3	54	9.60	518.40
	Movement	2	35	9.60	336.00
	Glass & Frame	2	40	9.60	384.00
Finish	Staining	2	20	$9.60	$192.00
	Coating	2	25	9.60	240.00
Quality Control	Machine	2	15	$9.60	$144.00
	Assembly	1	15	9.60	144.00
	Finish	1	10	9.60	96.00
	TOTALS	**28**	**564**		**$5414.40**

APPROVED BY:_____   DATE: _____

Table 10-3. A labor estimate identifies the total production department labor costs for one product. Listed are the number of workers in each division (or job), the number of hours they will work, their wage rate, and the total labor costs.

d. start-up costs associated with making special tools, buying new machines, writing computer programs, and making the prototype product.

5. **Master budget.** A master budget is formulated after each of the previous four budget estimates is completed. It combines and summarizes the sales projections, production expenses, selling

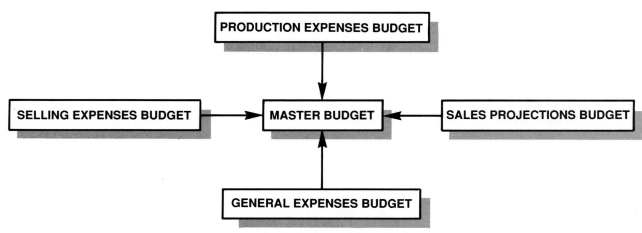

Figure 10-4. A master budget combines and summarizes the production expenses budget, sales projections budget, general expenses budget, and the selling expenses budget.

Manufacturing Costs across America

Running a manufacturing plant can cost millions of dollars. When a company decides to open a new plant in a certain city, it always considers the costs of doing business there. The following table compares the costs of running a manufacturing plant in different cities across America. The plant is 125,000 square feet in size, employs 300 workers, and manufactures 15 million pounds of metal products. Included in the table are labor, electric, and occupancy costs. Occupancy costs include taxes, insurances, other utilities (such as water, gas, telephone, and transportation), and other general expenses. Notice that labor is the largest expense. Also notice the difference between labor costs in Cleveland and Panama City. Why is there a difference of almost $2 million? Notice also the approximate $2 million difference between the total costs of the two cities.

Calculate the salary differences for one worker in each of the two cities. If you were looking for a manufacturing job, in which city would you want to work? If you wanted to own and operate a new manufacturing plant, which city would you consider?

CITY	LABOR COSTS (millions)	ELECTRIC POWER COSTS	OCCUPANCY COSTS (millions)	TOTAL COSTS (millions)
MANUFACTURING COSTS ACROSS AMERICA				
Cleveland, OH	$9.1	$198,000	$1.2	$10.5
Minneapolis, MN	8.8	139,000	1.3	10.2
Chicago, IL	8.4	267,000	1.3	10.0
Houston, TX	8.7	174,000	1.0	9.9
Boston, MA	8.4	227,000	1.2	9.9
New York, NY	7.9	342,000	1.4	9.7
Seattle, WA	8.3	111,000	1.1	9.5
Los Angeles, CA	8.0	214,000	1.1	9.3
St. Louis, MO	7.8	177,000	1.2	9.2
Atlanta, GA	7.8	195,000	1.0	9.1
Panama City, FL	7.2	160,000	0.9	8.2

The cost of running a manufacturing plant varies greatly across America. Why do you think these costs vary so much from city to city? Notice that the largest cost in manufacturing is labor.
(Copyright 1988, USA TODAY. Adapted with permission.)

expenses, and general expenses budgets in one document, Figure 10-4. Management uses the master budget to make decisions about whether or not the company should manufacture the product. Remember, the goal of manufacturing is to make products at a profit. If management thinks the company will not make a profit, they will probably decide not to produce the product.

Acquiring Money

After the finance department has established budget projections and management has decided to manufacture the product, the next step is to get money for all the inputs needed. For an ongoing enterprise, this money could come from sale profits of other products. Part of the profits should always be put back into the company to help fund future business. A new or start-up company does not have profits from sales. It must get money from other sources. When one person or several partners own the company, they can use some of their own savings to finance the enterprise. Larger manufacturing corporations can get money from three sources—loans, bonds, or stocks, Figure 10-5. A bank can lend money to a corporation. For the privilege of borrowing the money, the corporation must pay interest on the **loan**. When the company pays the bank for the loan, they must pay back more than was actually borrowed. The money paid above the amount of the loan is the **interest**.

Instead of borrowing money from a bank, a corporation can issue **bonds**. Bonds are like a loan, but a group of individuals provides the money instead of a bank. When a company issues, or sells, a bond certificate, individuals can buy the bond for a fixed price. In return, the corporation promises to pay back the amount of the bond plus a set amount of interest by a certain date.

When a manufacturing company acquires finances with a loan or with bonds, it is merely borrowing money. Stocks are a very different matter, Figure 10-6. When a company sells stock, it is actually selling a portion of the company to the stockholders. **Stock** represents

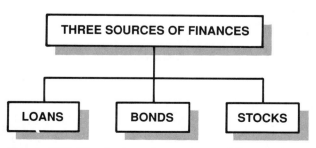

Figure 10-5. The three major sources of finances for manufacturing corporations are loans, bonds, and stocks.

Figure 10-6. Most large corporations acquire money for their operations by selling stock. A share of stock represents partial ownership in the corporation. *(Reprinted with permission from Harms, MANUFACTURING TECHNOLOGY ACTIVITIES, © 1988 by Delmar Publishers Inc.)*

ownership in the corporation. Anyone with the money to invest can buy partial ownership in a corporation that issues stock. As a partial owner, the stockholder is entitled to participate in the management decision-making process by voting at stockholders' meetings. Stockholders can find out the real risks and rewards possible in owning a company, Figure 10-7. People buy stock in the hope that the

Figure 10-7. Stockholders are the real owners of manufacturing corporations. Owning shares of stock entitles stockholders to a vote in the management of the company. *(Courtesy of Fleet/Norstar Financial Group)*

company will be **profitable** (make money) and the stockholders will receive dividends and increasing stock value. **Dividends** are money paid back to the stockholder out of the company's profits. As a second reward, the stock of a profitable company will often go up in value. A stockholder who bought shares in a company for $100 might be able to sell the shares later for more money if the company makes large profits. Along with the rewards of dividends and higher stock value, there are risks. Remember, stockholders are the real owners of the company. If the company loses money, the value of the stock might go down. Also, if the company goes out of business, it must pay all debts before the stockholders can get back any of their money. If all of the company's money is gone after paying the debts, the stockholders will probably not get back any of the money they invested in the shares.

The largest manufacturing corporations usually put together profits from product sales, bank loans, and the sale of bonds and stocks to finance their enterprises.

Fixed and Variable Costs

Finance departments divide manufacturing costs into two different groups—fixed costs and variable costs. **Fixed costs** stay the same, or fixed, for a company no matter how many products they make or sell. These costs include money spent for relatively permanent investments such as property, buildings, tools, machines, and furniture. Also included in fixed costs is money spent for workers and materials that do not actually make the product. This means all the expenses to run every department except production. Total fixed costs stay fixed for a certain time limit, usually a year, six months, a quarter, or one month. These costs might go up or down (probably up) after this time period. The relationship between total fixed costs and the number of products manufactured is very important to the finance department, Figure 10-8. Notice that the total fixed costs remain at a fixed level no matter what quantity of products are manufactured. This relationship will always hold true.

Variable costs will vary; that is, go up or down with the amount of products manufac-

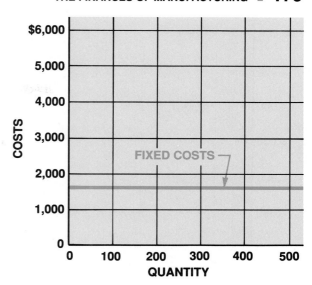

Figure 10-8. Fixed costs stay the same (remain fixed) no matter what quantity of products are manufactured. This graph shows total fixed costs for a company of around $1,700, whether they manufacture 100 or 500 products.

tured. Variable costs involve all the expenses directly associated with making the product. This includes wages for production department, workers, and the price of materials used in the product. Also included is money spent on tools and supplies used to make the product, such as sand paper, finishing materials, and ruined tools. When a company decides to manufacture more products, more production time is needed and more materials are used; therefore, total variable costs increase. If a company decides to produce fewer products, total variable costs decrease. Figure 10-9 shows the relationship between total variable costs and the quantity of products. Not that the total variable costs are directly proportional to the number of products made. For example, if product quantity is doubled or tripled, the total variable costs will also double or triple, respectively.

Companies include fixed costs and variable costs in the appropriate budget expense projections described earlier. They incorporate variable costs in the production expenses budget and fixed costs in the selling expenses budget and general expenses budget.

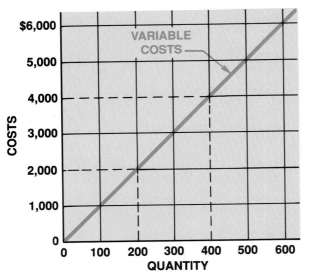

Figure 10-9. Variable costs go up or down (vary) with the quantity of products manufactured. Total variable costs are directly proportional to the amount of products manufactured. The proportion (percentage) of increase or decrease in amount results in the same proportion of increase or decrease in variable costs. In this graph, what happens to variable costs when the quantity of products jumps from 200 to 400?

Reducing Manufacturing Costs

Manufacturing companies are always looking for ways to cut costs. Because labor is one of the largest expenses in manufacturing, companies often try to cut labor costs with automation, such as robots. In comparison to the costs of paying a production worker, the robot

- replaces five or six workers;
- works without lunch, coffee breaks, or vacation;
- needs no sick leave;
- creates less wasted materials (reduced materials costs);
- is more productive (more products manufactured); and
- has a one-time cost to buy (no salary needed).

These factors make robots an appealing way to reduce variable costs in manufacturing.

Other ways manufacturing companies reduce costs include using cheaper materials, lowering the quality of the product, recycling scrap to reduce wasted materials, using

Why Do Manufactured Products Cost So Much?

How much profit do companies really make? What are the actual costs of manufacturing a product? Let's look at a simple product and see exactly what costs are involved. A mantel clock made by C & C Clock Corporation sells for $49.99. Cathie and Chris were the original owners of C & C. Before deciding to go into business, they acted as the market research and finance departments. They prepared budget forecasts for sales, production expenses, selling expenses, and general expenses. Once they decided to manufacture clocks, they formed the corporation.

First, the company needed a building and the necessary equipment. Cathie and Chris found a completely equipped manufacturing shop they could buy for

C & C Clock Corporation sells this mantel clock for $49.99. How much does it cost C & C to make this clock? *(Courtesy of Mason & Sullivan)*

$70,000. They did not have that much money available, so they decided to sell stock in the company. The C & C Clock Corporation sold 1,000 shares of stock at $62 per share for a total of $62,000. Cathie and Chris bought 501 shares of stock so they could still control ownership of the company. This money plus an $8,000 loan from a local bank gave C & C the finances they needed to start manufacturing clocks.

C & C was very successful in manufacturing and selling the mantel clocks. To help us understand why the clocks cost $49.99, Table 1, provided by C & C, shows us the actual cost to manufacture 1,000 clocks. Notice that the production expenses are given in **unit costs**. These are the costs to manufacture each unit, or one clock. By examining the fixed and variable costs, you can see every expense in producing the clocks.

Table 2 shows the income and profit from the sale of 1,000 clocks. Notice the profit on each unit. Only $6.46 of the $49.99 selling price is actual profit for C & C. Notice also that ten percent of the profits were held back for future plant

FIXED COSTS (total costs)		VARIABLE COSTS (per unit costs)	
SELLING BUDGET		**PRODUCTION BUDGET**	
Advertising	$ 350		
Shipping	150	Labor	$21.50**
Sales Commissions	1,750		
TOTAL:	$2,250	Materials	
		▪ wood	$ 4.35
GENERAL EXPENSES		▪ glass	.28
Wages	$6,350*	▪ glue	.25
Loan Payment	750	▪ fasteners	.45
Taxes	425	▪ finish	.15
Insurances	350	▪ hardware	.75
Utilities	270	▪ movement	2.50
Jigs & Fixtures	250	▪ face	1.25
Special Tools	85	▪ package	1.25
R&D Prototype	70	TOTAL:	$32.73/unit
TOTAL:	$8,550		

*Includes engineering, management, finances, human resources, and marketing personnel
**10 days × 8 hrs × 28 workers × $9.60/hr

	FIXED COSTS	VARIABLE COSTS	TOTAL COSTS
TOTALS	$10,800	$32,730	$43,530

Table 1. Here are C & C's fixed and variable costs to manufacture 1,000 mantel clocks. What is the largest cost for C & C ?

INCOME & PROFIT STATEMENT

	PER UNIT	1,000 UNITS
Income	$ 49.99	$ 49,990
Costs	− 43.53	− 43,530
Gross Profit	6.46	$ 6,460
10% Retained	− .65	− 646
Net Profit	$ 5.81	$ 5,814

$$\frac{\text{Net Profits}}{\text{Shares of Stock}} \quad \frac{\$5,814}{1,000} = \$5.81 \text{ Dividend per share}$$

Table 2. C & C's income and profit statement shows a net profit of $5.81 per unit after all costs are paid and ten percent is retained for future business. Stockholders in C & C Manufacturing received a dividend of $5.81 per share. Would you buy stock in C & C? Why or why not?

improvements. Based on the 1,000 shares of stock sold, stockholders would receive a dividend of $5.81 per share.

The profit on each unit might seem small. The company had to spend more than $43 on each clock to make only $6.46. In some manufacturing businesses, the profit might be less than a dollar per unit. However, if you sell 5 million units, it can add up to some nice profits.

Perhaps now you can better understand why manufactured products cost so much. There are many expenses the company must pay in order to produce and sell products.

cheaper nonunion labor, and moving to a place with lower overall operating costs. Any cost reduction technique can have trade-offs. Product quality could suffer, consumers might not buy the product, and cheaper labor might not have the right skills. Management must weigh the trade-offs when making decisions about cost reduction measures.

Summary

The finance department in manufacturing determines the financial needs of a company and acquires the needed money. To determine financial needs, expense projection budgets are made to spot all the costs of designing, producing, and selling a product. The costs of manufacturing are described as fixed and variable. Fixed costs include selling and general expenses, while variable costs include product materials and production labor costs. Manufacturing companies can obtain finances from several sources, including personal savings, profits, loans, bonds, or stock sales. Companies pay for these finances by paying interest on loans and bonds or dividends on stocks.

Money is an extremely important input for manufacturing. All inputs, including money itself, must be paid for with money.

DISCUSSION QUESTIONS

1. Four jobs of the finance department in manufacturing were discussed. Which of these do you think is most important? Which is least important? Why? Can a manufacturing company get by if the finance department does not perform all these jobs?

2. What is the relationship between the market research, finance, management, production, and engineering departments when it comes to creating the four budget projections that go into the master budget?

3. In this chapter, the idea of estimate ranges in budget projections was described briefly. Why would a company go through all the trouble of producing a low, a middle, and a high budget estimate? What would happen if only one estimate were used?

4. Manufacturing companies can finance their enterprise with savings, loans, bonds, or stocks. Play the role of a sole owner of a manufacturing company. What are the pros and cons that you can see for each of these sources of finance? Which would you use for your company?

5. Why would a bank lend money to a manufacturing company? Why would an individual invest or not invest money in the bond or stock of a manufacturing company?

6. One way manufacturing companies try to cut costs is by replacing human workers with robots. Do you think this is a good idea? Why or why not?

CHAPTER ACTIVITIES

 CALCULATING START-UP COSTS FOR MANUFACTURING

OBJECTIVE

Starting a new manufacturing company is very expensive. The largest costs for starting a new company are renting or buying the building, equipment, and tools. Once the plant has been set up, you will need to figure your company's financial needs by preparing budgets for sales projections, production expenses, selling expenses, and general expenses. All of these budgets are put together in a master budget.

In this activity, you will find the total start-up costs for your manufacturing company.

Your manufacturing lab is a fully equipped production facility. Look around the lab: The tools, equipment, and furniture there can be used for manufacturing. Do you know how much money was spent to build the building and buy all that equipment? When you and your classmates form a manufacturing company, how much money would you need to build and equip a manufacturing plant just like this lab? Find out by adding up the total replacement costs for the building, tools, equipment, machines, and furniture.

Once these items are bought, you will have expenses for the other inputs. You will need workers for the departments, materials for the products, and energy to run machines and lights. All this costs money. Manufacturing companies use budget projections to determine how much money they need to pay for these inputs. Remember, budget projections are estimates, or intelligent guesses. Use estimate ranges to estimate costs better.

MATERIALS AND SUPPLIES

1. Inventory lists (your teacher might provide this, or you might write your own lists as part of this activity)
   a. tools
   b. machines
   c. equipment
   d. furniture
2. Manufacturing or school supply catalogs
3. Calculators
4. Market research product information

PROCEDURE

1. Break the class into groups.
2. Your teacher will assign a task to each group. These tasks will be to figure start-up costs for the building, the tools, the equipment, and to make the budget projections.
3. Use supply catalogs to find the costs for all the tools, machines, equipment, and furniture in your lab.
4. Add up the start-up costs for each category of inventory items.
5. Add the total start-up costs for all items, including tools, machines, equipment, and furniture.
6. To figure the cost of building the lab, start by measuring the size of the lab in square feet.
7. Find the cost to build a new manufacturing plant the same size as your lab by using a fixed dollar amount, such as $30 per square foot. Ask your teacher for a fixed dollar amount based on building costs in your area.
8. Prepare a sales projection budget based on market research information.
9. Prepare a selling expenses budget for advertising, shipping, commissions, and so on.
10. Prepare a production expenses budget. You will need a bill of materials for the product and a labor estimate. Include labor costs and materials costs on a per-unit basis.
11. Prepare a general expenses budget. This should include:
    a. Wages for non-production personnel
    b. Utility expenses
    c. Other start-up costs, such as new tools, writing special computer programs, and prototype development by the research and development team
12. Prepare a master budget for the estimated start-up expenses for your company.

MATH/SCIENCE CONNECTION

Measuring square feet. Square feet (abbreviated sq. ft. or ft²) is a two-dimensional measure of an area. The two dimensions measured are length and width. To find square feet, do this:

1. Measure the length (in feet) and the width (in feet) of an area (like the floor area in your lab) using a tape measure.
2. Multiply the length times the width.
3. The answer will be in square feet.

Directly Proportional. Variable costs are directly proportional to the quantity of products sold. Remember, variable costs are given in per-unit costs, or the costs for one product. Directly proportional means that for every increase in the quantity, the variable costs will increase by the same proportion or percentage. Here is a formula that will help you:

$$\text{Variable costs per unit} \times \text{Quantity} = \text{Total variable costs}$$

RELATED QUESTIONS

1. What are the different types of budgets created by the finance department?
2. What is a budget projection? Why are estimate ranges used in budget projections?
3. What are the differences between fixed and variable costs in manufacturing?
4. What was the total start-up cost for your classroom manufacturing enterprise? What items cost the most or least?
5. How many square feet are in a lab with the following dimensions?

    Length = 52'9" (this equals 52.75')
    Width = 20'7" (this equals 20.583')

6. Variable costs for manufacturing a product are $12.50 per unit. What are the total variable costs for twenty products?
7. The total variable costs for 300 products are $2,500. What are the per-unit variable costs?

 ACQUIRING FINANCING BY SELLING STOCK

OBJECTIVE

One of the most important ways to acquire financing for a manufacturing corporation is to sell stock. Stock sales let a company acquire funds to purchase the inputs needed for manufacturing.

In this activity, you will sell stock shares in a newly formed manufacturing corporation.

The people who buy stock, or the stockholders, are the real owners of the corporation. Stockholders participate in the management decision-making process by voting at stockholder meetings. People who want to invest in stock certificates should consider the risks and rewards of stock ownership. If the company goes out of business or does not make a profit, the stockholders might lose all their money. However, if the company makes a profit, the stockholders will be rewarded with a part of the profits in the form of dividends.

Usually, a fixed number of shares of stock are sold at a certain price. The decision on how many shares to sell and at what price is based on the financial needs of the company. Also, the desired stock price should be considered. Keeping the stock price low will give more people an opportunity to buy the stock. If your company needs, for example, $600, then you might sell 200 shares at $3 each (or any other combination that adds up to $600). Just remember, stock sales should provide enough money for the company and still provide a reasonable dividend to the stockholders.

MATERIALS AND SUPPLIES

1. Stock certificates (handout)
2. Stockholders ledger (handout)

PROCEDURE

1. Form a manufacturing corporation with the members of your class.
2. Chose a product and establish a reasonable selling price.
3. Determine the financial needs for your manufacturing company to design, manufacture, and sell the product.
4. Decide how many shares of stock you will sell.
5. Set the selling price for the stock certificates.
6. Be sure to inform investors of the risks and potential rewards of owning stock in your manufacturing company.
7. Issue stock certificates to interested investors.
8. On a stockholders ledger, keep a list of the investors, the number of shares they purchase, and their total investment.
9. Deposit money from stock sales in an account for the company.
10. You now have the finances you need to start manufacturing your product.

MATH/SCIENCE CONNECTION

Price Per Share. Stock prices are given in price per share. This number is based on the total number of shares sold and the total value of the shares (the amount of money raised by selling all the shares of stock).

$$\text{Price per share} = \frac{\text{Total value of all shares of stock}}{\text{Total number of shares}}$$

RELATED QUESTIONS

1. Why do manufacturing companies sell stock?
2. What do we call the people who buy stock? Why would a person buy stock in a manufacturing company?
3. What are the risks and rewards of owning stock in a company?
4. A company wants to sell shares of stock for $15 per share. How many shares would it need to sell to raise $125,000 of start-up capital?

5. Company XYZ needs $30,000 to start manufacturing a new product. What would be the price per share if the company decided to sell 500 shares of stock?

6. Company ABC needs $500 to start a manufacturing enterprise. It's directors have decided to sell 175 shares of stock at $3 per share. Will they raise enough money?

CHAPTER 11

Time and Work Measurement

OBJECTIVES

After completing this chapter, you will know about:

- Why time and work measurements are important considerations of input.
- What work measurement is and its importance in determining job efficiency.
- The history of work measurement.
- Three common ways to measure work.
- The importance of recognizing worker uniqueness when doing time studies.

KEY TERMS

Allowances
Average
Basic motion time systems
Continuous
Cost-efficient
Downtime
Efficiency experts

Elements
Empowerment
Laws of probability
Qualified
Repetitive
Speed-up
Standardizing the conditions

Standard method
Standard pace
Time-motion studies
Time study
Wage incentive
Work measurement

Time as an Input

When considering manufacturing system inputs, time is an important factor. Adequate time is necessary for planning and setting up the production process itself. Calculating the time it will take to make something and whether it will be **cost-efficient** is an important part of input. Figuring cost-efficiency means determining the cost of the entire production system including the time involved. However, time is one of the most difficult variables to calculate. This chapter discusses several common ways to measure the amount of time workers need to do their jobs. **Work measurement** helps to predict the cost-efficiency of a product.

What Is Work Measurement?

For many athletes, the toughest competitor is time itself. Runners, swimmers, skiers, speed skaters, and bicyclists ultimately race against the clock. They spend many hours becoming as efficient at their sport as they can, Figure 11-1. A track and field hurdler carefully measures steps between hurdles; a swimmer counts strokes between turns. Saving energy through efficient strides or strokes takes down their time. This determines their progress or success if they are competing. Records are set and broken because of accurately timed performances, Figure 11-2.

One of the first concerns of production is conserving human energy through finding the most efficient way to do something. Efficient manufacture of goods means producing the most by using the least amount of energy and wasted movement. Human energy and wasted movement both add to the total amount of time it takes to do a job.

Work measurement is also called **time study** and refers to measuring the amount of time needed to finish a job. It finds the time a **qualified** worker needs, using a **standard method**, working at a **standard pace** to finish a task, Figure 11-3. A qualified worker is one

Figure 11-2. Athletes can win races and shatter records by shaving hundredths of a second off their times. Scott Tinley is a two-time champion of the Ironman Triathlon; he won in 1982 and 1985. *(Courtesy of Raleigh Cycle Company of America)*

who has been trained and has experience at a particular job. A standard method is a certain way of doing something that is repeated over and over in the same manner. Likewise, standard pace is a speed or rate of working that is constant. The time required for the task is called standard or allowed time.

The History of Work Measurement

What is the best way to do a job? What equipment should be used? What is a fair day's work? As the Industrial Revolution progressed during the early part of this century and manufacturing efficiency gained importance, questions like these were asked. Around 1880, Frederick Taylor, a foreman at a steel plant, tried to answer these questions. He studied various jobs to find the most efficient method. He then taught workers how to use the method, Figure 11-4. Working conditions were maintained so the workers could do the job properly. An average or standard time was set for completing the work. Then workers were paid a bonus for finishing the job in the given time and manner. This was the first example of work measurement. Ideally, it is a tool used to increase overall efficiency, making higher wages possible for workers and lower costs for consumers.

Figure 11-1. Accurate measurement of time, as well as achieving a high level of efficiency, are critical to competitive success in some sports. *(Photo by Kenneth A. Deitcher, M.D.)*

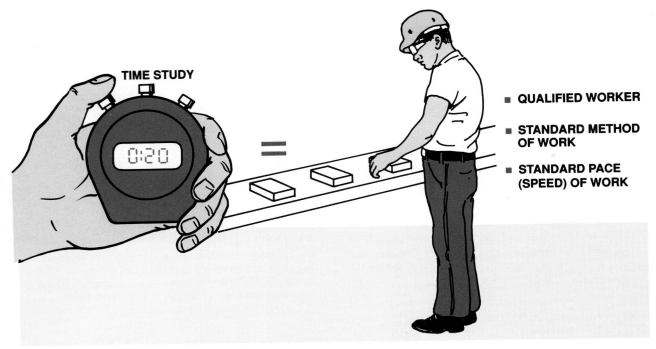

Figure 11-3. Time Study = Qualified Worker + Standard Method + Standard Pace

In the early 1900s, interest in work measurement was sparked by Lillian and Frank Gilbreth. They were engineers who wanted to find the most efficient way to do tasks. Their work resulted in what became known as **time-motion studies**. The Gilbreths became **efficiency experts**. They shared their ideas with many people, including plant managers who used their ideas in production lines. One of the Gilbreths' main concerns was worker attitude. They insisted that if workers helped make decisions about their jobs, they would take more interest in the jobs, Figure 11-5. This feeling of **empowerment** as well as matching skills and interests of workers with their jobs increased overall efficiency and worker satisfaction.

Ways to Measure Work

Today manufacturers use complex methods to measure work efficiency. This is because they are trying to outsell their competitors. Efficiency experts decide how to get the most output with the least input from workers. The following are the most common ways to measure worker efficiency.

Figure 11-4. Workers on a production line are often trained in the most efficient way to do their jobs. This practice was first introduced by Frederick Taylor during the Industrial Revolution. (Copyright 1987 Miles Inc. Used by permission.)

Work Measurement by Timing Device. Use of a stopwatch for measuring work was the original method introduced by Frederick Taylor. It

Prizes for Suggestions

We desire to secure improvement in all departments of our business, and to this end have adopted a plan whereby employees and others may have an incentive to make suggestions with the assurance that all such suggestions will have careful and impartial consideration. Should such suggestions prove of value, the suggester will thereby qualify to compete for a series of prizes to be awarded monthly to employees offering the best suggestions.

Suggestions are invited from all classes of employees. No suggestion need be held back because it appears to be of little importance. The simplest ideas are often valuable.

Suggestions lead to promotion and increased value. They show an interest in our work and organization, and a capacity for greater responsibilities. We invite suggestions upon methods or equipment, methods which will cause more speed, economy or better work, and other matters calculated to advance the interests of the business.

Rules Covering Suggestions

All suggestions submitted will be under the supervision of Frank B. Gilbreth, personally.

Write your suggestion and mail it to F. B. G. marked "personal."

Suggestions will be considered promptly. For each suggestion that is accepted, the Company will award the suggester the sum of one dollar, which will be sent to the employee when he is notified that his suggestion has been accepted. We will then be at liberty to adopt the suggestion at any time at our option.

Prizes

We will award monthly the sum of $20.00 for the most valuable suggestions received during the previous month. This amount will be divided as follows:

FIRST PRIZE $10.00
SECOND PRIZE 5.00
THIRD PRIZE 3.00
FOURTH PRIZE 2.00
	$20.00

Method of Awarding Prizes

On the first Monday of each month, employees who have made suggestions of the greatest value during the preceding month, will be awarded prizes in the order of the value of the suggestion.

As soon as the awards are made, the prizes will be paid in cash, and notices will be posted giving the names of the prize winners, together with a brief description of their suggestions.

Per Order

FRANK B. GILBRETH

Figure 11-5. The Gilbreths encouraged workers to make suggestions for improving efficiency in the workplace. *(Reprinted with permission from Spriegel and Myers,* The Writings of the Gilbreths, *Richard D. Irwin, Inc., 1953, p. 13)*

The Atomic Clock

Accurate time measurement is critical to many areas of technology including space exploration, satellite tracking, and scientific research. Critical time measurement is done with an atomic clock, which was invented during the 1950s.

An atomic clock does not look much like a normal clock. It has no clock face and does not tell time as we are used to. The atomic clock acts as a reference standard against which to calibrate other clocks. An atomic clock looks like a complex piece of laboratory equipment with vacuum pumps and electronic apparatus.

All atoms in their natural states give out and take in pulses of energy. This happens as electrons move from one energy level to another around the nucleus. When an electron moves from a high energy orbit to a lower orbit, a pulse of electromagnetic radiation goes out. Energy levels of an atom are the most constant phenomenon we know. They are not affected by temperature, pressure or gravity.

Elements with only one electron in the outer orbit are especially useful for atomic clocks. Those most commonly used include caesium, rubidium, and hydrogen. Their frequencies are fairly simple and easier to decipher than those from atoms with more electrons in this orbit.

Commercial atomic clocks are available, and are used in research laboratories and broadcasting stations. Industry is finding more and more uses for them. A typical portable caesium clock weighs about 65 lbs.

---

is still occasionally used today. More common are instruments like digital time study boards and other electronic time measuring devices, Figure 11-6. Regardless of which device is used, workers should always be informed of when a time study will be done and why it is needed.

Standardizing the conditions of a job is important because variation and change will affect the time a job takes. For example, changes in kinds, availability, or volume of materials can make accurate time studies difficult. For the best results a smooth, flowing production line with controlled materials flow and standardized jobs is desirable, Figure 11-7. In addition, if there are several workers doing the same job, neither the quickest nor the slowest should be selected for the time study.

When a job is being timed, it should be broken into separate parts. Each part should be timed. These parts are called **elements**. Each element contains a series of movements that

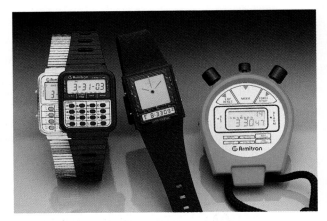

Figure 11-6. Digital timing devices are now commonly used to conduct time studies. *(Courtesy of Service Merchandise Co., Inc.)*

Figure 11-7. This stockpile of wood chips ensures a steady production flow of paper. *(Courtesy of Weyerhaeuser Company)*

OPERATION	Drill oil hole in shaft		OPER. NO.	30	
MACH. TYPE	Delta drill press	MACH. NO. 214		DEPT.	A17
PART NAME	Shaft	PART NO. PL138	OPERATOR	B. Alden	
STUDY NO.	A-112-56	ANALYST T.F. Jones	DATE		

WRITTEN STANDARD PRACTICE

ELEM NO.	LEFT HAND DESCRIPTION	RIGHT HAND DESCRIPTION	MACHINE ELEMENT	SPEED	FEED	STD. TIME
1	Get shaft from tote bag and place in jig	Wait for left hand				.111
2	Grasp jig handle and close jig	Advance drill to part				.203
3	Hold jig closed while drilling	Advance drill 1¼" during drilling	Drill ⅛"x1¼" deep hole	920		.747
4	Open jig	Raise drill				.058
5	Remove shaft from jig and place in tote box	Wait for left hand				.110
6	Remove chips once every 20 pieces	Assist left hand				.012

STANDARD PRODUCTION—PCS. / HR.	48.34	STANDARD TIME—MINUTES / PC.	1.241
SKETCH OF WORKPLACE	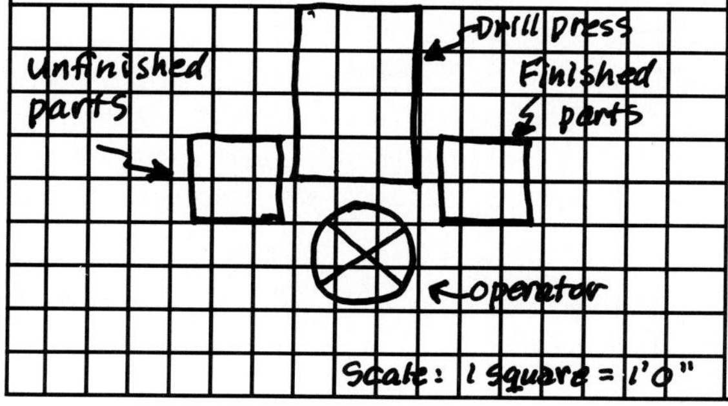	**SET-UP, TOOLS, JIGS, FIXTURES, GAGES—**	

Unfinished parts — Drill press — Finished parts — operator — Scale: 1 square = 1'0"

Jig No. DJ-532
⅛" high speed drill

Figure 11-8. Listed here are elements identified for the left and right hands while operating a Delta drill press.

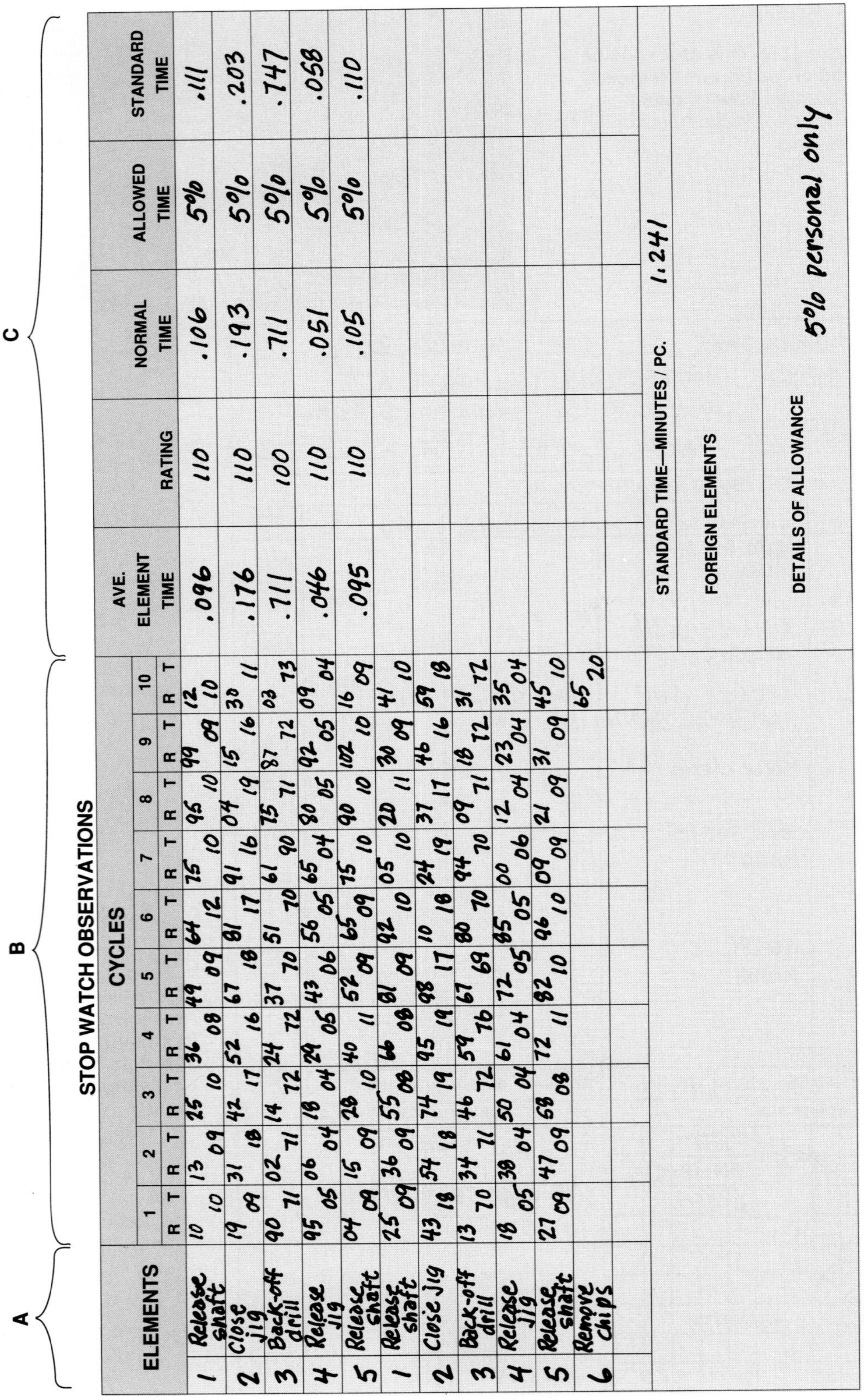

TIME STUDY OBSERVATION SHEET

ELEMENTS		C1 R	C1 T	C2 R	C2 T	C3 R	C3 T	C4 R	C4 T	C5 R	C5 T	C6 R	C6 T	C7 R	C7 T	C8 R	C8 T	C9 R	C9 T	C10 R	C10 T	AVE. ELEMENT TIME	RATING	NORMAL TIME	ALLOWED TIME	STANDARD TIME
1	Release shaft	10	13	09	31	25	36	09	49	18	64	75	95	94	12	09	10					.096	110	.106	5%	.111
2	Close jig	19	09	31	42	17	52	16	67	81	17	91	04	10	15	30	11					.176	110	.193	5%	.203
3	Back-off drill	90	02	71	14	24	72	37	51	70	61	90	71	87	03	13						.711	100	.711	5%	.747
4	Release jig	95	05	06	18	24	05	43	06	56	05	65	50	92	09	04						.046	110	.051	5%	.058
5	Release shaft	04	15	09	28	40	11	52	59	51	10	90	10	102	16	09						.095	110	.105	5%	.110
1	Release shaft	25	09	36	55	09	81	92	10	09	30	41	10													
2	Close jig	43	18	54	74	91	95	98	10	24	19	37	17	46	59	16	18									
3	Back-off drill	13	70	34	46	59	72	69	80	94	00	12	71	18	31	35	72									
4	Release jig	18	39	05	50	04	19	40	72	58	50	09	21	04	23	31	45	54	40	10						
5	Release shaft	27	09	47	68	08	72	82	10	09	09	69	09							65	20					
6	Remove chips																									

STANDARD TIME—MINUTES / PC. 1.241

FOREIGN ELEMENTS

DETAILS OF ALLOWANCE 5% personal only

Figure 11-9. This time study observation sheet includes (A) elements, (B) times for cycles, and (C) average times recorded.

can be identified and recorded. When separating a job into parts, it is easiest if the elements are as short as possible. Elements are then listed on an observation sheet in as much detail as possible, Figure 11-8.

There are two methods of timing the elements that make up a job. They are known as **continuous** and **repetitive** timing. In continuous timing, the timing device is started at the beginning of the job and allowed to run throughout. As each element is completed, the time is recorded on the observation sheet, Figure 11-9, section A. The time for each element is determined by subtracting the time at the start of the element from the time recorded at the end of the job cycle. In repetitive timing, the timing device is started at the beginning and stopped at the end of each element of the job. This procedure is repeated for as many cycles of the job as necessary to complete the observation sheet, Figure 11-9, section B.

After the times are recorded, the **average** time for each element is found by adding all the times for a particular element and dividing by the number of observations. This is the average amount of time needed for the element. Adding all the averages of the elements that make up a job results in the average time needed for completion of the job, Figure 11-9, section C. Note that the more the times recorded for a job vary, the more times the job must be observed and recorded for the data to be considered reliable.

After an average time is determined for a job, **allowances** must be added. An allowance is an amount of time added for interruptions like mechanical problems, personal needs of workers, and other uncontrolled delays. Typically, the allowance for personal needs of workers is about two to five percent of the time required by the job for light work and as much as 50 percent for heavy, more strenuous work, Figure 11-10.

Basic Motion Time Systems

Recently there has been increased use of predetermined or **basic motion time systems**. Basic motion time systems are based on the idea that the average time it takes to perform a

Figure 11-10. Workers should have enough time for personal needs and rest in order to work most efficiently and safely. *(Courtesy of New York State Department of Economic Development)*

basic motion (movement) varies little from person to person. There are many commercial basic motion systems available. They all consist of tables that list standard time values for basic motions. Some basic motions include reaching, positioning, and turning, Figure 11-11. Time values have been determined for most operations that can be broken into basic motions. This eliminates the need for a timing device.

When studying the basic motions of many jobs, it was found that many of the movements were similar. Two different operations with common basic motions were found to have similar standard (total) times. Operations with similar basic motions are often grouped into a family like drilling, cutting, milling, and so on.

A commercial basic motion time system sets standard times for operations at the outset of a manufacturing run. This makes it a quicker, cheaper, and more consistent method.

Work Sampling

Another method for measuring work was used in the English textile industry to determine the cause of **downtime** on looms. Downtime is any time a machine is not running when it is supposed to be. It can be because of mechanical problems, materials shortages, workers' per-

TABLE I – REACH – R

Distance Moved Inches	Time TMU				Hand In Motion		CASE AND DESCRIPTION
	A	B	C or D	E	A	B	
3/4 or less	2.0	2.0	2.0	2.0	1.6	1.6	A Reach to object in fixed location, or to object in other hand or on which other hand rests.
1	2.5	2.5	3.6	2.4	2.3	2.3	
2	4.0	4.0	5.9	3.8	3.5	2.7	
3	5.3	5.3	7.3	5.3	4.5	3.6	B Reach to single object in location which may vary slightly from cycle to cycle.
4	6.1	6.4	8.4	6.8	4.9	4.3	
5	6.5	7.8	9.4	7.4	5.3	5.0	
6	7.0	8.6	10.1	8.0	5.7	5.7	
7	7.4	9.3	10.8	8.7	6.1	6.5	C Reach to object jumbled with other objects in a group so that search and select occur.
8	7.9	10.1	11.5	9.3	6.5	7.2	
9	8.3	10.8	12.2	9.9	6.9	7.9	
10	8.7	11.5	12.9	10.5	7.3	8.6	
12	9.6	12.9	14.2	11.8	8.1	10.1	
14	10.5	14.4	15.6	13.0	8.9	11.5	D Reach to a very small object or where accurate grasp is required.
16	11.4	15.8	17.0	14.2	9.7	12.9	
18	12.3	17.2	18.4	15.5	10.5	14.4	
20	13.1	18.6	19.8	16.7	11.3	15.8	
22	14.0	20.1	21.2	18.0	12.1	17.3	E Reach to indefinite location to get hand in position for body balance or next motion or out of way.
24	14.9	21.5	22.5	19.2	12.9	18.8	
26	15.8	22.9	23.9	20.4	13.7	20.2	
28	16.7	24.4	25.3	21.7	14.5	21.7	
30	17.5	25.8	26.7	22.9	15.3	23.2	
Additional	0.4	0.7	0.7	0.6			TMU per inch over 30 inches

TABLE II – MOVE – M

Distance Moved Inches	Time TMU			Hand In Motion B	Wt. Allowance			CASE AND DESCRIPTION
	A	B	C		Wt. (lb.) Up to	Dynamic Factor	Static Constant TMU	
3/4 or less	2.0	2.0	2.0	1.7				
1	2.5	2.9	3.4	2.3	2.5	1.00	0	A Move object to other hand or against stop.
2	3.6	4.6	5.2	2.9				
3	4.9	5.7	6.7	3.6	7.5	1.06	2.2	
4	6.1	6.9	8.0	4.3				
5	7.3	8.0	9.2	5.0	12.5	1.11	3.9	
6	8.1	8.9	10.3	5.7				
7	8.9	9.7	11.1	6.5	17.5	1.17	5.6	
8	9.7	10.6	11.8	7.2				B Move object to approximate or indefinite location.
9	10.5	11.5	12.7	7.9	22.5	1.22	7.4	
10	11.3	12.2	13.5	8.6				
12	12.9	13.4	15.2	10.0	27.5	1.28	9.1	
14	14.4	14.6	16.9	11.4				
16	16.0	15.8	18.7	12.8	32.5	1.33	10.8	
18	17.6	17.0	20.4	14.2				
20	19.2	18.2	22.1	15.6	37.5	1.39	12.5	
22	20.8	19.4	23.8	17.0				C Move object to exact location.
24	22.4	20.6	25.5	18.4	42.5	1.44	14.3	
26	24.0	21.8	27.3	19.8				
28	25.5	23.1	29.0	21.2	47.5	1.50	16.0	
30	27.1	24.3	30.7	22.7				
Additional	0.8	0.6	0.85					TMU per inch over 30 inches

Figure 11-11. The MTM Association for Standards and Research is one example of a commercial work measurement system. *(Copyrighted by the MTM Association for Standards and Research. No reprint permission without written consent from the MTM Association, 16-01 Broadway, Fairlawn, NJ 17410)*

sonal needs, and so on. Work sampling is based on the **laws of probability**. The laws of probability support the idea that a random sample of observations of an event will follow the same pattern as a lengthy, continuous observation of the same event.

Work sampling takes a number of randomly spaced observations of the event being studied and finds how much time is devoted to each part of the operation. For example, the work of a drill press operator observed randomly and recorded on a tally sheet, Figure 11-12, shows the amount of work time versus idle or downtime.

Work sampling lets the observer work without a timing device. This method will avoid any inconsistencies that might result from using the device. On the other hand, observers will probably need more time to do a work sampling study, and will need an understanding of statistical analysis.

Time Measurement and the Individual

The people who make up the work force are individuals. They want to provide for themselves and their families. They have different backgrounds and ethics by which they live. Each is unique. Therefore, it is unrealistic to expect them to move identically and work at exactly the same rate. It is a matter of ethics for owners and management to give serious consideration to worker well-being. This includes seeing their uniqueness. If enough allowances are made for workers and their individual abilities, then time measurement is more likely to be met with enthusiasm, Figure 11-13. Worker attitude plays a large role in efficiency and product quality.

WORKER'S STATUS	TALLY	TOTAL
Working	〰〰〰〰〰〰 ///	33
Idle	〰 //	7
Total Observations		40

Figure 11-12. This work measurement tally sheet shows work time versus downtime.

Figure 11-13. Informing workers of time studies ensures that they will be more enthusiastic about participating. *(Courtesy of Barnes Group Inc.)*

Some companies have been accused of **speed-up**. Speed-up means decreasing the standard time for operations, perhaps cutting personal allowances, in order to increase productivity. If a work measurement **wage incentive** is used, the results may produce an unwanted result. A work measurement wage incentive increases a worker's pay for meeting or beating the standard time for an operation. Worker safety and product quality may suffer as a result. On the other hand, the use of appropriate standard times, with adequate personal allowances, in combination with the incentive wage can motivate workers. It is a delicate balance to maintain, Figure 11-14.

Summary

One of the first concerns of production is efficiency. To find the efficiency of a worker, time studies are done. The time measured for the task is the standard or allowed time.

Work measurement began with Frederick Taylor during the late nineteenth century. He studied various jobs to find the most efficient way to do them. He then taught these methods to the workers. A few years later Lillian and Frank Gilbreth, efficiency experts, did time-motion studies. They were also concerned with worker well-being and insisted that a satisfied worker is an efficient worker.

The following are the most common ways to measure worker efficiency.

- Work measurement by timing device
- Basic motion time systems
- Work sampling

The people who make up the work force are individuals. It is unrealistic to expect them to move identically at the same rate. If enough allowances are made for workers' individual abilities, then workers will accept work measurement with more enthusiasm.

Companies have been accused of speed-up in order to increase productivity. Speed-up can compromise worker safety and product quality. But the use of appropriate standard times for jobs in combination with a work measurement work wage incentive can be a source of motivation.

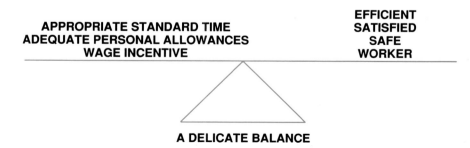

APPROPRIATE STANDARD TIME
ADEQUATE PERSONAL ALLOWANCES
WAGE INCENTIVE

EFFICIENT
SATISFIED
SAFE
WORKER

A DELICATE BALANCE

Figure 11-14. A delicate balance is necessary between appropriate standard times, wage incentives, and satisfied, safe workers.

DISCUSSION QUESTIONS

1. Describe an activity that you feel you can do efficiently (bicycling, computer games, washing dishes, and so on). What are the elements (basic motions) that make up this activity?

2. If you were a worker on an assembly line and were informed that you were to be the subject of a time study, what questions would you want to ask the efficiency expert?

3. Describe some of the allowances that should be considered when determining the standard time for a welder on an assembly line.

4. Would you like to be an efficiency expert? Why or why not?

5. What are the benefits of measuring work for a company? For a worker?

6. How has robotics affected time and work measurement?

CHAPTER ACTIVITIES

HOW LONG DOES IT TAKE?

OBJECTIVE

This activity will help you understand the job of efficiency experts. You will also see how they use time studies to predict the cost efficiency of a manufacturing enterprise.

MATERIALS AND SUPPLIES

1. Handouts: "Continuous Timing Observation Sheet" and "Repetitive Timing Observation Sheet"

2. Appropriate tools and machines for conducting time studies of a basic operation like drilling, cutting, sanding, and so forth

3. Timing device that measures seconds

4. Safety glasses

PROCEDURE

1. Review figure 11-9 in this text. It shows the use of continuous and repetitive timing observation sheets.

2. Working in pairs, choose a basic operation (drilling, cutting, sanding, and so on) using either hand tools or machines.

3. Obtain the tools you need for your operation and set up a work space. Follow and practice appropriate safety rules.

4. One person will play the role of efficiency expert, and the other will be a worker performing the operation. Identify the elements or basic motions that make up the operation. List them on the handouts.

5. Practice using the timing device to time the elements of the operation.

6. With the timing device, complete the handouts using the continuous and repetitive timing methods. Be sure to observe and time the operation at least eight times. You can figure total times and averages after you have recorded all your observations.

7. Exchange positions and repeat steps five and six above.

8. As a class, compare the two methods of timing and discuss any problems you had during the activity.

RELATED QUESTIONS

1. Which work timing method seemed more accurate? Why?

2. Did the average or allowed time differ between worker one and worker two? Why?

3. Which role did you enjoy more, efficiency expert or worker? Explain.

4. How did you feel when you were the worker? Did you try to hurry, or were you comfortable during the time study?

5. Based on your answer to question four above, do you think studies are an accurate gauge for determining the allowed time for a job? Explain.

WORK SAMPLING

OBJECTIVE

When you have finished this activity, you will have seen work sampling as a means to measuring downtime and worker efficiency. Work sampling is a sampling technique based on the laws of probability.

MATERIALS AND SUPPLIES

1. Handout "Time Study: Work Sampling"

2. Paper and pencil

PROCEDURE

1. Review the section on work sampling in the unit and study figure 11-12.

2. Working alone, go to the library and choose an individual whose work pattern you will observe. Try not to be noticed.

3. Follow the instructions to complete the handout "Time Study: Work Sampling." Record the work time versus the downtime of your chosen individual.

4. Compute the percentage of work time and downtime according to the following formula.

MATH/SCIENCE CONNECTION

$$(100)(WT) = (X)(TO)$$
$$(100)(DT) = (X)(TO)$$

Where

TO = total observation time
WT = work time observed
DT = downtime observed
X = percentage

RELATED QUESTIONS

1. Describe any problems you had while recording the information for this activity.
2. Do you think your work sampling experience truly reflects the work habits of your subject? Explain.
3. Describe a situation that might make the results of a work sampling time study false.
4. What is an advantage of using this time-study method?
5. Should the individual being observed know about the study? Why or why not?

SECTION THREE

MANUFACTURING PROCESSES

In this section, you will read about the various jobs related to designing, engineering, producing, and selling products. Chapter 12 follows a product from idea through sketches, mock-ups, prototypes, and working drawings. Chapter 13 then outlines the steps needed to produce a product. Chapter 14 describes how companies are owned and managed. Chapter 15 explains how materials are formed, separated, or combined to make a product. In Chapter 16, you will learn how the marketing department advertises, sells, and services a product. And in Chapter 17, you will see how companies track their profits and losses, payroll, dividends owed to stockholders, and the overall financial health of the company.

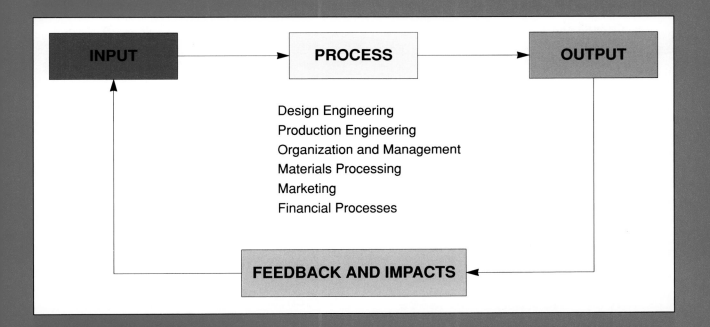

INPUT → PROCESS → OUTPUT

Design Engineering
Production Engineering
Organization and Management
Materials Processing
Marketing
Financial Processes

FEEDBACK AND IMPACTS

CHAPTER 12

Design Engineering Processes

OBJECTIVES

After completing this chapter, you will know about:

- The role of design engineering in a manufacturing enterprise.
- The six stages of the design engineering process.
- The use of design criteria as a set of guidelines in designing products.
- The sketching, drawing, and modeling processes designers use when developing a product idea.

KEY TERMS

Aesthetics	Development	Pure research
Applied research	Durability	Renderings
Assembly drawing	Ideation	Rough sketches
Design criteria	Mock-up	Thumbnail sketches
Design engineering	Planned obsolescence	Working drawings
Detail drawings	Prototype	

Design Engineering Processes

Engineers are the problem-solvers in manufacturing. They are responsible for two major activities: designing products and planning the most efficient manufacturing system to make the product. This chapter focuses on **design engineering**, that is, the process of designing products. The next chapter will focus on production engineering—planning an efficient manufacturing system.

Introduction to Design Engineering

If you had an idea for a new product and wanted to get it manufactured, what would you do? Well, first you would have to convince a manufacturing company that your product is worth making. To do that, you would have to improve and refine your idea into plans that could be used to communicate with the company. They would want you to answer the following questions:

- Can the product be made with our equipment?
- Will consumers buy the product?
- Can the product be sold at a profit?

This is the task of design engineering. Design engineers create ideas for products. They also develop these ideas into plans that tell a company if the product can be made and sold at a profit, Figure 12-1. The design engineering process begins with research and development of new product ideas. Engineers make designs, models, and engineering drawings to help them develop and test out their ideas.

Research and Development

Workers in research and development (called R&D) identify and develop new ideas for products, materials, and manufacturing processes. Most of the products that have the description "new and improved" are the result of manufacturing R&D. R&D is composed of two distinct areas—research and development.

Research. Research is a step-by-step search for new information, facts, ideas, or basic principles. Scientists, such as chemists, physicists, and mathematicians, work in the engineering department conducting much of this research. They use the scientific method to discover or gather new information.

There are two types of research—pure and applied. **Pure research** (also called basic research) is the search for new information without considering any practical uses for the information. **Applied research**, on the other hand, is the search for practical applications for the new information found through pure research.

NASA's research into the possibilities of manufacturing products in space points out the difference between pure and applied research. Before any products can be made in space, scientists must learn more about the effects of microgravity on people, materials, and processes. Their experiments in this field are examples of pure or basic research. NASA's pure research scientists try to learn how things work in the space environment, Figure 12-2.

Once NASA understands the characteristics of the space environment, research can begin into new ways of using that information. The new information developed through pure research is applied to the search for manufacturing processes that will work and new materials that can be produced in space. Putting information to practical use is applied research.

On earth, pure research is being done in manufacturing every day to learn more about materials, processes, products, machines, and even customers. Conducting market research

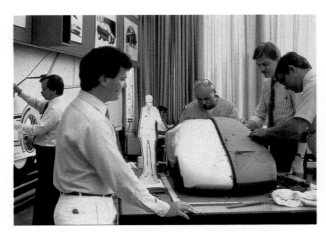

Figure 12-1. Design engineering develops product ideas by creating sketches, drawings, and models. *(Courtesy of General Motors)*

Figure 12-2. NASA's pure researchers study the characteristics of the space environment. *(Courtesy of NASA)*

Figure 12-3. The research scientist on the left is conducting pure research into the chemistry of new plastics materials. Design engineers take information gathered by research scientists and develop new products like this sailboard made from plastics. *(Courtesy of Amoco Corporation)*

to learn about consumers' needs and wants is another example of basic research.

Development. Development is a type of applied research that tries to create new products or new applications for existing products. Development takes new materials or product ideas discovered by researchers and creates new products. When plastics were first discovered by pure research scientists, product applications were needed. Workers in development took the new plastics materials and used them to create new products. Design engineers work in the development process. This is also called the design engineering process, Figure 12-3.

Stages in the Design Engineering Process

The design engineering process contains six important stages. These stages do not occur in a step-by-step manner. Rather, they may overlap each other throughout the entire design process. The stages in this process can take days or even years. This depends on the complexity of the product and the size of the company. When designing products for manufac-

turing, design engineers often pass through the stages listed in Figure 12-4.

1. Desire

Desire, also called motivation, is a very important stage in the process. Desire provides the fuel or energy needed by the design engineer

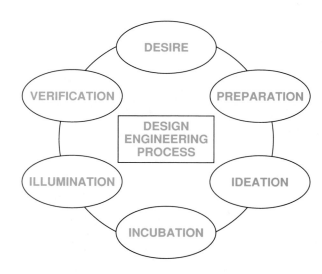

Figure 12-4. The six stages in the design engineering process.

throughout the entire design and manufacturing process. Desire is important in every step of the process, from identifying the design criteria through having the finished product come off the assembly line.

Desire is hard to create or force. A designer who chooses to work on a certain project will usually show more desire than one who is forced to work on a project. Management must realize the importance of desire. They should try to nurture it by giving the designer a sense of ownership in the product design. When design engineers have desire, creating new and improved products is easier and more enjoyable. However, without desire, trying to design may be a laborious and difficult task. Developing the personal desire to design the best possible product is an important stage in the design process.

2. Preparation

Preparation, or "doing your homework," is a stage of learning, exploring, and gathering information. To prepare themselves, designers often study existing products, talk to experts in the field, ask consumers what they like, or read about certain products. They must also study the tools, materials, and processes used to make products. Preparation gives the designer the information needed to create new and improved designs.

One important part of the preparation stage is developing a set of design criteria. The design criteria give the designer guidelines to follow when working on a design.

The Design Criteria. The goal of the design engineer is to develop quality products that meet human needs at a fair and reasonable price. Many factors influence the final design of a product. These include the materials selected, tools and machines needed for manufacture, and the production processes available in a company. Design engineers usually consider a list of selected **design criteria** when developing a product idea, Figure 12-5. These criteria guide the designer throughout the design process. The goal is to have a product that can be made and sold at a profit, while serving a useful function for the consumer.

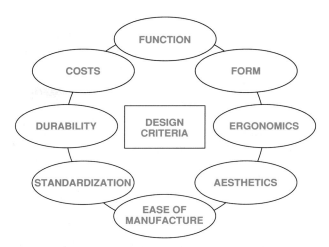

Figure 12-5. The design criteria give the design engineer a set of guidelines.

The design criteria are described as follows.

Function. The function of a product is usually one of the most important design criteria. After all, if a product does not function, it is useless to the consumer. Design engineers must design products that do the job for which they were intended. Of course, there are many different product functions. The designer must think about how consumers will use the particular product.

Form. There is a saying in design that states "Form follows function." This means the form (size, shape, and structure) of a product must match its intended function. The size, shape, and structure of a bicycle is designed to match its function of providing efficient and enjoyable transportation. A bicycle with an uncomfortable seat is not well designed for its function. Designers try to create a product form that matches function.

Ergonomics. Ergonomics is closely related to form and function. It can be defined as designing for human use. Ergonomically designed products have a form that matches the way people will use the products. An uncomfortable chair or a hand tool that causes muscle strain are not ergonomically designed.

One branch of ergonomics, called human factors engineering, has created a body of knowledge about average people. Drawings of people in different positions, such as standing, sitting, and reaching, have dimensions showing the minimum and maximum sizes for the average person. Design engineers must consider this information if they want their products to be ergonomically designed, Figure 12-6.

Aesthetics. **Aesthetics** are qualities that give beauty or visual appeal to a product or other object. An aesthetically appealing product is pleasing to view. Some people would say it has a certain beauty. Most products are designed to attract the attention of consumers aesthetically.

Engineering places less value on aesthetics than on function and form. A beautiful product that does not work is useless. Many manufacturing companies design aesthetically appealing products that do not function properly. Cheap products that imitate the looks of the original but not the operation are always being made and sold.

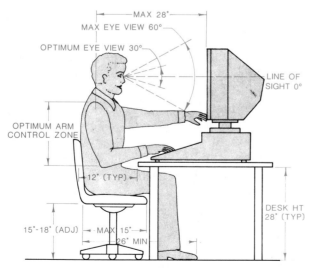

Figure 12-6. The field of human factors engineering has created a body of knowledge about the average person. This information is used to create ergonomic designs. *(Reprinted from* DRAFTING IN A COMPUTER AGE *by Wallach and Chowenhill, © 1989 Delmar Publishers Inc.)*

Ease of Manufacture. Design engineers must consider thé tools, materials, and processes needed to make a product. The engineers must ensure that workers have the skills needed to make the product with existing equipment. Of course, the company may decide to buy new equipment if they think enough consumers will buy the product.

The complexity of a product must also be considered. In general, the fewer and the simpler the parts, the easier a product will be to make. Manufacturing a product that needs hundreds or thousands of parts is difficult to manage.

Standardization. Standardization is closely related to ease of manufacture. Some manufacturers publish guidebooks of design standards. These guidebooks specify certain standards that design engineers must follow. The standards identify the tools, machines, and equipment the company has available for manufacturing products. As an example, standard sizes for tools such as drill bits and saw blades are listed in the guidebooks. This ensures that product features, such as drilled holes, match the existing tools.

Standardization also ensures that products are designed to be made from standard materials. Manufacturing a product with standard material sizes, such as plywood thickness or metal width, instead of nonstandard sizes takes less time and costs less money, Figure 12-7.

Durability. **Durability** relates to the expected life of a product. Durable products are made to last longer. Of course, they cost more money to make than products that wear out quickly. Luxury automobiles are very durable. They sometimes run for hundreds of thousands of miles. But they can cost ten times as much money as a typical economical subcompact car.

Some products are intentionally designed to fail after a certain time. This is called **planned obsolescence**. Parts are designed to wear out or break down after so many months or years. This ensures that the consumer will

Figure 12-7. Even futuristic automobiles, like this concept car, will use standard parts for bolts and screws, wheels and transmissions, and engines. *(Courtesy of General Mototrs)*

have to buy another product in the future. If products were made to last forever, manufacturers would never sell replacement products. Unfortunately, some companies abuse planned obsolescence by not giving their customers the best quality product available.

Costs. Cost is probably one of the most important design criteria. The cost of manufacturing a product must not prevent the company from selling it at a profit.

A specialized type of engineering, called value engineering, makes sure product costs are kept to a minimum. Design engineers must always consider the costs associated with making a product. Trade-offs are usually made between costs and the other criteria. In general, designers attempt to choose the most economical materials and components for the product that will still do the job and match the other criteria.

Trade-offs and the Design Criteria

Designers may receive a set of design criteria for a certain product from management, or they may develop their own set of criteria. By examining any one product, you can probably identify the trade-off decisions that were made to design that product. As an example, consider the criteria used to design automobiles. The criteria and possible trade-off decisions are listed in Figure 1.

Design engineers must make trade-off decisions about the product design. Obviously, the trade-offs involved in designing cars give rise to a wide range of different automobiles. The first step in designing a quality product is to develop a list of specific design criteria.

CRITERIA	TRADE-OFF DECISIONS
Function	Speed, economy, passengers
Form	Compact, full-size, wagon
Ergonomics	Ease of entry and exit, rider comfort
Aesthetics	Styling, colors
Ease of Manufacture	Accessories, options available
Standardization	Standard engines, wheels, parts
Durability	Reliable, breaks down
Costs	Economy or luxury

Figure 1. Here are some design criteria and trade-off decisions for automobile manufacturers. *(Photo courtesy of Pontiac Division, General Motors)*

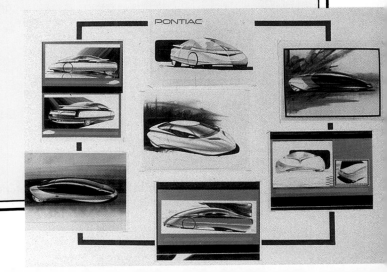

The materials, supplies, and components that go into a product are just one part of value engineering. Another consideration is the amount of labor needed to make a product. Complex products that need skilled workers are more expensive to make than simple products that can be made by automated equipment. Remember, labor costs are a big part of the total cost of a product.

3. Ideation

The third stage in the design engineering process is **ideation**. During this stage, the designer combines various bits of information learned during the preparation stage into new ideas. Techniques used by designers to create new ideas include brainstorming, sketching, and drawing. During brainstorming, a group of designers gathers to discuss the design problem. During the discussion, any and all ideas are spoken out and recorded. The list of brainstormed ideas is then evaluated. The best ideas are chosen for further development through sketching and modeling.

Sketching Ideas. The first sketches a designer makes are called **thumbnail sketches** or **rough sketches**. These are small sketches or doodles the designer uses to record any ideas on paper. Thumbnail sketches are not usually full sized. They can be of a complete product idea or of just a few details of the product, such as handles, knobs, or corners. For every aspect of the product, the designer puts any ideas down on paper, Figure 12-8.

Designers usually work as part of a design team. Individual team members create their own rough sketches. They then share their designs with the team. As a team, the designers review and select the best design ideas for the product.

Once the best ideas have been chosen, the rough sketches are improved or refined. These refined sketches show features of the product in more detail. Once these refined sketches are complete, designers begin to work with production engineers to discuss the ease of manufacture criteria. Tools, materials, and processes required to make each part are discussed. The production engineer tells designers whether or not the parts can be made with existing equipment.

Renderings. The next sketches created are called **renderings**. The designer takes the technical information provided by the production engineer plus ideas from other designers to form comprehensive sketches. These sketches show the finished product with all details included, such as color, purchased components, and hardware, Figure 12-9.

Renderings are reviewed by supervisors in the engineering, marketing, and finance departments, as well as by management. In these review meetings, they ask a number of questions, such as,

- Do we have the tools and people needed?
- Can we beat our competition to the market?

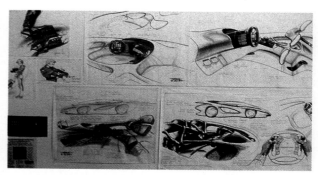

Figure 12-8. Thumbnail sketches and refined detail sketches are used to record and communicate a designer's initial ideas. (*Courtesy of Pontiac Division, General Motors*)

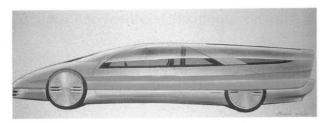

Figure 12-9. Renderings are comprehensive sketches of a finished product. *(Courtesy of General Motors)*

- Can we beat the price of our competition?
- Can we sell the product at a profit?

Everyone presents ideas. Management makes the final decision to continue with further development or to scrap the product idea. If management decides to go ahead with further development, the next step is the creation of scale models.

Creating Mock-ups. Models are made by highly skilled technicians to evaluate the product design. The first models created are called mock-ups. A **mock-up** is a scale model of the finished product. Mock-ups, which show the appearance of the product, are made from easily worked materials such as cardboard, balsa wood, styrofoam, or clay. Mock-ups do not have real working parts. For example, a mock-up of an automobile may have wheels, but they do not work. They are just there for appearances, Figure 12-10.

Designers and engineers use mock-ups to begin to make better estimates of the ease of manufacture, standardization, and value engineering aspects of the product. One of the most important reasons for making mock-ups is to analyze aesthetics. Marketing workers may even use the mock-ups to evaluate the appeal of the product to potential consumers.

4. Incubation

Often, designers reach a point in the design process when they become frustrated. They can not seem to find any new ideas, or their new ideas do not seem so great. During this time, it may be advantageous for the designer to take a break for a period of time. Taking a break from a difficult task is called incubation. The incubation stage can occur at any time in the design engineering process.

During the incubation stage, the designer should relax and become refreshed. Incubation helps renew the desire and motivation needed to solve a problem.

The incubation stage, provided it is not prolonged, should not be seen as a lazy stage. Every designer needs a stage of incubation.

5. Illumination

Relaxing during the incubation stage allows new ideas to be generated subconsciously. When a designer returns to work, these ideas

Figure 12-10. Here are three different automobile design mock-ups. Clay mock-ups for the exterior and interior are on the left and center. A plywood mock-up of the driver's seat is on the right. Notice the color sketch in the center photo. *(Courtesy of General Motors)*

seem to jump into mind. This is often called illumination. Another name for this stage is the "ah ha!" stage.

Working in groups, sharing ideas, and brainstorming are good ways to help illuminate the final ideas for a product design.

6. Verification

This is the stage in the design process when ideas are proved. Verification means making sure the product design actually works. During this stage, product sketches and mock-ups are turned into full-sized models called prototypes.

Prototype. A **prototype** is a fully functional full-sized model of the product. Prototypes are made with the actual materials and working components that will be used in production. With the prototype, engineers run tests to make sure the product works as it was designed. A number of factors are checked. These include ease of manufacture, durability, ergonomics, function, and operation, Figure 12-11.

Figure 12-11. A designer adds the finishing touches to a prototype automobile (top) before road testing begins. *(Courtesy of General Motors)*

Getting Management Approval on Product Designs

After a product design has been verified, the design team must get final approval from management to go to production. Just as the design sketches were reviewed by management during the ideation stage, the final prototype design must also be approved before the company can start producing the product. Management usually meets with the design team, as well as representatives from production, marketing, and finance, to discuss the product design. Each department brings a certain expertise to the meeting. Production engineers discuss ease of manufacture, market researchers discuss consumer reaction to the product, and finance personnel tell whether the product can be sold at a profit. If management approves the final product design, the product will be made.

Communicating Product Designs to Production

Before a product can be manufactured, the product design must be communicated to production personnel. A set of working drawings and a bill of materials are created by the design engineers for this purpose. Working drawings provide production with all the details and specifications they need to begin making the product. A bill of materials lists all the parts, components, and hardware used to make the drawing.

Working Drawings. **Working drawings** are a set of drawings and plans that communicate all the size, shape, and manufacturing information needed by the production department. A set of working drawings usually includes two different types of drawings—detail drawings and assembly drawings.

Detail Drawings. **Detail drawings** are usually orthographic, multiview drawings of the individual parts of a product. They contain all the information needed to make each part. Detail drawings are created by drafters in the engineering department using manual drafting tools or CAD systems.

Depending upon the complexity of the part, a detail drawing can include one, two, or more

Reducing Design Time with Computer Models

Designing, producing, and testing scale model mock-ups and full-size prototypes can take weeks, months, or even years. To reduce the time involved in refining product plans, designers have turned to computer-generated models. Computer-aided drafting and design (CADD) systems speed up the design process. CADD systems are programmed with information on the properties and costs of materials; the operation of moving parts; and the function of various components, such as electrical systems. When a product design is fed into the CADD system, the designer can specify materials and components. Then, simulated tests are performed on the design by the computer.

CADD systems are also programmed to calculate the total costs of manufacturing the product. Prices for individual components and materials are programmed into the computer. When the designer selects a component, the computer automatically creates a manufacturing cost estimate.

CADD systems give manufacturing companies a big advantage in beating their competitors to market. If a part does not work as planned, it can quickly be replaced on screen and retested. With actual prototypes, replacing parts can be a long, involved process. Computer simulation with CADD systems makes the time for R&D much shorter. This reduction in design time helps companies get their products to consumers as fast as possible.

Designers can reduce the time it takes for the design engineering process by utilizing CADD systems to design and test products by computer. *(Courtesy of Honeywell Inc.)*

views. The drawings show the shape and form of each part. Also included are dimensions that give exact information on sizes, shapes, and locations of various features, such as holes, slots, or cuts. Notes also appear that identify the materials to be used, tolerances on parts, and machining and finishing operations required, Figure 12-12.

Assembly Drawings. An **assembly drawing** shows what the final product will look like when it is assembled. Assembly drawings may be orthographic or pictorial. The most com-monly used pictorials are isometric drawings. Pictorial drawings have the advantage of showing the three dimensions of a part or product with one view, Figure 12-13.

Another common assembly drawing is the exploded assembly, Figure 12-14. In an exploded assembly, all the parts of a product are drawn as if they had exploded from the finished product. Each part appears as a pictorial drawing. Lines are usually drawn between parts to show assembly techniques. This type of drawing is commonly used in owner's

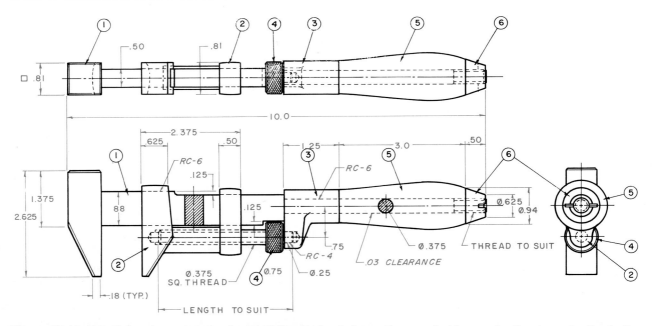

Figure 12-12. Detail drawings communicate all the design information needed by production to make the individual parts of a product. *(Reprinted from* TECHNICAL DRAWING AND DESIGN *by Goetsch and Nelson, © 1986 Delmar Publishers Inc.)*

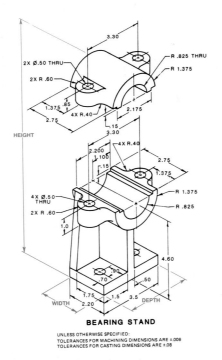

Figure 12-13. Pictorial assembly drawings show the height, width, and depth of a product in one view. *(Reprinted from* DRAFTING IN A COMPUTER AGE *by Wallach and Chowenhill, © 1989 Delmar Publishers Inc.)*

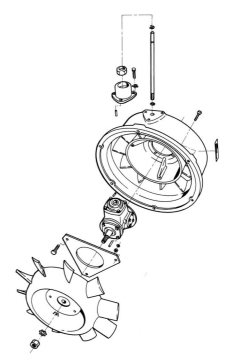

Figure 12-14. An exploded assembly drawing shows how all the parts of a product go together. *(Reprinted from* DRAFTING IN A COMPUTER AGE *by Wallach and Chowenhill, © 1989 Delmar Publishers Inc.)*

XYZ Manufacturing Co.

PRODUCT CODE		X-125-A	BILL OF MATERIALS			MODEL	08
QUANTITY		450				DRAWING	125

PART NO.	QTY.	PART NAME	DESCRIPTION	COST UNIT	COST TOTAL
1	1	Base	walnut, $1^1/8 \times 4^1/4 \times 10^3/8$	1.64	1.64
2	2	Sides	walnut, $5/8 \times 3^3/8 \times 7^7/8$	.48	.96
3	1	Case Top	walnut, $1/2 \times 4 \times 10^3/8$	.62	.62
4	1	Middle Top	walnut, $1/2 \times 3^5/8 \times 9^3/8$	.50	.50
5	1	Cap	walnut, $1/2 \times 3 \times 8^1/2$	.35	.35
6	4	Frame	walnut, $1/2 \times 1/2 \times 8$	.06	.24
7	2	Retainer	pine, $1/2 \times 1/2 \times 7$	.02	.04
8	1	Handle	#H-750, brass finish	.75	.75
9	1	Clock Face	#547CF, painted, Clock Co. Intl.	1.25	1.25
10	1	Movement	#629MV, battery, Clock Co. Intl.	2.50	2.50
11	1	Glass	$1/8 \times 8^3/16 \times 7^7/8$, City Glass	.28	.28
APPROVED BY: _____			DATE: _____	TOTAL	$9.13

Figure 12-15. The bill of materials is also used to communicate product design information to the production and finance departments.

manuals for products, such as bicycles and appliances, that are put together at home by the consumer.

Bill of Materials. Another method of communicating product information is through the bill of materials. A bill of materials is usually included as a component of the set of working drawings. It lists all the parts, components, and hardware needed to make the product. The bill of materials is used to tell finance workers what materials (standard stock, supplies, and so on) must be ordered and available for production. It may also be used to estimate the costs of a product, Figure 12-15.

Summary

Design engineering creates and develops product ideas. Design engineering processes usually begin with research and development. Research can be pure or applied. Pure research gathers information without considering any practical applications. Applied research takes the information gained through pure research and tries to find practical applications, usually in product designs.

The stages in the design engineering process include desire, preparation, ideation, incubation, illumination, and verification. These stages do not occur in a step-by-step order. Rather, they may take place in any order. Desire, the motivation of the designer, is a very important stage. A designer must have the desire to create quality products. The two other most important stages are ideation and verification. During the ideation stage, designers create sketches, rendering, and mock-ups to record and evaluate their ideas about products. During the verification stage, full-sized fully functional prototypes are created. The prototype is used to evaluate the product design and make decisions about possible production.

The final step in the design engineering process includes creating working drawings. Working drawings communicate the plans for a product design to the production department. Detail drawings and assembly drawings, as well as a bill of materials, are included in a set of working drawings.

Once a company completes the design engineering processes, it is ready to begin the production engineering processes. Production engineering involves creating and setting up a production line to manufacture a product.

DISCUSSION QUESTIONS

1. Describe or define design engineering. Identify the basic processes performed by a design engineer.

2. What is the difference between research and development?

3. What are the six stages in the design engineering process? Describe each stage.

4. What are the design criteria described in this chapter? Which do you think is most important?

5. What is planned obsolescence? How is it good or bad for manufacturers and consumers?

6. What is the difference between a mock-up model and a prototype?

CHAPTER ACTIVITIES

 SKETCHING PRODUCT IDEAS

OBJECTIVE

An important stage in the design engineering process is the ideation stage. During this stage, designers often draw sketches to record their product design ideas.

In this activity, you will sketch your ideas for a product to be manufactured by your class.

MATERIALS AND SUPPLIES

1. Drawing and sketching tools
2. Grid paper or drawing paper

3. Design criteria worksheet
4. Water colors or magic markers

PROCEDURE

1. As a class, decide what type of products you want to manufacture. This will be determined by the machines and equipment available in your lab.

2. To prepare for the design engineering process, study other similar products in local stores or department store catalogs. If possible, cut out several photos of the types of product you would like to make. The more product designs you study, the more ideas you will have to draw from.

3. In small design groups or as a class, list the design criteria for your product. Use the design criteria worksheet supplied by your teacher. Refer to Figure 1 as you fill out your worksheet.

DESIGN CRITERIA WORKSHEET	
DESIGN CRITERIA	**TRADEOFF DECISIONS**
Function	How will the product operate, be used?
Form	What size and shape will the product be?
Ergonomics	How will people use the product? What consumer safety factors must we consider?
Aesthetics	Will the product have an appealing appearance?
Ease of Manufacture	How many parts are needed? What tools and materials are needed?
Standardization	Will standard materials and supplies be used?
Durability	How long will the product last?
Costs	What is the product's price range?

Figure 1. Refer to this example as you fill out your worksheet.

4. Two of the most important criteria for a simulated classroom manufacturing enterprise will probably be ease of manufacture and costs. Pay special attention to these criteria.

5. Once you have developed a list of design criteria, begin to create thumbnail sketches of your design ideas. Make your sketches freehand. Use grid paper to make the sketching easier.

6. Meet with the members of your design group and review thumbnail sketches. Pick the best ideas and incorporate them into one comprehensive design.

7. Meet with the class production engineers or your teacher to make sure the product can be manufactured with the tools and machines available in your lab.

8. Once the design has been approved by production engineering or your teacher, draw renderings of the final product design. Be sure to include all details, such as color, dimensions, purchased components, and hardware.

9. Your renderings may be used in the next activity, "Verifying Product Designs with Mock-ups and Prototypes."

10. If you do not have enough time to finish your renderings in your manufacturing class, consider asking students who are taking drafting or art classes to make the sketches.

MATH/SCIENCE CONNECTION

Sketching products to scale. When product designs are sketched at their actual size, we say these sketches are at full scale. Often, product design sketches are drawn smaller than their actual size. They are drawn at a reduced scale. For the designs to be accurate, drawings must be made to scale.

Drawing an object to scale means all the dimensions on a reduced scale drawing are directly proportional to the same dimensions on the actual product. Product designs are often drawn to half scale or quarter scale. On a drawing, these scales are shown as follows.

Half Scale: $1/2" = 1"$ or 1:2

Quarter Scale: $1/4" = 1"$ or 1:4

In all cases, the number on the left corresponds to the drawing and the number on the right corresponds to the actual product. As an example, when a product with a height of twelve inches is drawn at half scale, the height of the drawing will be six inches. Each half inch on the drawing is equal to one inch on the actual object.

Making sketches to scale is easier with grid paper. Each square on the grid paper can be equal to some dimension, such as one inch. Here is an example that will help you see how designers figure the scale in a drawing. If an object has the actual dimensions listed at the left, its dimensions in a quarter scale drawing would be those listed at the right.

ACTUAL DIMENSIONS	QUARTER SCALE DIMENSIONS
Height = 14"	3.50"
Width = 9"	2.25"
Depth = 6"	1.50"

RELATED QUESTIONS

1. Other than studying existing product designs, what techniques could a design engineer use to prepare for designing a product?

2. Which design criteria do you think are the most important?

3. Why are the first sketches created by designers called "thumbnail" sketches?

4. Do you think sketching processes can be improved by the use of computers? Why?

⚙ VERIFYING PRODUCT DESIGNS WITH MOCK-UPS AND PROTOTYPES

OBJECTIVE

After product design sketches have been made, designers create mock-ups and proto-types. A mock-up is a scale model used to verify product design sketches. The most important criterion verified with a mock-up is the appearance. Other factors are also reviewed, such as ease of manufacture and standardization. Designers might produce several different mock-ups, changing various styling or other features.

Once the designers have reviewed mock-ups and chosen the final product design, a prototype is produced. A prototype is a fully functional, full-sized version of the product. Prototypes are made with the actual materials and components that will be used in the final product. Design engineers run tests with the prototype to make sure it works properly. Engineers also consider aesthetics, ergonomics, durability, and ease of manufacture at this stage.

In this activity, you will produce mock-ups and a prototype to verify your product design ideas. Based on these models, management will decide whether to manufacture the product.

MATERIALS AND SUPPLIES

1. Product design sketches and renderings
2. Mock-up modeling materials:
   - clay
   - cardboard
   - styrofoam
   - plywood
3. Design and modeling tools:
   - measuring scales
   - knives, razors, other cutting tools
   - hot glue guns, tape, other fastening tools
   - water colors, magic markers, paints
4. Prototype manufacturing tools. (These will be similar to the tools and machines used to manufacture products.)
5. Safety glasses

PROCEDURE

1. Choose the best product design sketches and renderings you developed earlier.
2. Work in small groups or alone to produce a mock-up of your design using an easily worked modeling material, such as clay or cardboard.
3. The mock-up should be made to scale. (The mock-up can be made at full scale if the product is small enough.) Remember, mock-ups do not have any real working parts. Moving parts can be simulated.
4. Hold a meeting with the various groups or students who produced mock-ups. Each group or student should present its product design to the class by showing and describing the mock-up. As a class, evaluate the various designs for aesthetic appeal. Choose the best product design based on the presentations of the mock-ups.

5. Produce a prototype of the approved product design. Remember, a prototype is a fully functional, full-sized version of the product. The prototype should be made from actual product materials. All operating parts should work when the prototype is complete.

6. *NOTE:* Your teacher might choose a small group of students from the class to make the prototype. This frees other students to make working drawings, conduct market research, or begin production engineering activities.

7. After the prototype is complete, test it to make sure all the parts work as planned.

8. Market research can be conducted with the prototype. Set up a table in the cafeteria during lunch and take a consumer poll. Ask students and teachers if they would buy the product and how much they would be willing to spend.

9. Those students in your class manufacturing company who are involved in finances should try to project the costs of manufacturing the product and the potential profits from sales.

10. The students who made the prototype should be consulted to learn about possible production problems. They should be able to discuss any parts or assembly tasks that were difficult, dangerous, or needed special tools.

11. Hold a meeting with management, production engineering, marketing, and finance to decide whether the product should be mass produced.

    a. Design engineering should bring information related to the aesthetic appeal of the product.

    b. Marketing should present information on consumer reaction to the product design.

    c. Finance should offer information on manufacturing costs and projected profits from sales.

(Courtesy of Keuffel & Esser Company, Parsippany, NJ 07054)

    d. Production engineering should present information on the ease or difficulty of manufacturing the product.

    e. Management will make the final decision to manufacture the product.

12. If management approves the product, create a set of working drawings, including detail drawings, assembly drawings, and a bill of materials.

13. You will continue to develop your product as you learn about the production engineering processes described in Chapter 13.

RELATED QUESTIONS

1. Why are mock-ups usually made at a reduced scale and from easily worked materials like clay?

2. What are the differences between a mock-up and a prototype?

3. How well did your prototype meet the design criteria you established before you began sketching your product ideas?

4. How can computers reduce the time a manufacturing company spends making mock-ups and prototypes?

CHAPTER 13
Production Engineering Processes

OBJECTIVES

After completing this chapter, you will know about:

■ The importance of production engineering processes in planning a productive system of manufacturing.

■ The methods engineering processes, including operation process charts, flow process charts, and operation sheets.

■ The manufacturing engineering process of plant layout, materials handling, and tooling.

■ The quality control engineering processes.

KEY TERMS

AGV
Bottlenecks
Cycle time
Debugging
Fixed-position layout
Flow process chart
Manufacturing engineering

Materials flowcharts
Materials handling
Methods engineering
Operation process chart
Operation sheet
Pilot run
Plant layout

Process layout
Productivity
Product layout
Tooling
Tooling up
Quality control engineering
Work station

Production Engineering Processes

Three important production engineering processes are methods engineering, manufacturing engineering, and quality control engineering. Each of these is important in planning the manufacture of a product. As the product design is being finished, production engineers start to plan the most efficient manufacturing system possible. They do this by identifying the processes required to make a product and then designing the best combination of tools, machines, processes, and people.

Two key factors in production engineering are productivity and costs. Production engineers try to improve productivity while lowering production costs. **Productivity**, which is a measure of efficiency, is found by dividing the number of products manufactured by some unit of time, usually worker hour, Figure 13-1.

$$PRODUCTIVITY = \frac{PRODUCTS\ MANUFACTURED}{TIME\ (WORKER\ HOUR)}$$

Figure 13-1. Productivity, a measure of manufacturing efficiency, is expressed as the number of products manufactured per worker hour.

The best way to improve productivity is to reduce product cycle time. **Cycle time** is the time between completion of one product and completion of the very next product, Figure 13-2. Each production engineering process focuses on increasing productivity, usually by decreasing cycle time, while lowering production costs.

Methods Engineering Processes

Methods engineering involves planning the sequence of processes needed to make parts and assemble a finished product. These planners create charts that show the product processing sequence graphically. The three most commonly used charts are the operation process chart, the flow process chart, and the operation sheet.

On the operation process and flow process charts, standard graphic symbols, developed by the American Society of Mechanical Engineers (ASME), identify each step, Figure 13-3. These symbols represent the five processes required to manufacture any product. Operations include materials processes, such as drilling, cutting, and assembling. Inspections are checks to make sure that product parts match the dimensions on working drawings. Transportations are the moving of materials or parts from one work station to the next. Delays are times when parts are waiting

◯	OPERATION	Object is changed in any of its physical or chemical characteristics, is assembled, or is disassembled.
▢	INSPECTION	Object is examined for quality or quantity in any of its characteristics.
⇨	TRANSPORTATION	Object is moved from one place to another, except when such movements are part of an operation or inspection.
◗	DELAY	Object is held for the next operation, inspection, or transportation.
▽	STORAGE	Object is kept and protected against unauthorized removal.
◯▢	COMBINED ACTIVITY	When activities are performed concurrently or by the same person at the same work station, the symbols for those activities are combined.

Figure 13-3. The American Society of Mechanical Engineers designed five symbols that can be used to create operation and flow process charts.

for the next process. Storages are when parts or products are held and protected. Methods engineers use the symbols for these processes during their planning.

Operation Process Chart

Methods engineers use the bill of materials, working drawings, and their knowledge of manufacturing processes to create **operation process charts**, Figure 13-4.

Each column on an operation process chart lists, in order, the operations and inspections performed on one part of the product. Transportations, delays, and storages are not included on an operation process chart. The bottoms of the columns are connected to show the assembly of individual parts into a finished product.

Operation process charts identify the number of tools, machines, and people needed to

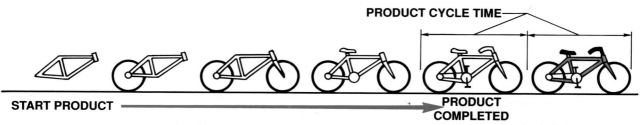

Figure 13-2. Product cycle time is the time between completion of one product and the completion of the very next product.

OPERATION PROCESS CHART

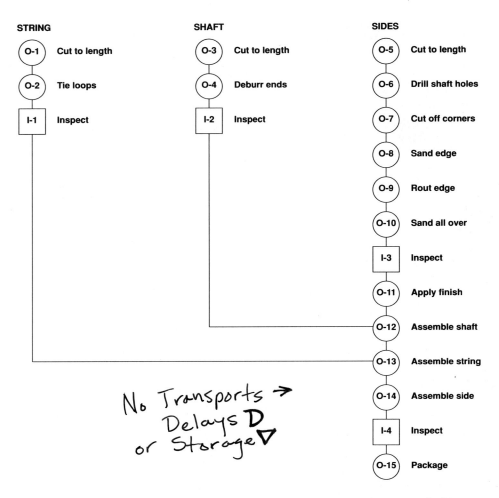

Figure 13-4. The operation process chart identifies all the processes needed to make one product.

make a product. Another purpose is productivity planning. The most productive operation process will have the fewest operations and the shortest cycle time. Several revisions are usually made to an operation process chart. During each revision, the engineer tries to combine or remove processes to reduce product cycle time.

Flow Process Chart

The operation process chart gives only part of the information needed to plan a productive

manufacturing system. The second chart, the flow process chart, gives more detailed information.

While the operation process chart lists the operations and inspections needed to make one complete product, a **flow process chart** lists all the processes needed to make each part in a product, Figure 13-5. One flow process chart is made for each part of a product. The exact order of operations, transportations, inspections, delays, and storages for each part are shown. This gives the engineer a more complete picture of the production system.

FLOW PROCESS CHART

SUMMARY	NO.	TIME		PRODUCT	Widget	DATE	
○ OPERATIONS	7			JOB/PART	Side #2		
⇨ TRANSPORTS	6			CHART BEGINS	O-1		
□ INSPECTIONS	1			CHART ENDS	T-6		
D DELAYS	1	25		CHARTED BY			
▽ STORAGES	0			APPROVED BY			

NO.	SYMBOLS	TASK DESCRIPTION	MACHINE	TOOLING
O-1	●⇨□D▽	Cut to length	Table saw	Stop block
T-1	○➡□D▽	Move to drill press		
O-2	●⇨□D▽	Drill shaft holes	Drill press	Drilling Fixture
T-2	○➡□D▽	Move to bandsaw		
O-3	●⇨□D▽	Cut off corners	Bandsaw	Bandsaw Fixture
T-3	○➡□D▽	Move to disc sander		
O-4	●⇨□D▽	Sand outside edges	Disc sander	Sanding Fixture
T-4	○➡□D▽	Move to routing work station		
O-5	●⇨□D▽	Rout edges	Router	Routing Jig
O-6	●⇨□D▽	Sand all over	Finish sander	
I-1	○⇨■D▽	Inspect shape, size, routing		Gage I-1
T-5	○➡□D▽	Move to finishing work station		
O-7	●⇨□D▽	Apply spray finish	Spray gun	Spray/Dry Rack
D-1	○⇨□●▽	Delay for drying		Spray/Dry Rack
T-6	○➡□D▽	Move to assembly work station		
	○⇨□D▽			
	○⇨□D▽			

Figure 13-5. The flow process chart identifies all the processes needed to make one part of a product.

Flow process charts are used to see how transportation, delay, and storage processes will change product cycle time. As with the operation process chart, engineers usually make several revisions to the flow process chart. With each revision they try to cut out transportations, delays, and storages.

Another factor reviewed with the flow process chart is the time needed for machining operations. During the revision process, engi-neers consider various materials processing options available for each operation. Figure 13-6 shows the potential time-savings for a variety of drilling processes. Methods engi-neers must know the various machining options available to make a product.

The flow process chart also identifies spe-cial equipment needed. Transportation sys-tems, such as conveyors or carts, are one example. A production system might also need

PROCESS TIME	OPTIONS— DRILLING OPERATION
	Worker lays out hole center, clamps stock, drills hole with manual hand drill.
	Center located with drilling jig, worker clamps stock, drills hole with power hand drill.
	Center located with drilling jig, worker clamps stock, drills hole with drill press.
	Center located with drilling jig, automated clamping fixture is used, worker drills hole with drill press.
	All operations automated.

Figure 13-6. Methods engineers must consider materials processing times. This chart shows the time-savings for a variety of drilling operations.

special jigs and fixtures. The flow process chart and a knowledge of machine processes help methods engineers spot the parts that need these special tools.

Operation Sheets

An **operation sheet** details the work to be done at each **work station**. Work stations are the places in a production line where operations occur. These include such places as machines and benches, Figure 13-7. The operation sheet lists the name of the operation, the machine and any special tooling required, and worker directions for layout and machining. Drawings may be included on the operation sheet to show any special setup, clamping, or materials processing procedures.

Manufacturing Engineering Processes

Manufacturing engineering involves planning the layout of tools, machines, and people on a production line. Once the engineers have made the operation process chart and flow process chart, manufacturing engineering can begin. Manufacturing engineers complete three planning tasks—plant layout, materials handling, and tooling.

Plant Layout

The **plant layout** is the arrangement of tools, machines, and other work stations throughout the factory. Manufacturing engineers draw the plant layout on a factory floor plan. The flow of materials and parts from work station to work station is drawn based on the methods engineer's process charts. Plant layout drawings are called **materials flowcharts** or flow diagrams, Figure 13-8. With the materials flowchart, the manufacturing engineer tries to design a smooth, uninterrupted flow of materials.

There are three different types of plant layouts—the fixed position layout, the process layout, and the product layout. Each system has advantages in certain manufacturing situations.

Fixed-position Layout. The **fixed-position layout**, also called the static layout, is used to make very large and complex structures, such as airplanes and ships, Figure 13-9.

The main structure, such as an airplane fuselage, remains in one place on the factory floor. All the workers, their tools, and the airplane components are brought to the main structure, where manufacturing takes place. Before Henry Ford introduced mass production in the early 1900s, cars were made in this way.

Fixed-position manufacturing systems need highly skilled workers and portable tools and machines. This type of manufacturing is best for low-volume custom manufacturing.

Process Layout. In **process layout**, machines and tools used to perform similar processes are grouped together, Figure 13-10. Rough machining processes are performed in the area nearest to receiving. Finish machining processes are performed near storage or shipping.

In a process layout, parts move through the plant in small batches. A batch of parts is machined in one area and then moved to the

OPERATION SHEET

Operation No.: O-5	Product: T.D.V.-12

Operation Name: Storage Hole Drilling

Part Name: Block
Part No.: 1
Quantity: 50
Stock/Material: Pine

Tools/Equipment: Drill Press
3/4" Spade Bit
Brush

Jigs/Fixtures: Jig O-5

Supplies: Inspection Gage O-5

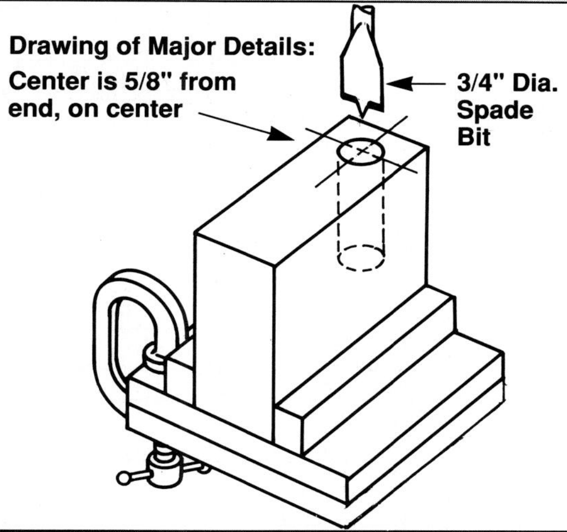

Drawing of Major Details: Center is 5/8" from end, on center — 3/4" Dia. Spade Bit

Operation Description:

Step No.	Description of Step	Materials	Machine	Tools and Equipment
1	Insert part in Jig O-5, turn on machine	Pine	Drill Press	Jig #2 3/4" Spade Bit
2	Drill hole 2.50 inches deep		Drill Press	Jig #2 3/4" Spade Bit
3	Remove part from jig, rotate 180° and drill other hole		Drill Press	Jig #2 3/4" Spade Bit Brush
4	Remove part from jig, inspect hole depth, diameter			Inspection Gage O-5
5	Place acceptable parts on conveyor			

Figure 13-7. The operation sheet details the work performed at a work station.

next area, where processing continues. The batch of parts usually stays in one machining area until all the machining is complete. This creates a long delay for the first part that was processed and a large volume of work in progress. Work in progress includes all partially completed parts or products. In addition to the delay, parts often backtrack through the process layout. This creates excessive and wasteful transportation distances and times.

Manufacturing with a process layout is best for intermittent or batch manufacturing. Since the focus is on manufacturing processes, skilled machinists are required.

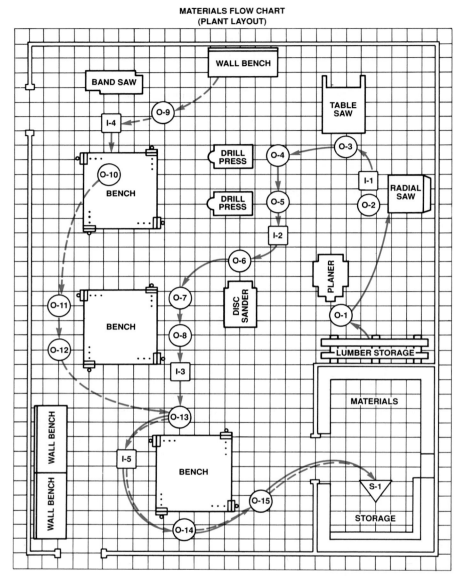

Figure 13-8. The flow of materials through a manufacturing factory is drawn on a materials flowchart.

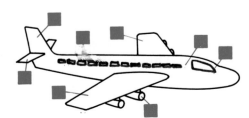

Figure 13-9. The fixed-position layout is used to manufacture large, complex products.

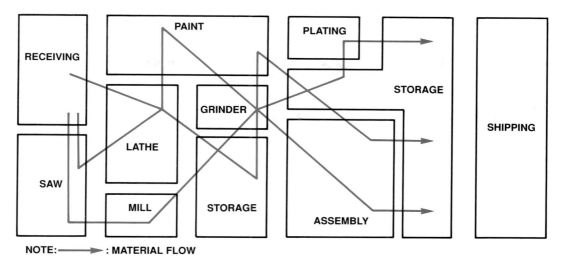

NOTE:——▶ : MATERIAL FLOW

Figure 13-10. Machines that perform similar processes are grouped in a process layout. Materials often backtrack in a process layout.

Product Layout. Product layout is characterized by a continuous flow from raw materials to finished product, Figure 13-11. In general, product layouts use factory floor space more efficiently, have shorter transportation times and distances, and have a shorter product cycle time than fixed position or process layouts.

The product layout was developed by Henry Ford in his mass production techniques. Operations at each work station are broken into their simplest parts. This creates the maximum division of labor. Work stations are arranged to match the sequence of operations identified on the operation and flow process charts. Long, continuous transportation systems, such as conveyor belts, are built between work stations to provide a smooth flow of parts through the factory.

Comparing Process and Product Layouts. Figure 13-12 illustrates the advantage of a product layout over a process layout for a

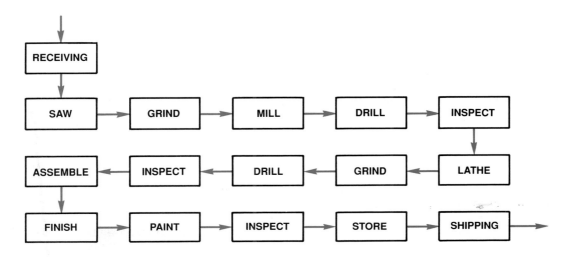

Figure 13-11. In a product layout, raw materials flow through the entire plant to a finished product.

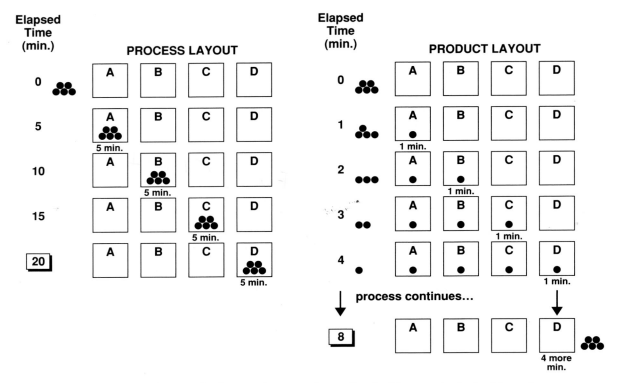

Figure 13-12. Substantial product cycle time savings can be realized with a product plant layout.

five-product cycle time. A batch of five products is manufactured in the process layout. In the product layout, products are processed one at a time. Each product requires four different operations, identified here as A, B, C, and D. The processing time for each operation is one minute per product.

The five-product cycle time for the process layout is twenty minutes, without transportation times. For the product layout, the five-product cycle time is only eight minutes. In this case, the product layout gives a forty percent savings in cycle time. This savings increases productivity, lowers production costs for the company, and lowers product prices for the consumer.

Engineering a Plant Layout. Manufacturing engineers create materials flowcharts to check for backtracking of parts, excessive transportation times and distances, and possible points of traffic congestion. Many revisions are made in the arrangement of work stations to improve efficiency. Because of the many revisions,

machine silhouettes or scale models are often used when engineering a plant layout. Silhouette cutouts of machines and work benches can easily be arranged and rearranged on a factory floor plan, Figure 13-13.

For very complex or automated manufacturing systems, computer-controlled scale models are often used to ensure synchronized timing of operations. The engineer in Figure 13-14 is adjusting the timing of events on a plant layout modeling system.

The main reason for planning a plant layout is to improve productivity. Other reasons include:

1. Safety. The system should be ergonomically designed for maximum worker safety, comfort, and efficiency. The possibility of accidental contact among workers, machines, and transportation systems should be eliminated.

2. Utilities. Work stations that need electricity, gas, or other utilities must be close to a source.

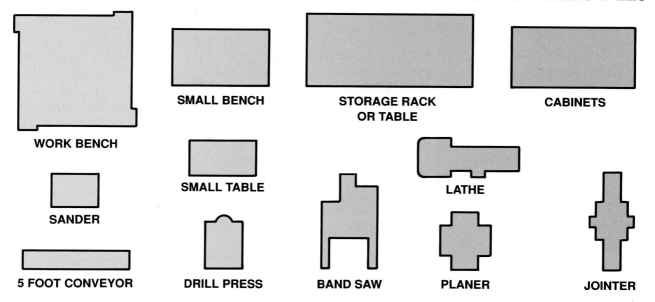

WORK BENCH

SMALL BENCH

STORAGE RACK OR TABLE

CABINETS

SANDER

SMALL TABLE

LATHE

5 FOOT CONVEYOR

DRILL PRESS

BAND SAW

PLANER

JOINTER

Figure 13-13. These silhouettes can be moved around on the factory floor plan to engineer a plant layout.

3. Ventilation. Good ventilation must be provided for work stations where hazardous air contamination, such as painting, sanding, and welding, are created.

4. Lighting. Certain operations, especially detailed assembly tasks, need extra lighting.
5. Waste disposal. Operations that create scrap materials must have a way to dispose waste. Adequate waste disposal is needed for good housekeeping.

Materials Handling

The second manufacturing engineering task involves planning for materials handling. **Materials handling** is the transportation system, such as conveyors and forklifts, that moves materials, supplies, and work in progress through a plant. Once the materials flowchart is created and plant layout begins, materials handling systems can be designed.

The two types of materials handling systems are fixed path and variable path. Fixed-path systems, such as conveyors, rail cars, elevators, tubes, and chutes, move materials on predetermined or fixed routes. Variable-path systems, such as forklifts, tractors, trucks, and cranes, can move materials on random or variable routes.

In general, fixed-path systems work better for continuous manufacturing (product layouts), while variable-path systems work better

Figure 13-14. Many manufacturers use computer-controlled models like this one to design and test a plant layout. *(Courtesy of Ford Motor Company)*

for intermittent manufacturing (process layouts).

Fixed-path systems usually run automatically without an operator. Variable-path systems are more expensive to operate because they need an operator. However, purchasing and installing fixed-path systems is more costly and provides less flexibility in moving materials.

Safety and Materials Handling. Safety is an important consideration in the design and operation of materials handling systems. Fixed-path systems should be located so they are not in the path of workers' movements. Moving parts, such as pulleys, belts, and motors, should be guarded so workers do not come in contact with them accidentally. Safety shut-off buttons are also included near work stations so workers can stop a system in case of an accident. Variable-path vehicles, such as forklifts, often have warning lights and bells so workers are warned of their presence.

Tooling

Tooling is special tools and devices used by production workers to help them make product parts of consistent size, shape, and quality. Tooling is a key factor in producing interchangeable parts. Manufacturing engineers design the tooling.

Types of Tooling. The most common types of tooling include jigs, fixtures, patterns, templates, and special tools. Jigs guide the path of a tool on a part being processed. They are usually attached to the part being processed, or the part is attached to the jig. Fixtures are attached to a machine and are used to position a part being processed in a specific location. A pattern is a copy of a finished part with allowances added for processing. The patterns used to make molds for casting are an example. A template is a two-dimensional outline of a part. A template guides the path of a tool during a layout or machining process. Drawing letters with a stencil template is an example.

AGV: Robotic Materials Handling Systems

One of the newest innovations in materials handling is the AGV. **AGVs**, which stands for automated guidance vehicles, are robotic materials handling systems. These computer-controlled vehicles carry materials and parts through a manufacturing plant without the aid of an operator. AGVs are programmed to follow fixed paths. Ways of identifying the path for an AGV include installing a wire or painting a line on the floor. In the first case, electromagnetic sensors on the AGV follow an electrical current passing through the wire. AGVs that follow painted lines have optical sensors. Some AGVs can be programmed to move on different paths by following lines of different colors.

One of the newest innovations in materials handling is the AGV. (Courtesy of FMC Corp, Materials Handling Systems Division)

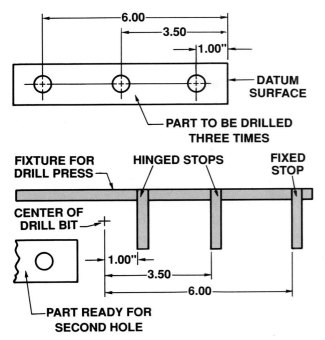

Figure 13-15. Locating drilled holes from a datum surface makes tooling more accurate.

ing out, and processing parts. Tooling must be made to precise tolerances by skilled workers. Accurate tooling is designed to maintain any critical dimensions. Locating the layout of several holes from one surface is an example, Figure 13-15. Being able to adjust tooling is also important to maintaining critical dimensions. The stop on the left in Figure 13-16 cannot be adjusted. By adding a thumb screw, the stop can be adjusted to maintain tolerances. Another factor related to accuracy is chip relief. Tooling should be designed to eliminate chips when they occur during operations.

3. *Safety.* Engineers must always remember the interaction between the worker and tooling. Tooling must be ergonomically designed. Tooling that clamps parts should not catch the fingers of an operator. In addition, clamps should apply enough pressure to keep the part from accidentally being ejected during cutting or drilling operations. However, clamping pressure should not cause parts made from flexible materials to buckle or become distorted.

4. *Speed.* The time needed to set up and use tooling must be kept to a minimum. The best way to keep speed up is to keep tooling simple.

5. *Costs.* The cost of making tooling devices must not be too high. Usually, simple tooling with few parts is inexpensive to make, easy to use, and cheap to maintain.

Any number of special tools might be needed, such as odd-sized drill bits or specially shaped router bits or shaper cutters.

Guidelines for Designing Tooling. Some of the guidelines manufacturing engineers follow when designing tooling include the following.

1. *Ease of operation.* The best tooling devices will have few moving parts and will be simple to set up and use.

2. *Accuracy.* Accurate tooling improves product quality by reducing the possibility of human error in measuring, lay-

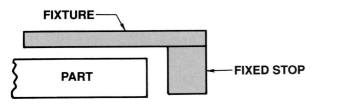

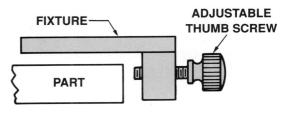

Figure 13-16. Adding a means of adjustment improves the accuracy of tooling.

Illustrating the Importance of Tooling

For an example of the importance of tooling, consider the following situation. A company needs 100 units of the part illustrated here. Without tooling a worker has to measure and lay out the location of each hole before it can be drilled. With tooling, the worker can position the part in a jig or fixture and drill the holes. The measurement and layout operations performed in the first case are built into the tooling.

What are the results? First, the possibility of human error in measuring and laying out four different holes 100 times is reduced. Second, since the possibility of human error is reduced, product quality will probably increase. Third, the time spent in measuring and layout is reduced. This reduces product cycle time, which reduces the costs of the part and final product. Fourth, without tool-

ing, the worker must be skilled in measurement and layout. With tooling, a less skilled worker, who receives less pay, can still do the job.

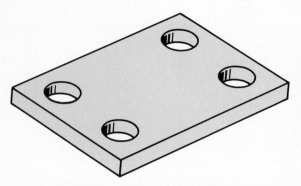

Locating and drilling the four holes on this part can be more accurate and less time-consuming with the use of tooling.

Quality Control Engineering Processes

Quality control engineering, the third type of production engineering, involves ensuring that the finished product matches the design in the working drawings. Quality control makes sure products work as they were designed. This is done by inspecting parts and products.

Quality Inspection

Quality must be built in during the manufacture of a product. It cannot be added in the inspection of a product. Inspections are not a substitute for accuracy in tooling devices and worker performance. Rather, inspections are used to spot problems so that they can be fixed.

Inspection involves measuring a part, comparing the measurement to specifications, and

making a decision about the quality of the match. There are three possible decisions—accept, rework, or reject. Acceptable quality means the part matches the tolerances specified in working drawings. Rework means the part does not match specifications, but it can be fixed. A reject part does not match specifications, cannot be fixed, and must be scrapped or junked.

Inspection Station Locations

There are four places where inspection occurs in manufacturing—incoming materials, purchased parts, work in progress, and finished products, Figure 13-17. The place where a defective part is found can affect the final costs of the product.

If a defect is found in incoming materials or purchased parts, there is no cost to the company. The supplier of the material or part created

Figure 13-17. Quality control inspects incoming materials, work in progress, purchased parts, and finished products.

the defect and must replace the parts. Similarly, if a defect is found immediately after processing, the part can be reworked or rejected. This prevents a defective part from getting in a final product and costs the company relatively little money.

On the other hand, if defects are not identified until after the product is finished, the entire product may have to be scrapped. Disassembling or reworking the defective part can be very costly, if not impossible.

Finally, if a consumer finds a defect, costs are highest. The manufacturing company has already spent money for manufacturing, shipping, and advertising. Depending on the warranty, the entire product might have to be replaced. In addition, the consumer might tell other potential consumers not to buy the manufacturer's products because of poor quality.

The best possible location for inspections would be after each and every operation. This is, of course, impractical and costly because of the number of inspection gages and people involved. The trade-off made is to inspect after operations that involve critical dimensions or parts with important tolerances. Often, accurate tooling will eliminate the need for excessive inspections. Another alternative is to inspect parts at random.

Inspection Gages

Quality inspection is made easier by using gages. The two types are indicating gages and fixed gages. Both types are used to measure parts.

Indicating Gages. With an indicating gage, an inspector measures a part; reads a numerical value (measurement) off the gage; compares the value to specifications; and makes a decision to accept, rework, or reject the part. Common indicating gages include micrometers, dial indicators, and rulers (see Chapter 7).

Fixed Gages. When an inspector measures a part with a fixed gage, it either matches specifications or it does not. Fixed gages have the minimum and maximum tolerance built in. Go–no go gages are an example, Figure 13-18.

Fixed gages reduce the chance of human error in reading measurements. They also

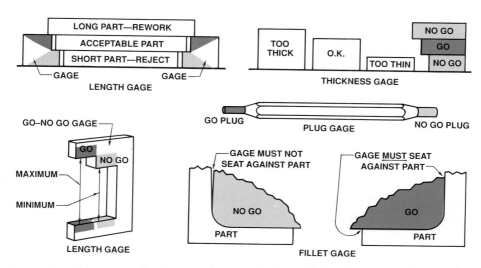

Figure 13-18. Here are fixed gages for quality inspection. Notice the red (no go) and green (go) colors on the gages.

Quality Inspection by Laser

Lasers have been used in manufacturing as quality control inspection devices. The laser can be used to find flaws or mistakes in parts.

The simplest technique is shown in Figure A. The laser illuminates the part. Optical lenses focus the light on a sensor. The sensor sends information about the light pattern to a computer where the light pattern is compared with quality standards that have been programmed into the computer.

Figure B shows a laser being used to check the alignment of parts in an assembly. The laser bounces off the part and reflects through the lenses onto a computer sensor. The location of the reflected light landing on the sensor tells the computer whether the part is within tolerances.

Laser inspection systems are highly precise and consistent in measurement. Many manufacturers use laser inspection systems to improve product quality.

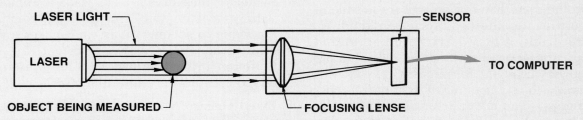

Figure A. This is the simplest type of laser quality control inspection.

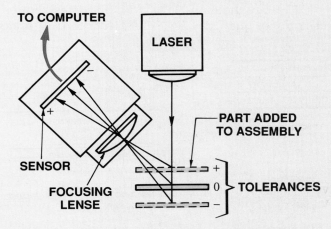

Figure B. Quality control inspection of assembly can be done with a laser.

reduce the time needed for each inspection. Fixed gages must be precisely made to match the tolerances being measured. Adding a means of adjusting or calibrating is often helpful. The screws allow the inspector to calibrate the gage precisely to minimum and maximum tolerances.

Tooling Up: Preparing for Manufacturing

Tooling up is the process of putting workers, the plant layout, tooling, and materials handling systems together in preparation for manufacturing. Engineers and production personnel work together to lay out the plant, set up work stations, and install jigs and fixtures. Once the tools and equipment are in place, the company usually has a pilot run. A **pilot run** is a practice session when the manufacturing systems are tested to make sure all systems are functioning as planned. During the pilot run, a number of factors are checked. These include the timing of events and the accuracy of tooling. Engineers want to find and remove any **bottlenecks** that might develop. A bottleneck is a point in a production line where parts back up and are delayed unintentionally. Bottlenecks extend product cycle time and lower productivity. The process of refining and tuning up the production system is called **debugging**. Once the system has been debugged, the actual manufacturing of products begins.

Summary

Production engineers plan, design, and implement the system that will be used to manufacture a product. Production engineering efforts are directed toward the creation of the most productive system possible. Productivity, which is a measure of efficiency, is best improved by reducing product cycle time and improving accuracy.

The three production engineering processes used to improve productivity are methods engineering, manufacturing engineering, and quality control engineering. Methods engineering involves planning the sequence of operations needed to make a product. Manufacturing engineering involves planning the plant layout, materials handling system, and tooling. Quality control engineering involves planning for the inspection of parts and products.

DISCUSSION QUESTIONS

1. What is production engineering? What are the three different types of production engineering processes discussed in this chapter?

2. What is the definition of productivity? What are three techniques that can be used to increase productivity?

3. How is cycle time important to production engineering processes and productivity?

4. What are the five symbols used on methods engineers' charts? What do the symbols stand for? Who created the symbols?

5. Methods engineers create three charts. What are they? What are the differences among these charts? Why are the charts created?

6. What are the three types of plant layout? How are they similar or different in terms of type of manufacturing done, productivity, and cycle time?

7. What is quality control? What are the two types of inspection gages used in quality control?

CHAPTER ACTIVITIES

☼ METHODS ENGINEERING: PLANNING MANUFACTURING PROCESSES

OBJECTIVE

Methods engineering involves planning the steps needed to manufacture parts and assemble a finished product. As you read in this chapter, methods engineers do their planning by creating a variety of charts. These charts give the engineer a graphic picture of the manufacturing processes needed.

In this activity, you will plan the sequence of processes needed to manufacture a product. You will create an operation process chart, flow process charts, and operation sheets. Before you begin, review the section in this chapter that describes how engineers use these charts.

MATERIALS AND SUPPLIES

1. Working drawings for a product to be mass produced
2. Graph paper
3. Blank flow process chart (handout)
4. Blank operation sheet (handout)
5. Drawing tools

PROCEDURE

1. Work in small methods engineering groups and divide the work load. Your class might also be running some manufacturing engineering and quality control engineering processes at the same time. Each of these engineering groups might need to work together to plan an efficient manufacturing system.
2. You can produce many charts and sheets. In general, the following are required:
   - One comprehensive operation process chart
   - One flow process chart for each part in the product
   - One operation sheet for each critical work station
3. Plan the sequence of processes needed to make each part on the product, including operations, inspections, transportations, delays, and storages.
4. Sketch a rough draft of the operation process chart. Include only the operations and inspections for each part.
5. Meet with your methods engineering group to review and revise the operations. Consult with your teacher on more efficient ways to make the product.
6. Revise your plans and draw a final operation process chart for the product.
7. Consider hiring a communications technology or drafting class to draw the operation process chart.
8. Your class will need one flow process chart for each part. Individual students or pairs can plan the flow process chart for each part.
9. Make a preliminary plan on a blank flow process chart provided by your teacher.

10. Some critical parts might need special tooling, such as jigs or fixtures. You can consult with the design engineer team making the product prototype or with your teacher to identify these parts. Be sure to note these parts on the flow process charts.

11. Work with your teacher to decide which work stations need operation sheets. Work stations where simple processes are performed might not need an operation sheet.

12. The operation sheet should list the step-by-step procedures performed at the work station. It should also give the operator an illustration of the important steps in the operation.

13. Remember three things when making your operation process chart, flow process chart, and operation sheets:
    ■ Planning manufacturing processes with these sheets may require revisions. Methods engineers usually make many revisions to these sheets.
    ■ Planning should aim toward improving productivity by lowering product cycle time and leaving no waste. Try to limit the number of delays, storages, and transportations.
    ■ This may be your first experience with methods engineering. You should choose a simple product for your planning efforts.

MATH/SCIENCE CONNECTION

Productivity is a measure of efficiency in manufacturing. Methods engineers represent productivity by the number of products manufactured over some period of time. The formula for measuring productivity is:

$$\text{Productivity} = \frac{\text{Products Manufactured}}{\text{Time (Worker Hours)}}$$

Productivity is usually expressed as the number of products manufactured for every work hour. As an example, if a manufacturing company made 240 products during an eight-hour shift, its productivity would be expressed as follows:

$$\text{Productivity} = \frac{240 \text{ Products}}{8 \text{ Hours}} \text{ or } \frac{30 \text{ Products}}{1 \text{ Hour}}$$

RELATED QUESTIONS

1. Why do methods engineers create operation process charts, flow process charts, and operation sheets? Could a company manufacture a product without making these?

2. What are the similarities and differences between an operation process chart and flow process chart?

3. What group of engineers develops the symbols used on operation and flow process charts?

4. Why is it important for methods engineers to coordinate their planning efforts with manufacturing engineering and quality control engineering?

MANUFACTURING ENGINEERING: PLANT LAYOUT AND MATERIALS HANDLING SYSTEMS

OBJECTIVE

Two manufacturing engineering tasks are planning the plant layout and implementing materials handling systems. The plant layout for your school manufacturing system will be based on the size and shape of the lab, as well as the type of equipment available. If the equipment in your lab is bolted to the floor, you will probably not be able to move machines to the exact locations desired to create a product layout. Rather, you will probably use a modified process layout.

If you use portable power tools (such as router tables, small drill presses, or a power miter box), they can be located between machines that are bolted down.

Many types of materials handling systems are used in manufacturing. You can make simplified versions of these systems for your school manufacturing lab. Usually, the simplest systems are the best. Figure 1 gives you some ideas for easy-to-make materials handling systems for your lab.

When you create a materials handling system, you must consider the various safety hazards involved. Any powered, moving parts, such as pulleys, belts, gears, or motors, should be guarded. Also, materials handling systems should be located so workers do not accidentally walk into them.

In this activity, you will act as a manufacturing engineer by designing a plant layout. You will then design and manufacture a materials handling system for your production line. The materials handling system will be used during mass-production activities.

MATERIALS AND SUPPLIES

For Plant Layout

1. Floor plan for the manufacturing lab. (If one is not available, sketch a floor plan on graph paper.)
2. Cut out silhouettes or templates for machines, tools, and benches in the lab (handout). Make sure the drawing scale for the machine silhouettes and the floor plan match. A commonly used scale is $1/4" = 1'$.
3. Drawing tools

For Materials Handling Systems

1. Depending on the type of materials handling systems you design and make, you might need the following:
   - electric motors
   - vacuum cleaner
   - gear reduction boxes
   - pulleys and belts
   - conveyor belt material (canvas, heavy cloth, rubber mat)
   - rollers (dowel rods, plastic pipe, conduit, coffee cans)
   - casters
   - various sizes of plywood and lumber
   - various sizes of angle iron and steel

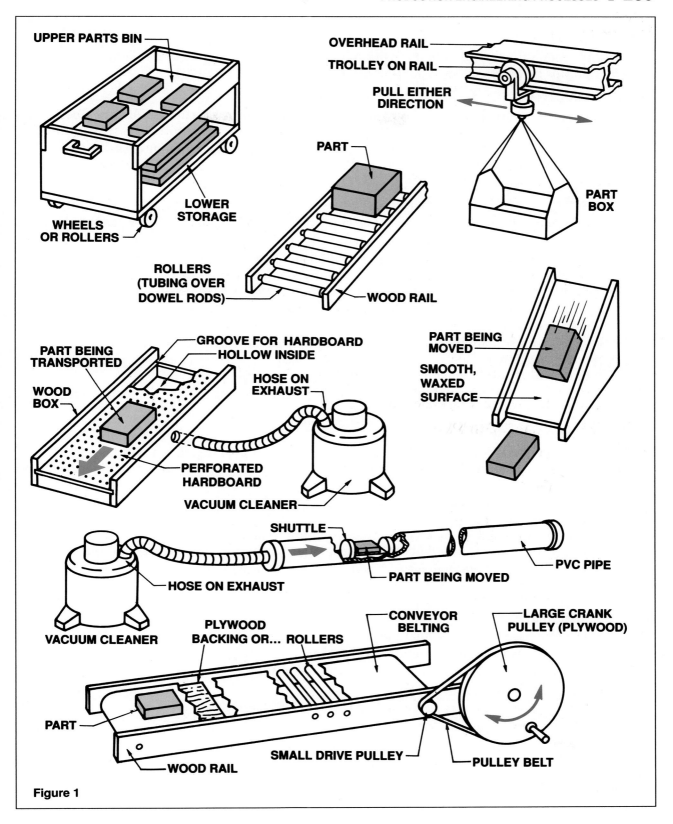

UPPER PARTS BIN

LOWER STORAGE

WHEELS OR ROLLERS

PART

ROLLERS (TUBING OVER DOWEL RODS)

WOOD RAIL

OVERHEAD RAIL

TROLLEY ON RAIL

PULL EITHER DIRECTION

PART BOX

GROOVE FOR HARDBOARD

HOLLOW INSIDE

PART BEING TRANSPORTED

WOOD BOX

HOSE ON EXHAUST

PERFORATED HARDBOARD

VACUUM CLEANER

PART BEING MOVED

SMOOTH, WAXED SURFACE

SHUTTLE

HOSE ON EXHAUST

PART BEING MOVED

PVC PIPE

VACUUM CLEANER

PLYWOOD BACKING OR... ROLLERS

CONVEYOR BELTING

LARGE CRANK PULLEY (PLYWOOD)

PART

WOOD RAIL

SMALL DRIVE PULLEY

PULLEY BELT

Figure 1

PROCEDURE

Work in small groups to divide the work load. One group can engineer the plant layout. Other groups can work on several different materials handling systems.

For Plant Layout

1. To engineer a plant layout, start with the operation process chart, a factory floor plan, and silhouettes for available equipment.
2. Design an efficient materials flowchart. Try to avoid backtracking, cross traffic, excessive transportation distances, and delays.
3. Keep these needs in mind:
   - Safety: Keep workers safe from moving machine parts.
   - Utilities: Do not lay extension cords across the path of traffic. Place machines close to needed utilities.
   - Ventilation: Place finishing and other operations that create hazardous contamination in well-ventilated areas.
   - Illumination: Be sure to provide enough lighting for detailed tasks.
   - Waste Disposal: Include waste cans in your layout. Scraps that build up can become a hazard.
4. Once you have planned a materials flowchart on paper, verify the efficiency of your plan by making a scale model. If you move machines and benches into place, you will be able to see how well your plan works.
5. Hold an evaluation meeting with production workers and management. Look for any unsafe conditions in your plan. Can you make any improvements?

For Materials Handling Systems

1. Review the flow process charts and materials flowchart. These charts will help you decide what materials handling systems you will need. Certain machines might be bolted down in your lab. If you are sure parts will flow between them, start designing materials handling systems for these machines first. You won't need to wait for the materials flowchart to be finished.
2. Focus on making two or three different materials handling systems. Try to make both fixed-path and variable-path systems. Figure 1 gives you some design ideas.
3. Remember these potential safety hazards as you plan your materials handling system.
   - A conveyor belt that moves too fast can shoot parts off the end and hit workers standing nearby.
   - Moving parts should be guarded.
   - Safety shut-off switches should be provided.
   - Variable-path vehicles should have warning lights or signals.

MATH/SCIENCE CONNECTION

Conveyor travel speed. The speed of movement for conveyor belts is given in feet per second. Short conveyors can travel four feet per second (4 ft./sec.), while longer belts can travel faster. A conveyor that moves too fast can create many safety hazards.

Converting conveyor travel speed to miles per hour. A rate of speed measured in feet per second is hard for people to visualize. We relate more easily to miles per hour. Feet per second can be converted to miles per hour with the following formula:

$$\text{Miles per Hour} = \frac{\text{feet}}{\text{second}} \times \frac{1 \text{ mile}}{5280 \text{ feet}} \times \frac{3600 \text{ seconds}}{1 \text{ hour}}$$

As an example:

$$\text{Miles per Hour} = \frac{4 \text{ feet}}{1 \text{ second}} \times \frac{1 \text{ mile}}{5280 \text{ feet}} \times \frac{3600 \text{ seconds}}{1 \text{ hour}}$$

Miles per Hour = 2.727

Gear reductions. Most electric motors turn too fast to be hooked directly to the drive roller on a conveyor system. Often, a gear reduction box or a system of pulleys and belts must be used to reduce the speed of the motor. Gear reductions are expressed as ratios, such as 2:1. The number on the left is the speed or number of revolutions of input, while the number on the right is the speed of output. If a gear reduction box has a 2:1 ratio, then every two revolutions of the motor (input) will turn the device attached to the gear box once.

RELATED QUESTIONS

1. What are the differences among fixed position, process, and product plant layouts?
2. Which engineers plan the plant layout and materials handling systems?
3. What are the advantages and disadvantages of fixed-path and variable-path materials handling systems?
4. What are some safety considerations related to the design and use of materials handling systems in manufacturing?

CHAPTER 14

Organization, Ownership, and Management Systems

OBJECTIVES

After completing this chapter, you will know about:

- The advantages and disadvantages of five different types of ownership.
- The organization of a basic corporation and the expanding role of corporations worldwide.
- The role of philosophy in determining ownership and management systems.
- The four primary jobs of managers.
- The importance of the concepts behind total quality control in manufacturing today.

KEY TERMS

Assets
Board of directors
Buy-outs
Bylaws
Controlling
Cooperative
Corporation
Directing
Dividends
Employee Stock Ownership
  Plans (ESOPs)

Export zones
Individual proprietorship
Inventory control
Investors
Liability
Management
Multinational corporation
Organizing
Partnership
Planning
Production control

Proxy
QC circles
Quality control
Stockholders
Stocks
Total quality control

Organization and Ownership

Every manufacturing enterprise must have a system of organization based on ownership and the relationship between owners and workers. Without some type of organization, it is questionable whether anything could be commercially produced. Somehow capital (money) must be raised. Appropriate buildings, tools, and materials must be acquired. And workers must be trained before production can begin. Of course, depending on the scale (size) of the enterprise, the amount and complexity of planning varies greatly.

Organization, ownership, and management of a manufacturing enterprise are part of an ongoing process that begins well before production. Organization and ownership decisions are basic to starting any type of business. The process of managing all the inputs of a company is central to the success or failure of the overall manufacturing system.

Figure 14-1. The individual proprietorship is the oldest form of business ownership. *(Photo by David Tuttle)*

The type of ownership and organization appropriate for a manufacturer depends on many factors. Some of the most important factors include

- the desired rate of production,
- the desired quality of the product,
- the amount of capital needed to start up, and
- the goals and philosophy of the individuals involved.

All of these factors are related. The desired rate of production and the desired quality of the product determine the amount of capital needed to get started. But the very foundation of choosing an ownership and organization system depends on the goals and philosophy of the individuals involved. The primary goal might be to make the largest profit possible, or to make the highest quality product possible, or to provide the most jobs possible, or simply to provide a good product at a reasonable cost to the consumer. Usually, the goal is a combination of these considerations and others that help determine the philosophic foundation of a business.

Individual Proprietorship

The least complicated type of ownership system is the **individual proprietorship**, Figure 14-1. This is a business owned by one person. It is the oldest form of ownership. It is still an important part of the economic structure in many parts of the world, especially in developing countries. In more developed countries, the role played by individual proprietorships has decreased markedly because of the amount of capital often necessary in manufacturing. Exceptions to this trend include craftspeople and artists like potters, jewelry-makers, and small-scale canning and clothing industries, Figure 14-2. Many individual proprietorships operate in the owner's home. Although individual proprietors in manufacturing usually produce a relatively small amount of products, they are often unique and of higher quality than mass-produced items. They also might cost more.

Figure 14-2. The individual proprietorship in manufacturing is mostly limited to craftspeople and cottage industries. *(Photo by Edith Raviola)*

Individual proprietorships offer two big advantages: they are easy to form and the owner has complete control over the operation. In addition, all the profits go to the sole proprietor.

The same advantages listed above can also be disadvantages for individual proprietors. Although the sole owner has the power to make all the decisions, he or she might not have enough knowledge and experience to handle all situations. And just as all profits may go into the pocket of the individual proprietor, all losses must come out of the same pocket, Figure 14-3. The owner has the **liability** for all debts of the business. Liability means responsibility. In the case of individual proprietors, if the business fails, creditors could take personal as well as business property to cover debts. In addition, it is often difficult to get loans because if something happens to the proprietor, the business no longer exists. In this sense, individual proprietorships can be rather unstable and often subject to **buy-outs**.

Partnership

A **partnership** is made up of at least two people who become co-owners of a business. As such, they share all of the profits. There can be any number of partners in a business partnership. A partnership can be formed in a written agreement or through an oral understanding between the people involved, Figure 14-4. There are two kinds of business partnerships—general and limited.

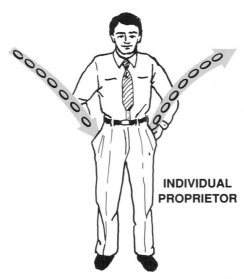

INDIVIDUAL
PROPRIETOR

Figure 14-3. The individual proprietor is directly affected by both profits and losses.

Figure 14-4. A partnership lessens the risk on the individuals involved. *(Courtesy of Cowen and Lobel)*

General Partnerships. The general partnership plays a large role in our economic system as well as those in most parts of the world. Each partner has full power to make decisions that bind the partnership as a whole. In this way, partners are also proprietors except that their actions affect all partners equally.

The general partnership has many of the same advantages as the individual proprietorship. It is easy to form and organize. Partners have full control of the business and the profits. In addition, it is usually easier for a partnership system of ownership to obtain capital. More people are liable for the business, so more credit may be available from **investors**. Investors are lending institutions, such as banks, or individuals with an interest in the company and money to invest, Figure 14-5.

There are also some disadvantages to a general partnership. The most serious one is that each partner has unlimited liability for the company. The decisions of one partner affect all partners equally. For example, if one partner commits the company to produce more than is possible or borrows more money than the company can pay back, all partners are held equally responsible. They might even have to pay out of their own pockets and personal property.

Figure 14-5. Banks and other financial institutions often put up the capital necessary for starting a business. *(Photo by Sonya Stang and Brent Miller)*

In any general partnership, all partners need to get along with each other. All decisions should be made as a group, with complete agreement and in writing. Disagreement can lead to a feeling of mistrust between partners. Mistrust can often bring disaster to the company.

Limited Partnerships. As you just read, the most serious disadvantage of the general partnership is the partners' unlimited liability. The limited partnership was created to attract investors who want to avoid such a risk. The limited partnership is made up of one or more general partners and one or more limited partners. The liability of the limited partners stops at the amount of capital they invest in the company. The limited partners are part-owners and receive a share of the profits. However, their limited liability status means that they do not have control over the management of the business or a voice in company decisions. The limited partner is a silent partner.

The main advantage of a limited partnership is that it can attract capital from investors who do not want unlimited liability. The personal assets of limited partners are not at risk in this type of ownership system, and the general partners might find it easier to raise capital this way.

The Corporation

The most popular form of ownership in developed countries is the **corporation**. Since the corporation is simply a form of ownership, any size business can incorporate, Figure 14-6. Corporations usually have many part-owners, called **stockholders**. Stockholders are individuals who invest in a company by buying **stocks**. Stocks represent actual ownership of a percentage of the business.

Large corporations may have thousands or hundreds of thousands of stockholders. Sometimes a single stockholder may own fifty-one percent of the stock of a corporation. This person can then make management decisions. Frequently, however, no one stockholder owns more than one percent of the stock. In such cases, the management of the corporation

Figure 14-6. Even small businesses can incorporate.
(Photo by Sonya Stang and Brent Miller)

sends out a **proxy**. A proxy is a signed declaration allowing the management to vote and make decisions as they see fit.

The advantage of becoming a stockholder is that individual liability stops at the amount of the stock investment. Liability is spread among many individuals who will lose only their stock value if the corporation fails. They will not lose any of their other personal property. Shares of stock can be easily traded without affecting the day-to-day operation of the

Figure 14-7. Stock is purchased and sold on Wall Street. *(Courtesy of New York Stock Exchange, Inc.)*

corporation, Figure 14-7. As a result, a corporation can easily raise the capital it needs to operate and grow.

Stockholders are the true owners of the corporation. They have some power both individually and as a group. As individuals they have the following rights:

- To receive their **dividends** (profits)
- To vote in stockholders' meetings
- To share in the **assets** (property) of the corporation if it fails
- To sell their stock or buy more
- To look at the records of the corporation

As a group, stockholders can participate in the following:

- Adopting and changing the **bylaws** (rules for guiding the management of the corporation)
- Electing the board of directors
- Selling the assets of the corporation
- Amending (changing) the charter with the consent of the state where the company was incorporated.
- Dissolving the corporation.

Board of Directors. The stockholders elect a **board of directors** who have final say in all corporate matters not reserved for stockholders. They are more directly involved with the overall policies and management of the corporation. There is no set number of directors, but state laws usually set a minimum number that varies from three to twenty, Figure 14-8. The term of office is typically three years, but directors are often re-elected over and over and serve many years on the board. Specific duties of the board of directors include

- electing the corporate officers including the president, vice-presidents, and so on;
- negotiating contracts for the corporation;
- paying dividends to stockholders;
- issuing corporate stock; and
- setting corporate policy.

All of these duties are important to the success of a corporation. Especially important are

Figure 14-8. Here is the board of directors of Woodward Governor Company. *(Photo by James Orlando)*

negotiating contracts and making corporate policy. It has become common in recent years for individuals to represent more than one board of directors at the same time. If these corporations are in any way related or competitive, a conflict of interest could arise. For example, an individual might serve on the

board of directors for a chemical manufacturing company and on the board for a company that runs a television network. Suppose the chemical manufacturer was creating a pollution problem through its waste disposal system. It might not serve this company's best interest if the public learns of this pollution problem. The board member in this situation has a conflict of interest. He or she might try to prevent news coverage of the problem, which would leave the public unaware. Some states have laws that prevent people from serving on more than one board of directors.

Corporate Officers. The board of directors is in charge of electing the corporate officers. The corporate executives in a manufacturing enterprise usually include the president, vice president(s), secretary, and treasurer, Figure 14-9.

The president must carry out the policies of the board of directors. This leader guides the other executives and reports to the board on how their policies are working and how business is in general.

A vice president was originally elected to take over for the president, if the need should arise. Large corporations usually have several vice presidents in charge of different functions, including the actual manufacture of the product or its marketing. The person designated to take over for the president is usually called the executive vice president.

BASIC ORGANIZATION OF A CORPORATION

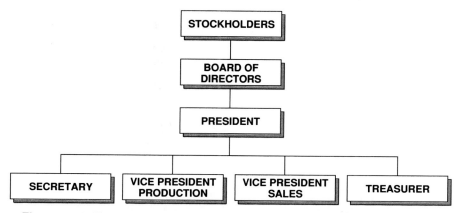

Figure 14-9. This is the basic organization of a corporation.

The secretary performs legal tasks that include filing reports with state and federal governments, keeping a list of stockholders, recording stock transfers, and notifying stockholders and board members of meetings.

The treasurer keeps all of the financial records, accounting for all corporate funds, and gives reports of the accounts to executives and board members.

The advantages of incorporating include the following:

- Clearly defined laws regulating the formation and organization of a corporation
- Limited liability on the part of stockholders
- Shares of stock easily traded without affecting the stability of the corporation
- comparably easy-to-raise capital

The main disadvantages of incorporating are as follows:

- There is state and federal control through taxes, laws, and reports.
- Stockholders may have little or no interest in the corporation beyond the amount of their dividend (profit).
- Profits are taxed twice, first as income to the corporation and again as income to individual stockholders.

Multinational Corporations. Multinational corporations are corporations located in several different countries. Most multinationals move their manufacturing enterprises to developing countries like Mexico, Taiwan, South Korea and the Philippines, Figure 14-10. The cost of labor in these countries is often a fraction of what it would be in developed countries. Host countries attract multinationals by promising special tax breaks and location in special **export zones**. Export zones may be exempt from local laws and regulations. Many developing countries do not have laws regulating worker health and safety or environmental protection laws. All of these incentives help lower the cost of production and increase profits for the corporation. The impacts of multinational corporations on people and our natural environment are discussed in more detail in Section Five.

Cooperatives

A **cooperative** is a form of private ownership that combines some of the aspects of the partnership with those of the corporation, but it has a completely different philosophic base. The cooperative is a form of worker ownership. In a cooperative, the workers not only own shares of the company, but also have an equal voice in its operation. They can also vote for the board of directors and take an equal share in the profits. In a true cooperative, all the workers get the same salary, regardless of their job. There is job rotation and job sharing so that no one always has the easiest or most difficult job. This helps to promote cooperation and to prevent job boredom, Figure 14-11. Furthermore, it helps workers understand the total operation and makes them valuable contributors to the cooperative.

Although not nearly as common as the other forms of ownership, the cooperative has been around for a long time. The first recorded producers' cooperative in this country was a smithy (a metal worker such as a horsesmith) that was bought out and run by its workers in the 1790s. Since then, many successful and

Figure 14-10. Multinational corporations have operations in more than one country and, in some cases, in many diverse parts of the world. *(Courtesy of Nalco Chemical Co.)*

Figure 14-11. A cooperative is a form of worker ownership. *(Courtesy of Southern States Cooperative, Inc.)*

not so successful cooperative ventures have been tried. Recently, a large corporation chose to shut down its asbestos mine in northern Vermont. The workers managed to raise two million dollars to take over the plant. They installed new pollution control devices, something the corporate owners had been unwilling to do. They kept production going smoothly. Within a year they had paid off their debts, paid out a 100 percent dividend to all worker-owners, and increased wages by nearly twenty percent. The dramatic turnaround was attributed to better attitudes and increased productivity because of increased worker motivation.

Cooperatives have proven that worker-owned companies can be successful over a long period of time. They also have shown that people can work together in a competitive world. Work democracy and self-government do not threaten successful business operation. In fact, worker ownership creates a sense of work pride and satisfaction often missing in other forms of ownership and management.

Employee Stock Ownership Plans

Employee stock ownership plans (ESOPs) are a form of worker ownership created by the federal government. ESOPs encourage corpora-

tions to give shares of stock to workers. In return, corporations receive tax breaks and investment privileges.

An ESOP begins with a trust set up for employees by a corporation. It consists of shares of stock that represent partial ownership of the company. However, the stock issued to employees is usually nonvoting stock, stock that will be voting stock only after a certain number of years, or stock that is controlled by a trustee appointed by management. In addition, most companies that use ESOPs do not turn over a controlling number of stocks (greater than fifty percent). Therefore, even with voting rights, the workers might not have much decision-making power.

Management

Individual proprietorships, partnerships, corporations, cooperatives, and ESOPs are different forms of ownership with a common need. They all need a system of setting goals and organizing people to meet those goals. During the early 1900s, Frederick Taylor learned as an apprentice and as a factory worker that productivity could be much higher if the operations were managed rather than just allowed to happen. He was concerned with the fact that workers were allowed to perform their jobs as they liked without having any standard method or procedure. Frederick Taylor's concerns led to his studies of work efficiency and to a general concern for management of manufacturing enterprise.

More recently, **management** has been defined as accomplishing goals through the work of others, Figure 14-12. It is concerned with the direction, coordination, and effort of people. People involved in management are called managers. In a traditional manufacturing enterprise, there are managers at all levels of an organization. Their jobs, their authority, and the problems they solve are all very different.

Ownership and Management

Prior to and during most of the Industrial Revolution, it was common for the owners of companies also to be the managers. As companies

Figure 14-12. Efficient, effective management is achieved through accomplishment of set goals through the work of others. *(Courtesy of Motorola Government Electronics Group)*

incorporated, a distinction between owners and managers evolved. As a result, many managers hold little or none of the stock of the company, but must accept responsibility for achieving the corporation's goals.

Of course, many small corporations are almost wholly owned and managed by one person. This person wears two hats, one as owner and one as manager.

The Functions of Management

All of the concerns of a manufacturing enterprise—engineering, purchasing, production, selling—require managing. The functions of management are generally defined as planning, organizing, directing, and controlling. This is true for whatever activity is being managed. In addition, the hiring and firing of employees is a function of management.

Planning. Planning is deciding what to do and how to do it. It demands the ability to analyze the conditions of a situation and make decisions about it. Managerial planning requires an understanding of the technical aspects of the operations being managed. This includes the tools, machines, materials, and processes. Other areas of management in a typical manu-

facturing enterprise might include engineering, accounting, and marketing.

Production planning is concerned with controlling the work-in-progress. Specific objectives of production planning are to establish routes and schedules for work that will ensure the most efficient use of tools, machines, materials, and people. Much of the planning and scheduling necessary for efficient production are done by process and production engineers. Engineering specifications, route sheets, schedule charts, PERTs, and other production planning strategies are discussed in Chapter 13.

There are two kinds of planning—long range and short range. Long-range planning involves trying to meet the long-range objectives of the company. This type of planning asks for futuristic thinking and realistic steps toward the company's objectives. Some companies have long-range objectives that span beyond five years. This type of planning is necessary if a company is to enjoy a long and profitable life.

Short-range planning involves the meeting of day-to-day and week-to-week objectives. Effective short-range planning is necessary in order to meet long-range objectives. Generally, the shorter the time period involved, the more specific the planning must be.

Organizing. Organizing a group of individuals to work together to achieve the goals of a manufacturer is also the work of managers. The main objective of the manufacturing organization is to develop an efficient teamwork system, Figure 14-13, page 252. Ideally, the organization of a manufacturing enterprise should prove that the whole is greater than the sum of its parts.

Organization of a company is based on the system of ownership and the production philosophy of the individuals involved. For example, a corporation is organized very differently from a cooperative. Regardless of which system is used and what philosophy is adapted, the organization must be clear and practical. All who work within that organization must understand how they fit in and contribute to the product. If parts of the organization do not

Participative Management

The small Quebec town of Bromont is increasingly becoming known as the home of the most advanced manufacturing facilities in Canada. The Canadian General Electric Company Bromont Compressor Airfoil Plant has been manufacturing compressor airfoils for the McDonnell Douglas DC-10, the Boeing 747, and the A-310 Airbus. Although the Bromont plant is full of sophisticated robots, machine vision, laser marking, and voice-entry data systems, the Bromont experiment goes far beyond technology. At its heart lies a radically different approach to organizing the workplace.

The system, called participatory management, is based on a set of positive assumptions about human nature. The basic tenet is that the more workers are required to be fully involved and solve the problems associated with their jobs, the less supervision and management are necessary. In order to create a sense of belonging, teams of workers are formed based on the plant's main production operations, machining, forging, and pinch and role.

Once production goals are set, the teams have the freedom to determine the best means to achieve them. In addition, the teams make their own rules, with plantwide regulations kept to a minimum. Teams also participate in the hiring process by being present at interviews and reserving the right to veto any new hire. This practice enhances team cohesiveness.

New employees go through a five-month training program. The program is designed to familiarize them not only with their own job responsibilities, but also with the entire manufacturing process and the plant management system. Employees are expected to master more than one skill, a policy known as multiskilling. Multiskilling at Bromont extends all the way to the top levels of management. It even includes the plant manager, who often lends a hand on the factory floor.

The entire work force at the Bromont plant is salaried. Enabling employees to share in the organization's success is critical in a participative system. Rather than the more common profit sharing system of employee participation, Bromont uses a system of gain sharing. Gain sharing rewards workers for cutting costs and production times. Productivity gains are translated into a dollar value. This is then divided according to the percentage of the total plantwide hours an individual has worked. The result is to foster a spirit of cooperation that involves the entire work force.

Size is a potential limiting factor for the Bromont style of participatory management system. Bromont employs about 400 people. It is believed that a plant of more than 800 would not be able to use this system. In addition, regions with a strong union influence might be more confined by work rules and job classifications. Proponents of the participatory management system at the Bromont plant stress that the main requirements of such a system are a fundamental change in attitude and a great deal of hard work.

Figure 14-13. Developing cooperation and teamwork in the workplace is an organizational goal of management. *(Reprinted courtesy of Eastman Kodak Company)*

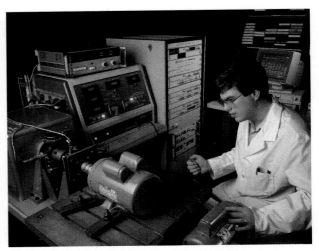

Figure 14-14. To ensure quality performance and accurate specifications, an engineer performs product evaluation on a motor. *(Courtesy of W. W. Grainger, Inc.)*

know how to work well together, the whole could turn out to be less than the sum of its parts.

Directing. Directing is actually the guiding and motivating of workers. Another word often associated with directing responsibilities is supervision. However, it has been proven over and over that effective supervision begins with positive motivation of workers. In general, workers perform better when they know what is expected of them and when they have good working knowledge of their task(s). They also appreciate knowing how their job fits into the total scheme of things. In addition, workers have shown that they perform better when they have some authority or decision-making power. Workers who feel they have some responsibility want to contribute to making the highest quality product possible, Figure 14-14.

Controlling. Controlling people, materials, machines, and money is essential in a manufacturing company. Regardless of what is being controlled, there are four steps that are followed.

1. There must be a plan or standard to be met.
2. A record of actual performance must be kept.
3. Actual performance must be compared with the plan.
4. When actual performance does not meet the plan, corrective action must be taken.

Generally, control is divided into three areas—**inventory control**, **production control**, and **quality control**.

Inventory control. Inventory control is the actual steps taken to maintain proper levels of raw materials and finished goods, Figure 14-15. Proper levels vary depending on the type of manufacturing system. For example, intermittent manufacturing enterprises typically have a very large inventory of raw materials. Just-in-time manufacturers try to have little or no inventory on hand at any one time. In either case, the accurate control of inventory affects both the production and the quality control of the operation.

Production Control. The role of production control is to ensure the optimum use of workers, materials, and machines to meet customer orders and delivery schedules, Figure 14-16. Production control involves routing the work through the plant, determining the production standards to be met, scheduling all phases of the work, monitoring the actual production

Figure 14-15. Inventory control affects both the production and the quality control of a manufacturing enterprise. *(Courtesy of Polytech, Inc.)*

called quality control. The quality standards adopted by a company should be determined by the consumer. Consumers usually decide which products to buy based on the cost of the product, consumer reactions, what country the product was made in, warranties, and the value of what one gets for what one pays. Therefore the manufacturer must design a product that will meet or exceed the standards that are acceptable by consumers. They must maintain that quality throughout the process and then react to consumer feedback about the product. All of this is part of a solid quality control program.

Quality control prevents defects in products and ensures that items are made properly the first time, Figure 14-17. Determining and maintaining the quality of products has traditionally been the job of a team of quality experts called inspectors. Quality inspectors may inspect all or just a certain percentage of the products. This might be done before or after certain steps in the manufacturing process, after the products are completed, or randomly throughout.

standards, and taking corrective measures or replanning if the standards are not being met. A rule of thumb reminds managers that the least control that accomplishes the objective is the best control.

Quality Control. Manufacturers have certain standards for the quality of their products. The steps they take to meet these standards are

Figure 14-16. Production control ensures the optimum use of workers, materials, and machines. *(Courtesy of AMP Incorporated)*

Figure 14-17. This employee keeps a watchful eye on quality on a half-gallon carton-filling line. *(Reprinted by permission of Dean Foods Company, © 1988. All rights reserved.)*

Figure 14-18. The Challenge Circle is just one of thousands of QC circles that are making important contributions to Toyota's operations. *(Courtesy of International Public Affairs Dept.)*

More recently, a system of **total quality control** has been gaining popularity as a more efficient method of maintaining quality. The system of total quality control has helped companies manufacture high-quality products in many parts of the world. Perhaps most noted for its use of this system is Japan. The idea behind total quality control is that quality in manufacturing starts with the attitude of each individual employee. Quality-mindedness in employees is not always easy to attain. The basic premise of this method is based on the philosophy that involvement of employees in the solving of quality problems will improve the overall quality of the product.

QC circles are composed entirely of workers who meet weekly to discuss and solve quality problems. They investigate causes, recommend changes, and take corrective action. All members receive training in problem analysis, brainstorming, and information collection and display techniques, Figure 14-18. In this way, workers are motivated to take pride in their work and become involved in maintaining quality standards. Waste from defectively made products is reduced dramatically, while productivity and quality are increased. The use of QC circles is being implemented by industries all over the world.

Summary

The system of ownership that is most appropriate for a manufacturing enterprise depends on many factors. Among the most important are the desired rate of production, the desired quality of the product, and the philosophy of the individuals involved. The five ownership systems described in this chapter include individual proprietorships, partnerships, corporations, cooperatives, and ESOPs. Besides ownership, all of these differ in scale, liability, complexity, worker responsibility, and basic philosophy. The corporation is the most common form of ownership in developed countries today, although both individual proprietorships and partnerships are still common. Cooperatives and ESOPs are alternatives that encourage worker ownership and involvement.

Management is a system of setting goals and organizing people to meet those goals. There are many different areas that need to be managed. These include production, accounting, marketing, and engineering. Regardless of what area is being managed, there are four major activities with which managers must be concerned. These include planning (both long range and short range), organizing, directing, and controlling.

Quality control is a major part of any manufacturing enterprise. Effective quality control can mean profit or loss for a company. Recently the trend has been toward the system of total quality control that involves workers in controlling the quality of their own work.

DISCUSSION QUESTIONS

1. Which type of business ownership is most common in your area? Why?
2. How do corporations raise money, and why is this easier for corporations than other types of ownership?
3. Why can there be a conflict of interest if a single individual is a board member for two competing companies?
4. Is there a food co-op or other cooperative business in your area? If so, what makes it different from other businesses?
5. Why do so many corporations go multinational? What potential problems do you see associated with this trend?
6. What is the difference between long-range planning and short-range planning?
7. What does a manager in manufacturing plant do?
8. Why is quality control important? Describe the system of total quality control.

CHAPTER ACTIVITIES

✸ STARTING A BUSINESS ENTERPRISE

OBJECTIVE

When you have finished this activity, you will be familiar with the procedures for starting a business, whether it is an individual proprietorship, a partnership, a corporation, or a cooperative. You will also know about the laws that affect each of these business ownership forms in your state.

MATERIALS AND SUPPLIES

1. Paper and pencils
2. Telephone book
3. Telephone
4. Transportation (if necessary)

PROCEDURE

1. Working alone or in small groups, select a product to manufacture. Try to select a product that is familiar and readily available for close inspection.
2. Make a list of goals and a statement of philosophy for the manufacture of your product. Include
   - desired rate of production;
   - type of manufacturing system (continuous, intermittent, job lot, etc.);
   - desired quality;

- amount of capital necessary for start-up;
- number of workers;
- any other considerations that you think will affect your product.

3. Based on the information stated above, select the ownership and organization system that seems to fit your needs the best.

4. Make a list of start-up steps, including
   - all laws, regulations, and local ordinances that apply to forming your business enterprise. You can look for this information at your local chamber of commerce or in the library. You might also talk to local business people for information.
   - the amount of money you need and possible sources for it.
   - the number of workers you need, their working conditions, and benefits.
   - descriptions of the tools, materials, and processes necessary to manufacture the product.
   - long- and short-term goals for the company.

MATH/SCIENCE CONNECTION

Math skills are central to operating any business. Regardless of the type of business enterprise, a sound working knowledge of accounting and bookkeeping is a necessity. Often, a person who specializes in these areas is hired to maintain the books and keep track of the financial matters for the enterprise.

RELATED QUESTIONS

1. How does the ownership of a company affect the way it acquires start-up money? How can different types of ownership make raising money easier?

2. Why has the corporation become the most common form of business organization and ownership?

3. The laws and regulations for starting a business vary from state to state. Do you think the laws in your state would attract certain industries? Why or why not?

4. Why has individual proprietorship become less common in the United States?

5. List a local business that is
   - an individual proprietorship
   - a partnership
   - a corporation
   - a cooperative
   - An ESOP company

 ## CORPORATE CHARTER AND BYLAWS

OBJECTIVE

The activities of a corporation are controlled by three things: the statutes (laws) in the state where the corporation was formed; the corporation's charter (or articles of incorporation); and the corporation's bylaws. In this activity, you will draft the necessary documents, as listed above, to form a corporation.

MATERIALS AND SUPPLIES

1. Handout on organizing a corporation
2. Paper and pencils

**ARTICLES
OF
INCORPORATION
of**

Mighty Manufacturing Co.
(name of corporation)

With principal offices to be located:

176 Dutch Hill Road
(street)

LaBelle, Pennsylvania
(city, state)

PROCEDURE

1. Working in small groups, read and discuss the handout on organizing a corporation.
2. Investigate the statutes for incorporation in your state by contacting your local chamber of commerce.
3. Based on the information in the handout and your state's statutes for incorporation, draft a charter that outlines certain facts about the proposed corporation. These are your articles of incorporation.
4. Based on the information in the handout and your articles of incorporation, outline your corporation's bylaws.
5. As a class compare your articles of incorporation and corporate bylaws.

RELATED QUESTIONS

1. Why do states have statutes regarding incorporation?
2. What is the difference between a corporation's articles of incorporation and its bylaws?
3. List three specific areas usually covered in corporate bylaws that might differ between corporations.
4. How did your small group make decisions about the articles of incorporation and bylaws?
5. Who designs and implements these documents in a corporation?

CHAPTER 15

Processing Materials

OBJECTIVES

After completing this chapter, you will know about:

- The definition of materials form-changing processes.
- The primary production form-changing processes in the manufacturing system.
- The secondary production form-changing processes in the manufacturing system.
- Materials-forming processes.
- Materials-separating processes.
- Materials-combining processes.

KEY TERMS

Annealing	Firing	Separating
Casting	Forming	Shearing
Catalyst	Hardening	Solutions
Chip removing	Industrial materials	Standard stock
Combining	Joint	Stretching
Components	Metering	Subassemblies
Compressing	Molding	Suspension
Conditioning	Plastic deformation	Tempering
Drying	Polymerize	Thermosetting plastic
Elastic deformation	Primary manufacturing	Work hardening
Final assemblies	Raw material	
Finished product	Secondary manufacturing	

Form-changing Processes

Materials processing occurs in the production department of a manufacturing company. Production workers use tools and equipment to change the forms of metallic, ceramic, polymeric, and composite materials to increase their economic value. Because of this transition, the new forms of materials (or finished products) can be sold by the manufacturing company for a much higher amount of money. In this way the company can make a profit. This is the primary goal of any manufacturing company.

This chapter was contributed by Dr. Leonard A. Colelli.

Materials processing occurs in three distinct stages: the **raw material** stage, the **standard stock** stage, and the **finished product** stage.

All raw materials that are used in the manufacturing system are obtained in a natural state from the air, earth, or water. Plant raw materials (polymers) are typically acquired through a process called harvesting. Animal raw materials (polymers) are secured through the process of catching wild animals or slaughtering domesticated animals. Mineral raw materials (metals, mineral fuels, or ceramics) are acquired through mining and drilling processes.

Once raw materials are obtained, they must be refined to separate wanted materials from unwanted materials. After raw materials are refined, they are converted into **industrial materials** that have standard shapes, sizes, and weights. These standard-sized and -shaped industrial materials are also called standard stock. Examples of standard stock include bolts of fabric; ingots of pig iron, steel, gold, or lead; sheets or rolls of paper and steel; coils of wire; sheets of plywood, hardboard, or particleboard; granules or pellets of plastic resin;

and bags of powdered flour or cement, Figure 15-1.

Many different kinds of processes can change refined raw materials into standard stock. For example, primary metals such as pig iron, steel, aluminum, or copper are converted into ingots, sheets, and coils using melting, casting, and rolling processes. Standard stock items almost always have to be further processed so that they can become useful consumer products.

Primary and Secondary Manufacturing

Manufacturing companies can be classified into **primary manufacturing** companies and **secondary manufacturing** companies. Primary manufacturing companies obtain and refine raw materials and produce standard forms of industrial materials. Examples of primary manufacturing companies include those producing metals (such as steel, aluminum, copper), textiles, lumber, glass, paper, and petroleum-based products or chemicals. The standard stock produced by these companies can be sold directly to individual consumers, or it can become material inputs to construction or secondary manufacturing companies, Figure 15-2.

Secondary manufacturing companies convert standard stock materials into products that can be bought by consumers in local stores. Product outputs of secondary manufacturing companies include such items as televisions, kitchen appliances, telephones, automobiles, medicines, furniture, and clothing. Secondary manufacturing companies first convert the standard stock purchased from primary industries into single-piece products or **components** of multiple-piece products using materials-forming and -separating processes. Components of multiple-piece products are then assembled into **subassemblies** and **final assemblies** with materials-combining processes, Figure 15-3.

Forming

Materials-**forming** processes convert standard stock (boards of wood, rolls or bars of steel,

Figure 15-1. Raw materials are usually converted into standard industrial material forms before final products are produced. *(Courtesy of Commercial Metals Company)*

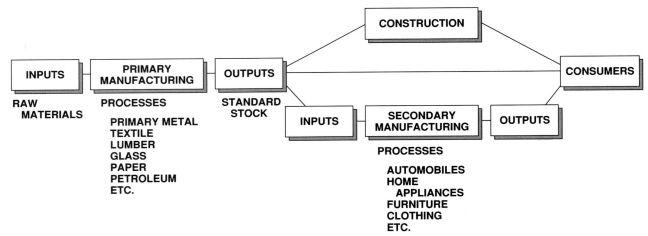

Figure 15-2. Primary manufacturing converts raw materials into standard stock, while secondary manufacturing converts standard stock into finished consumer products.

pellets of plastic, bags of ceramic cement or sand) into one-piece products or components of multiple-piece products. Forming processes can bring about internal or external form changes in metallic, ceramic, polymeric, or composite materials. External (outside) forms of materials can be changed through **casting** and **molding** and **compressing** and **stretching** processes. Internal forms of materials can be changed by using **conditioning** processes.

Casting and Molding

In casting and molding processes, industrial materials are melted, dissolved, or compounded into a liquid or semiliquid state. Then they are allowed to flow or are forged by pressure into a hollow cavity of a desired shape. Casting processes allow a liquid material to pour by gravity into a hollow cavity. Molding processes force liquid or semiliquid materials by pressure (injection) into a cavity, Figure 15-4. Metal materials like steel are melted in furnaces, ceramic materials like clay are dissolved in water, and plastic materials are compounded (mixed).

The five basic steps in casting or molding any material are 1) preparing a pattern, 2) preparing the mold, 3) preparing (melting, dissolving, compounding) the material, 4) introducing the material into the mold, and 5) removing the solid piece, Figure 15-5.

Casting and molding processes are usually organized by the permanence of the mold. Permanent mold techniques utilize reusable molds. Expendable mold techniques use molds that are destroyed after one use to remove the cast or molded material. Perhaps

Figure 15-3. Secondary manufacturing companies use forming and separating processes to change standard stock into one-piece products or components of multiple-piece products. Combining processes are used to turn components of multiple piece products into subassemblies and final assemblies.

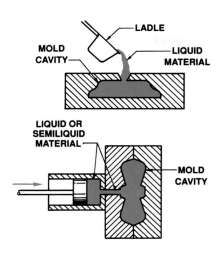

Figure 15-4. Casting occurs when liquid materials flow by gravity into a hollow cavity. Molding takes place when liquid or semiliquid materials are forced (injected) into a hollow cavity.

the greatest advantage for casting and molding processes is that they provide a direct route from industrial material to a semifinished product at a relatively low cost.

Compressing and Stretching

A second major way that forming can be done is by compressing or stretching materials. Compressing processes squeeze and stretching processes pull materials into desired shapes.

Compressing and stretching can occur when any of four different kinds of forces are applied to materials. These forces, shown in Figure 15-6, are compression, tension, shear, and torsion. These four forces are usually applied to materials with compressing or stretching devices such as hammers, presses, rollers, or drawing machines.

When a small amount of force is applied to a material, it first changes shape (deforms) elastically. An **elastic deformation** is not permanent. The material will return to its original shape when the force is removed. Rubber is an example of a material with a great ability to deform elastically. A rubber band can be stretched around a bundle of envelopes. When the rubber band is removed, it returns to its original shape. Many other materials deform elastically, but this nonpermanent change in shape may not be visible to the human eye. Bricks and ceramic tiles are examples of such materials.

If the force on a material continues to increase, the elastic limit will eventually be exceeded. The shape change will then become permanent. This permanent shape change is called **plastic deformation**. Each type of material needs a different amount of force for deformation to occur. Therefore, compressing and stretching tools (hammers, presses, rollers) are designed to provide just the right amount of force to cause plastic deformation of a material into a desired shape.

Plastic deformation is easier when materials are soft. If the materials are not softened enough before compressing or stretching, they could be easily fractured and ruined before the final desired shape is formed. Water is added to clay and wood; while plastics, metals, and glass are heated before compressing or stretching.

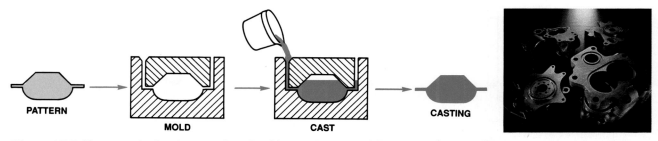

Figure 15-5. Here are the basic steps involved in casting or molding any material. *(Photo courtesy of Cross and Trecker Corp.)*

Figure 15-6. The four principal types of forces that can be applied to materials during compressing or stretching processes are tension, compression, shear, and torsion. *(Reprinted from* LIVING WITH TECHNOLOGY *by Hacker and Barden, © 1989 Delmar Publishers Inc.)*

There are seven basic ways to compress (squeeze) or stretch (pull) materials into desired shapes. These are squeeze forming, rolling, extruding, drawing, stretch forming, spinning, and bending, Figure 15-7. Although specific process names may vary depending on the type of material (metallic, ceramic, polymeric, composite) that is being formed, the seven basic processes are the same.

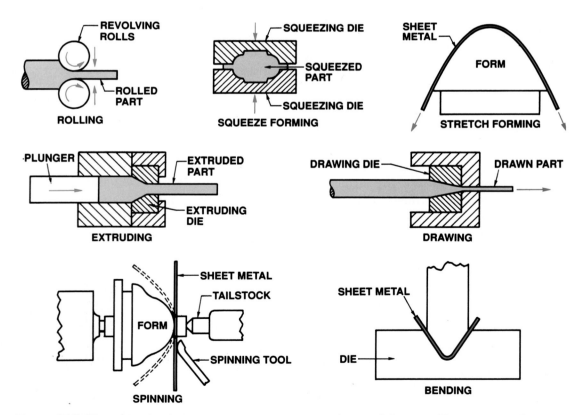

Figure 15-7. The seven basic ways to compress or stretch materials are rolling, squeeze forming, extruding, stretch forming, drawing, spinning, and bending.

Conditioning

Conditioning processes are the third major category of forming processes. Materials are conditioned to change their internal structures on a cellular or atomic level. These internal changes usually are not visible. For example, a malleable piece of carbon steel can be heated until it is cherry red, then plunged in water. The steel does not *look* any different, but profound changes have happened to its internal structure to make it stronger. The material properties that are changed through conditioning processes include hardness, brittleness, toughness, elasticity, plasticity, ductility, strength, and moisture content.

There are three basic reasons why materials are conditioned. First, properties may need to be changed so that materials are easier to process. Hard materials are commonly softened with heat so that they are more easily compressed, stretched, sheared, machined, or welded into desired shapes. Second, materials may be conditioned to relieve internal stresses and strains that can build up as they are processed. High internal stresses and strains can cause a material to become hard, brittle, and easily fractured. A third reason for conditioning is to give materials some special property or properties desired for the final product.

There are three major ways to condition materials—thermal conditioning, mechanical conditioning, and chemical conditioning processes.

Thermal Conditioning. Thermal conditioning processes use heat to change internal structures and properties of materials. Metallic and some ceramic materials are often thermally conditioned by a group of related processes called heat treating. Common heat-treating processes include hardening, tempering, and annealing. Clay-based ceramic materials are thermally conditioned by a process called firing. Wood materials are conditioned through a process called drying.

Hardening takes place when material (iron alloys such as steel) is heated above a critical temperature and is then very rapidly cooled or quenched. The critical temperature is a point at which the material will change from one crystal structure to another. Certain characteristics that allow a material to become harder (such as fine grain size and an even distribution of carbon throughout all molecules) can only take place above the critical temperature. The material is rapidly cooled to lock or freeze these desirable characteristics into the material. While the hardening process causes a material to become harder, it also leads to high internal stresses and brittleness.

A **tempering** process usually follows hardening. The material is heated to a predetermined point below the critical temperature and then is quenched. Tempering relieves internal stress, reduces brittleness, and provides toughness to materials. Low tempering temperatures result in less toughness. Higher temperatures lead to greater toughness.

Annealing means to soften. Materials are heated to a point above their critical temperature. They are then allowed to cool slowly. The slow cooling permits the grain size and distribution of carbon to return to normal. The annealing process can be used to remove any effects of thermal hardening or tempering as well as hardening caused by compressing and stretching processes.

Drying is a conditioning process that removes moisture from materials. This process is usually associated with wood and some ceramic materials. The kiln drying process removes excess moisture from most furniture grade lumber. Construction grade lumber is usually air dried. Freshly cut (green) lumber has about an eighty-five percent moisture content. The kiln drying process slowly reduces the moisture content to about eight percent. As the moisture content is reduced, the hardness, strength, and stability (resistance to warping) of the lumber is increased.

Clay-based ceramic materials are usually dried in an oven after they have been formed to prepare them for a firing process. The **firing** process cooks the clay product at extremely high temperatures. The product becomes hard, brittle, and permanently solid.

Mechanical Conditioning. Mechanical conditioning processes use physical force to change materials properties. Materials may be compressed, stretched, flexed, or hit to cause internal changes in the structure of the material. Mechanical conditioning may also be called **work hardening**. Work hardening occurs when compressing or stretching processes are performed on cold metal materials. The physical force transferred to the material by these processes changes the size and spacing of internal metal grains, Figure 15-8. The grains become elongated in this rolling process, and the overall hardness of the material is increased.

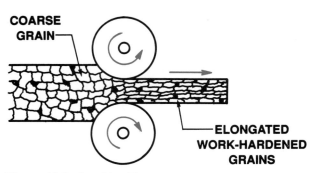

Figure 15-8. A cold rolling process mechanically compresses and elongates the grain structure of metal materials. An increase in overall hardness brought about by work-hardened (conditioned) grains would not have occurred if the material had been hot rolled.

Chemical Conditioning. Chemical conditioning processes cause chemical reactions to take place in materials. When this happens, the atoms inside a material rearrange themselves into a new chemical structure. The material that causes a chemical reaction to take place is called a **catalyst**. A catalyst material can be added to a **thermosetting plastic** material like auto body repair putty to cause it to quickly harden. The catalyst causes the thermosetting plastic to **polymerize** (combine) short molecular chains of atoms into longer, more stable chains. These changes cause the thermosetting plastic to become harder and much more stable than thermoplastic materials. Other chemical conditioning processes include leather tanning, as well as materials curing by exposure to gamma ray radiation.

Separating

Materials-**separating** processes are performed for the same basic reason as materials-forming processes—to convert standard stock into one-piece products or components of multiple-piece products. Separating processes differ from forming processes because they are used to cut down the size of materials by removing excess material. The material left over after all excess has been removed (separated) is the desired product or component. Forming processes result in products or components by changing the shape of the material without removing any material.

There are three basic ways to separate excess material from standard stock. The two commonly used groups of processes are shearing and chip removing. A third group represents special separating processes that are not used as often or are relatively new processes that do not fit into either the shearing or chip-removing categories. This third group of processes is simply called special separating processes.

Shearing

Shearing processes are used to cut excess material away from standard stock with no loss of material. Let's say that a twelve-inch-long piece of material was shear-separated into two six-inch-long pieces. If the two six-inch pieces were placed back together, they would measure the original twelve inches, Figure 15-9.

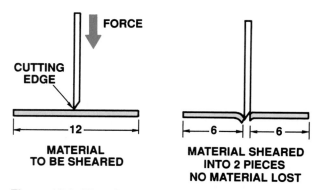

Figure 15-9. Shearing processes separate material without loss of any material.

Ion-Beam Implantation

Ion-beam implantation is an emerging materials-conditioning process that has been used to create up to a 1,000 percent improvement in the surface properties of materials. The material to be improved (for example metal punches) is called a target material. It is placed in an adjustable holder. A second material (nitrogen gas is often used) will be implanted in the target. This second material is converted into an ion cloud by charging it with electrons emitted from a tungsten filament. This process takes place in a metal box called an ion-beam generator.

Applications of the ion-beam implantation process are continually being developed and commercially introduced to consumers. Semiconductor manufacturers have pioneered ion-beam processing as a way to embed silicon semiconductor materials with elements that improve the electrical characteristics of microchips. This embedding process is called "doping." Surgical bone implants such as the artificial hip joint are implanted with nitrogen to improve their life expectancy from ten to fifteen years. Jet turbine bearings and raceways (which

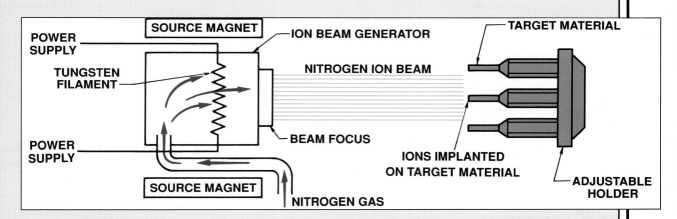

A combination of magnets and electric coils is used to focus and direct the cloud of ions into a concentrated, high-velocity beam. The beam of ions smashes into the target material and penetrates to a depth of about a few microns. The surface of the target material then becomes an alloy of the two materials and gains valuable properties of the implanted material that it did not previously have. When the metal punches are implanted with nitrogen ions, they become harder, last much longer, and are less affected by corrosion.

cost about $2,500.00 each) are implanted with chromium, molybdenum, boron, or a combination of these elements to make their service lives two to three times longer than those not conditioned with this process. Corrosion has been greatly reduced in the ink-spraying nozzles of high-speed electronic printers by using a chromium implant. Many new applications of this conditioning process are expected to emerge within the materials-processing industry over the next ten years.

Excess material that is shear-separated is usually recycled or can be designed for use in other products. Therefore, shearing processes are very material-efficient because little if any stock is wasted.

Shearing processes generally use two opposing surfaces to produce a fracture or break in the material. A movable shearing tool is brought into contact with the material. The shearing tool must be harder than the material being cut. Pressure is then applied, and the tool penetrates the material. As penetration continues, the material fractures and the part is separated.

Shearing processes are usually performed with one of three major kinds of cutting tools: shears and blades, punches and dies, and rotary cutters.

Shears and Blades. Shears and blades are often used for trimming books and magazines, shearing metal and plastic sheets, shaving whiskers, trimming tree branches, cutting wood veneer, and cutting extruded ceramic bricks to length before firing.

Punches and Dies. Punches and dies are often used to produce holes in sheet materials. Figure 15-10 shows a common punch and die setup. The punch forces the material down into the die. The size and shape of the separated material or the hole left behind is controlled by the shape of the punch and die. A paper hole puncher is a good example of how a punch and die works to shear-separate material.

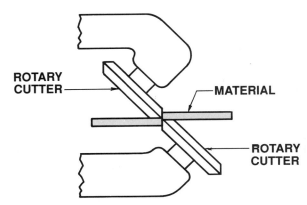

Figure 15-11. Here is a common rotary shearing setup for producing round or irregular shapes.

Rotary Cutters. Rotary cutters produce round and irregular shapes. Revolving circular cutters as well as roller-razor blade combinations, Figure 15-11, are used to cut rolls of metallic, plastic, paper, fabric, and other thin materials to finished sizes.

Chip Removing

Chip-removing processes, like shearing processes, are used to cut excess material away from standard stock. Chip removal, unlike shearing, results in a loss or waste of material in the form of chips (small bits of the stock). If a twelve-inch-long piece of material were chip-separated in half by a saw with a $1/8$-inch kerf, the result would be two $5\ ^{15}/_{16}$-inch-long pieces, Figure 15-12. If the two pieces were placed back together, they would measure $11\ ^7/_8$ inches long. A one-eighth-inch saw kerf of material would have been lost; it would have been turned into chips by the saw blade teeth.

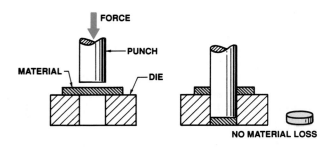

Figure 15-10. This is a common punch and die shearing setup.

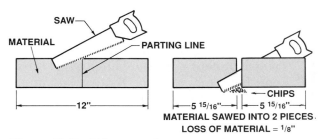

Figure 15-12. Chip-removing processes separate material with a loss of material in the form of chips.

Excess material that is chip-separated can be recycled or can be designed for use in other products; however, it is not a common practice to do so. Therefore, chip-removing processes are not as material-efficient as shearing processes.

Chip-removing processes separate materials by forming and removing chips. Chips are formed as a result of a cutting tool being fed into, along, or through a material. The tool compresses the material ahead of it. The material first changes shape elastically and then permanently deforms. Finally, the material fractures at a place called the shear plane, moves up and over the face of the cutting tool, and breaks away from the parent material in the form of a chip.

There are five basic ways to separate materials by chip removal. These are sawing, hole machining, turning, milling, and abrasive machining. (Refer to Chapter 7 to review the single-point and multiple-point tools used in these processes.)

Sawing. Sawing involves cutting material with a narrow cutting device called a saw blade, which is securely held in a tool or machine called a saw. The three major kinds of sawing processes are represented by straight blade sawing, continuous blade sawing, and circular blade sawing. Chapter 7 describes the various types of saws used in these sawing processes.

Hole Machining. Hole machining processes produce variously shaped holes in materials. A tool or machine called a hand drill or drill press is used. There are six common types of hole machining processes, Figure 15-13. These are drilling, boring, reaming, counterboring, countersinking, and tapping. Drilling easily and quickly produces a hole in a material with a drill bit. Boring accurately enlarges the diameter of a hole. Reaming accurately enlarges a hole, but also produces a very smooth surface finish. Counterboring enlarges a hole only partway along its depth to allow bolt heads or nuts to be hidden below the surface of the material. Countersinking produces a tapered surface in one end of a hole to allow flathead wood or machine screws to lie flush with the surface of the material. Tapping produces threads inside a hole.

Turning. Turning processes produce cylindrical or cone-shaped parts with a machine called a lathe, Figure 15-14. There are seven common

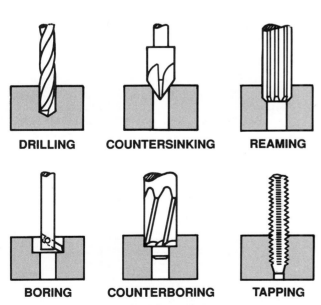

DRILLING COUNTERSINKING REAMING

BORING COUNTERBORING TAPPING

Figure 15-13. The six common types of hole machining processes are drilling, reaming, boring, counterboring, countersinking, and tapping.

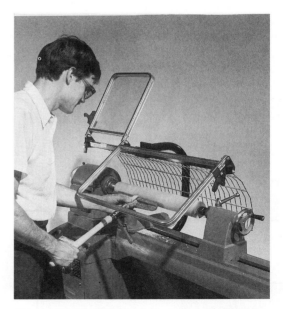

Figure 15-14. Wood lathes are used to make cylindrical objects, such as legs for tables and chairs. (Courtesy of Delta International Machine Corp.)

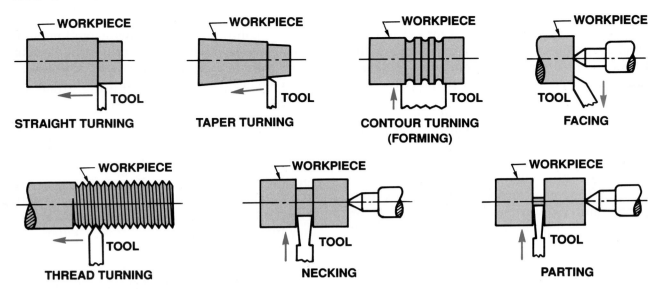

Figure 15-15. Seven common turning processes are straight turning, taper turning, contour turning, facing, thread turning, necking, and parting.

processes that can be used to turn metals, plastics, and woods. These are straight turning, taper turning, facing, contour turning, thread turning, necking, and parting, Figure 15-15.

Straight turning gives a uniform outside diameter to a material by feeding a cutting tool parallel to the work axis. Taper turning makes a part with a uniformly decreasing diameter

along its length by not feeding a tool parallel to the work axis. Contour turning can be done by either feeding the tool along an irregular (curved) path or by using an irregularly shaped tool to cut the material. Facing smoothes the end of the workpiece. Thread turning on a lathe (sometimes called thread chasing) will make very accurate or uniquely formed

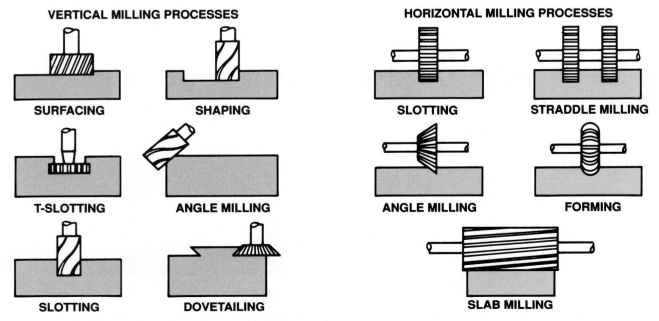

Figure 15-16. Here are some common vertical and horizontal metal milling processes.

threads with a specially shaped threading tool. Necking involves feeding a square-shaped tool directly into the work piece to a desired depth. Parting is the same as necking, except that the square-shaped tool is fed all the way through so that the workpiece is cut off.

Milling. Milling processes are used to square and contour wood, metal, or plastic materials. Most milling processes use one or more revolving multiple-point cutting tools to progressively remove layers of chips.

Metal milling, shaping, and planing processes are widely used to produce very accurate (thousandths of an inch or hundredths of a millimeter) flat surfaces, shoulders, grooves, keyways, T-slots, angles, and dovetails. Some common vertical and horizontal metal milling processes are shown in Figure 15-16.

Metal shaping and planing processes use a single-point tool and a back-and-forth cutting motion. In metal shaping processes, the cutting tool moves and the material remains stationary. In metal planing processes, the material moves and the cutting tool remains stationary.

Common wood milling processes include jointing, planing, shaping, and routing, Figure 15-17. Jointing is used to true (remove warps

or saw marks) an edge or surface of wood or plastic materials. Planing is used to reduce the thickness of wood materials. Shaping and routing are used to produce a contoured edge on a rectangular or curved piece of wood.

Abrasive Machining. Abrasive machining processes use small particles of natural or synthetic ceramic material to provide the cutting action that produces chips. There are three major kinds of abrasive machining processes. These are grinding, sanding, and loose-media processes.

Grinding processes use abrasive particles glued together in the shape of a wheel. Grinding wheels are specially designed for cutting soft materials like brass or aluminum, tough materials like steel, and very hard materials like cast iron, Figure 15-18. The five major types of grinding processes are off hand, surface, cylindrical, centerless, and tool grinding, Figure 15-19.

Sanding processes use coated abrasive sheets, belts, discs, and drums to remove fine chips of material. A glue or resin bonds the abrasive particles to a backing. Paper backing is generally used for sanding soft materials like wood, while cloth backing is used for sanding harder metal materials.

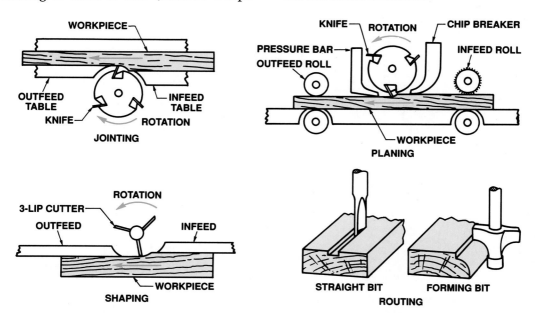

Figure 15-17. These are some typical processes for jointing, planing, shaping, and routing wood.

Figure 15-18. Notice the safety shields over the grinding machine and the safety glasses worn by the operator. Sparks and tiny particles of material can fly into the eyes unless proper safety precautions are taken. *(Courtesy of Delta International Machine Corp.)*

Loose-media processes use loose abrasive particles to machine materials or finish the surfaces of a material. The loose particles may be shot at high rates of speed with compressed air (sand blasting or jet machining) or may be vibrated in a water solution (ultrasonic machining). Loose-media abrasive separating is generally used in situations where conventional chip-removing processes will not work.

Applications of loose-media abrasive separating might include machining parts, frosting glass, cutting cemetery monuments, or producing decorative patterns in thin materials. A wide variety of metallic, ceramic, rubber, and plastic materials can also be placed into vibrating or tumbling machines filled with loose abrasive particles to remove burrs, sharp edges, tool marks, flash from castings, and scale from thermal conditioned parts.

Special Separating

Special separating processes are relatively new, not widely used separating processes that really do not fit into either the shearing or chip-removing categories.

There are eight different ways to separate materials by special separating processes.

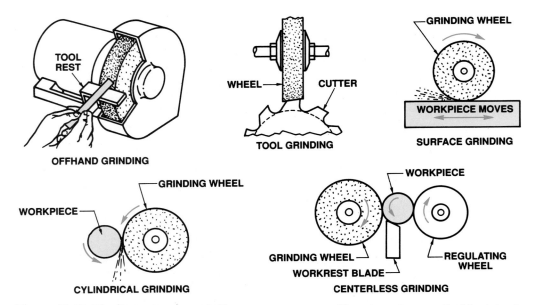

Figure 15-19. The five common grinding processes are offhand, surface, cylindrical, tool, and centerless grinding.

They are thermal (gas torch), electrical (electrical discharge machining, electron beam machining, ion beam machining), electrothermal (plasma arc cutting or machining), chemical (acid etching), electrochemical, light wave (laser), liquid (water jet), and induced-fracture separating, Figure 15-20.

Combining

Materials-**combining** processes are used to finish one-piece products and to assemble components of multiple-piece products into subassemblies and final product assemblies. Materials can be combined by mixing, bonding, coating, and mechanical fastening.

Mixing

Mixing is a combining process used commonly in food, petrochemical, and drug manufacturing companies. Mixing processes evenly spread molecules of gas, droplets of liquid, or particles of solid materials throughout the mixture.

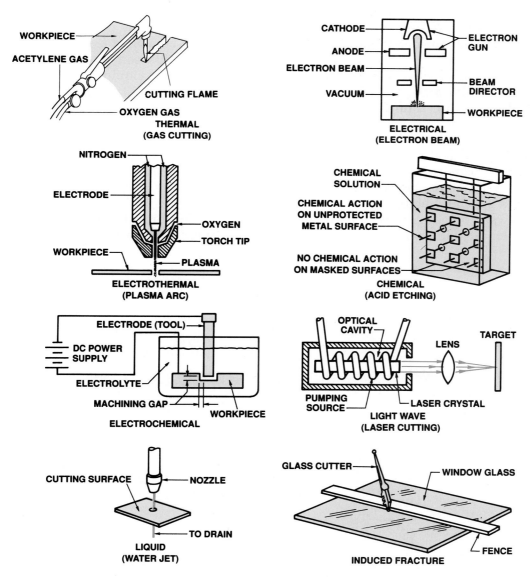

Figure 15-20. The eight major special separating processes are thermal, electrical, electrothermal, chemical, electrochemical, light wave, liquid, and induced fracture.

Dry (solid) materials are usually mixed by stirring, tumbling, mulling, and fluidizing. Correct portions of cement and sand are stirred with a shovel before water is added to make concrete. Entry postcards, balls, or other markers used in raffle, bingo, sweepstakes and lottery competitions are tumbled in drums so that all will have an equal chance of being selected. Mulling processes mix fine granular solid materials like metal casting sand and baking flour. The ingredients are placed in a circular tub. Power-driven wheels roll over the materials. This causes them to move sideways and mix together. Fluidizing occurs when air currents are blown through powdered ingredients, causing them to mix.

Liquid materials are typically mixed with pouring, shaking, blending, agitating, and vibrating processes. Thin liquids like water can be mixed by simply pouring them together. Thick liquids such as molasses or heavy-grade oils might need special vibrating, blending, or agitating processes to mix with other liquids. Liquid paint colors are mixed with a base liquid in a special vibrating machine at the local hardware or paint store. The food industry uses blending processes to make such products as breads, cakes, and ice cream in large quantities. Air can be bubbled through liquids to mix them in a process called pneumatic agitation.

Gases are mixed by a process called **metering**. Metering means to measure by volume. When gases are to be mixed, each gas is metered. The correct proportion (fraction) of each gas is then simply fed into a closed container. Since gas molecules move much faster than molecules of liquid and solid materials, the gases quickly mix themselves inside the container.

Many combinations of solids, liquids, and gases are also combined by mixing processes. Solid materials like salt or sugar can be mixed with water or other liquids by a process called dissolving. Mixtures that occur when solids are dissolved in liquids are called **solutions**. If the solid cannot be dissolved in a liquid, it becomes a **suspension**, which is evenly spread throughout the liquid. Sand and gravel are examples of materials that are suspended in a concrete mixture. Finally, gases and liquids are commonly mixed. Many soft drinks are carbonated by forcing carbon dioxide gas to dissolve into the liquid drink. When the bottle

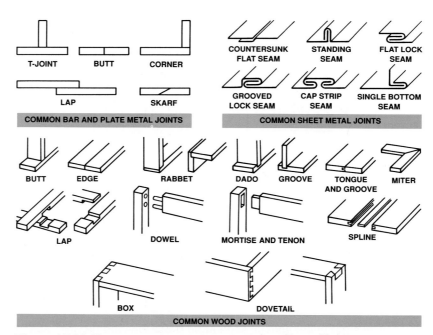

Figure 15-21. Here are some common metal and wood joints.

or can is opened, the gas bubbles rise to the surface.

Bonding

Bonding processes combine (assemble or join) solid materials together. The area of the material where the bond takes place is called a **joint**, Figure 15-21. The type of joint selected for use depends on the strength and appearance requirements of the product as well as the type of material that is to be bonded.

Bonding is a permanent combining process. Bonded joints are rigid so that parts that are bonded cannot move or be separated. Materials can be bonded by using either adhesive or cohesive processes.

Adhesive bonding processes use glues, cements, or some other adhesive to cause the joint areas of parts to stick together. The adhesive is applied in a thin layer at the joint area of the mating parts that are to be combined.

Adhesive bonding processes can be used to bond metallic, polymeric, and ceramic materials. Examples of adhesive bonding include gluing wood products, soldering copper pipes or components to printed circuit boards, cementing firebrick in kilns or furnaces, taping sheets of paper together, ironing patches onto clothing to cover holes, and pasting up wallpaper.

Cohesive bonding processes use heat, pressure, chemicals, or combinations of each to melt or soften parts at the joint. The molecules of the melted surfaces then move across the joint and cohere or mix together. This combining process is also referred to as fusion bonding.

Cohesive (fusion) bonding processes can be used to bond metallic, polymeric, and ceramic materials. Examples of cohesive bonding include many kinds of gas, electrical, and ultrasonic (vibration) welding processes that create heat. Also included are cold welding processes, which use tremendous amounts of pressure to force molecules to cross joint areas and cohere. Other examples of cohesive bonding include metal brazing (which differs from welding because filler materials that are very different than the base materials are used) and the use of special chemicals (such as ethylene dichloride) to soften and combine thermoplastic materials at joint areas.

Coating

Coating processes place one or more layers of one material on top of another material. Materials are coated to protect them from wearing out too fast, to decorate them so they will have an attractive appearance, to communicate information, to reduce noise, or to reflect heat or light. There are two major ways to coat one substance with another—(1) by applying a physical coating and (2) by converting (changing) the surface of a material, Figure 15-22.

Physical coating processes are used to apply a thin layer of coating material to the surface of another material by brushing, rolling, dipping, spraying plating, or printing. The coating material sticks to the surface of the part or product being coated.

Examples of physical coating include brush painting the outside of your house, roll painting your bedroom walls, spraying a piece of

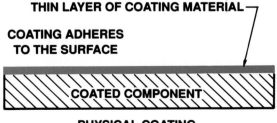

THIN LAYER OF COATING MATERIAL

COATING ADHERES
TO THE SURFACE

COATED COMPONENT

PHYSICAL COATING

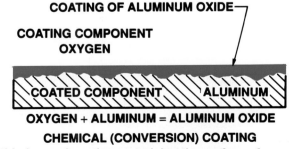

COATING OF ALUMINUM OXIDE

COATING COMPONENT
OXYGEN

COATED COMPONENT   ALUMINUM

OXYGEN + ALUMINUM = ALUMINUM OXIDE

CHEMICAL (CONVERSION) COATING

Figure 15-22. Physical coating processes are used to apply a thin layer of coating material to the surface of another material. A chemical (conversion) coating process called anodizing changes the exterior surface of the aluminum material to improve its appearance and wearability.

furniture with lacquer finish, dipping metal garbage cans in a zinc bath (galvanizing), and chrome plating an automobile bumper.

Conversion coating is used to change chemically the surface of a material. It includes dyeing, oxide coating, or phosphate coating. Conversion coating processes do not add additional material to the outside surface of another material. The outside layer of the material is simply changed to improve appearance or wearability.

Phosphate coating treats metals in a chemical solution that causes the surface of the material to become a very good undercoating for additional physical coatings of paint or some other exterior finish. Another conversion coating process called anodizing stimulates aluminum or magnesium metals to "grow" a clear or colored protective oxide coating.

Mechanical Fastening

Mechanical fastening, perhaps the oldest process used to combine materials, has been traced to the early cave dwellers' use of vines to lace stones and sticks together to produce crude tools and weapons. Examples of mechanical fasteners include staples, nails, screws, rivets, pins, nuts, bolts, thread, keys, shafts, hinges, and clamps. The two major kinds of mechanical fasteners are nonthreaded fasteners and threaded fasteners, Figure 15-23.

Mechanical fastening processes rely on physical force to hold parts together. Nonthreaded mechanical fastening processes such as nailing, tacking, or pinning compress (squeeze) the material that they enter. The pressure created by the compressing of the material holds the fastener in place by friction. Other examples of nonthreaded mechanical fastening processes include sheet metal seaming; spring clamping; the sewing and weaving of textile materials, flat or wire strapping; and fastening with rope, cable, or chains.

Threaded mechanical fasteners are much better holding devices than nonthreaded fasteners. The surface areas of threaded fasteners such as screws, bolts, and nuts are much larger than the surface areas of nonthreaded fasteners. Larger surface areas allow greater frictional forces to develop; therefore, parts can be held much better. Threaded fasteners also provide the advantage of nonpermanence. Products combined with threaded fasteners can be easily disassembled for repair or maintenance.

Summary

Materials are processed to change their forms so that their economic value is increased. The company can then sell the materials or finished products for a profit.

Primary manufacturing companies change the forms of raw materials into industrial materials with standard sizes, shapes, and weights (standard stock). Secondary manufacturing companies change the standard forms of industrial materials into one-piece products or components of multiple-piece products using materials forming and materials separating processes. Finally, secondary manufacturing companies use materials combining processes to turn components of multiple-piece products into subassemblies and finished final assemblies.

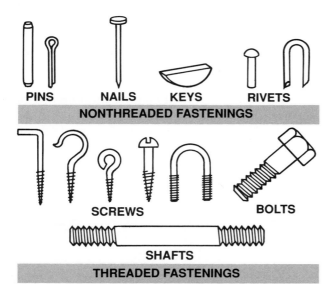

Figure 15-23. Here are common examples of threaded and nonthreaded mechanical fasteners.

DISCUSSION QUESTIONS

1. Describe the three distinct stages that materials go through as they are processed into finished products.

2. What is the major difference between primary and secondary manufacturing? Name at least four products that are produced by primary manufacturing companies and four products that are produced by secondary manufacturing companies.

3. What is the major purpose of materials-forming and materials-separating processes? What is the major purpose of materials-combining processes?

4. Identify at least one casting/molding, one compressing/stretching, and one conditioning process that was used to produce a product found in your home or school.

5. Identify at least one shearing, one chip-removing, and one special separating process that was used to produce a product found in your home or school.

6. Identify at least one mixing, one bonding, one coating, and one mechanical fastening process that was used to produce a product found in your home or school.

CHAPTER ACTIVITIES

 EXPANDABLE BEAD MOLDING

OBJECTIVE

Molding is a forming process often used in industry. In this activity, you will use a molding process to develop a prototype for a styrofoam bathtub toy for three- to six-year-old children. In addition, you will develop cost information for producing the toy.

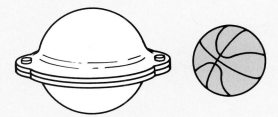

Figure 1

MATERIALS AND SUPPLIES

1. Expandable polystyrene beads
2. Aluminum mold
3. Kettle or pan large enough to hold the mold plus some boiling water

4. Stove or hot plate
5. Hot pads or tongs
6. Bucket of cold water
7. Safety glasses

PROCEDURE

1. Turn on the stove and heat the water to boiling. The amount of water in the pan is not important as long as there is some water. The steam created by the boiling water is what expands the beads. *NOTE:* Use caution as you work near boiling water! The steam can cause a burn as well as the water.
2. Fill the mold with a measured amount of expandable beads. Your teacher will tell you the correct amount to use for your mold.
3. Place the mold in the boiling water. Follow your teacher's instructions on how long to leave your mold in the water.
4. Periodically rotate the mold in the water to spread the beads out evenly in the mold.
5. Remove the mold from the boiling water and cool it in cold water. Allow the mold to stand in the cold water for at least five minutes. The cold must penetrate into the foam.
6. Remove the product from the mold.
7. Remove any flashing.
8. Develop a cost analysis for producing the toy using the following format. Charge for each quarter hour worked, but do not charge for the time you spent waiting for the water to boil. Charge only for the time you spent working on the prototype.

    Cost of the beads for the mold ....$ _____
    Total hours spent working on
      the prototype........................... _____
    Cost of labor per hour .... × _____ $5.00
    Total labor cost .... _____
      Total cost of producing the toy ....$ _____

MATH/SCIENCE CONNECTION

Volume is the amount of space inside an object. In molding, the volume is the space inside the mold. The volume of a square or rectangle can be found with the following formula:

$$\text{Volume} = \text{Length} \times \text{Width} \times \text{Height}$$

The formula for the volume of a cylinder is:

$$\text{Volume} = \pi R^2$$

The formula for the volume of a sphere (ball shape) is:

$$\text{Volume} = {}^4\!/_3 \pi R^3$$

RELATED QUESTIONS

1. The beads expand up to fifty times their pre-expanded volume. How many ounces, by volume, of beads would you need for a basketball mold with a diameter of 5 3/4"?
2. What causes the air in the beads to expand?
3. What perhaps is the greatest advantage of casting and molding processes?
4. What shape objects are particularly suited for expandable bead molding?

 **COLD CASTING**

OBJECTIVE

Casting is a valuable process for producing many kinds of manufactured goods. In this activity, you will produce polyester paperweights in a variety of shapes and colors. The paperweights must have smooth edges and be translucent.

MATERIALS AND SUPPLIES

1. Clear polyester resin
2. Polyester dye (coloring)
3. Mold release (silicon spray)
4. Casting mold
5. Polyester catalyst (MEK)
6. Mixing cup and stir stick

PROCEDURE

CAUTION: Polyester resins are highly flammable and give off potentially harmful fumes if inhaled directly. Use only in the finishing room with the ventilation fans on.

1. Select and clean the mold. Use soap and water to remove all traces of resin.
2. Spray on silicon mold release.
3. Fill the mold with water.
4. Pour the water from the mold into a measuring cup. This will tell you how much resin is needed for this mold.
5. Measure out the proper amount of polyester resin.
6. Add five drops of catalyst for each ounce of resin. Measure carefully. If you use too little catalyst the resin will not set up. Too much catalyst will create too much heat and ruin the resin.
7. Add drops of the desired color. The coloring agent is concentrated, so use it sparingly.
8. Stir up the mixture of resin, catalyst, and color with a stirring stick.
9. Pour the mixture into the mold.
10. Let the resin harden and remove from the mold.
11. Sand the edges of the casting.

RELATED QUESTIONS

1. What is the material called that causes a chemical reaction to take place?

2. A normal mixture is five drops of MEK catalyst to each ounce of polyester resin. If a mold calls for fourteen ounces of resin, how many drops of catalyst will you need to add for proper curing?

3. What is the purpose of applying a mold release to the mold before pouring the resin?

4. How might you embed an object like a coin or stone into the casting?

CHAPTER 16

Marketing Processes

OBJECTIVES

After completing this chapter, you will know about:

■ The activities included in marketing, which may all be considered "selling."

■ Marketing research as an input that helps to determine demand for a product.

■ The characteristics of the consumer goods market.

■ The characteristics of the industrial goods market.

■ The functions of marketing, including product planning, advertising, sales, and product service.

■ The problems (ethics) related to marketing techniques.

KEY TERMS

Advertising agencies	Made-to-order	Product service
Consumer goods market	Market research	Region-specific
Demand	Mass distribution	Sales forecast
False advertising	Mass media	Specialty items
Industrial goods market	Product planning	Subliminal

Marketing and Determining Demand

The hope that people will want to buy a product is too important to be left to chance alone. Too much is at stake for a company to concentrate solely on the manufacture of its goods. Therefore a great deal of attention is usually given to the ultimate sale of the product to the customer. The primary reason for commercial manufacturing is to sell, or market, the prod-uct. The marketing process involves many activities that occur during all stages of manufacturing. In a sense, all activities included in the process of marketing can be considered selling, Figure 16-1.

Section Two of this book discussed **market research**, an activity related to selling. Market research, an input to the overall manufacturing

Figure 16-1. Coca-Cola, the world's best-known trademark, symbolizes the company's presence in more then 155 countries. *(Courtesy of Helena Frost Associates, Inc.)*

system, is carried out even before manufacturing begins. This is done in order to find out exactly who, if anyone, is likely to buy the product. In addition, market research contributes to the overall selling of a product by

- keeping the business in touch with changes in its markets,
- uncovering new product ideas,
- assisting in managing sales, and
- measuring the potential of future markets.

Market research determines whether there is a need for the product. In some cases, a sense of need may be enhanced or created through advertising. Need is usually called **demand**. Demand for manufactured products varies widely. It depends on the types of customers and goods being produced, Figure 16-2.

Types of Markets

Generally, customers can be divided into two groups—consumers and industry. A consumer buys a product that is eventually consumed, or used. An industry may use the product to make yet other products. An example might be producing the actual machines that are needed to make consumer products. Selling techniques usually differ depending on whether the goods being produced are for consumers or industry.

The Consumer Goods Market

The following are characteristics of the **consumer goods market**:

1. It can be a nationwide or worldwide market, although many products are more **region-specific**. Region-specific products are appropriate for a particular region or climate. Examples include snow skis, surfboards, snow tires, and even tractors, Figure 16-3. There is not a great demand in New York City for tractors, plows, and other farming equipment. Goods such as clothing may be climate-specific or seasonal. Changing seasons are marked by reduced prices on bathing suits in late summer and winter's end sales on coats in early spring.

2. Consumer goods are often produced before orders are placed. This means that goods are made ahead of demand, or in anticipation of demand. Production ahead of demand must be based

Figure 16-2. Demand for manufactured goods varies depending on the type of customers and goods. *(Courtesy of Radio Shack, A Division of Tandy Corporation)*

Figure 16-3. Sleds and surfboards are products targeted for specific regions or climates. *(Photo by Edith Raviola)*

on careful market study. Imagine if production for a product like chewing gum were based only on orders received. Not only would it be nearly impossible to keep shelves stocked, but the price would be so high that few could afford to buy it. Anticipating demand involves some risk, but thorough market research can greatly reduce this risk.

3. According to most market research, consumers do not put much thought into economic values, efficiency, or long-run costs; they are not considered skillful buyers. Of course, as the price of the product goes up, more thought goes into a purchase. A consumer is much more likely to compare value and prices when shopping for a car or a house than when buying a comb or a box of tissues, Figure 16-4. Comparing the prices of various brands with quality and personal needs and wants are consumer skills that can be developed in order to become a more skillful buyer.

4. Most consumer goods have a small dollar value, because manufactured goods are usually mass-produced. This characteristic is similar to the one just mentioned. An attitude of the "time not being worth the effort" is common when consumers are comparing inex-

pensive nondurable items. This attitude is likely to change when inflation is high or if the consumer has little money to spend.

5. Many consumer goods are mass-distributed, Figure 16-5. **Mass distribution** means that the same brands of goods may be found in thousands of stores across the nation and even worldwide. **Specialty items** like gourmet ingredients and foreign cuisine food items that may appeal to small special-interest consumer groups are also found in most supermarkets. Although the majority of consumers may not purchase these goods, it is still economically profitable for companies to mass-distribute them.

Figure 16-4. The purchase of an automobile usually entails consideration and comparison. *(Courtesy of Dexter Corporation)*

Figure 16-5. Many varieties of fruit, though not locally grown, are available in most locations year-round. *(Photo by Ruby Gold)*

The Industrial Goods Market

The following are characteristics of the **industrial goods market**:

1. The demand for industrial goods tends to change often. When times are good for a business, aging equipment is replaced. When business is slow, equipment is repaired.

2. Because machines and parts for products are usually quite specialized, the number of customers is limited. A particular machine will be appropriate for a limited number of manufacturing operations. Therefore, manufacturers that make specialized machines may end up manufacturing a one-of-a-kind product. Although the industrial market is smaller than the consumer market, the individual cost of specialized products may more than make up the difference, Figure 16-6.

3. The buyers of industrial goods are skilled buyers with an in-depth knowledge of both the product to be purchased and its application. They carefully study the costs and safety of operation, the effect on productivity, and the quality of the product before making the purchase. In addition, it is common for several people to be involved in making decisions about major purchases.

4. Most industrial products are **made-to-order**. Rather than being produced in anticipation of a market, they are manufactured only after orders have been placed. It is for this reason that some plants may shut down or lay off workers temporarily during slow times.

Marketing techniques for consumer and industrial markets are quite different. The consumer market is often broad, while the industrial market is limited. Marketing for consumers involves reaching whole populations. Marketing for industries is pinpointed. We will refer to the differences between these two markets throughout this chapter.

Functions of Marketing

Marketing research has already been mentioned as a function of marketing. Market research begins well before production and

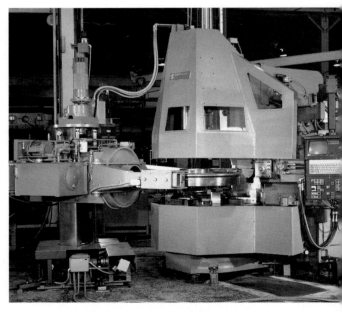

Figure 16-6. This diesel wheel boring machine was built by Simmons Machine Tool Corporation for the Burlington Northern Railroad. It was special-ordered at a cost of about $750,000. *(Courtesy of Simmons Machine Tool Corp.)*

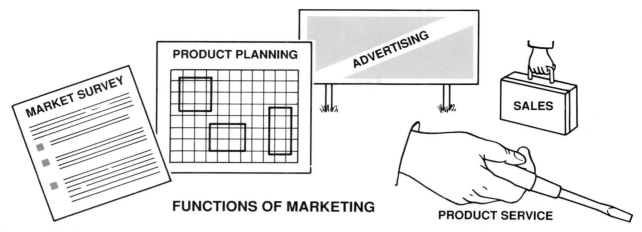

FUNCTIONS OF MARKETING

Figure 16-7. Marketing involves these functions.

continues throughout the manufacturing process. The other functions of marketing include product planning, advertising, sales, and product service, Figure 16-7.

Product Planning

Product planning ensures that new products are added, old ones discontinued, and questionable ones changed. Product planners work closely with marketing researchers to develop sales forecasts for each product. There is often a tendency to neglect product planning when business is good. The wise manufacturer does not wait for business to slow before planning new or revised products. Manufacturers must know how the customer feels about performance, appearance, price, and service.

The **sales forecast** plays an important role in running a business. Production schedules are based on forecasts. Errors in the forecast could be very costly. Forecasts are usually projected for a year and then broken into quarters, months, and even weeks. The forecast shows the commitment of the whole marketing department. It becomes a goal against which the success or failure of the department can be measured, Figure 16-8.

Advertising

Advertising makes consumers aware of the manufactured products they can buy. This is usually done in a way that tries to persuade the consumer to buy a certain product.

Advertisers can use a number of media to send their message. We have all seen advertisements on television and in magazines and newspapers. Companies who want to sell products buy time on television and space in newspapers and magazines. This, in turn, helps to pay for the programs and publications themselves. One essential element of advertising is good communication. In some way the manufacturers must communicate with potential customers.

Figure 16-8. Long-term strategic planning (forecasting) continues to be an important part of management. *(Courtesy of W. W. Grainger, Inc.)*

Figure 16-9. Advertising is aimed at a particular segment of the market. *(Reproduced with permission, © PepsiCo, Inc. 1989)*

The advertising medium may be thought of as the carrier of the message. Common media used by manufacturers include

- television,
- radio,
- newspapers,
- magazines (general magazines, trade journals, sports and hobby magazines, technical and professional journals, women's and men's magazines, and so on),
- direct mail,
- billboards,
- public transportation (on buses, trains, taxis, and in terminals),
- trade exhibits and displays, and
- free samples and trial use.

Probably no manufacturer uses all of these media. They try to select those that would most likely reach the targeted market segment, Figure 16-9. For example, a toy manufacturer might use television as its primary medium because of the amount of time children spend watching television. Especially popular for toy companies is the Saturday morning cartoon viewing audience. It is unlikely that a manufacturer of machine tools, targeting an industrial market, would choose this medium. They would probably have more success advertising in trade journals and at exhibits. Advertising for consumer and industrial markets is quite different. Most consumer-targeted ads appear in the **mass media** (TV, radio, newspapers, general magazines). Most industry-targeted advertising appears in trade journals, trade shows, and direct mailers.

Figure 16-10. Good advertising will present the product in a clever way to catch the eye of a potential buyer. *(Courtesy of Klein Bicycle Corporation)*

Marketing for Youth: Not Child's Play

Marketing for preteens can no longer be considered child's play. The profitability of marketing to children has steadily increased, especially with the purchasing power of the children of baby boomers. This has become a fact of business that will continue well into the 1990s. Households with older parents who are career professionals spend more on their children and encourage them to spend more themselves. In single-parent households, children are expected to behave more like adults and tend to spend more money.

The company that has been the pioneer of directing its advertising at kids for the longest, and has experienced the most success, is McDonald's Restaurants Inc. The fast-food giant has long recognized children as the key to long-term success. Their marketing approach has been based on three premises.

1. Directly appealing to children through such devices as fun-theme meal kits and parties

2. Using advertising that encourages family trips to the restaurants

3. Recognizing that children are the consumers of tomorrow (This future market is ensured by creating positive experiences in its restaurants, banking on the idea that these kids will not only come back on their own as they grow older, but also will eventually bring their own children.)

It is this future market that makes the strongest argument for appealing to the youth market. The U.S. Army, Marines, and Air Force have begun advertising in magazines such as *Boy's Life* and *Scholastic*. This way, they can appeal to kids before they begin making life decisions. Planting seeds in the minds of young people may be the key to long-term success for any product or service.

As business marketers become more conscious that kids are the consumers of tomorrow, more and more marketing campaigns will be targeted at them.

Most manufacturing companies do not do their own advertising. Instead, they use **advertising agencies**. These agencies help the manufacturer choose the right media. They also create ideas and themes for ads and prepare the actual advertisements, Figure 16-10. The fee for an agency's services is usually about fifteen percent of the total media costs.

Selling

All activities in a marketing department can be called selling. However, it is important to remember that some workers will actually visit prospective customers and "make the sell."

After the plans for the manufacture and distribution of goods have been made and the advertising campaigns implemented, these salespeople will make personal contact with customers and obtain orders. It has been found that nothing works as well in selling as the personal approach. Many customers make their final product choice based on how they feel toward individual salespeople, Figure 16-11. This is particularly true when there are competing products available. A primary job of salespeople is maintaining a close contact with past customers to ensure that they continue to buy products.

Figure 16-11. Salespeople are often ultimately responsible for selling. *(Courtesy of Walgreen Co.)*

It is crucial that a manufacturing company select and train good salespeople. A manufacturing company needs to recognize the following distinctions about the role of salespeople:

- Salespeople represent the goal of all prior planning and effort that has gone into the manufacturing enterprise. If the salespeople fail to sell the product, then the whole enterprise has failed.
- Salespeople represent the company and influence present and future business relationships.
- Salespeople are usually alone in their work and must make spot decisions on their own. They must possess good decision-making skills and have an in-depth understanding of their company and its products and policies.
- The job of a salesperson is often expensive because salespeople usually need to travel. Selling also creates expenses for lining up and maintaining clients. Companies often have trouble deciding how much money to spend on sales.

Product Service

Product service is important to the long-term success of a company. In providing quality and dependable product service, the manufacturer makes sure that all ethical and legal responsibilities for product performance are met to the

satisfaction of the customer. Product service helps ensure repeat business. It is also growing more important in sales. As products become more complex, proper installment and maintenance are critical for product performance, Figure 16-12. A customer may base the buying decision on continued product service.

The salesperson may also be responsible for product service. It is becoming more popular for salespeople to be highly trained engineers whose job includes not only sales, but also installation, maintenance training to the customer, and continued product service.

Marketing Ethics

There are many reasons behind the manufacture of products. Profit is perhaps the most obvious. Many manufacturers start with a unique idea for a product (an invention or innovation) that is hoped will appeal to at least a certain segment of consumers. Many ideas are in answer to a perceived need. It is hoped that the idea can be turned into profit. There are many companies truly interested in providing quality products to consumers at the lowest possible price. Unfortunately, some manufacturers meet only minimum consumer

Figure 16-12. One-of-a-kind products like this axle turning and burnishing lathe have a very specialized market and do not require marketing after production, except possible product maintenance. *(Courtesy of Simmons Machine Tool Corp.)*

safety regulations and use advertising techniques that are misleading. This is often called **false advertising**.

Consumer advocate groups try to monitor advertising. They are often helped by consumers themselves who may feel they have been deceived by false advertising, Figure 16-13. Legal standards in advertising help to ensure that we can believe what we hear and see about products. However, as consumers we need a healthy skepticism of advertising. We need to become more informed buyers, refraining from supporting those companies who misrepresent their products.

Forms of product advertising misrepresentation include substituting one material for another, usually a cheaper one for a more durable one, without telling consumers, and using **subliminal** advertising techniques. Subliminal advertising is advertising aimed at our subconscious mind. Advertisers who use this technique put images or messages in their ads that our conscious minds do not see. Even though we are not aware of these messages, they register in our subconscious minds. Several years ago, it was common for an image to appear on the TV screen for a fraction of a second. Viewers didn't actually have time to see the image, but it registered in their subconscious minds. For example, if an image of a

Arbitration involves the following steps:

1. The consumer takes the complaint to the businessman. If this fails, he goes to his local BBB.
2. The BBB tries to resolve the case informally. If the problem is not resolved, arbitration is offered to both parties.
3. The parties involved sign a binding agreement to accept the results of arbitration and submit to the BBB arbitration program.
4. An arbitrator acceptable to both parties is selected.
5. Where appropriate, an inspection of the product, repair job, or construction site is made.
6. Informal proceedings are conducted before the arbitrator. Both parties may be represented by an attorney or some other person, produce witnesses, and give supporting evidence.
7. Finally, a decision or award is made to resolve the issue.

Figure 16-14. Arbitration between consumers and businesses is suggested by the Better Business Bureau. (Reprinted from CONSUMER COMPLAINT GUIDE, 8th Ed. by Joseph Rosenbloom, copyright 1981 Joseph Rosenbloom, by permission of Macmillan Publishing Company)

Figure 16-13. Customers can return products with which they are dissatisfied. (Photo by Sonya Stang and Brent Miller)

certain soft drink were flashed, we might suddenly become thirsty for that soft drink without realizing why. This type of advertising has been banned, but other subliminal techniques are used in magazines and other printed material. It is harder to prove that an advertiser has used subliminal techniques in a printed medium.

If you think that you have been purposely misled by advertising, that the product was misrepresented, it is your right and duty as a consumer to report the product and its manufacturer to a consumer advocacy group. The Better Business Bureau is the best known of these groups. They are located in most large metropolitan areas in the United States, Figure 16-14.

Summary

The selling of products is too important to be left to chance alone. Marketing includes many activities related to selling. The goals of these activities are to determine markets and demand, make customers aware of the product, and ultimately to "make the sell."

Characteristics of consumer goods markets include

- nationwide or worldwide markets, although many products are region-specific;
- goods often produced before orders are placed, in anticipation of demand;
- consumers not considered skillful buyers;
- goods having a relatively small dollar value; and
- mass distributed goods.

Characteristics of industrial markets include

- An often-changing demand for particular goods,
- Possibly a limited number of customers,
- skilled buyers,
- made-to-order goods rather than mass-produced goods, and
- possible leasing rather than purchasing.

The functions of marketing include

- market research, an input that begins well before production in order to determine whether there is potential market for the product;
- product planning, which is necessary to make sure that new products are added, old ones discontinued, and questionable ones changed;
- advertising, which presents the product through the media in order to persuade people to buy it;
- selling, which employs the skills of salespeople whose job it is to make actual sales; and
- product service, which provides service during the initial installation as well as maintenance, often for the life of the product.

A few companies have been known to use false advertising techniques. There are consumer advocacy groups whose job it is to protect consumers from false advertising. These groups try to get companies to use honest and legal advertising. If you think that you have been purposefully misled by advertising, it is your right to report it to a consumer group in your area.

DISCUSSION QUESTIONS

1. Why would a company conduct market research prior to the manufacture of its product(s)?
2. List three differences between consumer and industrial markets.
3. Why is the role of the salesperson an important one for the overall marketing of a product?
4. What is product service, and why is it an important part of marketing?
5. Which function of marketing interests you most? Explain why.
6. What are some of the problems associated with advertising? What is subliminal advertising?

CHAPTER ACTIVITIES

☼ MAKING THE SELL

OBJECTIVE

In this activity, you will design and implement a marketing campaign for a selected manufactured product.

MATERIALS AND SUPPLIES

1. Handouts: *Market Inventory* and *Ad Campaign Critique*
2. Materials for brainstorming session (pencils and paper)
3. Materials for marketing campaign, including
   - posterboard
   - paints
   - markers
   - drafting tools
   - cassette tapes and player
   - video equipment and tapes
   - props for television commercial
   - examples of company logos and slogans

PROCEDURE

1. Form groups of two to four students.
2. Choose any readily available manufactured product to use for your marketing campaign.
3. Conduct market research by compiling the information you need to complete the handout *Market Inventory*.
4. Within your group, brainstorm the best medium for advertising your product to reach your targeted consumer group.
5. Design your complete advertising campaign using the medium you chose in step four. Your product should have a logo and a catchy slogan. In addition, you can use scripts for radio or television commercials and poster-size representations of billboards. If you have enough time and equipment, consider producing your radio or television commercial.
6. Present your campaign to the class and have them complete the handout *Ad Campaign Critique*.

RELATED QUESTIONS

1. Based on the targeted market for your product, what days and times would be most effective for airing television commercials?
2. What medium would you choose to advertise these products?
   - calculators
   - speed boats
   - toothpaste

■ incinerators
■ tractors

3. Would you like to work in marketing or advertising? Why or why not?

4. Describe an advertisement (from any medium) that effectively catches your attention. What makes it a successful marketing campaign?

5. How would you improve the marketing of your product if you were to repeat this activity?

⚙ PACKAGE DESIGN

OBJECTIVE

Most products need some kind of packaging. Package design is a key element of marketing. Manufacturers know that attractive packaging can influence a consumer to purchase a particular brand of a product.

New kinds of packages are always being developed. Aseptic (sterile) packages have long shelf lives. They can be used for milk and other products that are usually refrigerated. Glass jars are being replaced by plastic to reduce weight and shipping costs. Many companies are working to develop biodegradable plastic materials.

In this activity you will design a package for one of these products:

■ Brite White toothpaste
■ Johnson's Double Fudge Cookies
■ X-TRA Long Life Light Bulbs (they come with a five-year guarantee)

Packages serve several functions. They contain and protect the product. Most are designed to promote the product. Packages give useful information such as quantity or weight of the product. Government regulations sometimes require specific information, such as a list of ingredients for foods. Packaging for medicines must have carefully worded directions for use. Tamper-proof packaging is now used for certain products to protect consumers.

MATERIALS AND SUPPLIES

1. Paper
2. Color markers
3. Scissors
4. Cardboard
5. Clear tape and glue
6. Drafting tools
7. Illustration board or foam board
8. Transfer lettering

PROCEDURE

1. Select one of the products to package.
2. Make a list of the information that should be included on the package.
3. Make at least six rough sketches of the graphics for the package.

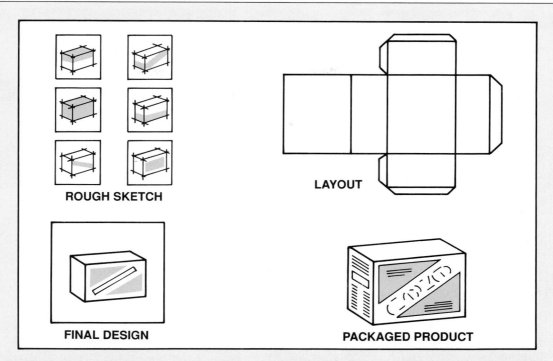

ROUGH SKETCH

LAYOUT

FINAL DESIGN

PACKAGED PRODUCT

4. With the help of your teacher, choose your best idea and make a final sketch. Your final design should make the consumer want to purchase your product.

5. Bring in several packages that might be suitable for your product. Carefully disassemble each package so you can see the layout of the package before it was assembled.

6. Decide what kind of package you want to use for your product.

7. Use drafting equipment to create a full-size layout on paper. Cut, fold, and assemble. Check for accuracy and make changes as needed.

8. Use light cardboard for the final package. Add the graphics using color markers. You can use transfer type to produce neat lettering.

9. Cut, fold, and assemble your package.

10. Make a display that includes your rough sketches, final design, and the layout on a large sheet of illustration board or foam board. Attach the finished package to the display so that it can be removed and replaced. You might try using Velcro® or small magnets.

RELATED QUESTIONS

1. Name several important purposes of packaging.

2. What other materials are used for packaging in addition to cardboard?

3. Solid waste disposal is a problem in many parts of our country today. How does packaging add to the problem? List several possible solutions.

4. What new kinds of packages do you think will become popular in the next few years?

5. Determine the cost of the cardboard for the package you designed. Assume that the material costs $.03 per square inch.

Financial Processes

KEY TERMS

Assets	EBIT	Purchase order
Balance sheet	General ledger	Purchase requisition
Bid	Gross pay	Purchasing
Bottom line	Income statement	Quote
Break-even analysis	Invoice	Stockholder equity
Break-even point	Liabilities	Unemployment
Credits	Net pay	compensation
Debits	Net worth	insurance
Deductions	Profit/loss statement	Vendor

Financial Processes

The main goal of a manufacturing company is to make products and sell them at a profit. The finance department performs those processes related to the company's money. In Chapter 10, you read about money as an input to manufacturing. Four main purposes were identified for the finance department.

1. Determining financial needs of the company
2. Acquiring adequate financing (money)
3. Spending money to pay for needed inputs
4. Reporting on the financial condition of the company

Chapter 10 described the first two purposes. This chapter will look at spending money and reporting on the company's financial condition.

The important processes related to spending money include calculating a break-even analysis, purchasing needed inputs, maintaining a general ledger, and calculating payroll. Two main reporting processes include creating a balance sheet and an income statement. Let's look at the spending processes first.

Spending Processes

Calculating a Break-even Analysis

Before spending money, companies analyze a product to determine its profit potential. Company managers want to know how much it will cost to make the product and how many products must be sold to turn a profit. The financial process used is called a break-even analysis. A **break-even analysis** finds the number of products a company must make to break even. At the **break-even point**, the company makes no profit and has no financial loss. The total of all money from the sale of products would be equal to the company's total costs. Remember from Chapter 10 that manufacturing costs are divided into fixed costs and variable costs. Fixed costs include

FIXED COSTS	VARIABLE COSTS

SELLING EXPENSES
  Advertising
  Shipping
  Sales commissions
 	
GENERAL EXPENSES
  Wages for management, engineering, marketing, finance, and human resources departments
  Loans
  Taxes
  Insurance
  Utilities
  R&D expenses
	PRODUCTION EXPENSES
	
	  Wages for production
	  Product materials
	  Production supplies
	  Packaging

Figure 17-1. A listing of the expenses for fixed and variable costs is needed to conduct a break-even analysis.

items in the general expense and sales expense categories. Variable costs include wages for production workers and the cost of materials in the product. Fixed costs are given as a total figure. Variable costs are given per unit (product). Figure 17-1 identifies expense items for fixed costs and variable costs.

There are two methods of calculating a break-even analysis—the algebraic formula method and the graphic method.

Algebraic Formula Method. An example of using the algebraic formula method to calculate the break-even point is shown in Figure 17-2. XYZ Manufacturing Company has fixed costs of $750 and variable costs of $2 per unit. Marketing researchers say consumers will pay $4 for the product. Using the algebraic formula, the break-even point for this product is 375 units. If XYZ made and sold exactly 375 units, they would break even—no profits and no losses. If they made or sold less than 375 products, they would lose money. However, if they sold more than 375 products, they would make a profit.

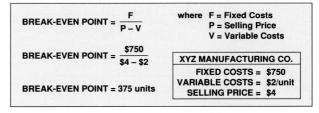

Figure 17-2. One way to calculate a break-even analysis is with an algebraic formula.

Graphic Method. In the graphic method, the break-even point is identified by plotting fixed costs, variable costs, and sales income on a graph. The process of determining the break-even point using the graphic method is shown in Figure 17-3. Starting with a piece of graph paper, follow these steps.

1. Draw the horizontal and vertical axes. The intersection of these two axes will be equal to zero, Figure 17-3A.
2. Mark the quantity of products along the horizontal axis. Start at zero and go

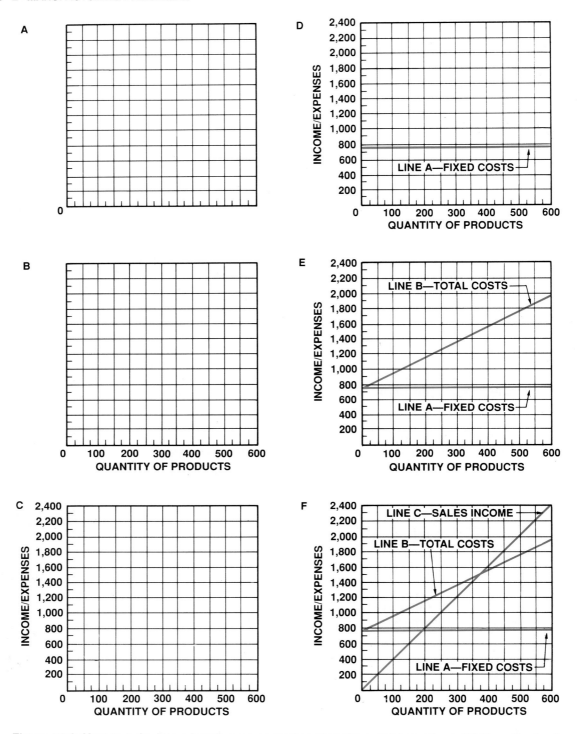

Figure 17-3. How to calculate a break-even analysis using the graphic method. (A) Draw the horizontal and vertical axes; (B) mark the quantity of products along the horizontal axis; (C) mark costs, sales income, and profits on the vertical axis; (D) plot the fixed costs line (fixed costs are constant regardless of the quantity of products); (E) plot the total costs line (total costs are equal to fixed costs plus variable costs for each quantity of products); and (F) plot the sales income line (sales income is equal to the selling price times the quantity of products sold).

to a quantity larger than the company plans to make. The quantity is stepped off in equal increments. In our example, multiples of 100 are used, Figure 17-3B.

3. Along the vertical axis, mark the dollar amounts representing costs, sales income, and profits. These figures also start with zero, but go to a maximum of the largest quantity (600) times estimated sales price ($4), or $2,400, Figure 17-3C.

4. Plot the fixed costs line. The fixed costs line represents fixed costs per each quantity. Two points are needed to plot the fixed costs line. The first point is for fixed costs at zero products, and the second point is for fixed costs at 600 products. Remember, fixed costs remain the same regardless of the quantity of products produced. In our example, fixed costs would be $750 for zero products and $750 for 600 products. A horizontal line identifying total fixed costs is drawn. This is line A on our graph, Figure 17-3D.

5. Plot the total costs line. The total costs line represents fixed costs plus variable costs for each quantity. Again, two points are needed—total costs at zero products and total costs at 600 products. At zero products, the company has fixed costs of $750, but no variable costs, because no manufacturing took place. At 600 products, total costs ($1,950) equal fixed costs of $750 plus variable costs of $1,200 ($2 per unit times 600 units). Line B is drawn to connect the two points, Figure 17-3E.

6. Plot the sales income line. The sales income line represents the product selling price times the quantity of products sold. If zero products are sold, there would be zero sales income. This is the first point. The second point is equal to 600 products times the sales price of $4, or $2,400. These two points are connected with a straight line to create the sales income line (line C), Figure 17-3F.

7. Find the break-even point. The intersection of lines B and C shows the break-even point. By dropping down to the horizontal axis, the quantity of products needed to break even can be found at 375. As we found with the algebraic formula, this company must make and sell 375 units to break even, Figure 17-4.

Notice the shaded areas below and above the break-even point in Figure 17-4. Below the break-even point (less than 375 units sold), the company would lose money. This area is called the loss zone. Above the break-even point (more than 375 units sold), the company would make a profit. This area is called the profit zone.

Computerized Break-even Analysis. Both the algebraic and graphic methods of break-even analysis have advantages, as shown in Figure 17-5. As with many other processes in manufacturing, people are using computers to per-

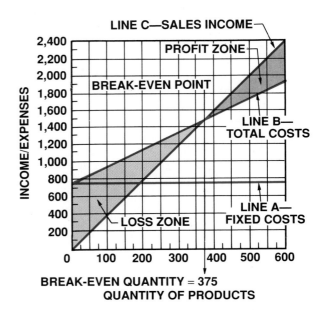

Figure 17-4. The intersection of the total costs line (line B) and the sales income line (line C) shows the break-even point.

ALGEBRAIC METHOD	GRAPHIC METHOD

More precise
Multiple calculations
  done easily, quickly
Multiple products done
  easily, quickly
	Easier to do
	Easier to read (visual)
	Easier to compare
	  different variables
	Graph makes comparing
	  different products easy

Figure 17-5. Both the algebraic and graphic methods of calculating a break-even analysis have certain advantages.

form break-even analyses with speed and accuracy. Computers are often used to make faster comparisons and to avoid calculation errors. With computers, accountants can see how different "what if?" situations will affect a break-even point. They can quickly change variables, such as product selling price, fixed or variable costs, and sales projections. Figure 17-6 shows a printout of a computerized break-even analysis for Small Manufacturing Company. Accountants input the fixed costs, variable costs, and the suggested selling price. The computer finds the break-even point. You can see on the printout that at a selling price of $49.99 the company must make and sell 626 products to break even. More powerful computer software can turn this data into a printed graph. Computers can give the finance department a break-even analysis with the speed and accuracy of the algebraic method *and* the reading ease of the graphic method.

```
=================================================================
                  SMALL MANUFACTURING COMPANY
 PRODUCT: #374-XYZ                          DATE: Oct. 26, 19XX
=================================================================
              VARIABLE COSTS --  PRODUCTION BUDGET
=================================================================
                        (per unit costs)
         Production Dept. Wages:    21.50
             Product Materials:     4.63     DIRECTIONS:  Input costs
           Production Supplies:     1.60     for items as requested.
                     Packaging:     1.25     Totals will be calculated
          Purchased Components:     3.60     automatically by program.
            Other Product Costs:    .15
         Other Production Costs:   0.00
                                  -------
      TOTAL PRODUCTION EXPENSES:   32.73/unit

=================================================================
                FIXED COSTS   -- SELLING BUDGET
=================================================================
                        (total costs)
          Advertising Materials:   300.00
             Sales Commissions:    400.00
               Shipping Costs:     275.00
         Other Marketing Costs:    100.00
                                  --------
      TOTAL MARKETING EXPENSES:   1075.00

=================================================================
              FIXED COSTS   -- GENERAL EXPENSES BUDGET
=================================================================
                       Wages:    7525.00   (all depts. except production)
                Loan Payments:     750.00
                        Taxes:     425.00
                   Insurances:     350.00
               Utilities Costs:    200.00
                R&D P rototype:     85.00
        Jigs, Fixtures, & Tools:   320.00
            Other General Costs:    70.00
                                 ---------
       TOTAL GENERAL EXPENSES:    9725.00

=================================================================
                    BREAK-EVEN ANALYSIS
=================================================================
| SELLING | FIXED  | VARIABLE| BREAK-EVEN |  DIRECTIONS:  Input suggested
|  PRICE  | COSTS  |  COSTS  |   POINT    |  SELLING PRICE. Computer will
|---------|--------|---------|------------|  automatically calculate the
|   49.99 |10800.00|  32.73  |   625.72   |  number of units needed for
|---------|--------|---------|------------|  the BREAK-EVEN POINT.
=================================================================
```

Figure 17-6. This printout is from a computerized spreadsheet program used to calculate a break-even analysis.

Changing Variables. As you read earlier, accountants can quickly play the "what if?" game by changing the variables in a break-even analysis. For example, what if Small Manufacturing Company raises its selling price by $5 per unit? Look at Figure 17-7 and notice the effect on the break-even point. The break-even point is now 486. This would make it easier for the company to be profitable in making this product, but the managers must ask themselves whether the consumer will pay $5 more for the product. Accountants can make similar changes to fixed and variable costs when they do break-even analyses. However, certain trade-offs will be made each time.

Purchasing Needed Inputs

Once a company has decided to make a product, the necessary inputs must be bought. Remember from Section Two that the inputs include workers, tools, materials, supplies, and more. The right inputs must be bought for the product being made. Materials must meet specifications. Qualified workers must be available. The right tools, machines, and supplies must be obtained. Manufacturing companies also buy services from other companies. For example, a transportation company might be hired to ship products to market, a communications company might be hired to produce high-quality working drawings using a CAD

```
|==============================================================================|
|                    SMALL MANUFACTURING COMPANY                               |
|PRODUCT: #374-XYZ                           DATE: Oct. 26, 19XX                |
|==============================================================================|
|                  VARIABLE COSTS --  PRODUCTION BUDGET                        |
|==============================================================================|
|                        (per unit costs)                                      |
|       Production Dept. Wages:    21.50                                        |
|           Product Materials:     4.63      DIRECTIONS:   Input costs          |
|          Production Supplies:    1.60      for items as requested.            |
|                    Packaging:    1.25      Totals will be calculated          |
|         Purchased Components:    3.60      automatically by program.          |
|           Other Product Costs:    .15                                         |
|        Other Production Costs:   0.00                                         |
|                                 -------                                       |
|    TOTAL PRODUCTION EXPENSES:    32.73/unit                                   |
|                                                                              |
|==============================================================================|
|                   FIXED COSTS  -- SELLING BUDGET                             |
|==============================================================================|
|                        (total costs)                                         |
|       Advertising Materials:    300.00                                        |
|           Sales Commissions:    400.00                                        |
|              Shipping Costs:    275.00                                        |
|        Other Marketing Costs:   100.00                                        |
|                                 -------                                       |
|     TOTAL MARKETING EXPENSES:  1075.00                                        |
|                                                                              |
|==============================================================================|
|              FIXED COSTS   -- GENERAL EXPENSES BUDGET                        |
|==============================================================================|
|                     Wages:     7525.00   (all depts. except production)      |
|             Loan Payments:      750.00                                        |
|                     Taxes:      425.00                                        |
|                Insurances:      350.00                                        |
|            Utilities Costs:     200.00                                        |
|              R&D P rototype:     85.00                                        |
|     Jigs, Fixtures, & Tools:    320.00                                        |
|         Other General Costs:     70.00                                        |
|                                --------                                       |
|      TOTAL GENERAL EXPENSES:   9725.00                                        |
|                                                                              |
|==============================================================================|
|                      BREAK-EVEN ANALYSIS                                     |
|=========|=========|=========|=============|==================================|
| SELLING | FIXED   | VARIABLE| BREAK-EVEN  | DIRECTIONS:  Input suggested      |
| PRICE   | COSTS   | COSTS   | POINT       | SELLING PRICE. Computer will      |
|---------|---------|---------|-------------| automatically calculate the       |
|  54.99  |10800.00 |  32.73  |   485.18    | number of units needed for        |
|---------|---------|---------|-------------| the BREAK-EVEN POINT.             |
|==============================================================================|
```

Figure 17-7. By raising their selling price by $5, Small Manufacturing reduced their break-even point from 626 to 486.

system, or a financial firm might be hired to handle the financial aspects of manufacturing.

The branch of the finance department known as **purchasing** buys these inputs, Figure 17-8. Their job is to find the **vendor** (supplier) who will sell the best quality items to the manufacturing company at the best possible price and will deliver the items on time. The purchasing process includes the following steps.

1. Submitting a purchase requisition. A **purchase requisition** (request) form is submitted to purchasing by production planners. The purchase requisition lists the items needed along with quality, quantity, and delivery time specifications.

Figure 17-8. Workers in the purchasing department buy the needed inputs for manufacturing.
(*Permission granted by Westvago Corporation/ Photography by Jeffrey Aranita*)

2. Securing bids and quotes. Purchasing secures bids and quotes from vendors. Bids and quotes are prices for items. A **bid** is a guaranteed price from a vendor. With a bid, the vendor tells the purchasing department that they will sell the item at the bid price, guaranteed. Bids usually specify a time limit. A **quote** is a price that is not guaranteed by the vendor. With a quote, the vendor tells purchasing the items may be sold at the quoted price, but there is not a guarantee.

3. Selecting vendors. Bids and quotes let purchasers compare vendors to find the best quality items at the best prices. Purchasers also consider the reputation of the vendor for on-time delivery at the bid or quote price. Purchasers may call vendors to negotiate a better price. Based on the bids, quotes, and vendor reputation, purchasers select the best vendor.

4. Sending purchase orders. After a vendor has been selected, the purchasing department sends purchase orders. A **purchase order** gives the vendor permission to send the materials. Once the vendor receives and signs the purchase order, it becomes a contract between the two parties. The vendor agrees to sell the items, and the company agrees to pay for them. The purchase order specifies price, quality, quantity, and date and place of delivery, Figure 17-9.

5. Receiving the items and invoice. The next step is for the vendor to send the items purchased, along with an invoice. An **invoice** is a sales bill. The purchasing department checks the invoice to ensure correct price and other specifications identified in the purchase order. For most items, a quality control inspector checks the items delivered to ensure proper quality from the vendor. Inferior tools or materials will be sent back, Figure 17-10.

PURCHASE ORDER

NO:

This number must appear on
invoices, packing lists and packages.
Invoice in duplicate.

SHIP PREPAID WITH INSIDE DELIVERY TO:

TO

DATE REQUIRED	SHIP VIA	YOUR QUOTE NO.	OUR REQUISITION NO.	ORIGINATED BY

ITEM	QUANTITY	UNIT	DESCRIPTION	UNIT PRICE	TOTAL PRICE

SPECIAL INSTRUCTIONS
FOR THIS ORDER ONLY

BUYER   DATE

INTERNAL NOTES

ORIGINATING DEPARTMENT(S)   ACCOUNT DISTRIBUTION

RECEIVING DATA			DATE/BY	ITEM	QUANTITY	DATE/BY	ITEM	QUANTITY	DATE/BY	ITEM	QUANTITY
DATE/BY	ITEM	QUANTITY									

**Figure 17-9. A purchase order gives the vendor permission to
send the needed materials to the manufacturing company.**

**Figure 17-10. An important part of the purchasing
process is quality control inspection of delivered
items.** *(Courtesy of Rockwell International/Ted
Horowitz)*

6. Authorizing payment. Once the invoice
and the purchased items have been
checked, the purchasing department
authorizes accountants in the finance
department to pay the vendor for the
purchase made by the company. This
completes the purchasing process.

Purchasing is an important part of the manufacturing enterprise. Workers in the purchasing department buy the best quality items at
the best possible prices. They also make sure
the production department has the inputs they
need to manufacture products. A big part of
the job of purchasing is to make sure items are
delivered on time. After the purchase order
has been sent, purchasing workers call the

vendor to ensure on-time delivery. As with every position in manufacturing, purchasing workers must do their job correctly if the company is to be successful and profitable.

Maintaining a General Ledger

The finance department must keep track of all money coming into and going out of the manufacturing company. Accountants use a general ledger to keep track of the inflow and outflow of money. A **general ledger** is a way to record all the financial transactions made by the company. General ledgers are similar to a personal checking account. Figure 17-11 shows a typical general ledger sheet. Each line on the ledger is for a different transaction. Each transaction is listed as a debit or a credit. **Debits** are payments made to other people for expenses. When checks are written, debits are subtracted from the balance in the last column. **Credits** are money put into the company account. When money from product sales or stock sales is put into the company account, credits are added to the balance. In order for the company to be profitable, the balance should remain a positive number. To maintain a positive balance, the total of all credits should be more than the total of all debits.

The general ledger is a simple yet effective way of keeping track of the daily financial condition of the company. As with many manufacturing processes today, these financial records are often kept on a computerized general ledger.

Calculating Payroll

Payroll is often one of the largest debits on an operating manufacturer's general ledger. Each worker must be paid for the number of hours worked. Large manufacturing companies employ thousands of workers. Payroll can be in the millions of dollars per year. The hours an employee works are kept on time cards. Time card machines record the starting and stopping time for each worker. There is a specific process for determining a worker's pay. Workers are usually paid an hourly rate, such as $10 per hour. The company is responsible for subtracting **deductions**, such as taxes, insurances, and retirement contributions, from workers' pay and sending that money to the proper recipients. Figure 17-12 shows some

NUMBER	DATE	DESCRIPTION OF TRANSACTION	DEBITS (PAYMENTS)	CREDITS (DEPOSITS)	BALANCE
	2/15	Stock Sale	$	$100,000 –	$100,000
	2/28	Bank Loan		50,000 –	150,000
100	3/1	Equipment Purchase	50,000 –		100,000
101	3/8	Payroll	7,525 –		92,475
102	3/8	Rent	1,000 –		91,475
103	3/10	Insurance	350 –		91,125
	3/31	Sales Income		11,250 –	102,375
104	3/31	Office Supplies	85 –		102,290
105	4/1	Utilities	200 –		102,090
106	4/5	Advertising	300 –		101,790
107	4/7	Tool Replacement	800 –		100,990
108	4/15	Shipping Contract	275 –		100,715
109	4/17	Materials Inventory	915 –		99,800
110	4/20	Taxes	425 –		99,375

Figure 17-11. Workers in the finance department record all financial transactions on a general ledger.

CALCULATING A WORKER'S PAY

PROCESS	FORMULA	CALCULATION	TOTAL
GROSS PAY			
Gross pay	Hourly wage rate × hours worked	$10 × 40	$400.00
DEDUCTIONS			
Social security	Gross pay × 7.51%* (up to annual maximum)	$400 × 7.51%	− 30.04
Federal tax	Taken from IRS tax tables*	NA	− 44.00
State tax	Gross pay × 2% (or applicable state rate)	$400 × 2%	− 8.00
Local tax	Gross pay × 1% (or local rate)	$400 × 1%	− 4.00
Unemployment Compensation Insurance	Gross pay × .1% (or applicable rate)	$400 × .1%	− 0.40
Other deductions (Health insurance, savings plan, union dues, etc.)	Based on contract agreement	NA	− 7.50
*1989 rates. Rates may change each year.		**NET PAY**	**$306.06**

Figure 17-12. Quite a few deductions come out of a worker's gross pay. The net pay is the amount of money workers receive in their paychecks.

examples of deductions a worker might see taken from a paycheck. The process of calculating these deductions includes the following steps:

1. Calculating gross pay. **Gross pay** is equal to the hourly wage rate multiplied by the number of hours the employee has worked.

2. Deducting Social Security. Social Security deductions are required by law. In 1989, workers paid 7.51 percent of their gross incomes, up to a preset annual maximum, to Social Security. The percentage rate and the annual maximum can change from year to year. In 1989, the maximum amount that could be deducted for Social Security was $3,672. To calculate the Social Security deduction in our example, multiply gross pay times 0.751 (7.51 percent), and subtract this amount from the gross pay.

3. Deducting federal income tax. Income tax deductions are also required by law. The Internal Revenue Service cre-

ates tables that employers use to determine the amount of federal income tax, Figure 17-13. These tables are based on gross wages and withholding allowances. The worker in our example earned gross wages of $400 and took one withholding allowance. Federal income tax is therefore equal to $44. This amount is subtracted from the gross pay.

4. Deducting state taxes. States have varying tax rates. The state tax rate used in Figure 17-12 is 2 percent. Multiply gross pay times 0.02 (2 percent), and subtract from the gross wages.

5. Deducting local taxes. Local taxes also vary by region. In Figure 17-12, 1 percent was used as the local tax rate.

6. Deducting unemployment compensation. **Unemployment compensation insurance** is deducted from the worker's pay in case of future layoff from the job. Workers who contribute to UCI and are unemployed because of layoffs collect money from the government. In

SINGLE Persons–WEEKLY Payroll Period

(For Wages Paid After December 1988)

And the wages are–		And the number of withholding allowances claimed is–										
At least	But less than	0	1	2	3	4	5	6	7	8	9	10
		The amount of income tax to be withheld shall be–										
$540	$550	$100	$90	$79	$68	$57	$50	$44	$38	$32	$27	$21
550	560	103	92	82	71	60	51	45	40	34	28	22
560	570	106	95	84	74	63	53	47	41	35	30	24
570	580	109	98	87	76	66	55	48	43	37	31	25
580	590	112	101	90	79	68	58	50	44	38	33	27
590	600	114	104	93	82	71	60	51	46	40	34	28
600	610	117	106	96	85	74	63	53	47	41	36	30
610	620	120	109	98	88	77	66	55	49	43	37	31
620	630	123	112	101	90	80	69	58	50	44	39	33
630	640	126	115	104	93	82	72	61	52	46	40	34
640	650	128	118	107	96	85	74	64	53	47	42	36
650	660	131	120	110	99	88	77	66	56	49	43	37
660	670	134	123	112	102	91	80	69	59	50	45	39
670	680	137	126	115	104	94	83	72	61	52	46	40
680	690	140	129	118	107	96	86	75	64	53	48	42
690	700	142	132	121	110	99	88	78	67	56	49	43
700	710	145	134	124	113	102	91	80	70	59	51	45
710	720	148	137	126	116	105	94	83	73	62	52	46
720	730	151	140	129	118	108	97	86	75	65	54	48
730	740	154	143	132	121	110	100	89	78	67	57	49
740	750	156	146	135	124	113	102	92	81	70	59	51
750	760	159	148	138	127	116	105	94	84	73	62	52
760	770	162	151	140	130	119	108	97	87	76	65	54
770	780	165	154	143	132	122	111	100	89	79	68	57
780	790	8	157	146	135	124	114	103	92	81	71	60
8			0			7	116	06				63
							1					6

Figure 17-13. Federal income tax deductions are required by law. The amount of the deduction is found in tables available from the Internal Revenue Service. This table shows rates applicable to single wage-earners during 1989.

our example, unemployment compensation is equal to 0.1 percent.

7. Other deductions. Deductions may also be made from a worker's pay for insurances, retirement funds, union dues, or other items. These deductions are based on agreements created between unions and companies.

8. After all the deductions have been subtracted from the worker's gross pay, the **net pay** is left. This is the amount of money the worker will receive in a paycheck.

Notice the amount of money deducted from the worker's gross pay in Figure 17-12. The company is responsible for paying this money to the proper recipients, such as the IRS, state tax bureaus, and insurance companies.

Computerized Payroll. Calculating a payroll is a complex process and leaves a lot of room for mistakes. Most manufacturing companies use computerized payroll systems to make the job easier. Figure 17-14 shows a computerized payroll printout for a small manufacturing company. With computers, the finance department worker in charge of payroll simply inputs the number of hours an employee has worked. The deductions and net pay are then calculated automatically.

Financial Reporting Processes

The finance department is also responsible for reporting on the financial condition of the company. Two of the more common reports created by accountants are the balance sheet and the income statement. With these two doc-

			SOC SEC	**FEDERAL TAX**	**STATE TAX**	**UCI**	**LOCAL TAX**	**OTHER**	**NET PAY**
WORKER	**HRS**	**GROSS**							
Jones	82	307.50	23.09	40.00	6.46	.31	3.08	3.08	231.49
Smith	82	307.50	23.09	40.00	6.46	.31	3.08	3.08	231.49
Jeffers	80	300.00	22.53	40.00	6.30	.30	3.00	3.00	224.87
Henry	80	300.00	22.53	40.00	6.30	.30	3.00	3.00	224.87
Carns	80	300.00	22.53	40.00	6.30	.30	3.00	3.00	224.87
Schmidt	80	300.00	22.53	40.00	6.30	.30	3.00	3.00	224.87
Elway	·80	300.00	22.53	40.00	6.30	.30	3.00	3.00	224.87
White	80	300.00	22.53	29.00	6.30	.30	3.00	3.00	235.87
Wilson	78	292.50	21.97	38.00	6.14	.29	2.93	2.93	220.25
Hseng	74	277.50	20.84	29.00	5.83	.28	2.77	2.77	216.00
Walker	72	270.00	20.28	35.00	5.67	.27	2.70	2.70	203.38
Ryan	42	157.50	11.83	17.00	3.31	.16	1.57	1.57	122.06
Samuels	35	131.25	9.86	13.00	2.76	.13	1.31	1.31	102.88
TOTALS:	**945**	**3543.75**	**266.14**	**441.00**	**74.42**	**3.54**	**35.44**	**35.44**	**2687.78**

PRODUCTION PAYROLL
C&C MANUFACTURING CO.

WAGE RATE: $3.75/hour   DATE: March 21, 1989

Figure 17-14. Most manufacturing companies use computers to calculate gross pay, deductions, and net pay for their workers.

uments, the finance department can show company managers and stockholders how well the company is doing financially. Each of these sheets is prepared at regular intervals, such as monthly, quarterly, and yearly. The balance sheet and income statement for a large corporation can be complicated and confusing. No matter how complicated, though, there are basic components always found in these reports. Let's look at the basic components for the balance sheet and income statement.

Creating a Balance Sheet

A **balance sheet** reports the financial condition of the company. All balance sheets have two main parts—assets of the company and claims against assets. The **assets** section lists the value of everything the company owns. The part that lists the claims against the company assets includes liabilities and stockholder equity. The **liabilities** section lists the value of what the company owes to other companies and businesses. Liabilities are claims made against the assets of the company by noncompany owners. **Stockholder equity** is the claim made against company assets by actual owners of the company—the stockholders. Stockhold-

er equity is equal to the value of stock issued by the company.

Figure 17-15 shows a balance sheet for the Mighty Manufacturing Company. The company assets include cash, accounts receivable (money owed to the company), investments, product inventory, land and buildings, and machines and equipment. Mighty's liabilities include credits (money the company owes to vendors), bank loans, bond payments, and taxes. Stockholder equity is equal to $15,000 because Mighty Manufacturing issued 3,000 shares of stock at $5 per share. Retained earnings are also included under stockholder equity. This is money the company keeps to reinvest in equipment, machines, new buildings, or other improvements for the company.

Notice that the total assets for Mighty Manufacturing equal the total liabilities plus stockholder equity. This is why this sheet is called a balance sheet. Total assets of the company should balance total liabilities. When company managers, stockholders, or potential investors look at a balance sheet, they want to know the net worth of the company. **Net worth** is equal to total assets minus total liabilities. This is the value of stockholder equity. Mighty

---

MIGHTY MANUFACTURING COMPANY
Balance Sheet
Year Ending December 31, 1989

ASSETS

Cash	$ 7,000
Accounts receivable	5,000
Investments	11,700
Product inventory	25,000
Land and buildings	24,000
Machines and equipment	27,300
Total Assets	**$ 100,000**

LIABILITIES

Credits	8,800
Bank loans	6,700
Bond payments	32,900
Taxes	6,500
Total Liabilities	**$ 54,900**

Stockholder equity

stock ($5 × 3,000 shares)	$ 15,000
Retained earnings	30,100
Total stockholder equity	**$ 45,100**
Total liabilities and stockholder equity	**$ 100,000**

Figure 17-15. One way manufacturing companies report their financial condition to stockholders is with a balance sheet. A balance sheet includes assets and liabilities. The net worth, or stockholder equity, of the company is equal to assets minus liabilities.

Manufacturing has a net worth of $45,100. Often, a balance sheet will compare two years of operation. Investors will compare balance sheets over two or more years to see if the company's net worth is growing.

Formulating an Income Statement

The **income statement** reports the financial success of the company over set time periods, such as monthly, quarterly, or yearly. Income statements are also called **profit/loss statements**. This is because they report how much profit the company made or how much money they lost. The income statement includes two main parts—income and expenses, Figure 17-16. The income section shows the amount of money the company took in by selling their products. This is called sales income. Also included are income from other sources, such as the sale of buildings, equipment, tools, waste materials, and services. The expenses section includes the following items:

1. Cost of goods sold. This is equal to the production department expenses or the total variable costs of the company. Remember, the production expenses include wages for production workers and the materials costs per product.

2. Gross profits. Gross profits are equal to total income minus the costs of goods sold. This is the profit before all

MIGHTY MANUFACTURING COMPANY
Income Statement
Year Ending December 31, 1989

INCOME
    Sales income .... $ 120,000
    Other income 20,000

        Total Income .... $ 140,000

EXPENSES
    Cost of goods sold 95,000

        Gross Profits .... $ 45,000

    Operating expenses
        Selling expenses 4,000
        General expenses 7,500
        Other expenses 2,700

    Earnings before interest and taxes (EBIT) .... $ 30,800

    Interest Expenses
    Bank loans 2,550
    Bonds 1,000
    Other 600

    Taxes 13,635

NET INCOME .... $ 13,015

Figure 17-16. Income statements, also called profit/loss statements, report how much money a manufacturing company has made or lost.

expenses (except for production expenses) are considered.

3. Operating expenses. Included here are the selling expenses, general expenses, and any other expenses the company has.

4. Earnings before interest and taxes (EBIT). **EBIT** is equal to gross profits minus operating expenses.

5. Interest expenses. Interest the company pays to banks, bond holders, or other groups are listed here.

6. Taxes. Just like individuals, manufacturing companies must pay income taxes on the money they make.

7. Net income. Subtracting interest expenses and taxes from EBIT equals the net income of the company. If this number is positive, the net income is a profit. If this number is negative, the net income is a loss. The net income line is often referred to as the **bottom line**. The bottom line shows how much money the company made for the month, quarter, or year. When company managers and investors want to know what the bottom line is for a company, they review the income statement.

Calculating Dividend Payments

At the end of each business cycle, such as a quarter or a year, profitable manufacturing corporations pay dividends to their owners—the stockholders. The amount of dividends paid to stockholders is found using information from the income statement and the balance sheet.

Dividends per share equal net profits (found on the income statement) divided by the number of shares issued (found on the balance sheet). Figure 17-17 shows how Mighty Manufacturing Company would figure its dividends based on its income statement and balance sheet. Companies paying high dividends will attract more investors. The more investors a company has, the more cash will be available for company improvements.

$$\text{DIVIDENDS PER SHARE} = \frac{\text{NET PROFITS}}{\text{NUMBER OF SHARES}}$$

$$\text{DIVIDENDS PER SHARE} = \frac{\$13,015}{3,000}$$

$$\text{DIVIDENDS PER SHARE} = \$4.34$$

Figure 17-17. The amount of dividends per share paid to stockholders is equal to net profits divided by the number of shares of stock issued.

Summary

In manufacturing, the finance department is responsible for keeping track of the money. This chapter examined two areas of responsibility for finance workers—spending money for needed inputs and reporting on the financial condition of the company. Purchasing workers are responsible for buying the inputs needed to make the manufacturing company run efficiently. However, before any money is spent, accountants conduct a break-even analysis to determine the number of products that must be produced to break even. All financial transactions are kept on a general ledger. The two main reporting processes include creating a balance sheet and an income statement. Workers in the finance department are just as important as workers in any other department. If the company is to be profitable, every worker must do the job correctly.

DISCUSSION QUESTIONS

1. Can you describe three reasons why the break-even analysis is an important financial tool for manufacturing companies?

2. What are the names of the two methods of calculating a break-even analysis? Describe the advantages and disadvantages of each method. Which would you prefer to use?

3. What are debits and credits? Can you give another name for each of these?

4. On a general ledger, what mathematical calculations are conducted with a debit or credit?

5. What are some of the items manufacturing companies list as assets and liabilities on a balance sheet?

6. Purchasing is an important part of a manufacturing enterprise. What are the steps in the purchasing process in manufacturing?

7. What are the different deductions made from a worker's gross pay each payday?

CHAPTER ACTIVITIES

⚙ CALCULATING A BREAK-EVEN ANALYSIS

OBJECTIVE

The break-even analysis is an important part of the financial processes in manufacturing. Before a company spends any money on production, a break-even analysis must be calculated with estimates for fixed costs, variable costs, and product selling price.

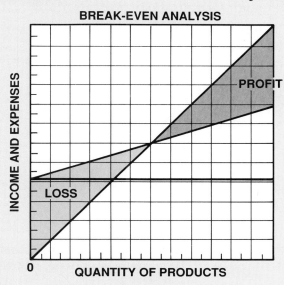

BREAK-EVEN ANALYSIS

In this activity, you and the members of your classroom manufacturing enterprise will select a product and calculate a break-even analysis. You will use one of the three methods discussed in this chapter—the algebraic method, the graphic method, or a computer program.

In order to calculate a break-even analysis, you will need three things: estimates for fixed costs, estimates for variable costs, and a suggested selling price. Remember, fixed costs include items in the general expense budget and sales expense budget. Variable costs include wages for labor in the production department and the cost of materials used to make the product. The market research group should provide the suggested selling price. Market researchers can interview potential consumers to get their opinions on selling prices, or they can compare their product with similar products already on the market.

MATERIALS AND SUPPLIES

1. Completed worksheets for fixed costs and variable costs (handouts)
2. Suggested selling price from marketing department
3. Depending on which method of calculation you will use, you will need the following:
   - ■ a calculator for the algebraic method

■ graph paper and drawing instruments for the graphic method
■ computer, software program, and printer for the computer method

PROCEDURE

1. Break the class into three different groups—one for the algebraic method, one for the graphic method, and one for the computer method. (If a computer is not available, use two groups or divide the work responsibilities differently.)
2. Complete the worksheets for fixed costs and variable costs (handouts).
3. Determine the suggested selling price using market research.
4. Calculate the break-even point for your product.
5. Compare the results among your three groups to ensure consistent, correct calculations.
6. Play the "what if?" game by changing the suggested selling price, fixed costs, or variable costs.

MATH/SCIENCE CONNECTION

The algebraic formula for calculating a break-even analysis is:

$$\text{Break-even Point} = \frac{F}{P - V}$$

Where: F = fixed costs
P = selling price
V = variable costs

PROBLEM: A company with fixed costs of $125,000 and variable costs of $12.75 per unit plans to sell its new product for $19.95. How many products must the company sell to break even?

SOLUTION:

$$\text{Break-even Point} = \frac{F}{P - V}$$

$$\text{Break-even Point} = \frac{\$125,000}{\$19.95 - \$12.75}$$

$$\text{Break-even Point} = 17,434 \text{ units}$$

(Actually, the break-even point is 17,433.75 units. However, the company really can't make and sell three-fourths of a product—who would buy an incomplete product?)

PROBLEM: As a follow-up, if the company sold exactly 17,434 products, how much profit would it make?

SOLUTION: The company would break even at $17,433.75 units. They sold 17,434 units. The difference between these two numbers times the selling price will give us the profit. The formula and solution look like this:

Profit = (17,434 units − 17,433.75 units) ($19.95)
Profit = (.25 units) ($19.95)
Profit = $4.98 (actually $4.9875, but who pay three-fourths of one cent?)

RELATED QUESTIONS

1. Why do manufacturing companies calculate break-even analyses?
2. What three factors are needed to calculate a break-even analysis?
3. What three methods can be used to calculate a break-even analysis? Which do you like best? Why?
4. What is the break-even point for a company that has $100 in fixed costs, $8 in variable costs, and a product selling price of $12.99?

 CALCULATING PAYROLL

OBJECTIVE

For many workers, the most important days in the month are paydays. Most people work to make money. Unfortunately, most workers also find something to complain about on paydays—the money taken from their pay for taxes and other deductions.

In this activity, you will learn more about the importance of payroll deductions by calculating the payroll for yourself and other student workers in your manufacturing class.

Many manufacturing workers are paid for the number of hours they work. Their gross pay equals the number of hours they worked times their hourly wage rate. The amount of money in a worker's pay check is net pay; that is, the gross pay minus deductions for taxes and social security.

Some companies give their workers incentive or bonus pay. Workers can receive the bonus money by producing or selling a certain number of products, by working overtime, or by keeping a perfect safety record. Companies also deduct money from worker's pay for insurances, retirement funds, and other items. These extra pay and deduction items are often negotiated between the workers and the company management.

MATERIALS AND SUPPLIES

1. Worker time cards
2. Calculators
3. Payroll worksheet, Figure 1

PAYROLL WORKSHEET

WORKER: _____

	_____	Hourly wage rate
×	_____	Hours worked
=	_____	**Gross pay**
−	_____	Federal tax
−	_____	State tax
−	_____	Local tax
−	_____	Unemployment insurance compensation
−	_____	Other deductions
=	_____	**Net pay**

Figure 1

PROCEDURE

1. Hold negotiation sessions between the workers and managers in your manufacturing company. (Your teacher might act as the chief executive officer for the company.) Consider negotiating for these bonuses and deductions:

   BONUSES
   - Perfect attendance
   - Perfect safety record
   - Performing extra lab work
   - Selling the most products
   - Scoring 100% on quizzes
   - Bringing in current event articles on manufacturing
   - Answering questions during class discussions
   - Class productivity incentive (making a set number of products)

   DEDUCTIONS
   - Not using safety glasses
   - Coming late to class
   - Excess absences
   - Neglecting clean-up
   - Neglecting tool storage
   - Misuse of tools/machines
   - Violating other rules established by teacher

   Payroll calculations will be easier if you make bonus pay and deduction items worth so many hours of work. For example, if a student has a perfect safety record, two work hours could be added to the total number of hours the student worked during the pay period.

2. Calculate worker pay using the payroll worksheet in Figure 1. (Review the processes described in the chapter for calculating gross pay, deductions, and net pay.)

3. If the IRS payroll deductions booklet is not available, you can use a straight percentage, such as 14%.

4. Ask your teacher what percentages you should use for state taxes, local taxes, and unemployment compensation insurance. Some areas might not have state or local taxes or unemployment compensation insurance.

5. Issue simulated pay checks for the workers in your class. Worker pay may be used for a number of different items. In some schools, manufacturing student-workers can use their pay to
   - invest in stock for the class manufacturing company.
   - purchase products made by the manufacturing company.
   - buy extra points on quizzes.
   - hire students to help on difficult assignments.
   - purchase materials for custom-manufactured products.
   - purchase food from the school cafeteria.

Mighty Manufacturing Co.	No. _____
Pay To The Order Of _____	$ [ ]
_____	**DOLLARS**
School Town Bank	_____

Some schools get savings coupons donated by bookstores, restaurants, record stores, or other businesses. Workers can then use their pay checks to purchase these coupons. Of course, you will have to negotiate with your teacher for the privilege of using your pay for any of the items above.

6. You can change this activity by hiring one student in the class to be payroll accountant or by using computer spreadsheet programs to calculate payroll.

MATH/SCIENCE CONNECTION

To calculate payroll deductions, you must multiply whole numbers by percentages. This can be a tricky operation for some people. One thing you must remember is that a percentage represents part of a whole expressed in hundredths. Therefore, a percentage can be expressed as a decimal. For example, 25% is actually 25/100. If you want to multiply a number by 25%, you must first divide 25 by 100.

$$\frac{25}{100} = .25$$

The resulting decimal (.25) is then multiplied by the number to get the product. For example, say you want to find 25% of $1,000. First, divide 25 by 100, then multiply your answer times $1,000. The calculations look like this:

$$\frac{25}{100} = .25 \qquad .25 \times \$1,000 = \$250$$

When calculating Social Security deductions for a worker's pay, you must multiply gross pay times the yearly percentage. For a worker with a gross pay of $350 in 1989, here are the calculations. (The Social Security rate was 7.51% in 1989.)

$$\frac{7.51}{100} = .0751 \qquad .0751 \times \$350 = \$26.285$$

Try these calculations on this problem.

PROBLEM: Calculate the following deductions for a worker whose gross pay was $425:

- Federal Taxes at 14.00%
- State Taxes at   1.50%
- Local Taxes at   0.10%

SOLUTION:

Federal Taxes

$$\frac{14}{100} = .14 \qquad .14 \times \$425 = \$59.50$$

State Taxes

$$\frac{1.50}{100} = .015 \qquad .015 \times \$425 = \$6.375$$

Local Taxes

$$\frac{10}{100} = .001 \qquad .001 \times \$425 = \$0.425$$

RELATED QUESTIONS

1. How do you calculate the gross pay for a worker?
2. What is the difference between gross pay and net pay?
3. What are some of the various deductions taken from a worker's pay?
4. Look at the sample problem again. The deductions for federal, state, and local taxes equalled $66.30. What percentage of the worker's gross pay was deducted for these taxes? Stated another way, $66.30 is what percent of $425?

SECTION FOUR

MANUFACTURING OUTPUTS

Section four discusses the outputs of manufacturing. Outputs are the results of manufacturing processes. They include products (goods) and the by-products of scrap, waste, and pollution. In this section, you will study the different types of manufactured products, including durable and nondurable consumer goods. You will also learn about the by-products of manufacturing, and how scrap, waste, and pollution can be turned into inputs through recycling.

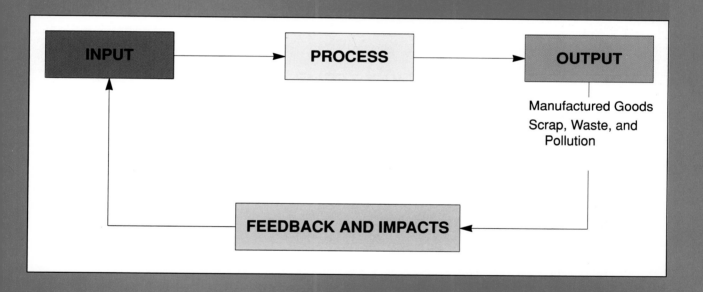

CHAPTER 18
Manufactured Goods

OBJECTIVES

After completing this chapter, you will know about:

■ The availability of manufactured goods as one of the variables that determine standard of living.

■ Classifying consumer goods as durable or nondurable.

■ The significance of industrial goods for all of manufacturing.

■ The impact of medical goods on quality and length of human life.

■ The impacts and consequences of military goods, both conventional and nuclear.

KEY TERMS

Antibody
Balance of power
Biotechnology
Built-in obsolescence
Conventional
Disposables
Durables

Food and Drug
   Administration (FDA)
Fission
Fusion
Generic
Genetic engineering
Nondurable

Nuclear
Over-the-counter
Pharmaceutical
Prescription
Standard of living
Styling cycle

Manufactured Goods

The most obvious output of manufacturing is the goods produced. After all, manufacturing companies exist for the very purpose of providing these goods. The products are the end result of all the previous planning, research, development, materials processing, marketing, and numerous other tasks.

A stroll through any department store shows the ingenuity and variety of manufactured goods. Products ranging from toothpaste to furniture to clothing can be found, Figure

18-1. There may be several brands of similar products. This allows customers to select according to price, quality, appearance, or simply personal preference. There may be as many as a dozen brands of coffee from which to choose. Perhaps the brand using the most creative advertising campaign will sell the best or perhaps the cheapest brand will. The luxury of selection is not worldwide. Coffee may be completely unavailable or too expensive for most people to buy in some parts of the world.

Figure 18-1. As consumers, manufactured goods are a part of our everyday lives. (Courtesy of Underwriters Laboratories Inc. [UL])

Availability of manufactured goods is one of the variables that determines people's **standard of living**.

When we think of manufactured goods, we most commonly think of consumer goods like those discussed above. Consumer goods do

make up a large part of the total of manufactured goods. However, if all of manufacturing produced only consumer goods, the act of manufacturing would eventually come to a halt. As machines wore out, they could not be repaired with new parts or replaced with newer models. The life-saving medical technologies, including vaccines and other drugs, that have deterred many diseases would eventually run out. The **balance of power** around the world would also change as weapons were used up or worn out without being replaced. Therefore, it is important and correct that we discuss not only consumer goods, but also industrial, medical, and military goods, Figure 18-2.

Consumer Goods

Consumer goods are those goods made for people to use in their daily lives. They are usually bought in stores or through catalogs. They are often marketed nationwide or worldwide. Some consumer goods appeal to a specific geographic region or ethnic group. Others are more **generic**, or general. Generic can also be used to describe products that do not have a trademark. Although often comparable in quality, generic goods are frequently less expensive because they are plainly packaged and go largely unadvertised, Figure 18-3. Goods designed and marketed for a specific group of

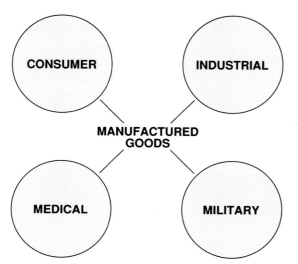

Figure 18-2. Four major categories of manufactured goods include consumer, industrial, medical, and military goods.

Figure 18-3. Private label goods are those marketed without a national brand name and are often less expensive to buy. (Courtesy of Price Chopper Supermarkets)

consumers or geographic region include items geared to a certain climate, and ethnic, religious, and cultural items. Of course, there are many more types of specialty goods. Most items are, however, made for the general public.

Consumer goods can further be divided into two categories: **durables** and **nondurables**.

Durable Consumer Goods

Durable goods are those that last for a long time or that wear out slowly. A car is a durable good, as is a bicycle. The length of time a durable product lasts is based on its intended use, the nature of its construction, and the materials used to make it. This length of time can be changed by the manufacturer. Sometimes the product is engineered to last a shorter period than might otherwise be possible. This means it will have to be replaced more often. This technique is called **built-in obsolescence**.

Figure 18-4. Some companies gain a reputation for quality products by producing goods that are durable and attractive. *(Courtesy of Mercantile Stores Company, Inc.)*

Styling cycles may also limit how long a durable good will last. A **styling cycle** is the amount of time something is considered to be in style. Durable goods can become nondurable by using styling cycles and built-in obsolescence.

Another characteristic of durable consumer goods is a generally higher cost. As a result consumers are more likely to research competing brands and buy more carefully than they would for nondurable goods. A consumer about to invest $15,000 in a new car, or even $200 in a bicycle, will probably "do some homework" before investing.

Some manufacturers of durable goods make a sincere effort to make quality, long-lasting goods. They refuse to set styling cycles or incorporate built-in obsolescence. These manufacturers gain a reputation for quality. Their product may last indefinitely, Figure 18-4. Informed consumers take into account these factors when buying. They may not mind paying higher prices for these very durable goods. They know that they will eventually come out ahead if they don't need to repair or replace the purchase for many years.

Nondurable Consumer Goods

Nondurable goods are those destroyed by use or shortly after use. They make up the majority of consumer goods. They can be purchased inexpensively. Most nondurables are intentionally made with less expensive materials and nonreplaceable and nonrepairable parts.

Today we live in a world of **disposables**. We have disposable diapers, disposable razors, disposable eating utensils, and even disposable cameras, Figure 18-5. Disposables are items that we throw out after use. The term "disposable" is misleading because it suggests that once an item is in the garbage truck, it is disposed of. But many of these nondurable disposables are made from plastics that do not easily biodegrade. As landfills fill up with these "disposables," it forces us to reevaluate the wide use of disposable nondurables.

Food is another example of nondurable goods. Since food is a basic human need, manufacturers are guaranteed a market. Competi-

Figure 18-5. Disposable consumer products are those that are thrown away after use. They typically have a short use-span. *(Courtesy of Constar International, Inc.)*

Figure 18-6. Foods containing natural ingredients and containing fewer additives and preservatives are recently more popular. *(Courtesy of National Nutritional Foods Association, Costa Mesa, CA)*

tion between brands is often intense. Food manufacturers compete to produce the tastiest, most appealing goods. The most common problems with manufacturing food items are the use of chemical additives to make foods stay fresh longer, and the use of nutrition-draining processes. The result has been the recent consumer demand for natural foods, Figure 18-6. People may be willing to pay more for organically grown food that has not been highly processed.

The line between durable and nondurable consumer goods is often fuzzy. As consumers learn more about our limited materials and energy resources, they ask for more durable, nondisposable consumer goods.

Industrial Goods

Industrial goods are used to produce other products. They also can be called either durable or nondurable. Nondurable industrial goods are mostly considered supplies, such as fasteners, adhesives, and lubricants. Durable industrial goods are the tools and machines used in industry. Many machines are specialized one-of-a-kind items that can take many months to design and make, Figure 18-7. Others are more generalized and have greater marketability. The machines in your technology laboratory are general machines with a wide market. Most durable industrial goods are manufactured on demand. This means that

Figure 18-7. This 300-ton wheel press is a one-of-a-kind industrial product made specifically for a particular customer. *(Courtesy of Simmons Machine Tool Corp.)*

Over-Tired

Americans generate some 240 million scrap car and truck tires per year. All of these add to an existing accumulation of as many as two billion tires. Two billion of anything is a lot. Two billion used tires is an eyesore and, worse yet, an environmental hazard. Most tires end up in a landfill or stockpiled, where they become a perfect breeding ground for mosquitoes and other pests. If they catch on fire, the flames can be almost impossible to extinguish. They sometimes smolder and smell for years. Tires are made of synthetic rubber and other artificial materials. They therefore take many decades to decompose. As a result, many landfills now refuse to handle tires at all.

Disposing of these "disposables" is not an easy task. It is possible to pay $2.50 or more for the local service station to take them off your hands. But more than seventy percent of tires disposed of in this manner will add to the country's growing tire heaps. However, recent innovations are making it possible to recycle these products. One foresighted company is already shredding tires to use as liners for leaky landfills and industrial roadways. Some states have developed or are currently developing tire disposal legislation. In Minnesota, tires have been completely banned from landfills. A chipping facility has been financed. Here the rubber is ground up and pressed into sheets for such products as carpet backing, molded rubber belts, and shingles.

Energy production is also becoming a real possibility as an alternative. This is because of the slow burning properties of discarded tires. In California, at the site of the country's largest scrap tire heap, the world's first fully tire-fueled power plant will soon serve more than 15,000 homes for at least the next fifteen years. Recycling alternatives such as these bring hope to an already over-tired society.

---

when there are no orders for new machines or equipment, production may slow down or stop until business picks up again. The overall market of industrial goods is much smaller in number than the consumer market, although the profitability of the business may be comparable.

Medical Goods

Medical goods are those produced to ease suffering and cure disease. They are also used for preventive health care. Medical goods include everything from bandages to X ray machines to the hundreds of medicinal drugs prescribed by physicians.

Using chemical substances to treat illness can be traced back to the use of opium as a pain killer. This was first documented among the Mesopotamians and Arabs around 1550 B.C. Today, **over-the-counter** drugs like aspirin, cough syrups, and many others are used by millions of people to relieve minor pain and discomfort, Figure 18-8. **Prescription** drugs, like penicillin and vaccines, are available only under the supervision of a doctor. All of these chemical substances have acted to increase the quality and length of human life.

As recently as the mid-1940s we have seen three major eras of **pharmaceutical** (chemical/medical) breakthroughs. The first era began when companies developed antibiotics to fight contagious diseases. The second era began when researchers discovered chemicals called beta blockers. These helped prevent high blood pressure and heart ailments. Both of these eras of medical advancement, through the use of chemicals, have helped to ease suffering and saved countless lives.

Figure 18-8. Over-the-counter pharmaceuticals, like Alka-Seltzer products, are a leading share of U.S. medicinal sales. *(Courtesy of Miles Inc.)*

Today, two major developments have led to the emergence of a third major era of chemical medicine. The two developments include inhibitors and cloned drugs made available through **biotechnology**.

Inhibitors are a preventive treatment that alters the body's chemistry to prevent ailments from starting. They represent a revolutionary strategy for fighting such common ailments as hypertension, high cholesterol, and diabetes. Beta blockers merely treat the symptoms, while inhibitors help prevent the disease in the first place.

Breakthroughs in biotechnology are now making it easier to treat diseases. Biotechnology is a term that describes the use of living cells to manufacture commercial products. Although often controversial, biotechnology offers the possibility of some of the most exciting breakthroughs in medical history. Especially important are breakthroughs in the areas of **antibody** production and **genetic engineering**.

Antibodies are the living cells that are our first line of defense against disease. They are naturally produced by our bodies and are made of protein. Biotechnology companies that manufacture these same antibodies are now able to produce them in large quantities. Antibodies are manufactured by combining a cell that produces antibodies with a cell that reproduces itself rapidly. The result is a new hybrid cell that reproduces itself quickly, complete with an antibody. Antibodies are very specific. They seek out certain viruses or cancer cells, leaving nearby healthy cells unaffected.

Genetic engineering involves the splicing and cloning of genes, which can give new life forms, Figure 18-9. Scientists have studied the different ways genetic engineering can be used in agriculture. Genetic research has also been done in the medical field. Companies are using gene-splicing and cloning techniques to produce new drugs that attack specific cells and viruses. Interferon, the first such drug commercially made, marked a new age in medicine. Recently, a new form of interferon was approved by the **Food and Drug Administration (FDA)** that is effective against one type of leukemia. Eventually several forms of interferon may be approved for treating other cancers, herpes, arthritis, and AIDS.

Figure 18-9. Recombivax HB is the hepatitis B vaccine made by recombinant DNA technology and the first genetically engineered vaccine for human use anywhere in the world. *(Courtesy of Merck & Co. Inc.)*

Other medical goods that have helped doctors make diagnoses and have reduced pain and suffering include the following:

- X rays provide a way to see the internal parts of the human body.
- The electrocardiograph machine photographically records and measures the electric currents flowing through the heart. It provides information about the weakness, regularity, and strength of the heart.
- Computerized axial tomography (CAT scan) is a machine that combines many single-range X rays into a single image.
- Advances in the manufacture of prostheses (artificial limbs) have helped to improve the quality of life for many people.
- Artificial hearts and other organs are increasing the chances of life for victims of genetic defects and disease while they wait for a compatible donor organ.
- The sophistication of the tools and techniques used by surgeons have made possible many medical procedures never even dreamed of before.
- Nuclear medicine, usually called radiation, traces and locates problems in the heart and arteries and treats some forms of cancer, viral infections, and blood diseases.
- Lasers are now used for quick and relatively painless outpatient surgery.

All of these examples of medical goods must be manufactured, Figure 18-10. Most large hospitals have some or all of these machines, so there is a reliable market for them.

Military Goods

Most countries around the world have a military that defends the country and its people. There are many views taken of the role of military and of the amount of resources that should be put toward it. Highly industrialized countries have the resources and technology to manufacture sophisticated defense systems. Less developed nations often purchase their military goods from the more affluent countries where they are produced. Generally, military goods can be described as **conventional** or **nuclear**.

Conventional Military Goods

Conventional military goods are all weapons, ammunition, transportation, and other items that do not carry nuclear warheads. These goods include everything from rifles to tanks to helicopters to C rations, Figure 18-11. Companies that wish to manufacture these items must bid on government contracts. Government contracts are usually fairly profitable because there is a guaranteed market that requires no advertising or expensive packaging. In addition, weapons systems require a consistent supply of replacement parts and ammunition. A company manufacturing these items may have a guaranteed source of business as long as the items do not become obsolete. Conventional military goods make up the majority of military goods produced. They are also the type of weapons purchased and used by most less developed countries in the world.

Nuclear Military Goods

Nuclear military goods include all weapons and related items that contribute to the stor-

Figure 18-10. Vasotec is used to treat high blood pressure. Here, a chemical operator does a processing step in the production of enalapril, the active ingredient in Vasotec. (Courtesy of Merck & Co. Inc.)

Figure 18-11. Dynalectron's Government Services Group maintains, modifies, and repairs military equipment for the U.S. armed forces. *(Courtesy of DynCorp)*

age, deployment, and delivery of nuclear weapons. Advances in aerospace vehicles, submarines, computers, chemical rocket fuels, communications, electronics, satellites, and global navigation all play a role in the nuclear weapons systems. Therefore a wide variety of companies are necessary to manufacture nuclear military goods. As in conventional weapons systems, private contractors must bid for government military contracts.

Chemical Weapons. One other type of lethal weaponry manufactured in small amounts is chemical weapons. A worldwide ban on the production, storage, and use of chemical weapons has not prevented continued research and manufacture of these chemicals.

The Implications of Manufacturing Military Goods

In 1945, a group of scientists who were working on what was known as the Manhattan Project tested the first nuclear fission device—the atomic bomb. **Fission** refers to the splitting of atomic nuclei, creating large amounts of energy. Three years later, the atomic bomb was used on Hiroshima and Nagasaki, Japan, to end World War II. By 1952, the first

nuclear fusion device, the hydrogen bomb, became a reality. **Fusion** refers to bringing together or merging hydrogen nuclei, which releases massive amounts of energy. This advanced weapon could be virtually unlimited in size and substantially reduce the amount of radioactive debris.

In barely a decade, humans created the means of threatening all of the life forms on earth. The rate of this weapons development was unprecedented. Throughout history, development of weapons had been slow, and never had resulted in so much destructive power.

If humans continue inventing and manufacturing more complex, sophisticated, and expensive military goods, the effects will extend far beyond national borders. Weapons production, both conventional and nuclear, affects people around the world and knows no political boundaries.

Summary

The most obvious output of manufacturing is the products themselves. Availability of manufactured goods is one of the variables that determines standard of living. If companies produced only consumer goods, most manufacturing would eventually stop. Industrial goods, including supplies and machines as well as replacement parts, are necessary for manufacturing to occur.

Medical goods are produced to ease suffering and cure disease. They are also used for preventive health care. Many chemical substances have acted to increase the quality and length of human life. Advances in biotechnology, especially in the areas of antibody production and in genetic engineering, have marked a new era in medicine.

Military goods can be classified as either conventional or nuclear. Most manufacturing of military goods consists of conventional, nonnuclear goods. The continued research into, and manufacture of, chemical weapons is also an issue. The implications of nuclear weapons production far outweigh those of conventional weapons.

DISCUSSION QUESTIONS

1. List as many disposable goods as you can. Next to each disposable good, describe a more durable item that could be used in its place.
2. Why is the term "disposable" misleading?
3. Industrial goods are the least obvious of manufactured goods. Explain the importance of industrial goods.
4. Describe an incident, either personally known to you or that you have heard about, that involves the use of sophisticated medical goods.
5. Biotechnology is the use of living cells to manufacture commercial products. Genetic engineering results in new life forms. Describe your feelings about these technologies.
6. Should conventional and nuclear weapons be manufactured?

CHAPTER ACTIVITIES

 CHILD-SAFE

OBJECTIVE

In this activity, you will design and build a child-safe toy according to specific guidelines from the Consumer Product Safety Council.

MATERIALS AND SUPPLIES

1. Obtain all or some of the following publications from the Consumer Product Safety Council (1–800–638–2772):
   - *You make the Difference—Product Safety Guide for Teachers of Grades 7–9.*
   - *Protect Your Child.*
   - *Guide for Manufacturers, Distributors, and Retailers.*
   - *Handbook for Playground Safety,* Vols. I and II.
   - *For Kids' Sake, Think Toy Safety.* (pamphlet)
2. Appropriate materials including wood, hardware, plastic, and so forth for individual child-safe toy designs.
3. Appropriate tools and machines for manufacturing child-safe toy designs.
4. Safety glasses

PROCEDURE

1. Investigate child-safe consumer guidelines as detailed in the publications you obtained and from your own common sense. Discuss these guidelines as a class.
2. Working individually, "sketch-storm" as many ideas and variations of possible child-safe toy designs as you can. Be sure to consider the age of the children your toys are designed for. A toy designed for a toddler will differ from that for a five-year-old.

3. Chose your best design and discuss it with your teacher and peers for additional input.

4. Prepare dimensioned drawings, specs, and a materials and procedure list for manufacturing your child-safe toy.

5. With approval from your teacher, begin making your toy. Be sure you have had proper instruction on how to use all tools and machines you will need. Follow all safety rules for working in your technology laboratory. Do not use a toxic finish on any toys that children might put into their mouths.

6. When you have finished your child-safe toy, let some children try it out. Record their reaction to it—how long it held their attention, if it was used as you designed it, and so forth. This is called field testing.

7. Present your child-safe toy and your log of its field test to your class for critique.

RELATED QUESTIONS

1. In your opinion, are the majority of toys found in toy stores safe for children? Give examples.

2. Are the regulations from the Consumer Product Safety Council strict enough? How could the regulations be improved?

3. If you could do this activity again, how would you change your child-safe design?

4. Of all the toys designed and built in your class, describe the toy you liked most. What is it that attracts you to this toy? Would this also be the toy most popular with children? Why or why not?

⚙ MANUFACTURING HEALTH CARE PRODUCTS

OBJECTIVE

When we think of twentieth-century manufacturing, we see the endless stamping of parts, the welding, fastening, and finishing products, perhaps a robotic arm moving products from station to station. The image of heavy industrialism can be strong in our minds.

Have you ever wondered where many of our every-day health care products come from? Do you know what processes are used to manufacture them? Products like toothpaste, soap, and hairspray roll off the production lines in huge quantities to satisfy an endless demand. This activity will introduce you to some of the production techniques used with these products. You will participate in the research, marketing, and production of health care products.

MATERIALS AND SUPPLIES

1. Powdered soap
2. Borax
3. Baking soda
4. Glycerine
5. Powdered pumice
6. Fragrances (rose water, food flavoring extracts)

7. Saw dust
8. Oatmeal
9. Corn meal
10. Fine sand
11. Baby oil
12. Liquid soap
13. Plastic storage containers
14. Balance scales or digital scales
15. Graduated cylinders
16. Mortar and pestle
17. Safety glasses

PROCEDURE

1. Form production teams of three students.
2. Mix together the following dry ingredients:
   - 198 g powdered pumice
   - 141 g powdered soap (not soap powder)
   - 35 g borax
   - 28 g baking soda

   Use the mortar and pestle. Try to achieve uniform particle size.
3. Add these liquids:
   - 15 ml glycerine
   - 342 ml water

   Add half the liquids to start mixing, then add the rest until you achieve a paste-like quality.
4. Test the basic product on your hands and evaluate it for texture, smell, cleaning ability, and how it leaves your hands. Use the soap with warm water. This is a mechanic's soap intended to remove dirt and grease from your hands. Do not use it on your face or other sensitive areas.
5. Change proportions and substitute ingredients until you feel you have a marketable product. Keep track of your formula as you go. You can make substitutions from the list of materials and supplies.
6. Develop a product survey sheet and field test your product using other students in your class.
7. Change your formula if the data from your survey indicates that you need to change it.
8. When you have a final soap formula, develop measuring jigs to make production easier.
9. Produce enough soap for each team in the class.

RELATED QUESTIONS

1. Describe some concerns that might need to be addressed when producing health care products that might not affect the production of industrial products.
2. What is the function of market research in the development of a product line?

3. What function did each of these ingredients perform in the basic hand soap formula?
   - pumice
   - glycerine
   - water
   - powdered soap

4. How might automation be used to produce health care items?

5. List some commercial products on the market today that would compete with your hand soap if you went into business.

CHAPTER 19

Scrap, Waste, and Pollution

OBJECTIVES

After completing this chapter, you will know about:

- How mass production is followed by mass consumption, which is usually followed by mass scrap, mass waste, and mass pollution.

- Scrap as an output for one manufacturer and an input for another.

- Post-consumer waste and recycling.

- Pollution as a direct and indirect output of manufacturing.

- The major air pollutants.

- Groundwater contamination and toxic waste chemicals.

- The difficulties associated with solving nonpoint source pollution problems.

- The modern historical shift from air and water disposal to land disposal of toxic waste chemicals.

KEY TERMS

Acid rain
Bioaccumulation
Carbon monoxide
Carcinogens
Chlorinated hydrocarbons
Curbside recycling
Deep well injection
Digester
Groundwater contamination
Hazardous waste

Heavy metals
Hydrocarbons
Nitrogen oxides
Nonpoint source pollution
Ozone
Particulates
Photochemical oxidants
Pollution
Scrap
Secured landfills

Smog
Source separation
Sulfur oxides
Surface impoundments
Synthetic organic chemicals
Tetraethyl lead
Toxic waste chemicals
Transfer station sorting
Waste

Scrap, Waste, and Pollution

If a society manufactures products in mass, it probably also consumes products in mass. Outputs of mass production include not only products but also scrap, waste, and pollution. To some degree, all manufacturers, directly or indirectly, create some form of scrap, waste, and pollution. This chapter will explore the by-products of manufacturing and consumption of products.

It is misleading to say that we have a "throw away" society, because we really can't throw away our scrap, waste, or pollution. Love Canal in Niagara Falls, New York, is a good reminder that there is no "away" for society's waste. A chemical company dumped 21,800 tons of toxic waste near Love Canal between 1947 and 1952. Large metal cans filled with toxic chemicals were buried in the landfill. Thirty years of rusting finally caused leaks in the metal containers. Chemicals seeped into groundwater as well as the land surface. After heavy rains, the chemicals rose to the surface in areas where children played. Many suffered acid burns. The terrible smell of pesticide lingered in the air. Miscarriages and birth defects increased. Trees and grass suffered burns. The air itself over Love Canal contained eighty-two different compounds, eleven of which were **carcinogens**. Carcinogens are agents that cause or promote cancer. Finally in August of 1978, the New York State Health Commission stepped in and bought 239 homes from residents of the area. The homes were boarded up, and families were forced to move from the area, probably forever. It might be safe to assume that the chemical manufacturing company could not forecast the impact of their dumping at the time. We now know, however, that nowhere is far enough "away" when it comes to waste, scrap, and pollution, Figure 19-1.

Scrap is an output of the manufacturing process that cannot easily or economically be reused by the manufacturer who creates it. **Waste** is that portion of the product the consumer throws away, never to be reused or recycled. **Pollution** is the direct or indirect output

Figure 19-1. The New York State Department of Environmental Conservation drills to monitor wells at the Love Canal site. They test groundwater for chemical contamination. *(Courtesy of NYS Dept. of Environmental Conservation)*

of manufacturing processes and other processes that cause any harmful physical, chemical, or biological changes of air, water, or land. An aluminum beverage can that is sent to a recycling center is considered scrap. That is, it will eventually be reused to make more aluminum cans or other aluminum products. However, if the same aluminum can is sent to a landfill, it is considered waste. That is, the material is never reused or recycled. And, if the can causes environmental problems when placed in the landfill, it is considered pollution.

Scrap

Scrap may take many forms, but it is usually associated with manufactured materials such as steel, aluminum, plastics, ceramics, textiles, wood, and so on. Although scrap cannot easily be used by the manufacturer that created it, it often becomes the materials input for another manufacturer. For example, the scrap created

Figure 19-2. A car body is lifted to the shredder at a scrap yard in Dallas, Texas, a metal processing plant that recycles steel. *(Courtesy of Commercial Metals Company)*

Figure 19-3. Landfills are running out of space for the millions of tons of solid waste generated each year. *(Photo by Helena Frost)*

from the manufacture of golf club heads becomes the raw material for tableware manufacturers producing spoons, forks, and knives. Scrap in the form of thermoplastics can be reformed into different products. An old automobile that is sent to a scrap yard may be crushed and eventually reformed into other steel products, Figure 19-2. Unfortunately, much scrap from manufacturing processes is contaminated and ends up in landfills, dumps, or incinerators.

Waste

Waste represents products that have already been consumed and discarded. The United States produces three billion tons of solid waste material every year. Many of the products that enter the waste stream can be reused or recycled. Steel, aluminum, plastic, glass, and paper are easily recycled but often go to landfills instead of being recycled, Figure 19-3.

Curbside recycling programs aid consumers in the recycling process. Consumers are asked to separate recycling materials at home and then take them to the containers. Periodically, the waste materials are picked up and transported to a recycling station. These

programs are becoming more popular because they promote **source separation**. Source separation simply means that consumers separate their wastes at home. The separated materials are transferred to a materials recycling center. They are then processed as raw materials that can be input back into the manufacture of products, Figure 19-4.

Another program that handles post-consumer waste is **transfer station sorting**.

Figure 19-4. Curbside recycling programs are being implemented around the country. *(Photo by Sonya Stang and Brent Miller)*

Consumer waste is collected by refuse trucks and taken to a transfer station, Figure 19-5. The waste collected in plastic garbage bags must be sorted. People stand on each side of a conveyor belt, open the bags, and sort out the recyclable materials. Organic waste must be transferred to a landfill or sent to a **digester**. A digester breaks down organic matter into an earthy brown product called humus. It can then be used as a landscaping fertilizer. Another type of digester produces methane gas, which is then used for heating or industrial processing.

Transfer station sorting has three drawbacks. The first is that consumers are not responsible for separating their own waste. Some people feel that if waste is created by consumers through their buying patterns then they should have some responsibility to help solve the solid waste problem through source separation. The second problem is that the sorting work at the transfer station may be dangerous and unhealthy because there is no control over possible hazardous waste that is put in the plastic garbage bags. The third problem deals with contaminated materials. Solvents, for example, may contaminate thermoplastics to a point where they cannot be recycled. Paper may also be contaminated to the point of not being recyclable. The contamination problem is solved by source separation.

Figure 19-5. This resource recovery plant will convert up to 2,000 tons per day of solid waste into a clean-burning fuel. *(Photo by Sonya Stang and Brent Miller)*

Pollution

Pollution is another output of manufacturing. There are two major categories of pollution related to manufacturing—air pollution and water pollution.

Air Pollution

Air pollution is a very serious output of the manufacturing process because clean air is one of the critical elements of life. Each day humans breathe approximately 23,000 times, typically inhaling about 525 gallons of air. Air is a mixture of gases, including nitrogen (78 percent), oxygen (20 percent), carbon dioxide (.03 percent), argon, helium, xenon, neon, and krypton. It is a life-sustaining resource often taken for granted while being shared by all of earth's inhabitants.

Major pollutants that are outputs of the manufacturing process include the following:

- Particulates
- Hydrocarbons
- Carbon monoxide
- Nitrogen oxides
- Sulfur oxides
- Lead and other heavy metals
- Ozone and photochemical oxidants

Pollutants are direct or indirect outputs of combustion. Air pollution occurs wherever fuel or other materials are burned. Combustion of fuel and other materials is common during manufacturing processes, including the acquisition of raw materials and the delivery of the products to market. Manufacturing processes often require great amounts of electrical energy that may be generated by fossil fuel power plants.

Particulates are little particles consisting mainly of carbon. They are emitted during combustion. We see these particles as smoke or haze. Particulates are so small that they remain suspended in the atmosphere for long periods of time. They occur from combustion of diesel engines, wood burning, and refuse incineration.

Hydrocarbons include materials in the organic volatile category such as gasoline, paint solvents, and organic cleaning solutions that evaporate and enter the atmosphere in a vapor state. Modern transportation is also a major contributor to the increase of hydrocarbons. Vapors from burning oil, gasoline spilled in the process of fueling, and the evaporation of gasoline in the tank increase hydrocarbon emissions.

Carbon monoxide is a molecule containing one carbon and one oxygen atom. It is the product of incomplete combustion of carbon in fossil fuels. Transportation of raw materials, parts, and products using the internal combustion engine as the power source increases carbon monoxide.

Nitrogen oxides are formed when air is used during the combustion process. Air is only twenty percent oxygen and seventy-eight percent nitrogen. At high temperatures during combustion, the nitrogen gas oxidizes and forms nitric oxide. Nitric oxide reacts with additional oxygen in air and forms the category nitrogen oxides. This pollutant absorbs light and is responsible for the brownish color of **smog.** Smog is the combination of smoke and fog that has resulted from the combustion of fossil fuels.

Sulfur oxides result when fuels or trash contain impurities that are emitted into the air during a burning process. Coal, in particular, contains 0.2 to 5.5 percent sulfur that, upon combustion, is oxidized and creates sulfur dioxide.

Lead and other heavy metals are serious pollutants. **Tetraethyl lead** is added to gasoline to achieve a higher octane fuel that reduces engine knock. It combines with another additive, ethylene dibromide, during combustion and escapes as a gas out of the exhaust as lead bromide.

Ozone and **photochemical oxidants** are known as indirect products of combustion because they are the result of other pollutants reacting together after combustion. Ozone is formed because of chemical reactions between nitrogen oxides and hydrocarbons. Sunlight supplies the energy necessary to cause the reaction. Because sunlight provides the necessary energy, these outputs are known as photochemical oxidants.

Another indirect result of combustion occurs when sulfur and nitrogen react. Sulfur dioxide and nitrogen oxides react with water vapor in the atmosphere to form sulfuric and nitric acids. The result is **acid rain** (see Chapter 20).

The five major pollutants shown in Figure 19-6 come from transportation (55 percent), power plants (17 percent), manufacturing (15 percent), agricultural fires (7 percent), and the incineration of solid wastes (4 percent), and other sources (2 percent). If the indirect pollution from power plant energy and the transportation of manufactured products to the market were added to the manufacturing section, the total pollutants produced by manufacturing would be closer to forty-five percent of the total.

Water Pollution

Water pollution related to manufacturing usually takes on the form of **groundwater contamination** by toxic chemical waste. Other major sources include

- inadequate landfills,
- leaking underground storage tanks,
- chemical pesticides and fertilizers,
- de-icing salt,
- waste oils,
- transportation spills,
- sewage, and
- chemical dumping.

Illegal dumping and inadequate disposal of chemical waste are considered the most serious problems. There are three main sources of chemical waste.

1. Chemical processes
2. Chemical solvents and cleaning fluids
3. Container residues and unused portions

Chemical Waste. Chemical processes produce certain wastes. The chemical processes associated with turning crude oil into synthetic organic chemicals used in plastics, coatings, pesticides, drugs, and so on generate thousands of by-products. These by-products are

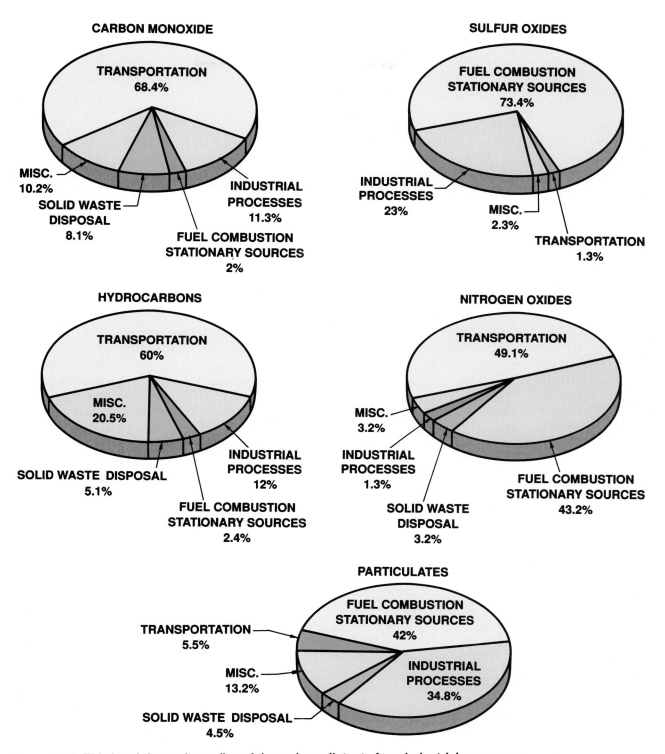

Figure 19-6. This breakdown shows five of the major pollutants from industrial processes.

Chlorofluorocarbons: Bite the Burger

Chlorofluorocarbons (CFCs) are a dangerous class of chemicals that have been associated with the destruction of the ozone layer in the atmosphere. CFCs migrate to the stratosphere when released. The stratosphere is the atmospheric zone extending from six to fifteen miles above the earth's surface. The stratosphere layer provides a global shield against the sun's harmful ultraviolet radiation. Crop damage, reduction of the human immune system, and skin cancer are environmental impacts of ultraviolet radiation. In 1978, the U. S. government banned the use of CFCs as aerosol propellants. However, the chemicals are still widely used in refrigerators, mobile air conditioners, polyurethane foam insulation, and fast food foam packaging and disposables.

CFCs are used as blowing agents in extruded thermoplastic foam. Foams include polystyrene (styrofoam), polyvinyl chloride (PVC), high-density polyethylene (HDPE), and polypropylene. The clam-shell hamburger containers that fast food restaurants use are an example of blown polystyrene foam that contains CFCs.

Scientists' concern has led to political action. On March 14, 1988, the U.S. Senate voted to strengthen the *Montreal Protocol on Substances that Deplete the Ozone Layer.* The original document was signed by twenty-four nations in September of 1987. The *Montreal Protocol* focuses on limiting the production of CFCs and CFC-blown foams. The first step is aimed at freezing the consumption of five CFC compounds to the 1986 level. The second step is to reduce the consumption of CFC foams by twenty percent by 1994. The third step is to reduce consumption of CFC foams by thirty percent by 1999.

Fifteen manufacturers that use CFCs in their food packaging announced their plan to phase them out by the end of 1988. The Foodservice and Packaging Institute is promoting a substitute blowing agent called hydrochlorofluorocarbon-22 (HCFC-22). HCFC-22's additional hydrogen atom causes it to be less stable. It breaks down more easily in the lower atmosphere. Therefore, it poses less damage to stratospheric ozone.

Pentane, butane, and propane are other alternatives in the form of hydrocarbon blowing agents. However, while they are safer in the upper atmosphere, hydrocarbon blowing agents have their own problems. They are extremely flammable, pose a threat to workers' health, and create hydrocarbon emissions that pollute the lower atmosphere.

In 1987, two national campaigns were launched to pressure certain fast food chains to stop using CFC-blown containers. The largest user of polystyrene foam containers consumes 70 million pounds of CFC foam containers per year. Citizen's Clearinghouse for Hazardous Waste organized a national grassroots campaign to reduce this type of packaging. On August 6, 1987, McDonald's Restaurants Inc. announced it would switch to non-CFC blown foam containers. The campaign however, is trying to persuade fast food chains to stop using polystyrene foam altogether and switch to biodegradable packaging.

either of no use or are not economical to separate, purify, or reuse. Process materials, such as chemical solvents and cleaning fluids, are also often discarded after use. Pouring dangerous chemical solvents "down the drain" is commonly done in manufacturing as well as households. The third problem results from unused portions of chemicals. A common example is paint that is left in closed containers. The containers are dumped. Over a period of time, they rust to the point that the liquid paint leaches into groundwater supplies and causes groundwater contamination, Figure 19-7. Many of these materials are classified as **hazardous waste**. Hazardous waste includes materials that are explosive or highly reactive; flammable; corrosive; or toxic, poisonous, or linked to causing long-term physiological problems. Toxic waste caused directly or indirectly by manufacturing processes is the main groundwater pollution problem.

Toxic waste chemicals can be divided into two categories—**heavy metals** and **synthetic organic chemicals**. Heavy metals are dense metallic elements in their pure form. Synthetic organic chemicals are unique arrangements of bonded carbon and hydrogen found in natural organic compounds.

Common heavy metals include lead, mercury, arsenic, cadmium, tin, chromium, zinc, and copper. Metal-processing industries and

Figure 19-7. Inappropriate disposal of paint, a household hazardous waste, can lead to groundwater contamination. *(Photo by Sonya Stang and Brent Miller)*

pigment industries create waste in the form of heavy metals. Other industries and manufacturers also create heavy metal by-products in the form of waste. These metals are soluble in water and may be ingested and absorbed into the body.

Mercury is a very dangerous toxic waste that is often discharged in water. In the 1950s, residents of Minamata Bay, Japan, who ate seafood with high levels of methyl mercury fell ill. Their symptoms included loss of muscle control, deafness, blurring of vision, clumsiness, and mental derangement. Seventeen people died and twenty-three were permanently disabled from mercury poisoning. "Mad as a hatter" is an expression used to describe the insane behavior of early-day hatmakers. It was later discovered that these hatmakers had used mercury in the manufacturing process and had poisoned themselves over a period of time. These tenth-century hatmakers lost their hair and teeth in addition to the mental derangement caused by mercury poisoning. Mercury is a by-product of manufacturing polyvinyl chloride (PVC). It is also discharged in water waste by chemical manufacturers, incinerators, and power plants. Mercury is found in dangerous levels in much of the drinking water in the United States. In fact, in 1980, mercury exceeded the national safety standard in over two-thirds of the drinking water.

Synthetic organic compounds have become the basis of all plastics, synthetic fibers, resins, drugs, pesticides, detergents, solvents, and many other products. **Chlorinated hydrocarbons** are a particularly dangerous subgroup of synthetic organic compounds. Such compounds are used in plastics, pesticides, solvents, wood preservatives, electrical insulation, flame retardants, and more. Consequently, these compounds are the waste of industries that produce them and of industries that use them. Two common pollutants in the chlorinated hydrocarbon category are polychlorinated biphenyls (PCBs) and dioxin, Figure 19-8.

Heavy metals and various synthetic organic compounds tend to bioaccumulate. **Bioaccumulation** refers to the increase of toxic

Figure 19-8. PCB-contaminated sediment is evaluated from the bottom of Baltimore Harbor, Maryland. *(Courtesy of USEPA)*

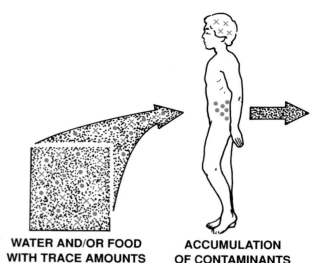

WATER AND/OR FOOD
WITH TRACE AMOUNTS
OF CONTAMINANTS

ACCUMULATION
OF CONTAMINANTS
IN BODY

Figure 19-9. Chemicals that are ingested with food and water accumulate in the body, concentrating in the liver and other organs until they reach dangerous levels.

chemicals in the body. The body acts like a filter and stores the toxic chemical. If a person drinks water and eats food that contains heavy metals and synthetic organic compounds over a long period of time, these chemicals build up in the body, Figure 19-9.

Modern History. Chemical waste was discarded as quickly as possible before the environmental laws of the 1960s and 1970s. Hazardous chemicals were flushed into natural waterways, and uncontrolled combustion polluted the atmosphere with many dangerous substances. Many streams and rivers, hazardous and void of life in manufacturing towns, became open chemical sewers. In 1970, the Clean Air Act was enacted. It was followed by the 1972 Clean Water Act. Manufacturers spent billions of dollars on pollution control equipment to remove chemical waste from air and water discharge. Toxic chemical waste shifted from air and water discharge to land disposal in the early 1970s. Surface water

quality and air quality increased. Unfortunately, groundwater pollution also increased because of the shortcomings of poorly designed and constructed land disposal systems. Although designs have improved, there are still problems associated with the main chemical waste land disposal systems.

Disposing of Chemical Waste. There are three main methods of disposing of hazardous waste on land. They are deep well injection, surface impoundments, and landfills.

Deep well injection handles approximately fifty-eight percent of hazardous waste that is disposed, Figure 19-10. A well is drilled into a porous material below the groundwater. Hazardous waste, in liquid form, is pumped into wells and is absorbed by the porous layer. In theory, it remains isolated from groundwater by impermeable layers. The major problem with this method is that there is no way to guarantee that the impermeable layer does not crack and allow hazardous waste to enter groundwater.

Surface impoundments contain about thirty-eight percent of the discarded hazardous

DISPOSAL OF HAZARDOUS WASTES BY DEEPWELL INJECTION

THEORY

A well is drilled into a dry porous layer and wastes are pumped in. A casing and seal are made around the portion of the well that penetrates groundwater in order to avoid contamination.

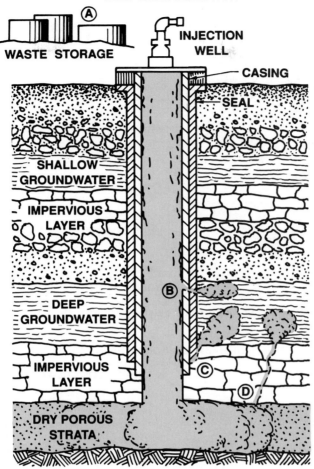

DANGERS

A. Waste spills or leaks at surface storage site

B. Casing corrodes and lets waste escape

C. Faulty seal lets waste back-flow

D. Fractures in the impervious layer allow waste to escape into groundwater. These fractures might already exist, or they could be caused by earthquakes or the introduction of fluids.

Figure 19-10. Injection wells are often used to dispose of large amounts of liquid waste, contributing to the problem of groundwater contamination.

waste, Figure 19-11. Large amounts of water that carry small amounts of waste are discharged into a sealed pit or pond. Water evaporates while the waste settles and accumulates. This is the least expensive method of the land disposal systems. Problems occur when exceptional storms cause overflows or seals break down and allow waste to leak into groundwater supplies.

Secured landfills are those landfills that are properly lined and covered with a means to remove drainage, Figure 19-12. Hazardous waste in concentrated forms is contained in drums and buried in secured landfills. Many changing variables, such as container break-

down and drainage failure, make this system the least desirable to contain hazardous waste. Experts feel that even the most secure landfills will eventually allow waste into groundwater supplies.

Nonpoint source pollution. This term describes pollution that cannot be traced back to a single source. It is characterized by two major problems. The first is that the pollution has usually been taking place for a long period of time. The second is that because it is almost impossible to find operators who have polluted, it is difficult to find anyone to pay for the cleanup. Two tragic examples are the acid rain

DISPOSAL OF HAZARDOUS WASTES IN SURFACE IMPOUNDMENTS

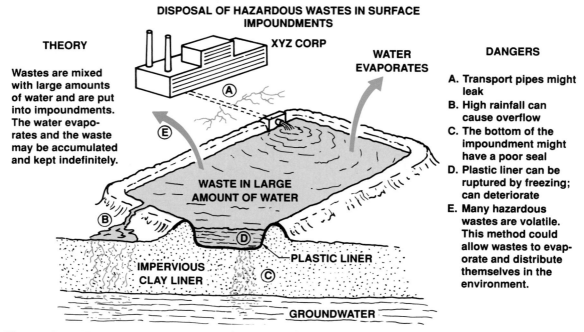

THEORY

Wastes are mixed with large amounts of water and are put into impoundments. The water evaporates and the waste may be accumulated and kept indefinitely.

XYZ CORP

WATER EVAPORATES

WASTE IN LARGE AMOUNT OF WATER

IMPERVIOUS CLAY LINER

PLASTIC LINER

GROUNDWATER

DANGERS

A. Transport pipes might leak
B. High rainfall can cause overflow
C. The bottom of the impoundment might have a poor seal
D. Plastic liner can be ruptured by freezing; can deteriorate
E. Many hazardous wastes are volatile. This method could allow wastes to evaporate and distribute themselves in the environment.

Figure 19-11. Hazardous waste can sometimes be disposed of in surface impoundments.

DISPOSAL OF HAZARDOUS WASTES IN LANDFILLS

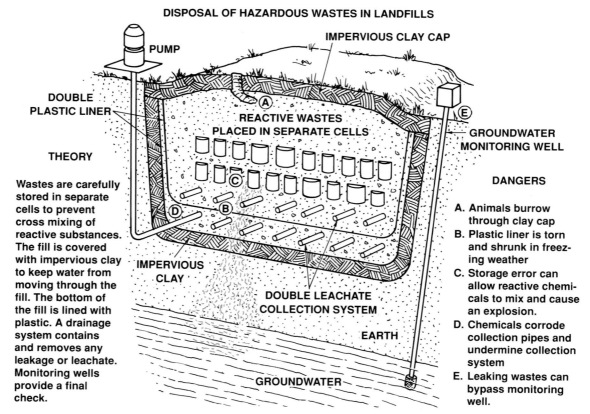

PUMP

IMPERVIOUS CLAY CAP

DOUBLE PLASTIC LINER

REACTIVE WASTES PLACED IN SEPARATE CELLS

GROUNDWATER MONITORING WELL

THEORY

Wastes are carefully stored in separate cells to prevent cross mixing of reactive substances. The fill is covered with impervious clay to keep water from moving through the fill. The bottom of the fill is lined with plastic. A drainage system contains and removes any leakage or leachate. Monitoring wells provide a final check.

IMPERVIOUS CLAY

DOUBLE LEACHATE COLLECTION SYSTEM

EARTH

GROUNDWATER

DANGERS

A. Animals burrow through clay cap
B. Plastic liner is torn and shrunk in freezing weather
C. Storage error can allow reactive chemicals to mix and cause an explosion.
D. Chemicals corrode collection pipes and undermine collection system
E. Leaking wastes can bypass monitoring well.

Figure 19-12. Secured landfills offer an alternate method for disposing of hazardous waste.

problem in the Adirondack Mountains and Canada and the high nitrate levels of groundwater in agricultural regions in the midwestern United States. Scientists believe that acid rain is caused by fossil fuel power plants, certain industries, and transportation emissions, Figure 19-13. It is difficult to trace what is happening in the Adirondacks to a specific source: No one source is held responsible for cleaning up the problem. Unfortunately, lakes and forests continue to die while governments try to analyze the situation. Acid rain, however, knows no political borders.

Groundwater in agricultural regions is being contaminated by years of pesticide and chemical fertilizer use. Because these chemicals took years to seep into groundwater systems, it is difficult to place blame on any one farmer. Groundwater systems may transport the pollution many miles from the source. This makes it impossible to identify the polluters. And, even if polluters were identified, who should pay? The consumers of the prod-

uct, the producers, or the government? This problem will continue to increase while governments balk at the actions necessary to curtail destruction. In the meantime, pollution control authorities continue to warn mothers and young children not to drink water supplies that have more than eleven ppm (part per million) nitrate levels.

To offset the costs associated with discarding toxic chemical waste, some unscrupulous manufacturers illegally dump waste by various means. Some toxic chemicals are left stacked high in abandoned warehouses, crudely buried on vacant lots or farms, sent to sanitary landfills, or poured directly into rivers and lakes. There have even been cases where toxic chemicals in drums have been dumped alongside roadways. Discarded pesticides and chemical fertilizers in drum containers are found in abandoned wells throughout farms across the United States. In most cases, the operators ensure that they will not be identified even after the waste they leave behind has been discovered. However, the impact of their actions is felt for years. The violators also need clean water to live healthy lives.

Household Wastes. Consumer dumping of hazardous waste is a serious problem that few people are aware of. Common hazardous waste that is often discarded in dangerous manners include

- paints,
- cleaners,
- wood preservatives,
- motor oil,
- antifreeze,
- solvents, and
- pesticides.

Paints can be divided into two categories—oil-based and water-based. Enamels, varnishes, lacquers, stains, and sealers are all oil-based paints. Latex paints are water-based. Paints contain solvents and metals that may enter surface and groundwater supplies if not properly disposed of. Serious pollution problems result when paints are poured down the drain, dumped in the ground, or thrown in the

Figure 9-13. Emissions from fossil fuel power plants are a major contributor to the problem of acid rain. *(Photo by Sonya Stang and Brent Miller)*

trash. If there is no outlet for unused paints, the proper action is to remove the lid of the paint and let the paint harden in a well-ventilated area, Figure 19-14. Paints will not seep into groundwater supplies in hardened form.

Cleaners with a label that says "flammable" or "poison" should not be poured down the drain. The best way to dispose of cleaners is to use them up for their intended purpose. Never mix cleaners with ammonia and chlorine bleach because the result will be toxic fumes.

Wood preservatives are products containing chemicals that are toxic to the organisms that cause wood to decay. Wood preservatives that contain pentachlorophenol mixtures are the most dangerous and have no safe means of disposal. Even a small amount of this substance will contaminate large amounts of groundwater. The best approach is to use the wood preservative up by applying a second or third coat if necessary.

Motor oil contains a number of contaminants, including organic chemicals and metals. Waste motor oil is often dumped on the ground. It then seeps into groundwater supplies. Waste motor oil can be recycled by a used motor oil recycling location. Since 1979, stores that sell oil must provide a collection tank for used motor oil or post a sign that indicates the location of the nearest recycling center. Most service stations will accept your oil because they sell it to recyclers.

Antifreeze is many times discarded on the ground during the flushing of an automobile radiator. This is often dangerous to small animals who are attracted to the sweet taste of antifreeze. The best way to discard antifreeze is to dump it in a sanitary sewer drain. Some automobile service stations will handle your used antifreeze.

Solvents can be flammable and poisonous, pose a serious health risk through skin absorption or inhalation, and pollute groundwater supplies if not properly disposed of. Once again the best way to discard leftover solvents is to use them up for their intended purposes. Never pour solvents down the drain.

Pesticides are chemicals designed to kill insects and rodents, Figure 19-15. Many have been found to cause long-range environmental damage. Pesticides should never be buried, mixed together, poured on the ground, dumped in the water, poured down the drain, or burned. Many pesticides have been banned. There is no safe way to dispose of pesticides. The nearest pollution control authority can advise users on how to store unused portions of pesticides.

Figure 9-14. Drying out leftover paint is important before appropriate disposal to prevent leakage. (Photo by Sonya Stang and Brent Miller)

Figure 9-15. The widespread use of pesticides in the production of food is a major source of groundwater contamination. (Photo by Andrew Horton)

Summary

Mass production is usually followed by mass consumption. Mass consumption is usually followed by mass scrap, waste, and pollution. This has been a characteristic of industrialized societies throughout modern history. Scrap, waste, and pollution are outputs of manufacturing.

Scrap is an output of manufacturing that becomes the material input to another manufacturer. Two-liter plastic beverage bottles may be reground and reformed to produce other plastic products. Waste, however, is a post-consumer output that is not reused or recycled and enters the waste stream. In this case, the plastic two-liter bottle would be sent to a landfill never to be reused. And, if during the decomposition of the plastic bottle there is damage to the environment, this would be pollution. Two programs to reduce waste and pollution are curbside recycling and transfer station sorting/digesting.

Two major forms of pollution come from direct and indirect manufacturing outputs—air pollution and water pollution. The major air pollutants related to manufacturing include particulates, hydrocarbons, carbon monoxide, nitrogen oxides, sulfur oxides, heavy metals, and photochemical oxidants. Groundwater contamination caused by the seeping of toxic waste chemicals is a serious problem. The three methods of disposing of hazardous wastes on land include deep well injection, surface impoundment, and secured landfills. No system of disposing of toxic waste is foolproof.

Nonpoint source pollution is unique because it is so hard to trace the pollution back to a single source. Groundwater contamination from years of pesticide and chemical fertilizers is one example. Acid rain, caused by fossil fuel power plants, automobiles, and manufacturing processes, is another example. A major problem of nonpoint source pollution is deciding who should pay for the environmental damage that is occurring now but has taken many years to produce. Lakes, forests, and groundwater systems continue to be polluted while political forces look at the problem. Unfortunately, pollution knows no political borders. This makes the problems of nonpoint source pollution more difficult to solve.

The Clean Air Act of 1970 and the Clean Water Act of 1972 forced manufacturers to change the ways they dispose of toxic chemical waste. The shift forced some operators to stop or limit the combustion and incineration of waste. It also forced manufacturers to stop dumping waste into rivers and lakes and look for land disposal alternatives. Unfortunately, some manufacturers still dump toxic waste chemicals illegally to avoid the rising costs of toxic waste disposal.

Hazardous wastes are produced in households as well as in manufacturing. They include paints, cleaners, wood preservatives, motor oil, antifreeze, solvents, and pesticides. There are proper methods for disposing of these common materials. Pouring unused portions of these chemicals down the drain is a dangerous practice.

DISCUSSION QUESTIONS

1. Describe how a plastic bottle may be scrap or waste or even pollution depending on how it is treated.

2. Describe the difference between curbside recycling and transfer station sorting. What is the preferred method and why?

3. Describe the scrap, waste, and pollution generated by local manufacturers. Discuss where the scrap, waste, and pollution from these manufacturers eventually end up.

4. Discuss and describe how smog is created.

5. List and describe three major air pollutants generated by combustion processes.

6. Describe how groundwater supplies may be contaminated by toxic waste chemicals.

7. What are three methods of land disposal of toxic hazardous waste? Describe the differences between the methods along with potential problems.

8. The Clean Air Act of 1970 and the Clean Water Act of 1972 forced manufacturers to change their waste disposal practices. Describe this change.

9. Illegal dumping of toxic waste is a dangerous problem. If you noticed that a local company was dumping waste into the ground or river, what would you do?

CHAPTER ACTIVITIES

THE THREE Rs—REDUCE, REUSE, AND RECYCLE

OBJECTIVE

In this activity, you will determine which common products can easily be reduced from the waste stream, reused, or recycled.

MATERIALS AND SUPPLIES

1. Recycled paper and pencils
2. One plastic garbage bag containing common household garbage. (Your teacher will supply the garbage and control its contents.)
3. Protective gloves

PROCEDURE

1. Form groups of four or five and select a team leader.
2. Each group should have one garbage bag full of common garbage (not household hazardous waste). You do not need to bring any garbage from home.
3. With protective gloves on, team members should open the garbage bags and inventory their contents. The team leader should record all of the waste removed from the garbage bag.
4. The research team should develop categories for the garbage and create a table for all of the garbage. Categories might include:
   - Organics (food scraps, etc.)
   - Plastics
   - Metals
   - Papers
   - Glass
   - Hybrids (products made from two or more materials)

5. After each waste item, list whether the item could be:
   a. reduced (do not consume the item, it is not necessary);
   b. reused (glass jars may be used to hold other products, a plastic bag may be reused to carry groceries from the store many times); or
   c. recycled (organic waste can be placed in a compost pile outside to biodegrade and become a fertilizer; aluminum, paper, glass, and most plastics can also be recycled).
6. List separately all items that cannot be reduced, reused, or recycled. Have your team leader present your results to the entire class.
7. Each student should develop a plan for reducing garbage that enters the waste stream through the plastic garbage bag. Concentrate on reusing and recycling products.

RELATED QUESTIONS

1. How can garbage generated by one household affect the entire region?
2. Try this mini research project. If organics are composted, and materials are reused and recycled, how much garbage would a family of four generate in one week?

 **USE IT—DON'T SCRAP IT**

OBJECTIVE

In this activity, you will study the different types of scrap that your manufacturing laboratory generates. You will then determine what products could be made out of the scrap or develop a plan for reusing or recycling the scrap.

MATERIALS AND SUPPLIES

1. Recycled paper and pencils
2. Scrap generated by your manufacturing laboratory.

PROCEDURE

1. Form groups of four or five and select a team leader.
2. Each group should have a sample of the scrap that is generated by the materials processing that is done in the laboratory. You might have wood cutoffs, sawdust, metal scrap, and plastic scrap.
3. Hold a brainstorming session with your group to develop other uses for the laboratory scrap. Ideally, the scrap should be turned into another product of high value.
4. If the scrap cannot be turned into a product of value, then each team must develop a reuse plan or recycling plan.
   NOTE: One criterion is that waste and scrap must be handled at the laboratory site. Therefore, sending waste to a landfill site is not an acceptable plan.
5. Team leaders will present their product ideas and reuse or recycling plans to the entire class. The class will vote on which plan to adopt for their manufacturing laboratory.
6. The plan should be implemented by the students.

RELATED QUESTIONS

1. Where does the scrap generated in your laboratory currently go? Trace where the various scrap products end up. Are these scraps polluting the local environment?

2. Try this mini research project. Visit a scrap yard and determine the potential for reusing materials found in the yard. Write a list of all the ways that reusing these materials could benefit the local community.

SECTION FIVE
MANUFACTURING IMPACTS

Section five describes the impacts manufacturing has on people and the environment. You will learn how feedback, or monitoring and adjusting, is used to control negative impacts. Chapter 20 explores the impacts of manufacturing on our natural resources, our air, and our water. Chapter 21 suggests some trends that might affect manufacturing in the future, including the possibility of manufacturing in space.

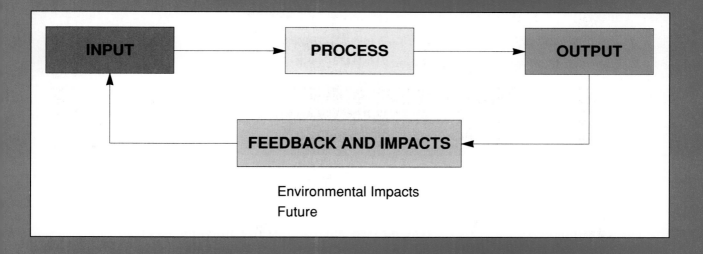

Environmental Impacts

OBJECTIVES

After completing this chapter, you will know about:

- The relationship between the Gaia Hypothesis and photosynthesis.

- The acid deposition problem and its long-term impact on aquatic ecosystems, forests, agriculture, materials, and humans.

- Acid deposition control options.

- The greenhouse effect and its long-term impact on ecosystems and climatic systems.

- The difficulty in control options to reduce the potential catastrophes of the greenhouse effect.

- The depletion of the ozone layer and its impact on ecosystems.

- The need to screen ultraviolet radiation in the stratosphere.

- Control options to reduce the depletion of the ozone layer.

- Carcinogenic substances found in groundwater supplies.

- Guidelines for environmentally soft manufacturing

KEY TERMS

Acid rain
Biosphere
Carrying capacity
Ecosystems
Environmentally soft
    manufacturers

Gaia Hypothesis
Greenhouse effect
Ozone
pH
Photosynthesis
Stratosphere

Symbiosis
Ultraviolet (UV)
    radiation

Environmental Impacts

The ancient Greek concept of Gaia, known as Mother Earth, has been developed into an important hypothesis. The **Gaia Hypothesis** reports that biological and chemical actions affect the earth's ability to support life.

Photosynthesis is a key ingredient in this hypothesis.

Photosynthesis is the process by which plants use the sun's energy to make sugars from water and carbon dioxide. The plants

Figure 20-1. Polystyrene containers for packaging fast food products add to environmental problems. *(Photo by Sonya Stang and Brent Miller)*

must use elements in the soil base to build plant tissue. Microorganisms in the soil break down dead plant and animal matter. This process provides the nutrients for other plants. Animals, including human beings, depend on photosynthesis for survival. Plants also depend on photosynthesis for survival. All food that is consumed by people can be traced directly back to photosynthesis.

Simply defined, the Gaia Hypothesis is the interrelationship of the earth's physical and chemical processes that create the possibility of a biosphere. The **biosphere** is the thin life zone that includes air (atmosphere), land (lithosphere), and water (hydrosphere). When we harm any of the air, land, or water, we

harm the entire planet. If, for example, we change the ozone layer in our atmosphere by using too many chlorofluorocarbons (CFCs), we might harm the entire earth's ecosystem. Just one CFC polystyrene hamburger container adds to the problem, Figure 20-1. The Gaia Hypothesis claims that every action can have an impact on the whole globe's ecosystem.

Manufacturing outputs, therefore, are also important to the Gaia Hypothesis. Many large-scale environmental problems that affect much of the biosphere can be directly or indirectly traced back to local actions, including manufacturing processes.

Impacts of Air Pollution

The Acid Deposition Problem

Acid deposition is acid precipitation and fallout of dry acid particles. This includes **acid rain**, acid snow, acid fog, and dry acid particles that fall to earth. These particles have a **pH** level lower than 5.6. To determine the acid/base content of water, pH tests are done, Figure 20-2. Although rain is usually acidic, excess acidity is derived from certain air pollutants, namely sulfur dioxide and oxides of nitrogen.

Neutral water has a pH value of 7. A basic substance has a pH greater than 7. When pH changes one value lower on the scale, it represents a tenfold increase in acidity. Rainwater with a pH of 5 is ten times more acidic than rainwater with a pH of 6; a pH value of 5 is 100 times more acidic than the neutral pH

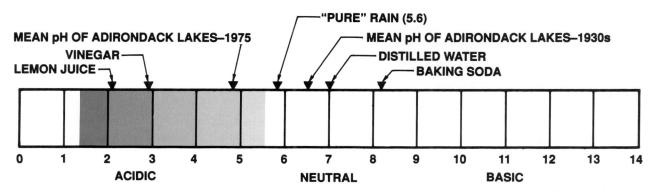

Figure 20-2. A pH scale indicates acid-base level.

value of 7. In acid rain, sulfur dioxide and nitrogen oxides combine with water to form sulfuric acid and nitric acid.

Acid deposition comes from two sources—natural and technological. Natural sources include forest fires, bacterial decay, and volcanoes. Technological sources encompass many forms of combustion, including coal-fired power plants. Technological sources also include manufacturing combustion processes and transportation systems. According to the Environmental Protection Agency (EPA), the United States produced twenty-two metric tons of sulfur dioxide and about nineteen million tons of nitrogen oxides in 1980. The EPA warns, however, that these levels will increase to around twenty-six million metric tons of sulfur dioxide per year and twenty-five million metric tons of nitrogen oxide per year by the year 2000.

Acid-forming pollutants can be carried long distances. They affect ecosystems hundreds of miles away from the source, Figure 20-3. An **ecosystem** is a group of plants, animals, and other living organisms that interact with each other and their environment in a symbiotic manner. **Symbiosis** is the healthy and helpful

Figure 20-3. Standard smokestacks of this coal-burning power plant have been replaced by new 1,000-foot stacks to aid in the dispersion of pollutants in the atmosphere. This might cut down on local problems, only to create more widespread ones. *(Courtesy of TVA)*

relationship of different living things. The Adirondack Mountains in upper New York State suffer from acid deposition, even though they are hundreds of miles from the tall stacked coal-fired power plants in the Midwest. Adirondack lakes and forests are dying day by day because acid deposition is able to travel there from the Midwest. Sweden is also acid drenched, though it is hundreds of miles away from the industrial centers of Western Europe. The movement of acid deposition over hundreds of miles creates a hard problem to solve. Coal-fired power plants generate steam to turn turbines that drive electric generators. These plants burn 10,000 tons per day. Common bituminous coal, with a sulfur content of three percent, puts 600 tons of sulfur dioxide in the air every day. In one year, a plant of this size sends out 220,000 tons of sulfur dioxide. Most of the largest emitters are in the midwestern and eastern parts of the U.S., but they affect the northeastern region the most, Figure 20-4.

Impacts of Acid Rain on Ecosystems. Ecosystems are affected in many ways. Acid deposition affects aquatic ecosystems, forests, agriculture, materials, and humans.

Aquatic ecosystems are lakes and rivers and their life forms. Different species can live with different pH levels. When the pH level drops to 5.0, many species die and others have a hard time surviving. Reproduction of some fish species is impaired, and some aquatic plants die. As the levels reach 4.0, all organisms die except certain types of algae. Acidic lakes are very deceptive in appearance. They can be clear blue and look especially clean. Under the surface, however, the lake might have no life, Figure 20-5.

Melting snow in the spring can quickly dump large amounts of acid into lakes, Figure 20-6. This can result in an acid shock that kills fish. Spring is the time when fish, frogs, and other animals spawn. Their eggs are very fragile. When fish die, they leave a gap in the complex food chain, and other life-forms are affected. For example, in dead Adirondack Mountain lakes, loons and other waterfowl have left or died because they cannot find

Figure 20-4. Note the locations of the largest coal-fired power plants in the United States.

enough fish to eat. Other birds that feed on insects have had their populations drastically reduced. Even populations of raccoons and many other mammals have been reduced in acid rain regions.

Forests and agriculture are also affected severely by acid deposition. In the Green Mountains of Vermont, there has been a fifty percent decline in the growth rate of spruce trees. A large number of trees are being invaded by insects and disease. Scientists say this problem is due to acid deposition. The wax-like protective layer of leaves is damaged by acid rain. Plants become easier to attack for insects and fungi. Acid deposition hits hard

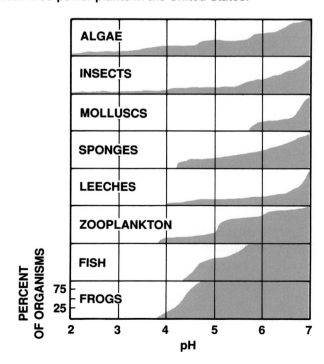

Figure 20-5. The pH level affects the survival of various organisms.

Figure 20-6. The movement of melting snow into lakes contributes to the acid level of lakes.(Photo by Edith Raviola)

and fast as natural lime buffering capacities are used up. For example, a 1980 study showed that fifty percent of the fir trees on the border between East Germany and Czechoslovakia were healthy. Only two years later, ninety-eight percent of the trees were dead or dying. Forests are the habitats for wildlife. As forests are destroyed, wildlife populations grow smaller and other dramatic changes happen. The loss of forests causes soil erosion, flooding, and sedimentation of waterways. Forests are also the economic base for many people.

Limestone and marble materials are also eroded by the corrosive effects of acid deposition. These materials are used for buildings and monuments. Acid rain also deteriorates roads and bridges that use concrete. Concrete contains lime, which deteriorates with increased acid deposition. Metals and paint also suffer from the corrosive impact of acid deposition.

Acid deposition impacts the health of humans. Inhalation of the highly acidic fog particles has caused respiratory problems during periods of smog. However, the most severe impact on humans will be the catastrophic loss of lakes and forests. Although their economic value can be measured, the ecological and aesthetic values are priceless.

Control Options. There are six main strategies for control. They are 1) alternative power plants, 2) fuel switching, 3) coal washing, 4) scrubbers, 5) fluidized bed combustion, and 6) passive decentralized energy systems.

Alternative power plants that could replace the energy capacities of the coal-fired plants include large-scale hydroelectric and nuclear plants. These two systems, however, can also harm the environment.

Fuel switching to low-sulfur coal also has some problems. Most low-sulfur coal is located in the western part of the United States. Transportation of this coal is very expensive. It is also a finite resource.

Coal washing before the coal is burned removes some of the sulfur but not enough of it. Chemical techniques for removing sulfur have also been proposed. They have not yet been developed on a commercial scale.

A scrubber is a filter that uses a liquid spray, Figure 20-7. Lime is used in a spray to

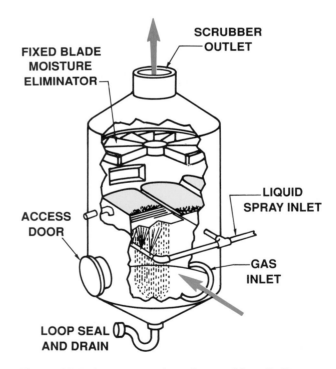

Figure 20-7. A cross-section of a scrubber. Sulfur dioxide can be removed from flu gases by passing the furnace exhaust through a spray of alkaline solution. (Redrawn with permission from W. W. Sly Manufacturing Co.)

Environmental Checklist

Conserving materials conserves land, forests, and energy and reduces stress on living systems. Check your conservation awareness.

In my house I
_____ recycle newspaper
_____ recycle plastic
_____ recycle glass
_____ recycle aluminum cans
_____ recycle aluminum foil
_____ reuse paper bags
_____ use hand-me-downs
_____ use recycled paper
_____ take my own bags to the grocery store
_____ repair and reuse things
_____ compost kitchen scraps

In my house I conserve energy by
_____ having adequate insulation
_____ keeping the thermostat at or below 65°F in the winter
_____ wearing warm enough clothing for the above
_____ using hot water sparingly
_____ avoiding air conditioning
_____ avoiding unnecessary electrical gadgets
_____ using high-efficiency electrical appliances
_____ using electricity sparingly in lights, range, tv, radios, and so on

To reduce pollution in my house, I
_____ do not dispose of toxic substances in the trash or down the drain

_____ use phosphate-free soap
_____ do not use pesticides
_____ clean windows with vinegar and water, not chemicals
_____ follow guidelines for disposing of waste products
_____ compost organic matter in an outdoor compost pile
_____ grow an organic garden using recycled compost as fertilizer

In my transportation, I
_____ have a high miles-per-gallon car
_____ maintain efficient exhaust emissions control
_____ keep the car tuned up
_____ carpool when feasible
_____ walk or bike for short trips when feasible
_____ recycle used motor oil
_____ recycle used tires
_____ use public transportation

In my shopping, I
_____ decline excess packaging from merchants
_____ avoid styrofoam
_____ cut back on disposable products
_____ read labels and buy least toxic products
_____ avoid buying unnecessary products
_____ buy products that can be repaired easily
_____ buy durable products that may cost a little more but last much longer

buffer the exhaust from coal combustion. Lime reacts with sulfur dioxide and forms calcium sulfate. Although scrubbers are expensive and hard to install, they do lessen some of the acid deposition problems associated with the burning of coal.

Fluidized bed combustion is a system that removes sulfur dioxide during the combustion process. This system operates by forcing sand and lime, which is kept in a fluid state, into the combustion chamber.

Nonpolluting decentralized energy systems include passive solar, photovoltaic, wind, wood, microhydro, biogas, and other systems. These systems have proven to be useful in specific places where enough natural resources are available. To make such systems work, consumers need to conserve energy. Many manufacturing processes would need to be scaled down to take advantage of passive decentralized energy systems. The entire manufacturing system would have to be assessed and retooled. Some scientists believe this is the most promising approach to solving long-term environmental problems associated with acid deposition.

The Greenhouse Effect

The **greenhouse effect** is also known as the carbon dioxide effect. A south-facing parked car that has the windows rolled up shows the greenhouse effect. Sunlight passes through the glass and strikes the interior of the car. This ultraviolet radiation is absorbed by the material and turned into infrared radiation or heat energy. In the summertime, the inside of the car warms up to extremely high temperatures, sometimes higher than 150 degrees. Glass lets one form of energy (ultraviolet) pass through. After it changes its form to infrared heat radiation, it blocks the energy from escaping. This trapped heat energy causes the entire inside of the car to increase in temperature, Figure 20-8.

Figure 20-8. Heat is trapped inside the car and warms the interior despite the cooler temperature outside.

The carbon dioxide in the atmosphere performs the same function as the glass in the car. It lets sunlight pass through to strike the earth. The infrared energy then radiates outward and is absorbed by the carbon dioxide. As the carbon dioxide absorbs the infrared radiation, the earth's atmosphere is warmed. The more carbon dioxide, the greater the warming of the earth's atmosphere. Although only 0.034 percent, or 340 parts per million (ppm), of the earth's atmosphere is carbon dioxide, it provides an adequate warming blanket in the temperate climates we enjoy on earth. However, as we increase the amount of carbon dioxide, too much warming will occur over the next thirty to eighty years. This trend will cause many other drastic climate changes.

An imbalance in the carbon dioxide cycle first occurred when humans started the Industrial Revolution around 1760. The combustion of fossil fuels, coal, oil, and gas was the beginning of this imbalance. During the Industrial Revolution there was an estimated 260 ppm carbon dioxide level compared to 360 ppm in the late 1980s. We have added thirty percent more carbon dioxide to the atmosphere since the Industrial Revolution. Unless there is a dramatic change in the world consumption of fossil fuels, it is projected that we will reach 600 ppm by 2025. Other pollutants also absorb infrared radiation. Methane, hydrocarbons, nitrogen oxides, and freons also add to the greenhouse effect.

Impacts of the Greenhouse Effect. Scientists fear that as the atmosphere warms, the polar ice caps will melt. This will raise ocean water levels about eighty feet (twenty-five meters). Massive flooding of coastal and low regions will probably be common. Climatologists have indicated that warming will probably be between three and eight degrees Fahrenheit. In polar regions, warming may be as high as eighteen degrees Fahrenheit. Regions near the equator will warm only two to four degrees Fahrenheit. With a new temperature difference between the poles and equator, wind patterns will change. When wind patterns change, all elements of the climate change. Some areas

Figure 20-9. During the drought of 1988, a farmer inspects a crop that is usually knee-high by the fourth of July. *(Courtesy of U. S. Department of Agriculture)*

will have increased annual rainfall, while others will have decreased annual rainfall. The 1988 summer drought in the midwestern United States stirred debate on the greenhouse effect and brought back memories of the 1930s Dust Bowl, Figure 20-9.

The Dust Bowl was then the greatest natural disaster in United States history. It was actually a loss of topsoil created in farming areas by a lack of soil conservation. This state was made worse by severe drought. Farmers had planted an extra forty million acres in the U. S. to offset the loss of farm lands in Europe during World War I. But they overestimated the demand for these crops. As their harvests increased, a glut developed in the market and prices fell.

The farmers tried to produce even more to make up their losses. But they went too far, overplanting and ignoring the need to let the land lie fallow, or unused. Farmers need to let a portion of their land lie fallow each year to conserve the topsoil.

A drought hit hard. Loose, dry topsoil was swept away by the winds. These windstorms made clouds of black dust, which gave the name "Dust Bowl" to this era. Scientists fear that the greenhouse effect could produce an even more severe dust bowl if climatic patterns continue to change.

Control Options. It is hard to control the greenhouse effect because it creeps up on us very slowly. It is also a global problem related to human behavior throughout many industrial and developing countries. Do wealthy industrialized countries have the right to tell developing countries that they should not develop their industrial base? The greenhouse effect is also a very difficult problem to study. Even during the 1988 drought, some researchers believed it was the first sign of the greenhouse effect, while others denied it.

Global conservation is a very difficult goal to obtain, but it might be the only control method that can turn back the greenhouse effect. As the countries of the world become more connected through trade and communication, decision-making becomes more complex. The concerns of many different nations and cultures must be considered when we think about the greenhouse effect. Complex global problems are more difficult to solve than local problems.

Ozone Layer Depletion

The **stratosphere** is the atmospheric layer ranging from about six to fifty miles above the earth's surface, Figure 20-10. The presence of **ozone** in this layer is concentrated at an altitude of about twenty-five miles. It is important to all life because it screens out dangerous ultraviolet radiation. Some pollutants, such as chlorofluorocarbons and nitric oxide, reduce ozone in the stratosphere. Ironically, we have two major problems with ozone. There is too much ozone in the lower atmosphere, but the ozone layer in the stratosphere is being depleted. Because there is little mixing of the two layers, these problems can exist at the same time.

Knowing about **ultraviolet (UV) radiation** is important to understanding the full impact

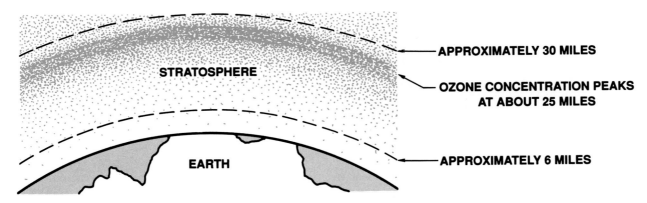

STRATOSPHERE

APPROXIMATELY 30 MILES

OZONE CONCENTRATION PEAKS
AT ABOUT 25 MILES

EARTH

APPROXIMATELY 6 MILES

Figure 20-10. The earth's stratosphere ranges from about six to fifty miles above the earth's surface. The highest concentration of ozone is at about 25 miles.

of depleting the ozone layer. UV radiation is an invisible radiation from the sun. The wavelength of UV radiation is slightly shorter than that of visible light, but has more energy. UV radiation penetrates living tissue. Proteins or nucleic acids (that is, DNA) absorb the UV radiation. Because of its high energy content, the chemical bonds of the molecules break down. This radiation is very harmful to human tissue. In the United States, 600,000 cases of skin cancer per year result from UV radiation passing through the atmosphere and damaging human tissue. Luckily, ninety-nine percent of UV radiation is absorbed by the ozone layer in the stratosphere. Without this protective shield, the biological damage to plants and animals would be catastrophic. Most life-forms could not exist on earth.

Control Options. The greenhouse effect is a problem that will not wait for a solution. There is a lag time between production of chlorofluorocarbons and depletion of the ozone layer. Even if manufacturers stopped production today, there would be emissions for the next twenty years. Chlorofluorocarbons in the lower atmosphere will take many years to reach the stratosphere. We have no way to remove chlorine from the atmosphere. Another aspect of this problem is that the depletion of the ozone and its impacts are global. Countries that do not produce and use these pollutants will also be affected. For example, France still manufactures chlorofluorocarbons used in

aerosol cans. Aerosol cans that emit chlorofluorocarbons are a major contributor to ozone depletion. Many of the refrigerants in common air conditioners and refrigerators also add to the problem. Who is willing to give up air conditioners and refrigerators that use chlorofluorocarbons? Do we depend too much on these products to be able to give them up?

Limited alternatives exist. For example, solvents using these compounds can be replaced or contained and recycled. Compressor units in air-conditioners and refrigerators could be changed to use heat transfer materials instead of dangerous refrigerants. As limited as they are, manufacturers and consumers resist these alternatives.

Impacts of Water Pollution

Chloride, nitrates, heavy metals, and hydrocarbons are the major groundwater contaminants (see chapter 19). Chlorinated hydrocarbons of low molecular weight are carcinogenic in humans and animals. Carcinogens are those elements that cause cancer. About 4.5 trillion liters (1.2 trillion gallons) of contaminated water enter the groundwater in the United States every day. Industrial waste and impoundments (evaporation ponds) are the largest sources of groundwater pollution. Solid waste disposal is also a large source.

The resource of good water was once taken for granted, but it will soon become a precious commodity. Many people who have had their

Figure 20-11. More people are buying purified water to avoid the risks of groundwater contamination. *(Photo by Ruby Gold)*

water tested have been forced to buy purified water, Figure 20-11. If trends continue, a large portion of the United States groundwater supplies will be undrinkable by the year 2000.

Control Options. Some states have passed laws to regulate nonpoint water pollution. Local governments have passed zoning rules to protect groundwater from agricultural and urban sources. In 1948, the Water Pollution Control Act provided financial help to build waste water treatment plants. By September of 1981, 4,000 plants were in operation, with 7,000 more scheduled to begin work throughout the 1980s.

Conservation is another way to controlling groundwater contamination. The five-gallon flush toilet is very wasteful. A number of new toilets have come on the market that conserve water. In addition, shower heads are now being produced that reduce water consumption, Figure 20-12.

Specific chemicals found in groundwater affect human health in different ways. Figure 20-13 shows these various effects on health.

Environmentally Soft Manufacturing

The scale or size of an organization also affects the degree of environmental impact. A manufacturing company that produces 10,000 bicycles per day will probably do more harm to the environment than one that produces 200 bicycles per day. Traditionally, scale was set by the market and economics. If a manufacturer could find additional markets, it would increase the scale of its operation regardless of the impacts on humans or the natural environment. Unfortunately, some operations have reduced the local environment's carrying capacity. The **carrying capacity** of a region is its maximum ability to support life-forms in a healthy way. If the life-forms grow beyond the carrying capacity, the entire ecosystem can suffer. For example, a lake that is being slightly polluted has a natural buffering ability. This buffer acts as a pollution filter. At a certain point, however, the natural buffer cannot filter out any more pollution. The lake's carrying capacity will then be lowered, and a large fish kill may result.

Manufacturing organizations that show special sensitivity for the natural environment are

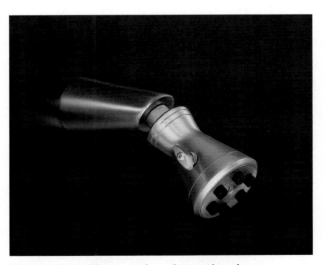

Figure 20-12. Water-saving shower heads are becoming more popular as people become aware of potential water shortages. *(Courtesy of Kohler Co.)*

TOXIC, SYNTHETIC ORGANIC COMPOUNDS FREQUENTLY FOUND IN CHEMICAL WASTES

Chemical	Known Health Effects	Causes Mutations	Carcino-genic	Birth Defects	Causes Still Births	Causes Nervous Disorders	Liver Disease	Kidney Disease	Lung Disease
Benzene	X	X	X		X				
dichlorobenzenes	X				X	X	X		
hexachlorobenzene	X		X	X	X	X			
Chloroform		X	X		X		X		
Carbon tetrachloride		X			X	X	X	X	
Ethylene									
chloroethylene (vinyl chloride)	X	X				X	X		X
dichloroethylene	X	X			X	X	X	X	
tetrachloroethylene		X				X	X	X	
trichloroethylene	X	X				X	X		
Heptachlor	X	X			X	X	X		
Polychlorinated biphenyls (PCBs)	X	X	X		X	X	X		
Tetrachlorodibenzo dioxin	X	X	X		X	X	X		
Toluene	X				X	X			
chlorotoluenes	X	X							
Xylene				X	X	X			

Figure 20-13. Here are examples of toxic synthetic organic compounds frequently found in chemical wastes and their effects on humans. *(From* Hazardous Waste in America, *by Samuel Epstein, Lester Brown, & Carl Pope. Copyright © 1982 by Epstein, Brown, & Pope. Reprinted with permission of Sierra Club Books.)*

called **environmentally soft manufacturers**. They follow a list of operating guidelines. These guidelines include

- appropriately scaled production,
- manufacture of only needed products,
- the use of indigenous (local) resources,
- the use of renewable energy, and
- the development of an environmental code of ethics.

Figure 20-14. It is important that appropriate forest management be implemented to preserve this precious renewable resource. *(Courtesy of Weyerhaeuser Co., Inc.)*

Appropriately Scaled Production. Appropriately scaled production uses a limited number of workers to produce a limited number of high-quality products, regardless of market conditions. These manufacturers decide against increasing the scale of their operations even if there is a market to absorb the potential production increase. The appropriately scaled production level depends on many factors, such as product type, local market, quality, worker skill, and tool and machine processing.

Make Only Needed Products. Manufacturing only needed products is a guideline that questions the social relevancy or need of a product. Luxury products are not produced because they serve only a small fraction of the population. These products do not satisfy a real social need. Manufacturers who follow this guideline decide whether a new product is socially relevant or not. A product design critique panel is sometimes set up to evaluate new products and decide whether society really needs them. This can be a very subjective decision, however. It may eliminate an individual's right to establish his or her needs. These manufacturers are very sensitive to the great amount of

Ecotopia: A Guide to Environmental Survival

A California writer's ecological novel is winning a new generation of admirers. Written by Ernest Callenbach and published in 1975, *Ecotopia* is an environmentalist's utopia. The fictional story is set in 1999, just 20 years after the states of Washington, Oregon, and most of California seceded from the United States, sickened by environmental degradation, overzealous military spending, and high inflation. What Ecotopians care most about is their air, their land, their water, and one another. Polluters get stiff jail sentences because environmental crimes are considered just as life-destructive as assaulting another person and should be punished similarly.

What Callenbach created in *Ecotopia* was a stable-state system that recycles food and sewer wastes into fertilizer used to grow more food. They outlawed the internal combustion engine and banned a host of consumer products, from microwave ovens to electric can openers. All waterfront land is expropriated to be publicly accessible to all. Plastics are made from plants. Thus they are biodegradable.

Aluminum and nonferrous metals are banned. All garbage is recycled. Electric power is supplied by solar voltaics and thermal-sea power plants. All companies are small, worker-owned cooperatives. Ecotopians are freed from "isolating technologies" like cars, television, and huge corporate institutions. The distinction between work and play has disappeared.

When Callenbach wrote about this utopian society that sacrificed conspicuous consumption to ensure survival, he was unable to find a publisher. So he borrowed money from friends and published it himself. Now, after seasons of ozone smog, sewage and medical wastes washed up on beaches, and fears of the greenhouse effect, the book is winning new popularity. Scientists have given Callenbach credit for the technical accuracy of his novel. If we survey our own daily diet of chemical-laden food, our polluted air and water systems, and our hazardous waste-strewn environment, we might wistfully ask, "When and how might I move there?"

---

unneeded products already in the marketplace. They do not want to add to the problem.

Use Local Resources. By using indigenous resources, manufacturers utilize resources that can be found locally or regionally. Imports are kept to a minimum because of the wasted energy in transporting raw materials over great distances and the problem of increased dependency. Local materials keep the local economy healthy because money is used over and over again. When materials are bought outside of the region, the money that pays for the materials rarely returns to the local economy. When local materials are used, the community builds its sense of local history. This guideline, however, must also be practiced with natural limitations. For example, oak hardwood furniture manufacturing must not deplete the local resources faster than it can replace them.

These manufacturers should have a 100- or 200-year forestry management survey done so they can balance hardwood growth patterns with harvesting, Figure 20-14.

Use Renewable Energy Sources. Using renewable energy sources is another guideline that helps keep the environment safe. The use of solar, solar photovoltaic, wind, biogas, small-scale hydro, and wood systems avoids the large risks associated with the combustion of fossil fuels. As future energy resources dwindle, more and more manufacturers will try to switch to renewable alternatives. Renewable energy systems work in harmony with nature's timetable and usually require new processing techniques. A furniture manufacturing company located next to a river could retool equipment to run on compressed air. The compressor could be powered by microhydro power from falling water.

Develop an Environmental Code of Ethics. Developing an environmental code of ethics is a guideline that should be followed by all manufacturers. A manufacturer should develop a code of ethics that exceeds the federal and state guidelines. This code should deal with material inputs, processing, and outputs. Outputs, such as hazardous waste, should have strict guidelines that must be enforced. Workers who live in the community develop a sense of respect for the natural environment when an environmental code of ethics becomes company policy. A code of ethics also focuses on material scrap, waste, and pollution. A reuse and recycling plan should be part of the policy along with an environmentally safe method to deal with hazardous waste that the company uses or generates.

Summary

The Greek concept of Gaia, known as Mother Earth, has been developed into an important hypothesis. The Gaia Hypothesis reports that the earth is a living interactive system sometimes called the biosphere. The biosphere is the symbiotic relationship between the land, water, and air support systems. If, by human action, one part of the system is harmed, all parts are damaged. The ability of plants to use the sun's energy in photosynthesis is an important part of the Gaia Hypothesis. All life is traced back to photosynthesis.

Acid deposition occurs when pollutants such as sulfur dioxide and nitrogen oxides cause water, snow, and dry particles to have a high acidic level. Coal-fired power plants and automobiles are the prime sources of acid deposition. Forests and lakes in the northeastern United States are being destroyed by sources as far away as the midwestern United States. There are six options to control acid deposition—alternative power plants, fuel switching, coal washing, scrubbers, fluidized bed combustion, and passive decentralized energy systems.

The greenhouse effect is caused by increased carbon dioxide in the atmosphere. Increased levels of carbon dioxide may increase the earth's temperature. Carbon dioxide acts like a blanket and keeps the earth's warmth from escaping into the atmosphere. Scientists are afraid that the polar ice caps may melt and cause widespread flooding. As the global industrial base continues to expand, it becomes harder to control the greenhouse effect. Some scientists fear that the drought of 1988 is related to the greenhouse effect.

Ozone layer depletion is a very dangerous problem that increases the ultraviolet radiation reaching the earth's surface. Skin cancer, which is increasing, and mutations are a result of ultraviolet radiation. It is caused by chlorofluorocarbons emitted into the atmosphere. Although legislation has been enacted by some countries to control the use of chlorofluorocarbons, ozone depletion continues to be a serious global problem.

Carcinogens are contaminating groundwater supplies. Chloride, nitrates, heavy metals, and hydrocarbons are the main contaminants. Clean water is becoming a scarce commodity.

Environmentally soft manufacturing is a promising system of guidelines that can reduce the severe environmental problems facing industrialized societies. These guidelines include appropriately scaled production, the manufacture of only needed products, use of indigenous resources, and development of an environmental code of ethics. If manufacturing systems develop an environmental code of ethics, future generations can enjoy the resources we have taken for granted.

DISCUSSION QUESTIONS

1. What is the importance of the Gaia Hypothesis and photosynthesis to life on earth?

2. Describe the difficult problems associated with solving the acid deposition problem. Why is acid deposition also a serious political problem?

3. The greenhouse effect could eventually melt the polar ice caps. What are the environmental and human impacts if the polar ice caps melt? Describe one possible scenario.

4. What are the difficulties in solving the potential catastrophes of the greenhouse effect?

5. Describe how the ozone layer of the stratosphere is being depleted. How can industry help solve this problem?

6. List the products that cause ozone depletion and the potential health effects on humans.

7. Our groundwater supplies are being threatened by toxic chemical waste. What are some of the health effects associated with groundwater pollution?

8. List and describe guidelines that promote environmentally soft manufacturing.

9. Describe a few things in your life that you could do to help keep the environment safe.

CHAPTER ACTIVITIES

 ENVIRONMENTAL CODE OF ETHICS

OBJECTIVE

In this activity, you will establish a set of environmental policy guidelines that your manufacturing laboratory will adopt through a voting process. Once adopted, this environmental code of ethics must be strictly followed and enforced.

MATERIALS AND SUPPLIES

1. Recycled paper and pencils
2. Research materials such as a copy of local ordinances

PROCEDURE

1. Form groups of four or five and select a team leader.
2. Discuss and then write a comprehensive approach to reducing the environmental impacts occurring from your manufacturing laboratory. Address these concerns:

   a. Air quality: Will your lab adopt a smoking policy, a dust control policy?

   b. Water quality: How will you control the disposal of liquid hazardous waste? List products that should not be dumped down the drain. Will you adopt a water conservation policy?

  c. Solid waste reduction: You might write guidelines limiting what materials may be thrown away. How will you treat paper, glass, metal, wood, plastics and other scrap?

  d. Noise reduction: How will you address the problem of noise pollution? Recommend a policy to reduce the noise.

  e. Energy conservation: You might draft an energy conservation policy that mandates turning off lights when leaving the room, using hand tools instead of machine tools for small jobs, and so forth.

  f. Other: Add to your code any guidelines related to environmental impacts that you feel are important.

3. Divide the work load. The team leader should ask each team member to draft one section of your code. Team members should choose the categories they are most interested in. If team members cannot decide, the team leader may assign each member to a different category.

4. Study your local ordinances and other research materials to see how these documents are organized.

5. Draft the section of your code that you chose. Try not to mimic the legal jargon you have read. Keep your writing clear and precise so it is easy to understand.

6. Your team leader will call a meeting to edit and modify any sections of your code.

7. Your team leader will present your entire code to the class.

8. The class will vote to choose one team's environmental code of ethics. That code will become laboratory policy. The code should be enforced and violations should be penalized.

RELATED QUESTIONS

1. How do local small-scale manufacturers handle hazardous waste?

2. Does your entire school have a comprehensive recycling program or energy conservation program? If not, why? Perhaps your class can draft an environmental code of ethics for the entire school. Is your principal interested in reducing negative environmental impacts from your school?

 **ACID RAIN**

OBJECTIVE

In this activity, you will learn about acid rain. You will measure the pH level of local rainfall to determine if acid rain is a problem in your community. You will also produce simulated acid rain and observe its effects on seedlings and materials.

BACKGROUND

Acidity is measured on the pH scale, which ranges from 0 to 14. A pH of 1 is very acidic, while a pH of 13 is very alkaline. The pH of several common products is shown in Figure 2. Rainwater normally has a pH of about 5.6. Rain with a pH below this level is considered to be acid precipitation.

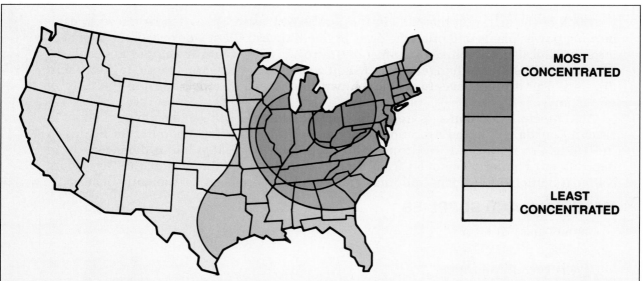

Figure 1. This map shows the relative concentrations of acid rain in regions throughout the United States.

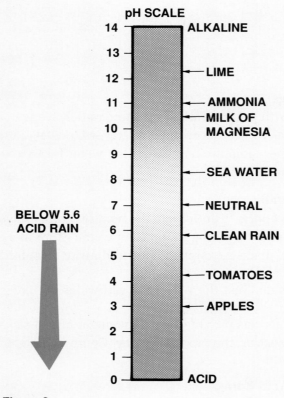

Figure 2

Much of the acid rain that falls in the Northeast United States can be traced to coal-burning power plants and other factories in the Midwest. Giant smokestacks designed to minimize local pollution send sulfur and nitrogen oxides into the upper atmosphere. These chemicals are changed by sunlight and mix with water vapor to form acid droplets. The droplets eventually fall to earth hundreds of miles away in the form of rain or snow.

Acid precipitation damages trees and crops and increases the acid content of lakes. In eastern Canada and in the Adirondack mountains, lakes that were popular for fishing in the 1970s are now dead. Buildings and monuments are also being damaged. Acid deposits are regularly removed from bronze and stone monuments at the Gettysburg National Battlefield. Ancient buildings in Greece have also been permanently damaged.

MATERIALS AND SUPPLIES

1. Safety glasses
2. Package of radish seeds
3. Package of plastic cups
4. Vinegar
5. Distilled water
6. Four test tube racks and 16 test tubes
7. pH meter, or test strip kit
8. Strips of copper, aluminum, steel, galvanized sheet metal
9. Magnifying glass

PROCEDURE

PART I: Growing Seedlings
1. Fill ten plastic cups with potting soil. Plant three radish seeds in each cup.
2. Label the plants so that you can keep accurate records.
3. Provide light and proper moisture using distilled water for two to three weeks.
4. Record the height of each plant.

PART II: Monitoring Rainfall
1. Follow local weather reports to anticipate the next two rainy days.
2. Clean three plastic cups by washing in distilled water. Store in a clean plastic bag.
3. On the next rainy day, place the cups outside and away from buildings and automobile traffic.
4. Bring the samples inside. Test the pH of the rainwater by using a pH meter or pH test strips.
   NOTE: Follow the directions provided with the meter or test strips.
5. Record your data. Repeat on the next rainy day. Compare results. Determine if your local rainfall is acid rain.

PART III: Seedlings and Acid Rain
1. Complete this part of the activity two to three weeks after planting the radish seeds.
   NOTE: Wear safety glasses during this part of the activity.

2. Use household vinegar and distilled water to make solutions with pHs of three, four, five, and six. Store the solutions in clean, labeled containers.

3. Treat two plants with each pH solution for ten days. Provide only distilled water to two plants as a control.

4. Keep a log that includes the heights and general appearances of the plants each day.

5. After about a week, summarize the results in your log and share this information with your class.

PART IV: Effects of Acid Rain on Materials

1. *NOTE*: Wear safety glasses during this activity. Use distilled water and vinegar to prepare solutions with pHs of three, four, five, and six.

2. Cut $1/4" \times 1^1/2"$ strips of copper, aluminum, steel, and galvanized sheet metal.

3. Set up and label four racks of test tubes. One sample of each metal should be placed in a test tube with each pH solution. Record your observations each day.

4. After a week, remove the samples one at a time. Wash with water and use a magnifying glass to examine each sample. Record your results.

MATH/SCIENCE CONNECTION

The pH scale is logarithmic. A pH of four is ten times more acidic than a pH of five. It is 100 times more acidic than a pH of six.

Researchers are studying ways to reduce the acid rain problem. Scrubbers are used to remove sulfur oxides from exhaust before it leaves smokestacks. The sulfur content of coal can be reduced by washing the coal with water. Several lakes have been restored by liming. To do this, large quantities of lime are added to the lake to reduce the pH. This is expensive, but it seems to work.

RELATED QUESTIONS

1. Describe two ways that power plants can reduce sulfur oxide emissions.

2. Why do you think power companies resist using low-sulfur coal as a fuel?

3. Who should be held financially responsible for the damage done to lakes in eastern Canada?

4. Is acid rain a problem in your community? If not, should you be concerned about acid rain? Why or why not?

5. What do you think can be done to reduce the damage acid rain causes to buildings?

CHAPTER 21

The Future of Manufacturing

OBJECTIVES

After completing this chapter, you will know about :

- Several important trends that may influence the future of manufacturing.

- The basic research being conducted and the promise of manufacturing in space.

- The options available for citizens to decide and plan for appropriate futures.

KEY TERMS

Appropriate technology	Hard technology	Simulation
Capital intensive	Labor intensive	Soft technology
Exponential rate of growth	Levitator	Superalloy
	Mapping	Trend
Forecasting	Microgravity	Trend analysis
Futurists	Microspheres	
Global competition	Scenario	

Manufacturing Trends

What will the future hold? No one can know for sure, but we can find some clues by looking at the past and extending recent trends to the future. A **trend** is a pattern in recent events in society. Throughout history, one important trend is that manufacturing has been important to the development of societies. In the future, manufacturing will continue to help shape the standard of living and financial health of our society. The only thing we can say for sure is that the future will be different from our world today. Change is the only constant. It is sure to occur in every area of society. Look, for example, at the trend in shortening the length of the average work week, Figure 21-1. In the early 1900s, people worked sixty to seventy hours per week. Today, the average work week lasts about thirty-five to forty hours. If we extend this trend to the future, people may work only fifteen to twenty hours a week in the year 2070. We may not be able to predict the exact number of hours, but

TREND—DECLINE IN AVERAGE HOURS IN A WORK WEEK

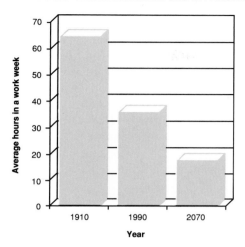

Figure 21-1. Over the last 80 years, the average number of hours in a work week has declined from 65 or 70 hours to 35 or 40 hours. If this trend continues over the next 80 years, people may only work 15 to 20 hours per week.

there is a pretty good chance that the trend toward fewer hours will continue. Today's trends can help us predict the future.

Exponential Rate of Growth

Futurists are people who study the future. They look at trends and try to predict future events. An important factor they must consider is the increasing rate of change in our technological society. The time it takes for new technologies to be accepted and used is rapidly decreasing. For example, the Wright brothers flew the first powered aircraft in 1903. By 1969, a span of sixty-six years, Neil Armstrong flew to the moon and back. In 1946, ENIAC, the first electronic computer, was invented. Today, less than fifty years later, having a personal computer at home is common. Finally, the first laser was invented in 1960. Today, less than thirty-five years later, lasers are commonly found in grocery store checkouts and compact disk players. The time between the invention of a new technology and its common use is getting shorter.

The decade of the 1980s saw more changes in technology than any other decade since the 1780s, when the Industrial Revolution began in Great Britain. At the beginning of the 1990s, experts say the amount of information in our technological world doubles every four to five years. This was not always true. Before the Industrial Revolution, change was very slow, taking hundreds or even thousands of years. Figure 21-2 shows the rate of growth of technology before and after the Industrial Revolution. The increasing rate of growth of

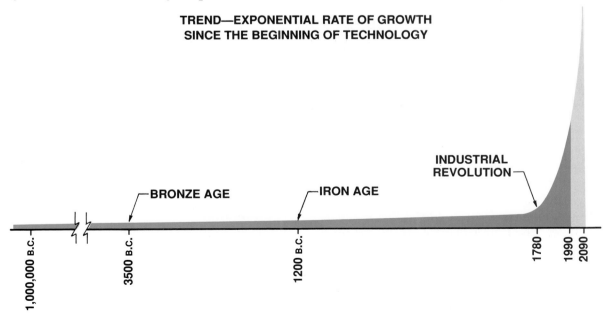

Figure 21-2. Technology is growing at an exponential rate.

Forecasting the Future

Humans have been trying to predict what might happen in the future since the beginning of time. **Forecasting** is a "tool" used daily by all of us, from planning our day to anticipating a changing traffic light. What has happened in the past is our only guide to what might happen in the future. Therefore, because we have seen a traffic light change on a regular basis from green to yellow to red, we can safely assume that it will continue to do so in the future. If you catch the school bus at 7:30 A.M. every day, you can assume this trend will go on. This way of forecasting is called **trend analysis**. Past and present trends are studied and forecasted into the future. However, knowing the past does not automatically tell us what will happen in the future. We often use our knowledge of the past to shape future events. But to create something based only on the past is a difficult process.

Making up stories about the future is another method of forecasting. A "made-up" story about the future is called a **scenario**. Science fiction stories are scenarios. A scenario begins to take shape when we ask, "What would happen if...?" We all use a form of scenario when we imagine ourselves in a particular situation. For example, ask yourself "What would happen if I were the principal in this school?" Writing a scenario is not hard. An imagination and knowledge of the basic facts related to the topic are all you need.

Another way to forecast the future is to ask experts. People who know about a subject are often asked for their opinions about the future of their particular field. Often, a person involved in one job for a number of years begins to see the trends that may give some hint of the future. By asking a group of experts, you can get an average of their opinions on the future.

Mapping is another way to predict a possible future. This method can be as simple as making a list or as complex as a family tree or computer flowchart. By making a map of some event, such as a computer program, the person creating the map is predicting a future event.

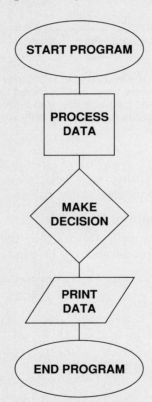

A computer programmer's flowchart is an example of mapping or predicting the future.

Simulation, another forecasting technique, is a broad term for activities like role-playing, modeling, and gaming. When children pretend to be doctors, play with toys, or play board games, they are simulating an activity that they have seen and might do some day. In your manufacturing class, you may be asked to join in a simulation of a manufacturing enterprise. You may play the role of a manager, production worker, accountant, or some other manufacturing worker. The manufacturing lab for your class is actually a model of the real thing.

By playing the role of an actual worker in your manufacturing class, you are involved in a future forecasting technique called simulation or role-playing. *(Courtesy of NASA)*

technology in this figure is called an exponential rate of growth. As we discussed in Chapter 9, an **exponential rate of growth** is an ever-increasing rate.

Today's exponential growth rate in technology is impressive. Almost ninety percent of all our technology has been invented in the last fifty years. The trend of exponential growth will probably continue in the future.

Throughout this text, several trends in manufacturing were described. Let's look at a few of these trends and see what impact they might have on the future of manufacturing.

Trend #1: Decrease in Labor-intensive Manufacturing. In the past, manufacturing was **labor intensive**. That is, large numbers of people were hired as workers, Figure 21-3. Manufacturing was based on human muscle power and physical skills. In Chapter 10, you read that labor is the largest expense in manufacturing. Production payroll can cost a company thousands or even millions of dollars each year. Because of this, manufacturing companies have been reducing the number of human workers in recent years. Many large companies, which have traditionally employed thousands of workers, have been replacing humans with robots and other auto-

mated equipment. Automated equipment often improves product quality while it reduces labor costs.

Most of these unemployed workers are finding new jobs in the service sector, particularly in information-processing jobs. Today,

Figure 21-3. In the past, manufacturing was labor intensive. Large numbers of people were hired to perform physical jobs. *(Courtesy of Ford Motor Company)*

and for the near future, many new jobs will involve collecting, processing, storing, retrieving, and analyzing information. For this reason, we often say that we live in an information age. The manufacturing industry also expects more jobs for workers who process information, such as engineers, technicians, and marketing personnel. Eventually information-processing jobs will also be automated, leading to a decline in labor-intensive information processing. Remember, change is the only constant, Figure 21-4.

Trend #2: Increase in Capital-intensive Manufacturing. Capital-intensive manufacturing is based on tools, machines, and equipment, particularly computerized and automated tools. This trend is directly related to the first trend. Increasingly, computers, robots, and automated assembly machines are replacing human workers. For the manufacturing company, computerized and automated equipment increases productivity, reduces labor costs, and often improves the quality of products. In the long run, after these expensive machines have been paid for, capital-intensive manufacturing should make more profits for the shareholders.

A related trend is the need for people who can learn to set up, operate, and maintain these sophisticated machines. As you read in Chapter 5, these new areas of employment will be in knowledge-intensive jobs that require mental skills. In the future, more technologists, workers like engineers and technicians, will be needed. A good technologist should be able to learn to operate new technological tools, manipulate information, and interact with other technologists on the job. Also, computer and math skills will be important in the future. Capital-intensive manufacturing will require workers who have knowledge and skills in technology. These new workers must be technologically literate.

If some future predictions come true, we might not need any workers in manufacturing, or any other industry for that matter. The totally automated factory, where robots and computers do all the work, may become prominent in the future. There are already a few totally automated factories. These factories can run twenty-four hours a day with fewer than a dozen workers for monitoring, maintaining, and servicing automated equipment, Figure 21-5.

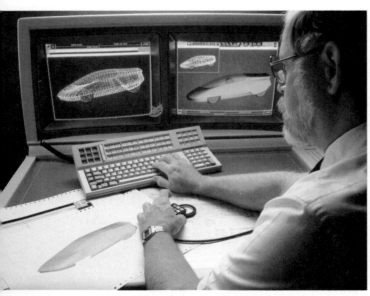

Figure 21-4. In the future, many physically demanding jobs in manufacturing will continue to be replaced by mentally demanding jobs that involve information processing. *(Courtesy of Ford Motor Company)*

Figure 21-5. An important trend in manufacturing is the development of the totally automated factory. *(Courtesy of ABB Robotics, Inc.)*

Trend #3: Increase in Global Competition. From the early 1900s until recently, the United States was the world leader in manufacturing. Increasing competition from foreign manufacturers has recently undermined this leadership. The manufacture of video equipment is a good example. The video cassette recorder (VCR) was invented in America. Today, however, not a single VCR is totally manufactured in this country. In less than two decades, Japan has improved its technology to the point where it is a respected world leader in manufacturing, especially in the field of electronic components. With the growth and development of Japanese manufacturing technology, American manufacturers have lost part of the market for their products. But not even Japan will be safe in the future. Right behind Japan are developing countries like Korea, Taiwan, and China, who are improving their technological base in manufacturing. There will be more and more **global competition** among manufacturing companies.

Another factor related to the increase in global competition is the trend for American manufacturing companies to open plants in developing countries. Many American companies have moved production operations to countries that have lower standards of living. Workers in these countries are more willing to work for lower hourly wages than those wages expected by American workers. In addition, these countries usually don't have labor laws or unions to protect workers. Finally, governmental regulatory organizations, such as OSHA or the Environmental Protection Agency (EPA), are not found in less developed countries. Operating a manufacturing plant under these conditions can save a company millions of dollars and increase profits for stockholders. Critics of this system say that it weakens the U. S. economy. Thousands of Americans are put out of work, and foreign countries learn to use our technology. Often, the decision to move a production plant to another country is made purely on the basis of increasing profits and dividends. Continuing this trend in the future may have an important impact on the American standard of living and economic base.

Trend #4: Decrease in Demand for Unskilled/Semiskilled Labor. As technology grows and develops, it becomes more sophisticated, that is, harder to learn, understand, use, analyze, and maintain. As this trend continues, workers will need more mental skills and fewer physical skills. Those people who do not have the knowledge and skills to understand and operate the technology of tomorrow will find themselves unemployed or working at difficult, boring jobs. More and more manufacturers are using complex, computer-controlled equipment. To run this type of equipment, an employee must be technologically literate. Historically, manufacturing employed large numbers of unskilled and semiskilled workers. With the improvements in technology, these people will find it harder to get a good job, Figure 21-6.

Trend #5: Increase in Depletion of Natural Resources. There is a limited supply of natural resources in our world. As global competition

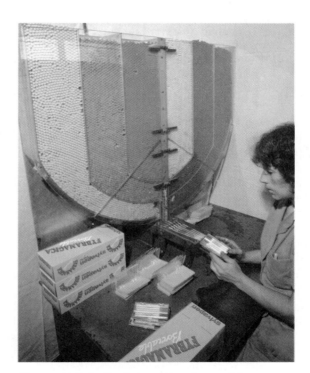

Figure 21-6. In the future, the demand for unskilled and semiskilled workers will continue to decrease as manufacturing companies use more automated equipment. *(Courtesy of Gillette Company)*

Figure 21-7. Recycling materials, like this aluminum ingot made from recycled beverage cans, has many advantages. The rate of depletion of natural resources will slow down, less energy will be used, and manufacturing companies will save money. *(Courtesy of Reynolds Metals Company)*

increases, the rate at which the world's natural resources are used will increase. Take Brazil for example. With its huge forests, Brazil is considered a valuable resource for lumber. Some call Brazil the "lungs of the world" because its vast forests produce a large percentage of the oxygen the world needs to survive. Development in Brazil is ruining thousands of acres of forest every day. Environmentalists are concerned that this deforestation could harm the ecological balance in our environment. Not only would this decrease the supply of wood available, but it would also reduce the amount of oxygen being produced.

Industry is the largest energy user in our society. As industries expand and grow, so do their energy needs. More manufacturing means more of our natural resources will be used to generate energy. Increasingly, manufacturers will be forced to conserve energy. Technologies like cogeneration will help save natural energy resources. In the area of natural materials, we will need to recycle more. Materials like aluminum, glass, and paper can be recycled at a fraction of the costs of manufacturing from natural materials (in terms of money spent and natural resources consumed), Figure 21-7.

Trend #6: Decrease in Mass Employment by Corporate Giants. At one time, many Americans dreamed of working for one of the giant manufacturing corporations that employed millions of people. Recently, and in the future, people are less likely to work for giant manufacturing firms and more likely to work for small entrepreneurial companies. More than ninety percent of new jobs are found in small businesses with fewer than 100 employees. These businesses are started by entrepreneurs. As you read in Chapter 5, Henry Ford was an entrepreneur, as are Steve Jobs and Steve Wozniak, the founders of Apple Computer. People like these will continue to create new jobs for the future of manufacturing.

These are just a few of the important trends that will help shape the future of manufacturing. Another bright area is the possibility that someday products may be manufactured in space.

Figure 21-8. One possibility for producing oxygen for people who work in space is to produce oxygen from ilmenite mined from the moon. *(Courtesy of NASA)*

Manufacturing in Space

For several years now, the National Aeronautics and Space Administration (NASA), has been predicting that someday products may be manufactured in space. As you probably know, a space station would be built to orbit the earth. One of the main uses of the space station will be to conduct manufacturing experiments.

The biggest problem with the space station is providing the basic life-support systems humans need. The space environment is very different from that found on earth. In the space station, a man-made environment must provide all the oxygen, food, water, and energy needed. A number of plans have been proposed, including transporting these necessities to the space station in the space shuttle. Long-range plans call for oxygen to be produced in space from other substances. One possibility is making oxygen from a material found on the

Figure 21-10. This mock-up of one module for the space station is about the size of a bus. Modules will be built for sleeping, working, and recreation activities. *(Courtesy of NASA)*

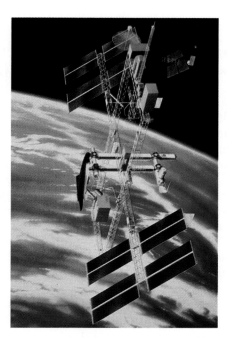

Figure 21-9. The space station will provide astronauts with a home in space where experiments in manufacturing can be conducted. The eight blue rectangles on the ends of the station are solar photovoltaic panels that will produce all the electricity the astronauts need. *(Courtesy of NASA)*

moon called ilmenite. Moon miners would extract this mineral from the surface of the moon and process it to produce oxygen. Without the gravity of earth, mining will be much easier on the moon, Figure 21-8. Energy is the easiest problem to solve. NASA has spent years developing solar photovoltaic panels. Photovoltaic panels convert the light energy of the sun into electrical current. Huge panels would be needed to meet all the electrical needs of the space station, Figure 21-9.

The space station would be made up of modules about the size of a large bus (44.5 feet by 13.8 feet), Figure 21-10. Astronauts would have different modules for work, sleep, and recreation. Another plan, separate from the space station, calls for an industrial spacecraft to be built, Figure 21-11. Under normal circumstances, no life-support systems would be provided on this craft. Experiments and processes would be performed automatically by robots and computers. Every few months, astronauts would fly to the industrial spacecraft in the shuttle and provide new raw materials, check out production, and make any necessary adjustments. When hooked to the shuttle, the industrial spacecraft would provide full life support for the astronauts.

Putting a space station or industrial spacecraft in orbit around earth is just the first step to a long process of manufacturing in space. Engineers have identified three phases in their plans for space industrialization.

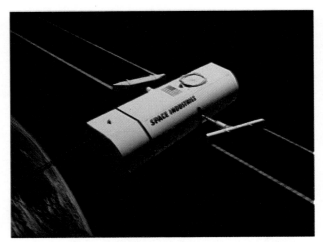

Figure 21-11. This industrial spacecraft, which will be smaller than the space station, would house automatic and robotic equipment, not people. *(Courtesy of NASA)*

Phase 1: Basic Scientific Research

Scientists can't accurately predict exactly how things will work in the space environment. In space, the effects of gravity are virtually nonexistent. There is a very small amount of gravity in space. Astronauts and aerospace engineers call it **microgravity.** As an example, something that weighs 200 pounds on earth would not be totally weightless in space, but it would weigh less than one-half ounce.

We don't know all the effects that microgravity will have on people working in space or on manufacturing processes. Microgravity has been simulated on earth using airplanes flying in parabolic curves, Figure 21-12.

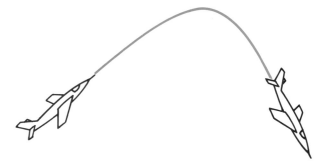

Figure 21-12. Planes flying in parabolic curves in the earth's atmosphere can be used to simulate microgravity. As the plane descends, microgravity is artificially produced for twenty to sixty seconds.

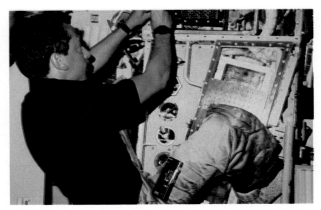

Figure 21-13. This astronaut must adapt to working in a weightless atmosphere. *(Courtesy of NASA)*

During descents, microgravity has been achieved for twenty to sixty seconds. Astronauts train in these airplanes to learn to function in microgravity, Figure 21-13. Most of the early experiments in space will help scientists and engineers better understand the effects of microgravity.

Phase 2: New Technology

Once we better understand how things work in space, engineers will design and create new technology that will use microgravity. From tests that have already been done, many new tools and equipment have been developed. An obvious example is portable power hand tools. In space, astronauts can't just string out an extension cord for electrical power. The popular cordless, portable, battery-powered screwdrivers and drills are examples of spinoff from space research. Another example is the furnaces that will be used to melt and process materials in space. Melting materials, like glass or metal, will be very different in space. For one thing, in microgravity, molten materials will not pour or spill out of a container. So, containerless materials processing can be done. In fact, some levitators have already been developed. A **levitator** is a system for processing materials without containers. On earth, containers like crucibles can contaminate melted materials. No matter how clean, small particles of the crucible can mix with the molten material and cause defects, Figure 21-14. In space, levitators will use acoustical

Figure 21-14. On earth, molten materials always pick up contaminants during processing. *(Courtesy of Allegheny Ludlum Corporation)*

energy (sound waves) to levitate or suspend molten glass or metal in mid space while it is being processed. Without containers, there will be no contamination. Other types of levitators would use electricity or magnetism to suspend materials.

Many other types of tools and machines will have to be created. Look around at the tools, machines, and equipment in your manufacturing lab. They might not work the same way in space.

Phase 3: Product Manufacturing

Once the new tools have been created, manufacturing industries will start to produce new products. Based on past space experiments, NASA expects the first developments to be in new and improved materials. Research in metals, glass, and crystals manufacturing has shown much promise.

Manufacturing Metals in Space. By combining two or more different metals, a new metal alloy can be produced with improved qualities. On earth, some alloys cannot be made. A good example is lead and aluminum. If these two metals were combined, a long-lasting, self-lubricating alloy would be produced. However, because of the difference in the weights of lead and aluminum, the lead/aluminum alloy cannot be made. Lead is four times heavier than aluminum. When these two metals are heated together for melting, the lead sinks to the bottom of the crucible while the

aluminum rises to the top, Figure 21-15. Mixing the molten metals in the crucible does not help. In space, however, because of microgravity, the difference in weights would not exist. In microgravity, lead and aluminum should mix to create a new **superalloy**. Engineers and scientists expect to create up to 400 new superalloys by combining two or more metals that cannot be combined on earth. These superalloys could greatly improve the strength, cost, weight, and wear characteristics in many of our manufactured products.

Manufacturing Glass in Space. Any glass made on earth, no matter how perfect, has impurities and imperfections. As mentioned before, the molten glass picks up impurities from the crucible. Also, gravity will cause molten glass to resolidify (harden) in uneven densities, causing imperfections. In space, the combined benefits of containerless processing using levitators and microgravity will permit the production of super-pure glass. This super-pure glass could be made into fibers for improved fiber-optics communication technology. In fact, futurists believe that pure glass fibers may some day replace metallic circuitry

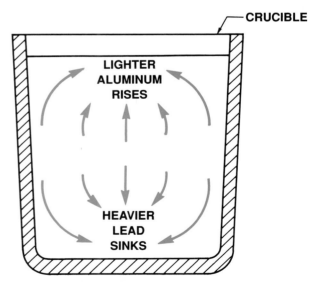

Figure 21-15. Because of the gravity on earth, certain metals cannot be alloyed. Lead and aluminum are examples. The heavier lead sinks, and the lighter aluminum rises; mixing doesn't help. In the microgravity of space, this alloy and hundreds of others will be possible.

Figure 21-16. Research into glass manufacturing in space may someday lead to fiber-optic cables and light replacing wires and electricity in computers. *(Courtesy of US Sprint Communications Company)*

Figure 21-17. Perfect crystals have already been grown in space. These crystals are used to manufacture computer chips. *(Courtesy of NASA)*

producing computer chips is high. Once again, microgravity and containerless processing will mean perfect crystals for computer chips. Astronauts have already demonstrated this by growing perfect crystals in space on several space shuttle missions.

Manufacturing Plastics in Space. The first products actually manufactured in space were tiny plastic beads called **microspheres**. These beads are $1/2{,}500$th of an inch in diameter (about

in computers. This would lead to the development of supercomputers that might use light instead of electric circuitry, Figure 21-16.

Manufacturing Computer Chips in Space. Computer chips are made from silicon crystals. Cylinder-shaped crystals are grown by melting a batch of silicon in a crucible, putting a cool "seed" crystal in the batch, and letting the silicon grow off the seed, Figure 21-17. As with glass and metals, no matter how clean the workplace, there are always some impurities in the crystals. Another problem is gravity. During the melting and resolidifying cycle, the hot silicon rises, while the cool silicon sinks. This heating and cooling cycle creates tensions in the crystals that can cause flaws and cracks. Usually, only twenty-one percent of these crystals are usable for computer chips. This means almost eighty percent of the crystal growth must be thrown out by the manufacturers. With such a high amount of waste, the cost of

Figure 21-18. Microspheres made in space are perfect in size and shape. These microspheres were the first product manufactured in space. *(Courtesy of NASA)*

1/40th the diameter of an average human hair). Fifteen million microspheres can be placed in a tube about the size of your index finger. Astronauts made millions of microspheres in space during several space shuttle missions dating back to 1982. These tiny beads have many uses as measurement instruments for processes such as calibrating microscopes and other precision instruments and measuring paint pigment and gunpowder particles. As with other space-manufactured materials, each microsphere produced on the shuttle was perfect in size and shape. On earth, making perfect microspheres is impossible because of the effects of gravity, Figure 21-18.

Manufacturing in space seems to hold great promise for the future. Many new and better products will be made. But setting up a space station and doing the necessary research will cost billions of tax dollars and take many years.

Can Technocracy Replace Democracy?

One possible future would find our society and citizens controlled by a small, elite group of people who understand and operate technology. This society would be called a **technocracy**. In our present democracy, we all have an opportunity to decide how technology will be used in the future. In a technocracy, the future would be decided by **technocrats.** Technocrats would use their understanding of technology to control other citizens (technocrats would be technologically literate). Those people who were technologically illiterate would be called **technopeasants**. The technopeasants would do all the work for the technocrats.

Today, our technology is becoming more and more sophisticated and complicated. It seems that only people with scientific and engineering degrees can understand how certain technologies work. If this trend continues, could our democracy be replaced by a technocracy? And if a technocracy developed, would you be a technocrat or a technopeasant?

One possible scenario for the future is a society called a technocracy. The technologically literate technocrats would control the technologically illiterate technopeasants. (© *Walt Disney Company. Nova City from a scene in the Walt Disney World EPCot Center Horizons Pavilion presented by General Electric)*

Deciding Which Future

Some futurists say technology may grow in two possible directions in the future—hard technology or soft technology. Figure 21-19 compares hard technology and soft technology. **Hard technology** is often equated with high technology that is based on improving productivity and profits without considering the human, environmental, and social consequences. **Soft technology** is referred to as **appropriate technology** (meaning choosing and using technologies that are "best" suited for a particular situation). Soft technology is concerned with productivity and profits; but the impacts of technology on people, the environment, and society are always considered. While hard technology would replace human workers with automated equipment, soft technology would keep people working. Hard technology would cause large amounts of pollution, deplete our natural resources, and consume much energy. Soft technology would create smaller pollution levels, recycle natural resources, and use less energy.

The future probably won't use only hard or only soft technology. It will more likely use some of each, with certain tradeoffs. The only way to know for sure is to wait for the future. Or is it? Every individual can help shape the future. In our society, every citizen can participate in the decision-making processes that will determine which path technology will take. Some individuals, particularly entrepreneurs, inventors, manufacturing managers, and political leaders, can play an even bigger role in determining the future. In order for you to participate in deciding the future, you must be a technologically literate citizen. Without technological literacy, you won't have the knowledge, skills, and attitudes you need to make decisions about the future of technology.

HARD TECHNOLOGY	SOFT TECHNOLOGY
Capital intensive	Labor intensive
Environmentally harmful	Environmentally safe
Large energy input	Small energy input
High pollution	Low pollution
Depletes natural resources	Recycles resources
Worldwide trade	Regional trade
Technocrats/ technopeasants	No technocrats/ technopeasants
Quantity production	Quality production
Frequent, serious technological accidents	Few, less serious technological accidents
Operation too complex for lay person to understand	Operation understood by everyone

Figure 21-19. Futurists predict two extreme paths for the future of technology—hard technology and soft technology.

Summary

No one can accurately predict the future. The only thing we know for sure is that the future will be different from today. The exponential rate of growth in knowledge causes technology to double every four to five years. This trend will probably continue to allow dramatic technological breakthroughs in the future. Several trends that may have an impact on the future of manufacturing were examined in this chapter. Studying these trends suggests that manufacturing in the future will use more automated machines and equipment (capital intensive) and fewer human workers (labor intensive). The people who will work in manufacturing in the future will probably work for smaller entrepreneurial companies. They will probably need more skills and knowledge than manufacturing workers of the past. Increasingly, American manufacturing companies will be forced to compete with smaller countries that are currently developing strong manufacturing bases. The trend of increasing the consumption of natural resources for manufacturing, and other uses, will probably continue. A final trend that was examined was the possibility that someday manufacturing companies may be operating in space. Manufacturing research conducted by NASA has shown much promise, especially in the area of producing materials with superior qualities over those made on earth.

DISCUSSION QUESTIONS

1. Of the six trends in manufacturing that were discussed in this chapter, which do you think will be most important in determining the future? Why?

2. Do you think technology can continue to grow at an exponential rate? What might stop or slow down this tremendous growth?

3. What are the advantages and disadvantages of a decline in labor-intensive manufacturing and an increase in capital-intensive manufacturing?

4. Should American companies that start production facilities in foreign countries be permitted to put thousands of American people out of work to increase company profits? Should American workers or the government try to stop this trend?

5. What will happen to all the workers who cannot find work when manufacturers use total automation? Do manufacturing companies have a responsibility to keep people working?

6. Do you think the products of manufacturing in space are worth the possible high costs?

APPENDIX

YOUR CLASSROOM MANUFACTURING EXPERIENCE

Most of the information presented in this book is about the tools, materials, processes, people, and ideas used in manufacturing technology. Human and environmental impacts of manufacturing are also considered. You can apply this information in a typical technology laboratory. Whether your laboratory area is designed primarily for woodworking, metal working, plastics, or has a general shop format with a little of everything, your class can perform a simulated manufacturing run.

This book follows the systems approach to studying technology. The systems approach organizes manufacturing into inputs, processes, outputs, and feedback/impacts. In this way, a complex and technical topic can be studied in an organized and sequential way.

In practice, however, the inputs, processes, outputs, and feedback/impacts cannot be done in the step-by-step order shown in this book. If a manufacturing enterprise followed exactly the order presented in this book, it might never get off the ground. With effective organization, many activities happen at the same time in an order that might not fit easily into the systems model. To start and run a manufacturing enterprise efficiently, several processes should be performed at the same time. These processes will need various inputs, will give various outputs, and will constantly react to feedback and impacts. For example, raising capital, doing market surveys, and planning for production are all important for start-up. Therefore, a manufacturing activity in your technology laboratory might address the different parts of the manufacturing systems model in a number of ways.

Every Situation Is Unique

This appendix describes one way to organize and run a manufacturing enterprise in the school technology laboratory setting. It is certainly not the only method. Every class is different in size, course length, meeting schedule, laboratory and classroom set-up, budget (or fundraising possibilities), and any number of other variables. Therefore, each classroom manufacturing experience will be different. For more specific information about each input, process, and output, refer to the units listed under the headings that follow. Here are some suggestions to help you get started.

Getting Started: Inputs to Consider

Planning a manufacturing run begins with making decisions about what to make; how to form, organize, and manage the company; how many products to make, and so on. This kind of planning is called production planning. In addition, production planning involves deciding how a product will be manufactured, with consideration for necessary inputs to the system as a whole. Good production planning identifies the many inputs that help ensure a smooth, efficient manufacturing run.

People (Chapters 4 and 5)

People are the most important input for any manufacturing system. Some of the people who help in the early stages of planning a manufacturing run are manufacturing engineers, who plan the production process, and production engineers (or technologists), who carry out the plans and maintain the system. Without these key people, a manufacturing enterprise might never get off the ground. In addition to these people, designers are needed to ensure that a desirable product is manufactured. They may also research and develop new or related products. The workers who actually make the products and the people who manage their work are the backbone of any manufacturing enterprise.

Materials Resources (Chapters 6 and 15)

Depending on the nature of the products you will manufacture, you must think about the specific materials you will use and how you will get them. You will need to make many other decisions about manufacturing materials as well. These decisions may be based on criteria such as desired quality, characteristics of your lab (tools and machines), and available money. Choosing between oak, maple, bass, or pine is an example of a decision student designers and engineers may have to make.

Tools and Machines (Chapters 7, 13, and 15)

Tools and machines are a basic input to any manufacturing enterprise. You must have tools to process the materials you need to make the product. You should consider the equipment in your technology laboratory as well as the possibilities of purchasing or borrowing additional tools when you select and manufacture your product. Often you will need many of the same tools to avoid bottlenecks at busy points in the production line. The use of portable hand power tools may solve your bottleneck problems.

Some of the most important tools used in manufacturing processes are jigs, fixtures, and gages. These tools are used to ensure precise processing of materials for quality control. In your classroom experience, your teacher might design and build the jigs and fixtures. It is a precise task that can take years of experience.

Energy (Chapter 8)

The energy sources and costs might not seem important to you in your laboratory simulation, but they are crucial considerations for most large-scale manufacturers who use tremendous amounts of electricity. Schools pay energy costs and are always trying to find ways to reduce them. You might not be able to determine exact energy costs in your laboratory experience. However, your teacher might develop a formula to charge the class for energy costs.

Information (Chapter 9)

Information about tools, machines, materials, and processes is central to manufacturing. In addition, creating a safe work environment and a knowledge of safety in the workplace should be a key consideration. Designing a safe laboratory experience is everyone's responsibility. You must have proper eye protection and other appropriate safety equipment before you start any laboratory activity. Safety should be central to all production planning. Assigning students to be safety managers is one way to ensure that safety never lapses.

You will also need information from market research before you begin production. Market research determines who will buy a product, how much money they will spend, who the major competitors are, and various other information about the market.

Finances (Chapters 10 and 17)

Finances are a key element in making decisions about the selection of inputs, from materials selection to the design of the entire production line including tools, machines, and processes. Adequate money is necessary for any manufacturing endeavor. Financial backing for your manufacturing company may be accomplished in a variety of ways including selling stock, getting a loan from the school principal, or venture finances generated from previous classes. A company must have people who understand financial matters.

Time (Chapter 11)

The time you need for manufacturing must be carefully determined. You can do this by making time studies of all the individual steps in your production run, giving consideration to the number of products to be manufactured, and calculating probable downtime. Bottle-necks will probably occur in the production line. These problems should be solved by workers, supervisors, and engineers.

Processes

The processes part of the systems model means action. In a classroom manufacturing experience, you need to know about and appreciate possible inputs, but the activity begins with the implementation of processes. As mentioned earlier, there are a number of ways to start up a manufacturing simulation. The method you choose will depend on the specific characteristics of your class and laboratory. Following is a description of one method that has proven successful in many technology laboratories.

Engineering (Chapters 3, 12, and 13)

The first step in a manufacturing run is to decide what product to make. After you make this decision, the type of manufacturing system most appropriate for production should be selected (custom, job lot, intermittent, or continuous). If time permits, you might spend several weeks developing product ideas. For the sake of experience, all students should participate in many aspects of production planning, including design and engineering activities. Design teams of two or three students may come up with their own prototypes to present as possible products to be manufactured.

Design teams should have dimensioned working drawings of products, and a detailed materials list. Teams should also have a procedure, or list of steps that includes necessary tools, machines, and processes listed in a sequential manner. A good way to present the steps and sequence of steps necessary to manufacture a product is with operation process and flow process charts. These charts show visually all the key processes and operations required in a production cycle.

For more information about operation process and flow process charts, review Chapter 13 on production engineering. All of this preparation is part of research and development, or R & D. Presentations of prototypes is

actually a selling job as the class may vote for the products they would most like to manufacture. You can also subcontract students in communications technology classes to do drawings, charts, and other visual presentations.

Ownership and Management (Chapter 14)

Another process begun early in the planning stage of the manufacturing run are decisions about ownership and management of the company. The first step may be to form the company, complete with democratic elections of president, vice-presidents, treasurer, and so on. If the corporate model of organization is selected, the responsibility of elected officials should be stressed. Review Chapter 14 for alternatives to the corporate model. Although the corporate model is the one most often simulated, partnerships and cooperatives can also be valuable learning experiences.

At some point during the production run, it is possible that non-management workers could unionize and decide to strike if they feel that working conditions are not adequate. This is a good learning experience if the problem is solved through negotiation in a day or two.

Materials Processing (Chapters 3, 13, and 15)

Materials processing is the changing of materials into a more usable form. It is the actual manufacture or making of the product. Many of the details related to the processing of materials in your class experience may have been calculated by the original design team. The list of materials, as well as a detailed process chart provided by the design team, makes the job of production easier. Tools, machines, and processes must be set up in the most efficient manner to accomplish each phase of the manufacturing run. Production engineers, with the teacher's help, may design and set up jigs and fixtures. This makes materials processing easier, more efficient, and precise.

If possible, setting up a conveyor system for at least part of the production run would be helpful in replicating a real manufacturing situation. In addition, the use of programmable robots for some of the operations would be ideal. In some laboratory settings, robots have been used to move parts or products from one station to the next. However, it is recognized that many schools do not have access to conveyors or robots. It is very possible to have a successful experience without them.

It is important to set up tools, machines, and processes in a sequence that will move the product smoothly down the line. In the laboratory setting, it might be hard to rearrange machines that are fixed in a particular spot. However, you will need to plan carefully for the smoothest manufacturing line in your laboratory setting.

The processing of materials is at the center of the production process and includes activities like cutting, drilling, boring, fastening, assembling, and finishing. With proper production planning and management, you might be able to manufacture your product within several days. Your time will depend on how complex your product is and how many you want to make. You can carefully maintain the desired quality of the products by thorough inspection by quality control specialists (possibly members of the original design engineering team).

Marketing (Chapters 9 and 16)

Students who will market the product must also begin their work early in the production process. As soon as product ideas are introduced, students can begin doing market research to determine how many people might buy the product. Market surveys could be used as a tool to select what product to manufacture. In addition, after the product has been chosen, marketers design a marketing campaign that includes advertising. This might be done with school newspapers, flyers, the school intercom system, or a student-produced video ad aired during lunch. Designing an eye-catching logo and packaging might also be the job of students involved in marketing.

Accounting (Chapters 10 and 17)

Accounting for the money used in the production process is an important part of any successful manufacturing enterprise. Students in charge of keeping the accounts of the company should be organized and familiar with bookkeeping. You will need to keep records of all money spent on materials, on the buying and replacement of tools, machines, and parts, and of orders and payments received from customers. Accounting is a process begun at the outset of the project and continued throughout.

Assessing Outputs Based on Feedback/Impacts

(Chapters 18–21)

As in industry, the outputs of any classroom manufacturing experience include the manufactured product and all scrap, waste, and pollution made during the run. Assessment of the product may be based on customer reactions, as well as that of the students involved in the project. You might hold a brainstorming session to come up with suggestions for improving future laboratory manufacturing experiences.

The kinds of scrap, waste, and pollution that you create is an important consideration. Leftover materials that may be recycled or reused are considered scrap. Waste materials are those that cannot easily be reused or recycled. Pollution may be in the form of chemical waste (like finishes and solvents), fumes or heat in the air, or even loud noise pollution.

A tremendous amount of scrap, waste, and pollution is costly for industries and might mean that production is not running efficiently. Figuring out ways to reuse scrap and reduce or dispose of waste materials can change production costs greatly. Pollution is a very real and serious problem faced by many manufacturing industries. Its impact on people and on our environment can be dramatic. You must weigh the effects of your pollution against the gains of the entire production run itself.

At the school level, you may be encouraged to use scrap to make other smaller products and projects. Or scrap and waste may be donated or sold (as kindling wood for example). In any event, your class should plan carefully for disposal. In addition, the decibel level of excessively loud machines might be recorded and a plan made for reducing the noise level. Designing the product and its manufacture with scrap, waste, and pollution reduction in mind is an essential part of the production process.

Summary

You can apply the information in this book to real life manufacturing enterprises as well as to your technology laboratory experience. Regardless of the technical areas your lab is designed for, a laboratory production run is possible.

You can apply the systems approach to studying manufacturing to your laboratory experience. However, the exact order of activities and operations will be different from that presented in this book. The sequence of processes will also differ from classroom to classroom. Class size, meeting schedule, laboratory set-up, available money, and other variables will affect the design of classroom manufacturing runs.

It is important to think about all of the inputs to a manufacturing system before you start production. Inputs for manufacturing include people, materials, tools and machines, energy, information, finances, and time. You should review the appropriate units in the book to understand better the importance of these topics.

Action begins with implementing various processes, including:

- designing and building prototypes of possible products;
- product selection;
- production planning, including selecting the best type of manufacturing and creating flow process and operation process charts that detail production operations;
- creating marketing and advertising campaigns; and
- structuring company organization and management systems.

Many of these activities happen at the same time. You will need to do detailed planning for a successful learning experience.

As in industry, the outputs of a classroom manufacturing experience are the products themselves and by-products, including scrap, waste, and pollution. Addressing the problems created by scrap, waste, and pollution is central to any manufacturing enterprise, including yours.

The impacts of manufacturing on people and on our natural environment is a concern that begins during the earliest stages of planning and continues throughout the production run.

PRODUCT PLANS

INTRODUCTION

There are two different types of product plans in this section—*fully developed product plans* and *product ideas requiring further development.* The fully developed plans include most of the information your classroom manufacturing enterprise needs to start manufacturing engineering (plant layout, materials handling, and tooling) and quality control engineering (inspection). The fully developed plans include drawings of the product and parts, a parts list, and an operation process chart.

Most of the design engineering and methods engineering processes have been completed with the fully developed plans. However, your teacher might ask you to make prototypes of the products to verify specifications. You will also need to complete certain methods engineering processes, such as flow process charts and operation sheets. Also, your class might decide to change the product designs, substitute materials, change the combining processes suggested, or improve the efficiency of the operation process chart.

If your class decides to use additional product plans provided by your teacher, the fully developed plans will serve as a guide, giving you some hints for presenting product design ideas.

The product ideas vary in their development. Most of these plans include the basic information you need to complete the necessary design engineering and production engineering processes, such as working drawings, mock-ups and prototypes, operation process charts, plant layout, and tooling. Here is a list of the product plans.

MEMO MINDER

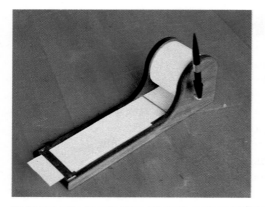

PARTS LIST

Part	Qty.	Part Name	Description
A	1	Base	1/2 T × 3 1/2 W × 13 L Wood
B	2	Sides	1/2 T × 4 1/2 W × 5 5/16 L Wood
C	1	Dowel	1/2 Dia × 3 1/2 L Dowel
D	1	Rod	3/16 Dia × 3 L Welding Rod
E	1	Cutter	.02 T × 1/2 W × 3 3/8 L Brass/Sheet Metal
F	1	Pad	1/16 T × 2 7/8 W × 6 3/8 L Plastic
G	1	Pen	Pen and holder

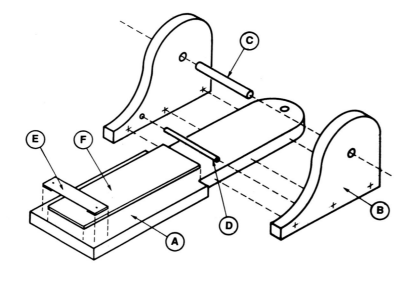

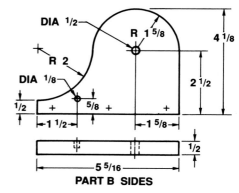

PART B SIDES

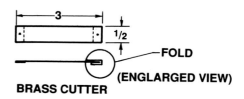

FOLD

(ENGLARGED VIEW)

BRASS CUTTER

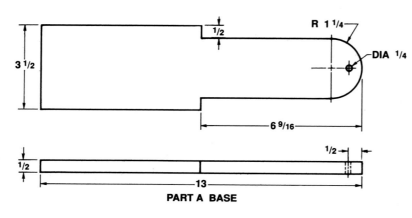

PART A BASE

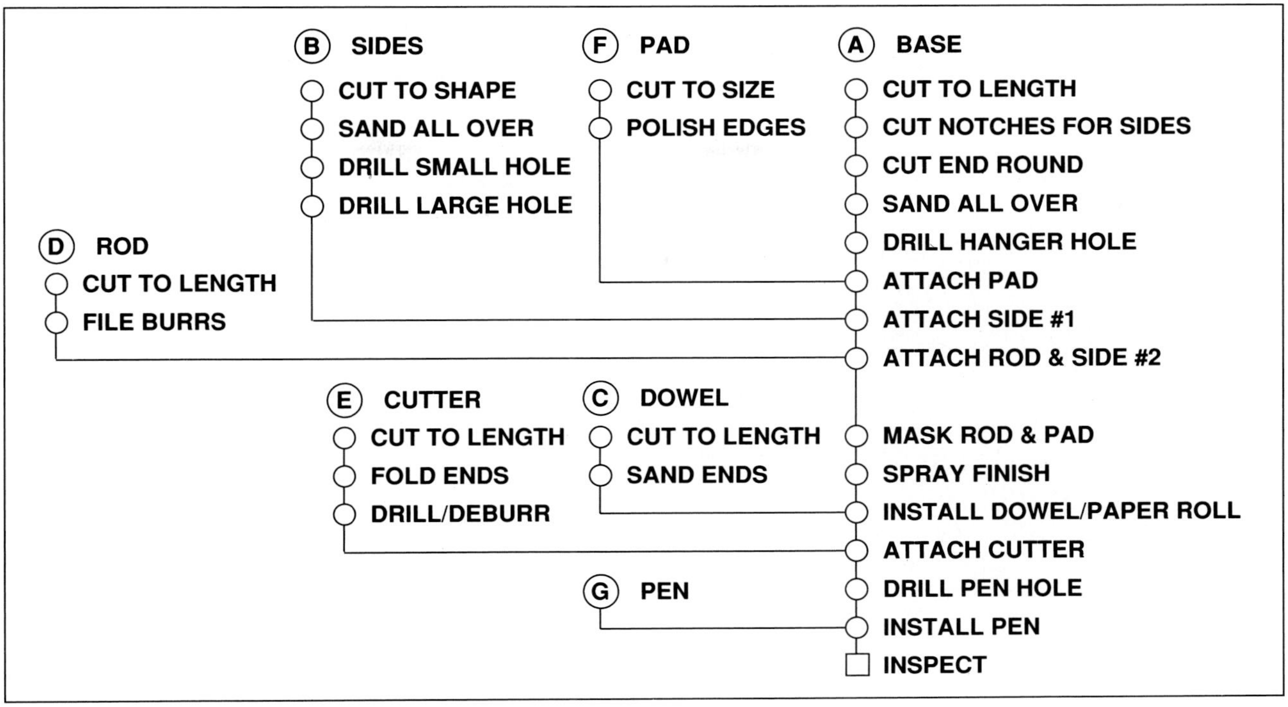

B SIDES
- CUT TO SHAPE
- SAND ALL OVER
- DRILL SMALL HOLE
- DRILL LARGE HOLE

F PAD
- CUT TO SIZE
- POLISH EDGES

A BASE
- CUT TO LENGTH
- CUT NOTCHES FOR SIDES
- CUT END ROUND
- SAND ALL OVER
- DRILL HANGER HOLE
- ATTACH PAD
- ATTACH SIDE #1
- ATTACH ROD & SIDE #2

D ROD
- CUT TO LENGTH
- FILE BURRS

E CUTTER
- CUT TO LENGTH
- FOLD ENDS
- DRILL/DEBURR

C DOWEL
- CUT TO LENGTH
- SAND ENDS

- MASK ROD & PAD
- SPRAY FINISH
- INSTALL DOWEL/PAPER ROLL
- ATTACH CUTTER

G PEN
- DRILL PEN HOLE
- INSTALL PEN
- INSPECT

MANTEL CLOCK

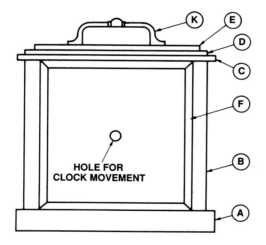

HOLE FOR
CLOCK MOVEMENT

NOTES: 1. A AND C SECURED TO SIDES B WITH
WOOD SCREWS
2. HANDLE K SECURED TO TOP WITH
WOOD SCREWS THROUGH C D AND E
3. PARTS F AND H INSTALLED WITH HOT
GLUE

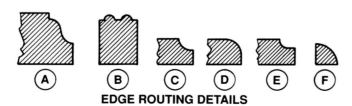

EDGE ROUTING DETAILS

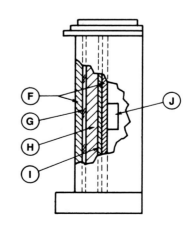

Ⓔ CAP
- CUT TO LENGTH
- ROUT
- SAND

Ⓓ MIDDLE TOP
- CUT TO LENGTH
- ROUT
- SAND

Ⓒ TOP
- CUT TO LENGTH
- ROUT
- DRILL
- INSPECT/SAND

Ⓑ SIDES
- CUT TO LENGTH
- ROUT
- SAND

Ⓐ BASE
- CUT TO LENGTH
- ROUT/EDGE ENDS
- DRILL 4 HOLES
- SAND/INSPECT HOLES
- DRILL ASSEMBLY
- INSPECT SQUARE/ SECURE SCREWS
- ASSEMBLE TOPS/HANDLE

Ⓚ HANDLE
- MASK WITH TAPE

Ⓗ SPACER
- MITER TO LENGTH
- SAND
- SPRAY FINISH

Ⓖ GLASS
- CUT TO SIZE
- INSPECT

Ⓕ RETAINER (FRONT)
- ROUT QTR. RD.
- MITER TO LENGTH
- SAND

- INSTALL FRONT RETAINERS
- SAND
- SPRAY FINISH
- INSTALL GLASS
- INSTALL SPACER

Ⓕ RETAINER (REAR)
- ROUT QTR. RD.
- MITER TO LENGTH

Ⓙ CLOCK MOVEMENT
- INSPECT PARTS

Ⓘ CLOCK FACE
- ASSEMBLE MOVEMENT TO FACE

- INSTALL FACE/MOVEMENT
- INSTALL RETAINERS
- REMOVE MASKING

SMALL TOOL BOX

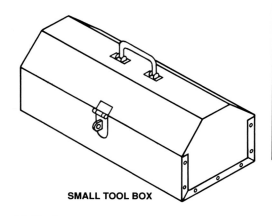

SMALL TOOL BOX

PARTS LIST

Part	Qty.	Part Name	Description
A	1	Btm. and Sides	$10\,^7/_8 \times 14\,^1/_2$ 24 Ga. Galv.
B	1	Top	$6\,^3/_8 \times 14\,^1/_2$ 24 Ga. Galv.
C	2	Ends	4×5 20 Ga. Galv.
D	1	Hinge	$13\,^1/_4$
E	1	Handle	
F	1	Latch	

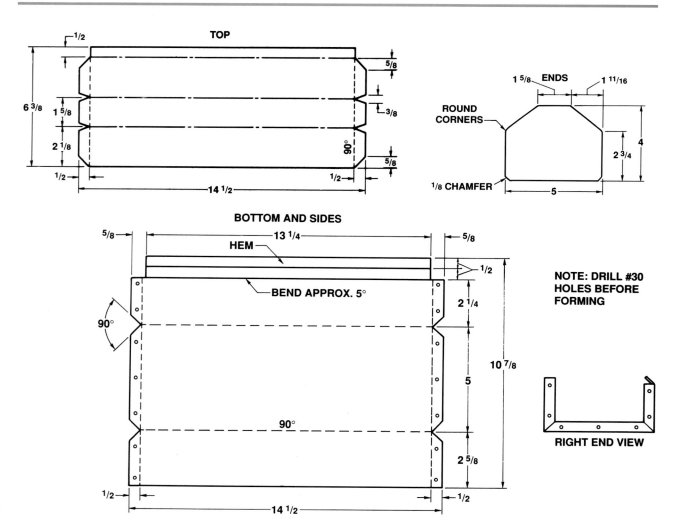

TOP

ENDS

$1\,^5/_8$ $1\,^{11}/_{16}$

ROUND CORNERS

$6\,^3/_8$ $1\,^5/_8$ $2\,^1/_8$ $^1/_2$ $^1/_2$ $^1/_2$ $^5/_8$ $^3/_8$ $90°$ $^5/_8$ $^1/_2$

$14\,^1/_2$

$^1/_8$ CHAMFER

4   $2\,^3/_4$ 5

BOTTOM AND SIDES

$^5/_8$ $13\,^1/_4$ $^5/_8$

HEM

BEND APPROX. 5°

$^1/_2$

$90°$

$2\,^1/_4$

$90°$ 5 $10\,^7/_8$

$2\,^5/_8$

$^1/_2$ $^1/_2$

$14\,^1/_2$

NOTE: DRILL #30 HOLES BEFORE FORMING

RIGHT END VIEW

B TOP
- CUT TO SIZE
- NOTCH ENDS
- FOLD END HEMS
- DRILL HANDLE HOLES
- DRILL HINGE HOLES
- RIVET HINGE TO TOP
- FOLD TOP
- RIVET HANDLE

C ENDS
- CUT TO SIZE
- CUT CORNERS
- ROUND UPPER CORNERS
- CHAMFER BOTTOM CORNERS
- DRILL RIVET HOLES

A BOTTOM/SIDES
- CUT TO FIT
- CUT HEM
- NOTCH FOR BENDS
- DRILL RIVET HOLES
- FOLD HEM
- FOLD END SEAMS
- BEND BOTTOM
- RIVET ENDS TO BODY
- RIVET TOP TO BODY
- DRILL LATCH HOLES
- RIVET LATCH TO BODY

D HINGE
- ☐ INSPECT PARTS

E HANDLE
- ☐ INSPECT PARTS

C LATCH

LOUNGE CHAIR

PARTS LIST

Part	Qty.	Part Name	Description
A	2	Inside Leg	$7/8$ T × 2 $1/4$ W × 45 L Oak
B	2	Outside Leg	$7/8$ T × 2 $1/4$ W × 35 L Oak
C	2	Arm Rest Support	$7/8$ T × 4 W × 18 $1/4$ L Oak
D	2	Arm Rest	$7/8$ T × 2 $1/4$ W × 16 L Oak
E	2	Head/Foot Rest	$7/8$ T × 2 $1/4$ W × 24 $3/8$ L Oak
F	1	Leg Rest	$7/8$ T × 3 $1/2$ W × 25 $3/4$ W Oak
G	2	Leg Tie	$7/8$ T × 2 $1/4$ W × 17 $1/8$ L Oak
H	1	Back Leg Cross	$7/8$ T × 2 $1/4$ W × 25 $7/8$ L Oak
I	1	Seat Material	16 $1/2$ W × 58 L Canvas

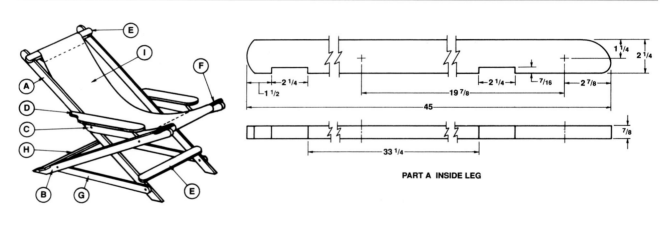

PART A INSIDE LEG

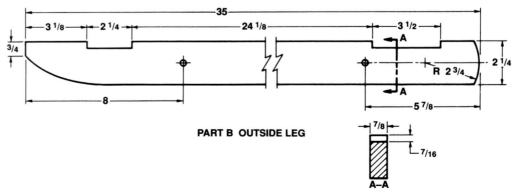

PART B OUTSIDE LEG

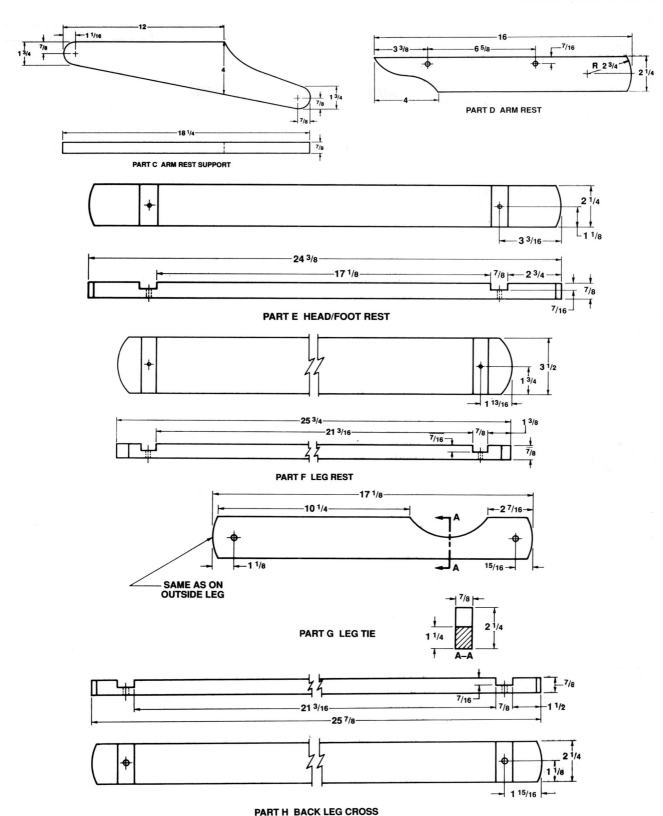

PART C ARM REST SUPPORT

PART D ARM REST

PART E HEAD/FOOT REST

PART F LEG REST

SAME AS ON
OUTSIDE LEG

PART G LEG TIE

A–A

PART H BACK LEG CROSS

OFF-ROAD TRUCK

PARTS LIST

Part	Qty.	Part Name	Description
A	4	Wheels	2 T × 4 Dia. Wood
B	4	Suspension	1/4 T × 1/2 W × 6 3/16 Plexiglas® Rod
C	1	Front Bumper	5/8 Dia. × 6 3/4 L Plexiglas® Rod
D	1	Cab	3 1/2 T × 5 1/2 W × 7 L Wood
E	1	Bed	3/4 T × 4 1/2 W × 6 L Wood
F	1	Tail Gate	1/2 T × 1 3/16 W × 4 1/2 L Wood
G	2	Bed Sides	1/2 T × 2 W × 5 1/8 L Wood
H	1	Rear Bumper	5/8 Dia. × 6 3/4 L Plexiglas® Rod
I	1	Roll Bar	5/8 Dia. × 27 L Plexiglas® Rod

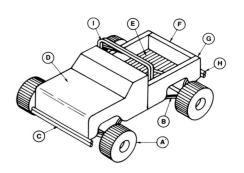

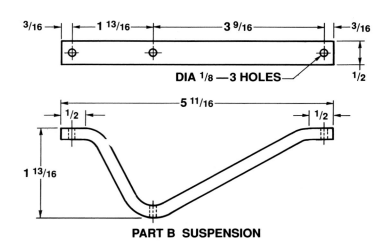

PART B SUSPENSION

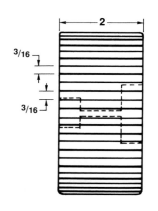

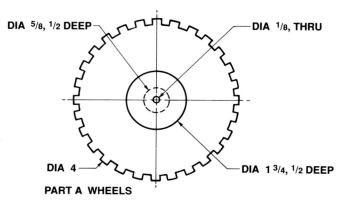

DIA 5/8, 1/2 DEEP

DIA 1/8, THRU

DIA 4

DIA 1 3/4, 1/2 DEEP

PART A WHEELS

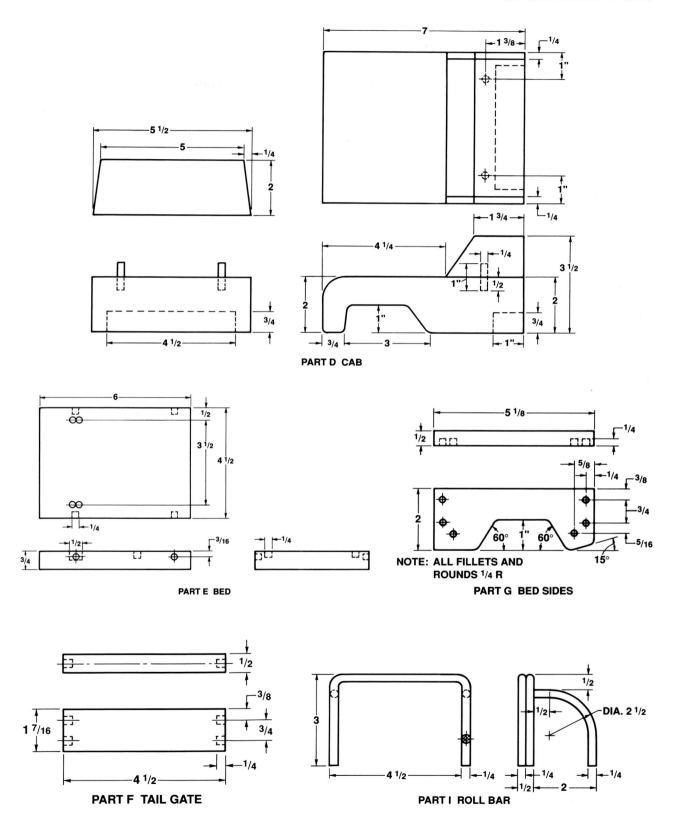

PART D CAB

PART E BED

PART G BED SIDES

NOTE: ALL FILLETS AND
ROUNDS 1/4 R

PART F TAIL GATE

PART I ROLL BAR

DIA. 2 1/2

SLEIGH CENTERPIECE

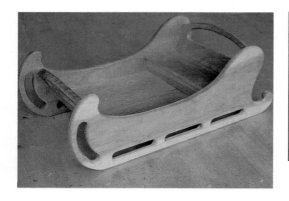

PARTS LIST

Part	Qty.	Part Name	Description
A	1	Front	1/2 T × 4 1/2 W × 8 1/2 L Wood
B	1	Back	1/2 T × 5 1/2 W × 8 1/2 L Wood
C	1	Bottom	1/2 T × 8 1/2 W × 10 1/2 L Wood
D	1	Seat	3/8 T × 3 1/8 W × 8 7/16 L Wood
E	1	Seat Front	1/2 T × 1 1/8 W × 8 1/2 L Wood
F	2	Sides	1/2 T × 6 1/2 W × 18 L Wood

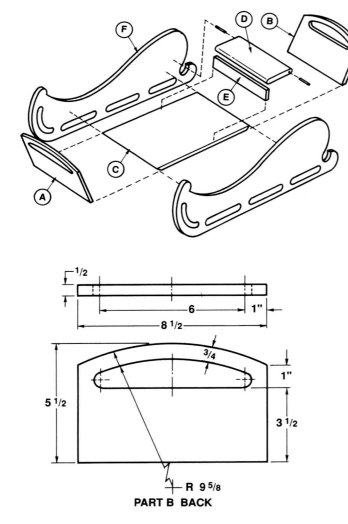

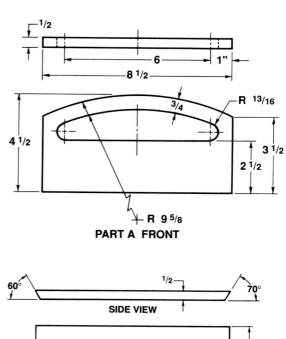

PART A FRONT

PART B BACK

PART C BOTTOM

SIDE VIEW

TOP VIEW

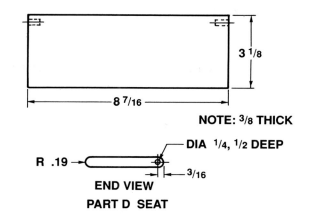

NOTE: ³/8 THICK

END VIEW
PART D SEAT

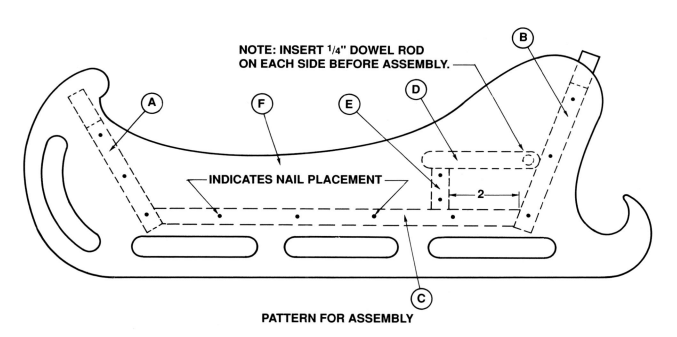

NOTE: INSERT ¹/4" DOWEL ROD
ON EACH SIDE BEFORE ASSEMBLY.

INDICATES NAIL PLACEMENT

PATTERN FOR ASSEMBLY

KITCHEN CANISTER

PARTS LIST

Part	Qty.	Part Name	Description
A	1	Back	$3/4$ T × 7 $1/2$ W × 10 $1/2$ L Wood
B	2	Sides	$3/4$ T × 6 W × 7 $1/4$ L Wood
C	1	Front	$3/4$ T × 7 $1/2$ W × 5 $7/8$ L Wood
D	1	Bottom	$1/8$ T × 6 $5/8$ W × 6 $5/8$ L Hardboard
E	1	Back Edge	$3/4$ T × 1 $1/4$ W × 7 $1/2$ L Wood
F	1	Front Molding	$1/2$ T × 1" W × 8 $1/2$ L Wood
G	2	Side Molding	$1/2$ T × 1" W × 8 L Wood
H	2	Lid Sides	$3/4$ T × 1" W × 6 L Wood
I	1	Lid Back	$3/4$ T × 1" W × 7 $1/2$ L Wood
J	1	Lid Front	$3/4$ T × 1" W × 7 $1/2$ L Wood
K	2	Hinge	$1/2$ T × $3/4$ W × 1 $1/4$ L Wood
L	2	Pins	$1/4$ Dia. × 2 L Dowel
M	1	Glass	$1/8$ T × 4 $1/2$ W × 5 $3/4$ L Glass

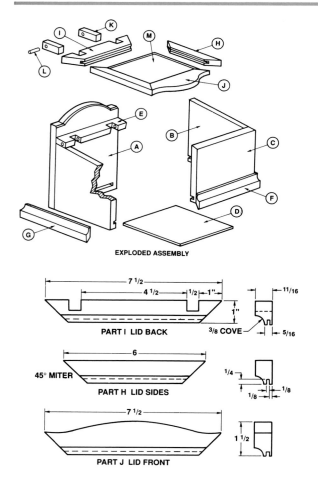

EXPLODED ASSEMBLY

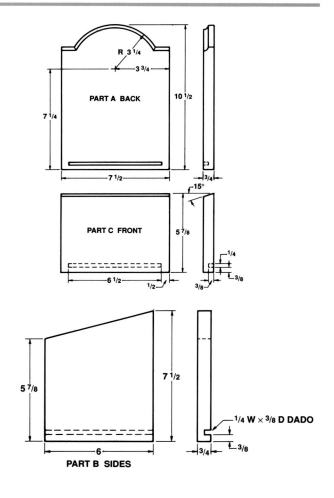

PART A BACK

R 3 $1/4$

3 $3/4$

10 $1/2$

7 $1/4$

7 $1/2$

$3/4$

PART C FRONT

15°

5 $7/8$

6 $1/2$

$1/2$

$3/8$

$1/4$

$3/8$

7 $1/2$

4 $1/2$

$1/2$

1"

$11/16$

1"

PART I LID BACK

$3/8$ COVE

$5/16$

6

45° MITER

PART H LID SIDES

$1/4$

$1/8$

$1/8$

7 $1/2$

1 $1/2$

PART J LID FRONT

5 $7/8$

7 $1/2$

6

$1/4$ W × $3/8$ D DADO

$3/4$

$3/8$

PART B SIDES

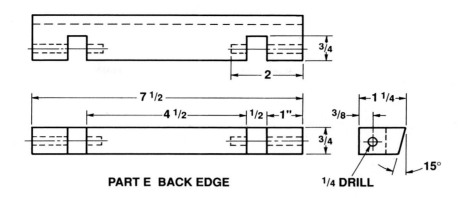

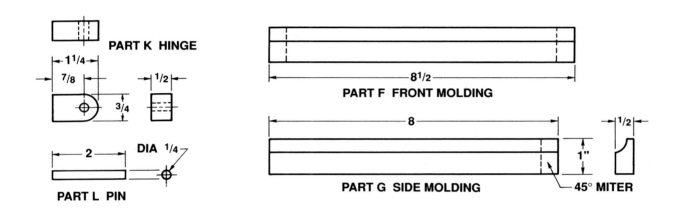

PART E BACK EDGE

¹/₄ **DRILL**

15°

PART K HINGE

1¹/₄

7/8

1/2

3/4

2

DIA ¹/₄

PART L PIN

8¹/₂

PART F FRONT MOLDING

8

1"

1/2

PART G SIDE MOLDING

45° **MITER**

BREAD BOX

PARTS LIST

Part	Qty.	Part Name	Description
A	1	Top	3/4 T × 5 1/2 W × 17 3/4 L Wood
B	1	Bottom	3/4 T × 11 W × 17 3/4 L Wood
C	2	Sides	3/4 T × 10 1/4 W × 10 1/4 L Wood
D	1	Top Facing	3/4 T × 1 1/2 W × 16 1/4 L Wood
E	13	Roll Top Slats	3/8 T × 3/4 W × 15 3/8 L Wood
F	1	Back	1/4 T × 15 1/2 W × 10 1/4 L Hardboard
G	1	Bottom Slat	3/8 T × 1 1/4 W × 15 3/8 L Wood
H	1	Handle	3/4 T × 3/4 W × 3 1/2 L Wood
I	2	Roll Top Backing Cloth	3/4 W × 11 L Roll Top Backing Cloth

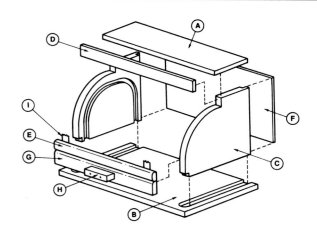

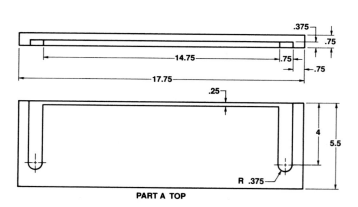

PART A TOP

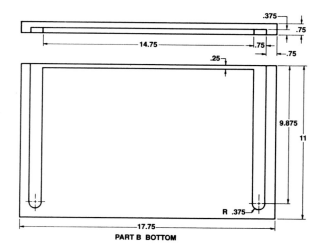

PART B BOTTOM

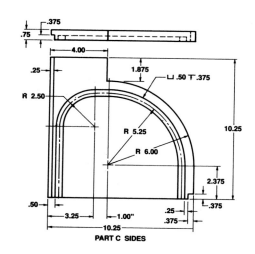

PART C SIDES

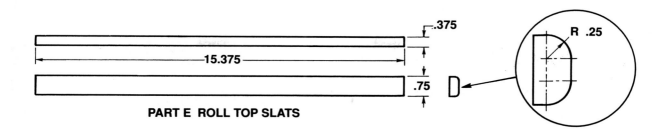

.375

15.375

.75

R .25

PART E ROLL TOP SLATS

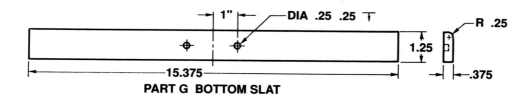

1"

DIA .25 .25 ⊤

R .25

1.25

15.375

.375

PART G BOTTOM SLAT

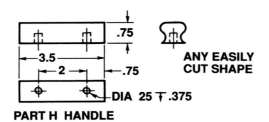

.75

3.5

.75

2

DIA 25 ⊤ .375

**ANY EASILY
CUT SHAPE**

PART H HANDLE

JEWELRY BOX

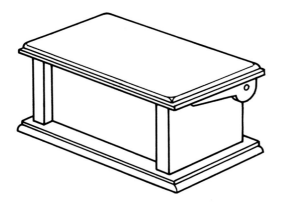

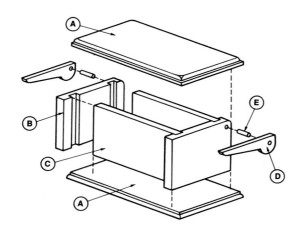

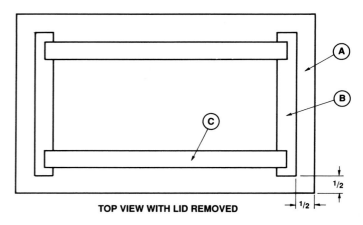

TOP VIEW WITH LID REMOVED

DETAIL OF EDGE ROUTING

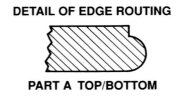

PART A TOP/BOTTOM

5/32 **DRILL**

HINGE PATTERN

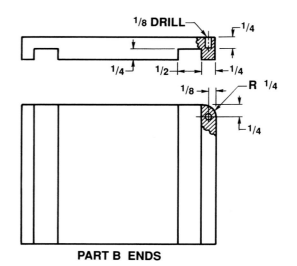

1/8 **DRILL**

R 1/4

PART B ENDS

NEW ENGLAND CLOCK

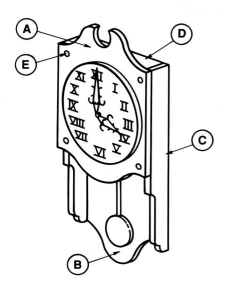

PARTS LIST

Part	Qty.	Part Name	Description
A	1	Face	3/4 T × 10 W × 11 L Wood
B	1	Back	3/4 T × 8 1/2 W × 10 L Wood
C	2	Sides	3/4 T × 2 1/2 W × 13 1/2 L Wood
D	1	Top	3/4 T × 2 1/2 W × 8 1/2 L Wood
E	4	Plugs	Wood Taper or Button
F	1	Movement	Pendulum, Battery Operated
G	1	Bezel/Dial	Glass/Brass

SHELF CLOCK

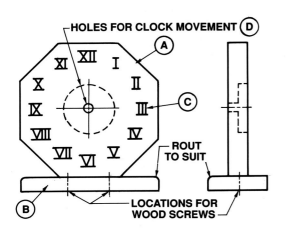

HOLES FOR CLOCK MOVEMENT

ROUT TO SUIT

LOCATIONS FOR WOOD SCREWS

PARTS LIST

Part	Qty.	Part Name	Description
A	1	Face	3/4 T × 8 W × 8 L Wood
B	1	Base	3/4 T × 2 1/4 W × 8 L Wood
C	1 set	Numerals	Plastic Stick-on (Black/Brass)
D	1	Movement	Battery Operated

401

DRAFTING TABLE

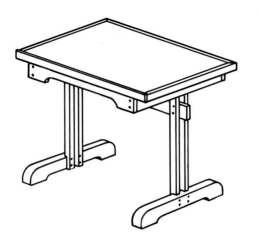

PARTS LIST

Part	Qty.	Part Name	Description
A₁	1	Drafting Mat	5 Ply T × 24 W × 36 L Vinyl Plastic
A₂	1	Table Top-Hardboard	1/4 T × 24 W × 36 L Hardboard
A₃	1	Table Top-Plywood	1/2 T × 24 W × 36 L Plywood
B	1	Table Lip	3/8 T × 1 1/4 W × 36 L Wood
C	1	Long Trim	3/4 ID × 7/8 × 36 L Vinyl J-Channel
D	2	Short Trim	3/4 ID × 7/8 × 24 L Vinyl J-Channel
E	2	Frame Ends	1 1/4 T × 5 1/2 W × 21 1/2 Wood
F	2	Frame Front/Back	3/4 T × 5 1/2 W × 33 3/8 Wood
G	1	Stretcher	1 1/4 T × 5 1/2 W × 33 3/8 Wood
H	4	Legs	1 1/4 T × 1 1/4 W × 29 3/4 Wood
I	2	Feet	1 1/4 T × 5 1/2 W × 22 1/2 Wood
J	1	Brace	1/8 T × 1 1/4 W × 30 3/4 Steel

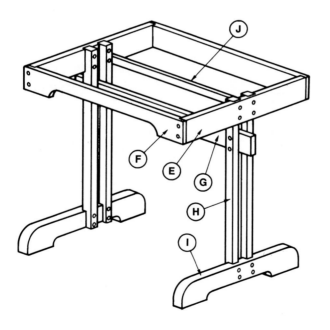

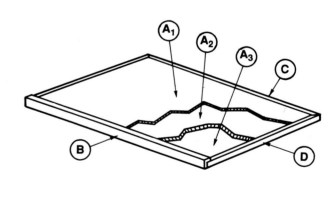

SPINNING TOP

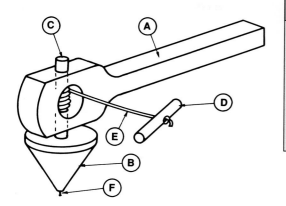

PARTS LIST

Part	Qty.	Part Name	Description
A	1	Handle	3/4 T × 1 1/2 W × 7 1/2 L Wood
B	1	Top	2 3/8 Dia. × 2 L Wood
C	1	Spindle	5/16 Dia. × 2 1/2 L Dowel
D	1	Pull	3/8 Dia. × 2 L Dowel
E	1	String	18 L String
F	1	Tack	Rd. Head Brass Tack

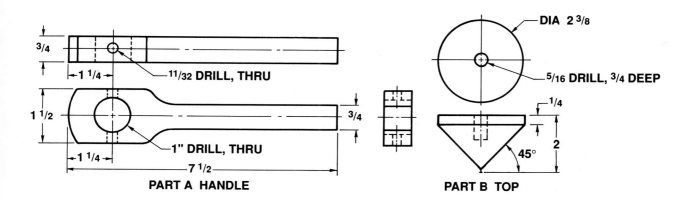

PART A HANDLE

PART B TOP

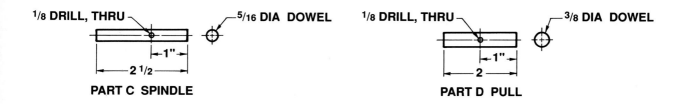

PART C SPINDLE

PART D PULL

HEART CANDLE HOLDER

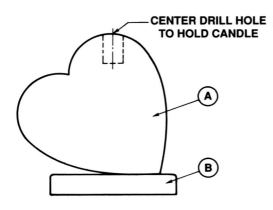

CENTER DRILL HOLE
TO HOLD CANDLE

PARTS LIST

Part	Qty.	Part Name	Description
A	1	Heart	1 1/2 T × 5 1/2 W × 5 1/2 L Pine
B	1	Base	1 1/2 T × 3 W × 4 1/2 L Pine

STEREO SPEAKER

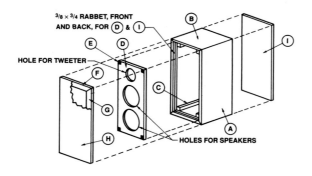

3/8 × 3/4 RABBET, FRONT AND BACK, FOR D & I

HOLE FOR TWEETER

HOLES FOR SPEAKERS

PARTS LIST

Part	Qty.	Part Name	Description
A	2	Sides	3/4 T × 9 W × 22 3/4 L Wood
B	2	Top and Bottom	3/4 T × 9 W × 10 1/4 L Wood
C	4	Cleats	3/4 T × 3/4 W × 7 1/2 L Wood
D	1	Speaker Panel	3/4 T × 9 1/2 W × 22 L Wood
E	4	Hook/Loop Connector	1" Sq (Velcro)
F	2	Cover Frame Top and Bottom	3/4 T × 1" W × 10 1/4 L Wood
G	2	Cover Frame Sides	3/4 T × 1" W × 22 3/4 L Wood
H	1	Cover Fabric	12 1/2 × 24 1/2
I	1	Back Panel	3/4 × 9 1/2 W × 22 L Wood

TILT MIRROR

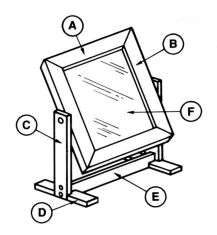

PARTS LIST

Part	Qty.	Part Name	Description
A	2	Short Frame	3/4 T × 1 1/2 W × 8 L Wood
B	2	Long Frame	3/4 T × 1 1/2 W × 12 L Wood
C	2	Supports	3/4 T × 1 1/2 W × 7 5/8 L Wood
D	2	Feet	5/8 T × 1 1/2 W × 4 1/2 L Wood
E	1	Span	1 1/2 T × 1 1/2 W × 8 1/4 L Wood
F	1	Mirror	Cut to fit frame

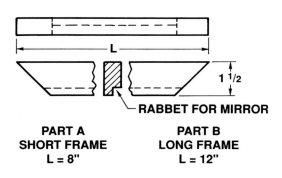

L

1 1/2

RABBET FOR MIRROR

PART A
SHORT FRAME
L = 8"

PART B
LONG FRAME
L = 12"

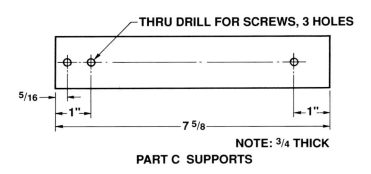

THRU DRILL FOR SCREWS, 3 HOLES

5/16

1"

7 5/8

1"

NOTE: 3/4 THICK

PART C SUPPORTS

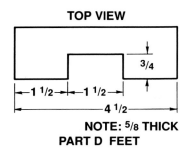

TOP VIEW

3/4

1 1/2

1 1/2

4 1/2

NOTE: 5/8 THICK

PART D FEET

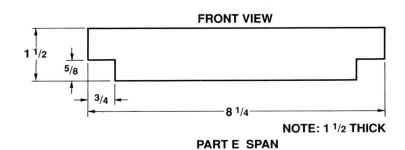

FRONT VIEW

1 1/2

5/8

3/4

8 1/4

NOTE: 1 1/2 THICK

PART E SPAN

LOG HOLDER

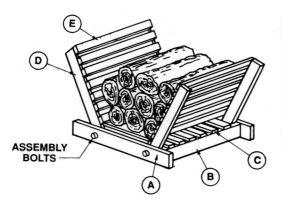

ASSEMBLY BOLTS

PARTS LIST

Part	Qty.	Part Name	Description
A	2	Ends	3/4 T × 3 W × 18 L Wood
B	2	Base	3/4 T × 3 W × 24 L Wood
C	9	Base Slats	3/8 T × 2 W × 14 L Wood
D	4	Angle	3/4 T × 2 W × 16 L Wood
E	14	Angle Seats	3/8 T × 1 3/8 W × 23 1/2 L Wood

CASSETTE TAPE RACK

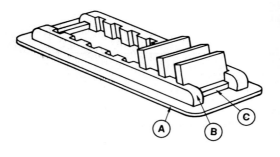

PARTS LIST

Part	Qty.	Part Name	Description
A	1	Base	1/2 T × 5 3/4 W × L Wood
B	2	Sides	3/4 T × 1 1/2 W × L Wood
C	2	Ends	1/2 T × 3/4 W × 3 3/4 L Wood

Notes: 1. Length of A and B can be varied.
2. Round corners on A and B as desired.
3. Fasten B and C with wood screws.

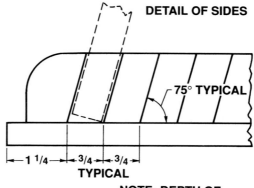

DETAIL OF SIDES

75° TYPICAL

1 1/4 3/4 3/4

TYPICAL

NOTE: DEPTH OF GROOVES CUT TO 3/8"

COMPUTER TABLE

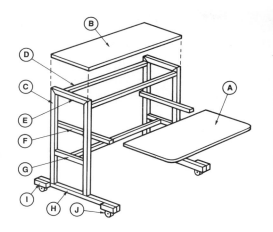

PARTS LIST

Part	Qty.	Part Name	Description
A	1	Desk Top	$3/4$ T $\times$ 22 W $\times$ 35 $7/8$ L Counter Top
B	1	Shelf	$3/4$ T $\times$ 14 W $\times$ 35 $7/8$ L Counter Top
C	4	Legs	1" Sq. Tubing $\times$ 30 L
D	3	Span Brace	1" Sq. Tubing $\times$ 36 L
E	2	Upper Brace	1" Sq. Tubing $\times$ 13 L
F	2	Shelf Support	1" Sq. Tubing $\times$ 18 L
G	2	Lower Brace	1" Sq. Tubing $\times$ 11 L
H	2	Feet	1" Sq. Tubing $\times$ 26 L
I	4	Caster Base	1" Sq. Tubing $\times$ 4 L
J	4	Caster	2" Casters

LAP DESK

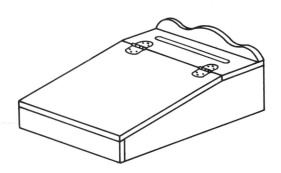

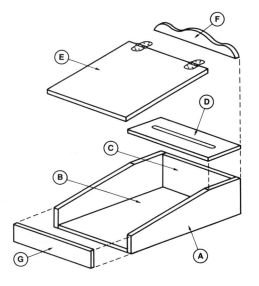

PARTS LIST

Part	Qty.	Part Name	Description
A	2	Sides	$3/4$ T $\times$ 4 W $\times$ 12 L Wood
B	1	Bottom	$3/4$ T $\times$ 11$1/4$ W $\times$ 11$1/2$ L Wood
C	1	Back	$3/4$ T $\times$ 4 W $\times$ 11$1/2$ L Wood
D	1	Top	$3/4$ T $\times$ 4 W $\times$ 13 L Wood
E	1	Lid	$3/4$ T $\times$ 9 $3/4$ W $\times$ 13 $3/4$ L Wood
F	1	Apron	$3/4$ T $\times$ 2 $3/4$ W $\times$ 13 L Wood
G	1	Front	$3/4$ T $\times$ 2 $5/16$ W $\times$ 13 L Wood
H	2	Hinges	

TOOL TRAY

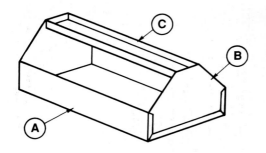

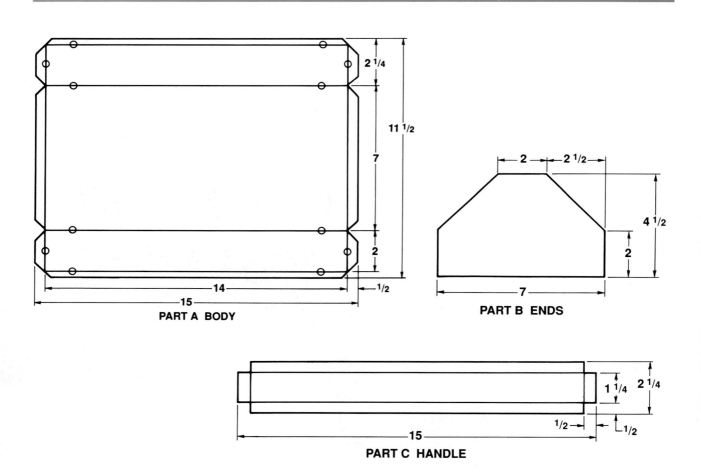

PART A BODY

PART B ENDS

PART C HANDLE

PLANTER BOX

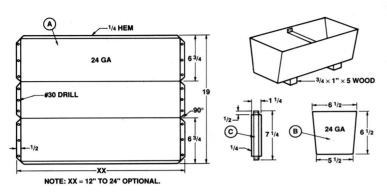

NOTE: XX = 12" TO 24" OPTIONAL.

PLANT STAND

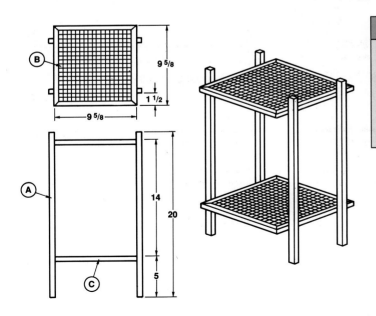

REBAR LOG HOLDER

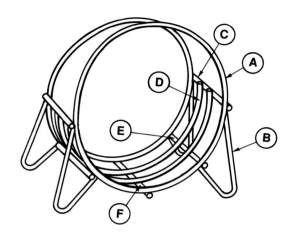

PARTS LIST

Part	Qty.	Part Name	Description
A	2	Frame	Rebar–120 L
B	4	Legs	Rebar–32 L
C	2	Short Cross	Rebar–9 L
D	2	Supports	Rebar–56 L
E	2	Mid. Cross	Rebar–14 L
F	1	Long Cross	Rebar–17 L

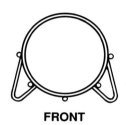

FRONT

SIDE

SHEET METAL BOX AND TOP

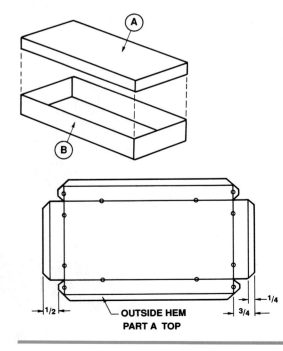

PARTS LIST

Part	Qty.	Part Name	Description
A	1	Top	5 3/4 × 9 30 Ga. tinplate
B	1	Box	4 3/8 × 7 5/8 30 Ga. tinplate

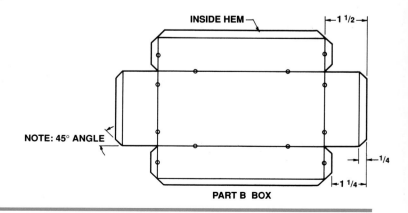

OUTSIDE HEM

PART A TOP

1/2   3/4   1/4

INSIDE HEM   1 1/2

NOTE: 45° ANGLE

PART B BOX

1/4   1 1/4

WIND CHIMES

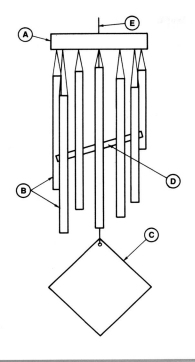

PARTS LIST

Part	Qty.	Part Name	Description
A	1	Base	4" Dia. circle, 3/4" thick Wood
B	12	Rods	Two 8" Long Rods, Two 5" Long Rods
C	1	Wind Catcher	4" Sq. Sheet Metal or Acrylic Sheet
D	1	Center Disk	2 1/2" Dia. C. Al.
E		Twine	

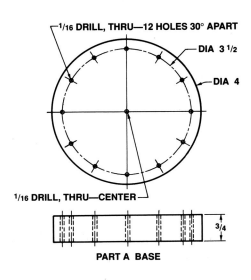

1/16 DRILL, THRU—12 HOLES 30° APART

DIA 3 1/2

DIA 4

1/16 DRILL, THRU—CENTER

3/4

PART A BASE

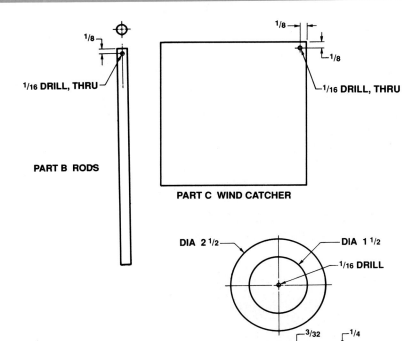

1/8

1/8

1/16 DRILL, THRU

PART B RODS

1/8

1/8

1/16 DRILL, THRU

PART C WIND CATCHER

DIA 2 1/2

DIA 1 1/2

1/16 DRILL

3/32

1/4

PART D CENTER DISC

411

FOLDING TABLE

PARTS LIST

Part	Qty	Part Name	Description
A	4	Legs	3/4 T × 1 3/4 W × 27 1/2 L Wood
B	4	Table Supports	3/4 T × 1 3/4 W × 13 1/2 L Wood
C	2	Leg Braces	3/4 T × 2 1/2 W × 17 1/2 L Wood
D	2	Table Top	3/4 T × 7 W × 17 1/2 L Wood
E	1	Long Rod	3/8 Dia. × 14 L Aluminum
F	4	Short Rod	3/8 Dia. × 1 1/2 L Aluminum

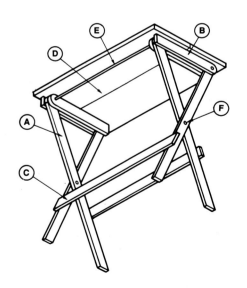

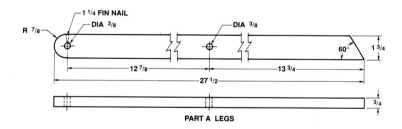

PART A LEGS

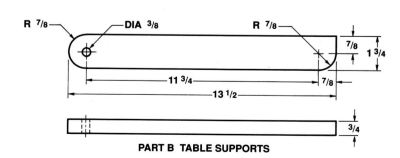

PART B TABLE SUPPORTS

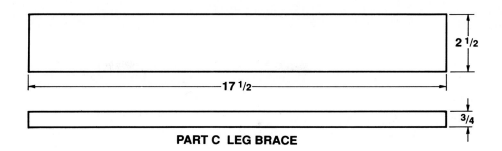

PART C LEG BRACE

2 1/2

17 1/2

3/4

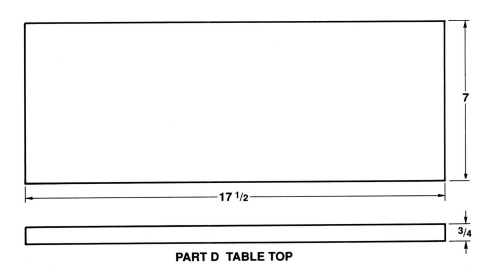

PART D TABLE TOP

7

17 1/2

3/4

TURKEY CALL

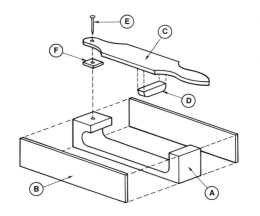

PARTS LIST

Part	Qty.	Part Name	Description
A	1	Body	$1\,3/8$ T × $1\,7/8$ W × $7\,1/8$ L Hardwood
B	2	Sides	$3/32$ T × $1\,7/8$ W × $7\,1/8$ L Hardwood
C	1	Cover	$1/4$ T × $1\,1/2$ W × $8\,3/8$ L Hardwood
D	1	Chalkboard	$1/4$ T × $1/2$ W × $1\,1/2$ L Hardwood
E	1	Roofing Nail	$1\,1/4$ L
F	1	Rubber	$1/8$ T × $1/4$ Square

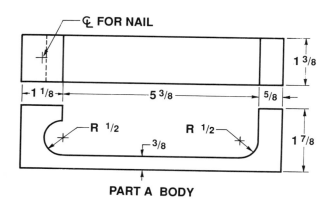

₵ FOR NAIL

$1\,3/8$

$1\,1/8$ — $5\,3/8$ — $5/8$

R $1/2$ R $1/2$

$3/8$

$1\,7/8$

PART A BODY

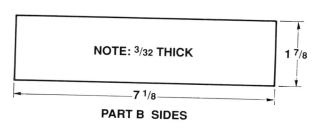

NOTE: $3/32$ THICK

$1\,7/8$

$7\,1/8$

PART B SIDES

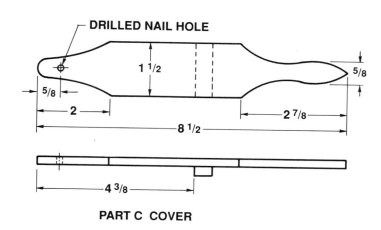

DRILLED NAIL HOLE

$1\,1/2$

$5/8$

$5/8$

2

$2\,7/8$

$8\,1/2$

$4\,3/8$

PART C COVER

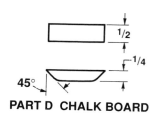

$1/2$

$1/4$

$45°$

PART D CHALK BOARD

SCHOOL CLOCK

PARTS LIST

Part	Qty.	Part Name	Description
A	1	Face	3/4 T × 12 1/2 W × 12 1/2 L Wood
B	2	Sides	3/4 T × 3 1/8 W × 19 L Wood
C	1	Window	1/4 T × 7 W × 11 L Hardwood or Veneer Plywood
D	1	Glass	1/8 T × 4 3/4 W × 6 1/4 L Glass
E	1	Upper Base	3/4 T × 3 5/8 W × 9 1/4 L Wood
F	1	Mid. Base	3/4 T × 3 1/8 W × 8 1/4 L Wood
G	1	Lower Base	3/4 T × 2 5/8 W × 7 1/2 L Wood
H	1	Top	3/4 T × 3 W × 7 1/4 L Wood
I	1	Back	1/4 T × 7 W × 11 L Hardboard
J	1	Movement	Pendulum, Battery Operated
K	1	Bezel/Dial	Glass/Brass

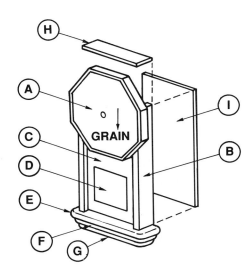

FILING BOX

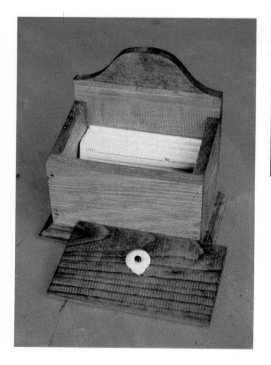

PARTS LIST

Part	Qty.	Part Name	Description
A	1	Front	1/2 T × 3 1/2 W × 6 1/4 L Wood
B	2	Sides	1/2 T × 4 1/2 W × 3 L Wood
C	1	Bottom	1/2 T × 4 1/2 W × 7 1/4 L Wood
D	1	Back	1/2 T × 7 W × 6 1/4 L Wood
E	1	Lid	1/2 T × 3 5/8 W × 6 1/4 L Wood
F	1	Knob	Ceramic, Brass, or Wood

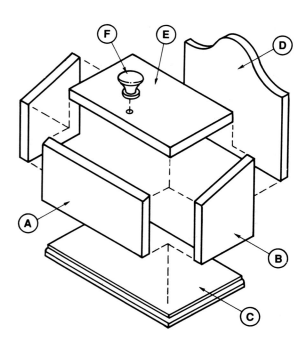

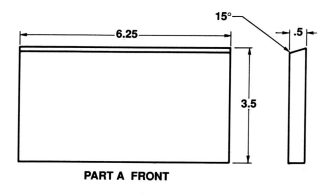

PART A FRONT

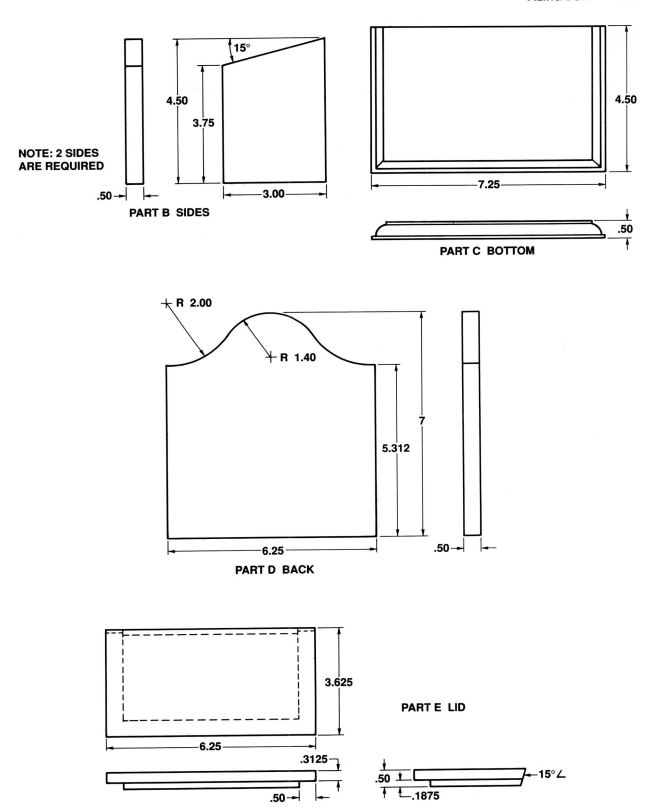

**NOTE: 2 SIDES
ARE REQUIRED**

15°

4.50

3.75

.50

3.00

PART B SIDES

4.50

7.25

.50

PART C BOTTOM

R 2.00

R 1.40

7

5.312

6.25

.50

PART D BACK

3.625

6.25

PART E LID

.3125

.50

.50

.1875

15°∠

SCROLL NAME SIGN

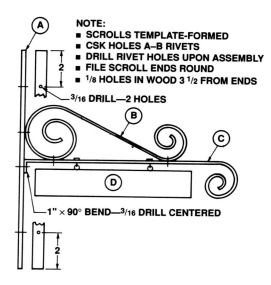

NOTE:
- SCROLLS TEMPLATE-FORMED
- CSK HOLES A–B RIVETS
- DRILL RIVET HOLES UPON ASSEMBLY
- FILE SCROLL ENDS ROUND
- $1/8$ HOLES IN WOOD $3 1/2$ FROM ENDS

$3/16$ DRILL—2 HOLES

$1" \times 90°$ BEND—$3/16$ DRILL CENTERED

PARTS LIST

Part	Qty.	Description
A	1	$1/2 \times 3/4 \times 12$ HRS
B	1	$1/8 \times 3/4 \times 29$ HRS
C	1	$1/8 \times 3/4 \times 23 1/2$ HRS
D	1	$3/4 \times 2 1/4 \times 14$ pine
		$3/16 \times 1/2$ RH SI rivets
		#208 eye bolts

NAME SIGN POST

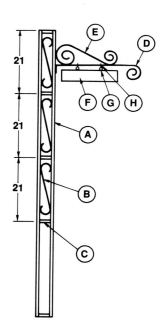

PARTS LIST

Part	Qty.	Description
A	2	$1/2 \times 1/2 \times 96$ HRS
B	3	$1/8 \times 1/2 \times 24$ HRS
C	5	$1/2 \times 1/2 \times 2 1/4$ HRS
D	1	$1/8 \times 1/2 \times 22 1/2$ HRS
E	1	$1/8 \times 1/2 \times 29 1/2$ HRS
F	1	$1/2 \times 2 1/2 \times 14$ Pine
G	2	#108 Eye Screws
H	2	#2 $\times 3/16$ Eye Bolts

418

TECHNOLOGY STUDENT ASSOCIATION

The Technology Student Association (TSA) is a national organization for students in technology education (industrial arts, industrial technology, industrial education). Technology students in middle schools, junior high schools, and senior high schools can join TSA. There is even an association similar to TSA available for college students.

TSA begins in the classroom and lab. Students can organize a TSA chapter, elect officers, hold meetings, and plan school, community, and social activities. Students can meet with other TSA chapters at state and national conferences. Most states in the United States are affiliated with the national TSA organization. The national conference is held each summer in a different city. State conferences are usually held in the spring. At both the state and national conferences, students can meet and compete with other TSA students.

These students are observing a computer-controlled lathe used in manufacturing. (Photo by Arvid Van Dyke)

Purpose and Goals of TSA

The main purpose of TSA is to prepare students to live and work in our technological society. The TSA motto is "Learning to live in a technical world." The specific goals of TSA include the following:

Leadership. TSA promotes leadership by asking students to plan and run club meetings, competitive events, and school, community, and club activities.

Technology. TSA helps students understand the impacts of technology on their future and prepares them to function in a society dominated by technology.

Knowledge. TSA promotes the development of consumer and career knowledge. Also, many of the competitive events in TSA give students opportunities for in-depth study in technology, the development of craftsmanship and creativity, and the development of interests in leisure and recreational activities related to technology.

Respect. TSA promotes respect for the dignity of work, for quality craftsmanship, and for the worth of individuals as they contribute to group efforts.

Motivation. TSA motivates students to excel in their scholastic efforts, to be the best they can be, and to prepare for the challenges of living in our technological world.

Choices. TSA gives students the information they need to help them make meaningful and informed decisions about their future educational and occupational choices.

Transition. TSA helps students make the transition from the classroom to the community as workers, consumers, and involved citizens.

A student's entry in a TSA Technology Processes Contest. *(Photo by Arvid Van Dyke)*

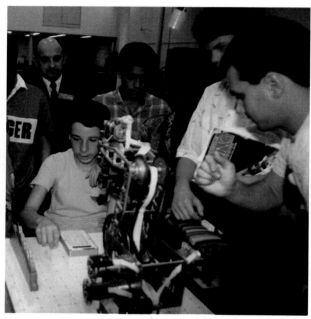

These students are using a robot to simulate a manufacturing procedure. *(Photo by Arvid Van Dyke)*

Manufacturing-Related TSA Activities

Many TSA chapters are involved in activities in the school and community. These activities can be related to manufacturing. TSA chapters organize tours of local manufacturing plants or invite people from industry to speak at local or regional meetings. Your TSA chapter could provide a service to the school and raise money for club activities by mass-producing school products, such as bookcases, desk sets, or products that display the school mascot. During Technology Education Week or a school's open house, TSA students can demonstrate a mass-production line for other students, teachers, administrators, and parents.

Some TSA chapters get involved in civic and community activities. In November and December, TSA students mass-produce toys for children. In the spring, TSA students make benches or garbage cans for a local community park. Some TSA students even join in community clean-up activities and take aluminum cans or newspapers to recycling centers.

Of course, many of the competitive events held at regional, state, and national levels can be related to manufacturing. Speeches, research papers, technology process display, and projects can focus on high-interest topics in manufacturing. Many states even have contests where students compete for the best mass-production run or enterprise activity.

If your school does not have a TSA chapter, organize one. If there is a TSA chapter in your school, join and become an active participant in an organization dedicated to preparing students to live and work in our technological society.

GLOSSARY

Abrasive papers—Used to smooth or finish the surfaces of materials.

Acid rain—Rain having a pH level of less than 5.6.

Adhesive—A type of bonding process that uses glue, cement, or some other tacky substance to cause materials to stick together at a joint area.

Aesthetics—The beauty or visual appeal of a product or object.

Age of Automation—The era resulting from increased innovation and invention that is characterized by machines on the production line.

Age of information—The dramatic increase in knowledge and information, especially in recent years.

Alloy—A combination of two or more metals.

Alternative energy sources—Sources of energy that are not usually used; such as wind, water, and solar power.

Arc welders—Tools that use heat from electrical flow to combine materials.

Assembly drawing—A drawing of the final product when assembled. It may be an orthographic or pictorial drawing.

Assembly lines—Workers standing side by side in long lines, each doing a task.

Assets—The value of everything the company owns; listed on the balance sheet.

Automated guidance vehicle (AGV)—a robotic materials handling system.

Average timing—The average time for an element is found by adding all the times for the element and dividing by the number of observations. The average time for a job is found by adding all the averages of the elements that make up the job.

Balance sheet—A report of the financial worth of the company; includes assets and claims against assets such as liabilities and stockholder equity.

Bartering—Trading by exchanging goods without using money.

Basic motion time systems—Predetermined systems for setting time standards for operation.

Batch manufacturing—See *intermittent manufacturing*.

Bid—A guaranteed price from a vendor.

Bill of materials—Lists every part of a product, gives exact specifications on each part, identifies the costs for each part and the total cost for each product. The bill of materials is included in the production expenses budget.

Bioaccumulation—The accumulation of toxic chemicals in the body from eating and drinking food and water that contains heavy metals and synthetic organic compounds.

Biosphere—The air (atmosphere), water (hydrosphere), and land (lithosphere) that together make up the earth.

Biotechnology—Using living cells to manufacture commercial products.

Bits—Separating tools used to make round holes by removing chips from materials; see *drills*.

Board foot—Standard measure for selling lumber, equal to one inch thick, twelve inches wide, and twelve inches long.

Bonding—Materials combining processes that join solid materials by cohesively mixing their molecules or by adhesively gluing or cementing them.

Bonds—Similar to a loan, but a group of individuals provides the money instead of a bank.

Break-even analysis—Graphic or algebraic calculations to find the break-even point.

Break-even point—The number of products a company must sell to break even; no financial profit or loss is made.

Brittleness—The property that shows how easily a material can be broken by the force of a sudden impact.

Budget projections—Estimates of the expenses a manufacturing company should expect from making and selling the product.

Buffer inventory—Extra inventory sometimes kept on hand to cover problems and unforeseen shortages.

By-laws—Rules adopted for guiding the management of a company or corporation.

CAD—Computer-aided drafting; computer systems used by drafters to create technical drawings of product plans.

CAD/CAM—Computer-aided drafting/computer-aided manufacturing; CAD/CAM results when CAD systems in the engineering department and CAM systems in the production department are tied together.

CADD—Computer-aided drawing and design; systems used by engineers to draw, design, and test product plans on a computer.

CAM—Computer-aided manufacturing; tools and machines are controlled by computers.

Capital intensive—Manufacturing that is based on tools, machines, and equipment; particularly computerized and automated tools.

Carbon monoxide—A molecule containing one carbon atom and one oxygen atom. It is the product of incomplete combustion of carbon in fossil fuels.

Carrying capacity—The maximum ability of the region to support life in a healthy way.

Carrying charges—The cost to keep materials in inventory, including warehouse costs and warehouse workers' wages.

Casting and molding—Materials forming processes in which an industrial material is either melted, dissolved, or compounded into a liquid and allowed to flow by gravity into a hollow cavity of a desired shape.

Catalyst—A special material that is mixed with thermosetting plastic resins to create a chemical reaction that solidifies the resins into permanent shapes.

Ceramics—A classification of manufacturing materials that includes clays, pottery, china, porcelain, and glass.

Chemical refining—Processes that use chemicals to refine raw materials.

Chip removing—Materials separating processes that cut excess material or reduce the size of standard stock with special single and multiple point cutting tools. These processes create a loss of material in the form of chips.

Chisels—Tools with single, straight cutting edges; most commonly used as hand tools in working wood.

Chlorinated hydrocarbons—A subgroup of synthetic organic compounds that are particularly dangerous, including PCBs and dioxin.

CIM—Computer integrated manufacturing; a central computer system links the management, engineering, production, finances, marketing, and human resources departments in manufacturing.

Clamps—Tools used to hold parts during processing.

Cogeneration—An energy generating technique that uses one energy source to supply two or more energy applications.

Cohesive—A type of bonding process where heat, pressure, chemicals, or combinations of these are used to cause molecules of materials to cross a joint area and permanently mix or cohere.

Collective bargaining—The process used for creating satisfactory labor agreements.

Combining—All mixing, bonding, coating, and mechanical fastening processes that are used to finish one-piece products and put parts of multiple-piece products together in subassemblies and final product assemblies.

Communication skills—The ability to read and write, to listen and take instructions, and to learn new techniques and processes when technology changes.

Composite—A classification of manufacturing materials that are combinations of materials. Examples of composites are plywood and fiberglass.

Compression strength—The ability of a material to resist crushing or compressive forces.

Computer—A programmable machine that accepts, processes, and displays data.

Conditioning—Materials forming processes that use heat, mechanical pressure, or chemicals to change internal molecular structures and improve properties of materials such as hardness, toughness, ductility, and moisture content.

Consumer—Anyone who buys and uses manufactured products.

Consumer Protection Agency (CPA)—The federal agency that sets and enforces safety standards for products manufactured for consumers.

Continuous flow—The uninterrupted movement of materials and parts at a constant rate of speed along an assembly line.

Continuous manufacturing—The product is moved continuously along the production line, usually through the use of a conveyor system.

Continuous timing—A method of timing elements in which the timing device is started at the beginning of the job and allowed to run throughout.

Conversion coating—A type of coating process where the surface of a material is chemically changed using dyeing, oxide coating, or phosphate coating processes.

Conveyor system—A machine that moves materials and parts along an assembly line at a constant rate of speed.

Cooperative—A form of private ownership that gives workers part ownership of the company, as well as a voice in its operation and an equal share in its profits.

Cost-efficient—A product or process that is profitable to a manufacturing company because it makes good use of time and money.

Cottage industry—A manufacturing enterprise operated out of the home.

Credits—Money put into the company accounts.

Curbside recycling—Consumers separate materials (glass, aluminum, paper, and plastics) at their homes and place them in containers that are periodically collected and transported to a recycling station.

Custom manufacturing—One or just a few products are manufactured by a single person or several people who work on the products from beginning to end.

Cutters—Used to process materials to a certain thickness, to cut grooves, or to make special edges; they have two, three, or more cutting points.

Cycle time—The time between completing one product and completing the very next product.

Debits—Payments made to other people for expenses.

Deductions—Money subtracted from a worker's gross pay for items such as taxes, insurances, retirement contributions, and other items.

Deep well injection—Liquid hazardous wastes are pumped into wells and absorbed by a porous layer below; a major source of ground water contamination.

Degree of freedom—The number of ways a robot arm can move; more degrees of freedom means more movements.

Depreciate—To lessen in value, wear out, or fall behind in style.

Design criteria—A list of factors considered by the designer, including function, form, ergonomics, aesthetics, ease of manufacture, durability, and cost.

Design engineering—Creating ideas for products by drawing sketches, creating models and prototypes, and preparing working drawings.

Detail drawings—Orthographic drawings of the individual parts of a product, a part of the working drawings.

Die—Tool used to form materials; it has a metal surface with a shape matching the surface shape wanted on the finished piece of material.

Dielectric—A material that does not conduct electricity.

Digester—A device that breaks down organic wastes into an earthy brown matter called humus that is then used as a fertilizer.

Disposables—Goods manufactured to be used just once and then discarded.

Distribution—Marketing department division responsible for identifying the most economical and efficient way to transport the product to the consumer.

Diverse product line—Many different related or unrelated products manufactured by a single company.

Dividends—The money paid back to the stockholder out of the profits from the company.

Division of labor—A system of organizing people to work together that includes dividing work into simple tasks.

Downtime—Any time a machine is not operating when it should be.

Drills—Separating tools used to make round holes by removing chips from materials; see *bits*.

Ductility—A property that indicates how well a material can change shape (flow) without breaking as a result of stretching, compressing, twisting, or shearing forces.

Durable—Goods that are designed to last a long time and wear out slowly.

Earnings before interest and taxes (EBIT)—Equal to gross profits minus operating expenses found on the income statement.

Economic order quantity (EOQ)—The appropriate lot size for a manufactured product (determined by carrying charges and set-up costs).

Ecosystem—A grouping of plants, animals, and other living organisms interacting with each other and their environment in a symbiotic manner.

Efficiency rating—The percentage of energy output from an energy converter based on the amount of energy input to the converter. The formula for calculating efficiency is: OUTPUT ENERGY/INPUT ENERGY × 100.

Elasticity—The property that shows how well a material can withstand stretching, compressing, twisting, or shearing forces and still return to its original shape.

Electrical discharge machine (EDM)—A machine that uses an electric spark for accurate separation of metal materials.

Electrolyte—A liquid material that conducts electricity.

Employee Stock Ownership Plans (ESOPs)—A form of worker ownership created by the federal government that encourages corporations to give shares of stock to workers in return for tax breaks and investment privileges.

Energy—The ability to do work.

Energy conservation—Using energy wisely to avoid wasting it.

Energy consuming sectors—The categories of society that use energy; commercial, residential, transportation, and industrial sectors.

Energy converter—A device used to change energy from one form to another more usable form; the more common energy converters are generators, turbines, engines, and motors.

Engine—An energy converter used to change the thermal energy of burning gasoline or diesel fuel into the mechanical energy of rotary motion.

Entrepreneur—One who organizes a business undertaking, assuming a financial risk for the sake of future profits.

Environmentally soft manufacturing—Manufacturing that promotes a healthy natural environment and a healthy working environment.

Equal Employment Opportunity Act—Federal and state laws that require all employees and applicants to be treated fairly without regard to race, color, sex, age, marital status, religious belief, or national origin; protects workers and people looking for jobs from any type of discrimination.

Ergonomics—Designing systems for people; in the work place the focus is to improve the efficiency, safety, and well being of the worker.

Factory system—A form of organization for production that uses special buildings and machines for manufacturing.

Fatigue strength—The ability of a material to resist failure after repeated forces in opposite directions.

Feedback—The use of information about the output of a system to modify the system's output.

Ferrous—Metals that contain iron as the primary element.

Files—Hand tools with rows of cutting edges used to remove small amounts of metal, wood, or other materials.

Finances—A term used in business and industry to mean money.

Fission—The splitting of atomic nuclei.

Fixed costs—Manufacturing expenses that remain the same, or fixed, for a company no matter how many products it makes or sells. Fixed costs remain fixed for a limited time period.

Fixed position layout—Plant layout used to manufacture large structures, such as airplanes; also called static layout.

Fixtures—Tools attached to a machine and used to position a part being processed in a specific place on that machine.

Flexible manufacturing—The use of machining centers that let a company make many versions of the same product to meet specific consumer demands.

Flow process chart—Graphic display of the sequence of operations, transportations, inspections, delays, and storages performed on each part of one product.

Food and Drug Administration (FDA)—The federal agency whose job it is to test, approve, or ban pharmaceuticals.

Forming—All casting, molding, compressing, stretching, and conditioning processes that bring about internal and external form changes in metallic, ceramic, and polymeric materials.

Fossil fuels—Fuel that developed from millions of years of decay and pressure exerted on the fossils of plant and animal life.

Fracture—The point where a material breaks or separates when an excessive stretching (tensile), compressing, twisting (torsion), or shearing force is applied.

Free trade zones (FTZs)—Special locations for multinational corporations in host countries where local rules and regulations may not apply and where only foreign investors may locate.

Friction—The resistance to motion between two surfaces that are touching each other.

Fusion—Bring together, or merging, atomic nuclei.

Gages—Tools used to check sizes and dimensions on the parts of a product.

Gaia hypothesis—A modern scientific hypothesis that states that biological and chemical actions on earth affect the ability of the planet to support life.

General expenses budget—Includes wages for the management, finance, human resources, and engineering departments; utility expenses, insurance payments, and start-up costs.

General ledger—A form used by the finance department for recording all the financial transactions made by the company; similar to a checking account ledger.

Generator—An energy converter used to change mechanical energy into electrical energy.

Generic—Products that bear no trademark, are simply packaged, and generally less expensive.

Genetic engineering—Using gene-splicing and the cloning of genes to produce new life forms.

Global competition—Worldwide competition for manufactured goods, increased number of products being produced in small or developing countries.

Go-no go gage—Tool used during quality control inspections for measuring parts.

Greenhouse effect—Also known as the Carbon Dioxide Effect; carbon dioxide in the atmosphere lets sunlight pass through and strike the earth. This infrared energy radiates outward and is absorbed by the carbon dioxide. As the carbon dioxide absorbs the infrared radiation, the earth's atmosphere is warmed.

Grinding wheels—Used on power hand tools or machines called grinders; used primarily on metals.

Gross pay—A worker's pay before deductions are made; equal to the hourly wage rate multiplied by the number of hours the employee has worked.

Hard technology—Technology that is based on improving productivity and profits without considering the human, environmental, and social consequences; often equated with high technology.

Hardwood—A classification of wood that comes from deciduous trees with broad leaves, such as oak, cherry, and walnut.

Hazardous wastes—Materials that are explosive, flammable, corrosive, toxic, or that may cause long-term physiological problems.

Heavy metals—Serious pollutants emitted from the combustion of high octane gasoline and coal burning power plants. Common heavy metals include lead, mercury, arsenic, cadmium, zinc, and copper.

Hierarchical order—One type of management structure for manufacturing; headed by the CEO.

Hydraulics—A fluid power system that uses liquids, usually oil, under pressure to perform work.

Hydrocarbons—Materials that evaporate and enter the atmosphere in a vapor state including gasoline, paint solvents, and organic cleaning solutions.

Ideation—The stage in the design engineering process when the designer combines various bits of information learned during the preparation stage into new ideas.

Impact strength—The ability of a material to absorb energy during impacts, also called toughness.

Income statement—Report of the money made by a company over predetermined time periods, such as monthly, quarterly, or yearly; also called profit/loss statements.

Individual proprietorship—A business owned by one person.

Industrial materials—Raw materials that have been refined and converted into standard shapes, sizes, or weights by primary manufacturing companies.

Industrial Revolution—A period of tremendous industrial change that occurred in England between about 1750 and 1850.

Innovators—People who make an existing product better or combine several ideas to create a new and different product.

Input—In a manufacturing system, input includes all the resources needed to make a product such as tools, machines, materials, people and energy.

Interest—Money the company pays to a lender, such as a bank, for the privilege of borrowing money.

Intermittent manufacturing—This type of manufacturing processes products in limited numbers.

Inventors—People who create or discover new ideas or products, called inventions.

Inventory control—The steps taken to maintain proper levels of raw materials and finished goods.

Investors—Lending institutions such as banks, or individuals with an interest in a company and money they are willing to invest in it.

Invoice—A sales bill sent to the purchasing department by the vendor; identifies price and other specifications.

Jigs—Special tools used to guide the paths of other tools on a part being processed.

Jobbing—See *intermittent manufacturing.*

Job lot—See *intermittent manufacturing.*

Job rotation—Line workers may rotate, or change jobs, on an hourly, daily, or monthly basis to make work more interesting.

Joint—A point of contact between solid materials or parts of a product that are being combined by bonding or mechanical fastening processes.

Just-In-Time (JIT) manufacturing—A system that can be applied to continuous, intermittent, and custom manufacturing that manufactures and delivers products just in time to be sold.

Kanban—A Japanese inventory replenishment system developed by Toyota (similar to JIT manufacturing).

Kilowatt—Equal to 1,000 watts.

Kilowatt hours—The number of hours that an electrical device is used over a period of time. The formula for calculating Kilowatt hours is KILOWATT HOURS = KILOWATTS × HOURS OF USE.

Labor estimate—An estimate of the number of workers needed to produce the product, the total worker time spent making one product, and the total cost for production labor wages.

Labor relations—The conditions of employment arranged between employers and groups of employees.

Labor union—Organizations for workers that obtain and protect the workers' rights.

Laser—Light Amplification by Stimulated Emission of Radiation. A tool that amplifies and intensifies light into a narrow beam that can melt and vaporize material.

Lathe—Machine used to add threads to or to cut cylinder-shaped objects to size.

Laws of probability—The idea that a random sampling of observations of an event will follow the same pattern as a lengthy, continuous observation of the same event.

Levitator—A system for processing materials in the space environment without containers like crucibles; will use acoustical, magnetic, or electrical energy to raise materials.

Liabilities—The value of everything the company owes to other companies and businesses. Liabilities are claims made against the assets of the company by non-company owners.

Limited (nonrenewable) energy sources—Sources of energy that will eventually be completely consumed; primarily coal, petroleum, natural gas, and uranium.

Loan—Money given to a company on a temporary basis. For the privilege of borrowing the money, the corporation must pay interest on the loan.

Lots—The specific number of products made when manufactured intermittently.

Malleability—The ability of a material to be pounded, rolled, and formed into sheets.

Manufacturing engineering—Planning the layout of tools, machines, and people on a production line including plant layout, materials handling, and tooling.

Market research—Research done to determine who is likely to buy a product.

Mass distribution—Products that are widely marketed, perhaps in stores across the nation or even worldwide.

Mass media—Any medium used in advertising that is likely to reach a large group of people. Examples of mass media are television, radio, newspapers, and magazines.

Mass production—Another term for continuous manufacturing; the product is moved along the production line continuously.

Master budget—Combines and summarizes the sales projections, production expenses, selling expenses, and general expenses budgets in one document.

Materials flowcharts—Drawings of the plant layout, also called flow diagrams.

Materials handling—The transportation systems used to move materials, supplies, and work in progress through a plant.

Materials requirements planning (MRP)—A technique used to aid in the ordering of raw materials, parts, and sub-assemblies.

Mechanical advantage (MAf)—An increase in a force.

Mechanical energy—The energy found in moving objects, such as a rotating saw blade or a turning drill bit.

Mechanical fastening—Materials combining processes that use threaded (screws, nuts, bolts, clamps) or non-threaded (fabric thread, pins, nails, straps) devices to create a physical force that holds materials together.

Mechanical refining—Processes that use mechanical forces to refine raw materials.

Metal shaper—A machine used to cut straight and angular surfaces, such as keyways and slots in metal.

Metallic—A classification of manufacturing materials that includes metals, such as iron, steel, and aluminum.

Methods engineering—Planning the sequence of processes needed to make parts and assemble a finished product.

Microgravity—The very small amount of gravity found in the space environment. Microgravity is the key to manufacturing improved products in space.

Micrometer—Tool used for accurate measurements to a thousandth of an inch on precision parts.

Microspheres—Tiny plastic beads $1/2,500$ of an inch in diameter (about $1/40$ the diameter of an average human hair); first products ever manufactured in space.

Mixing—Materials combining processes that evenly spread molecules of gas, droplets of liquid, particles of solid materials, or combinations of gases, liquids, or solids throughout the mixture.

Mock-up—A scale model of the finished product, usually made from easily worked materials, such as cardboard or clay.

Molding—See *casting.*

Motor—An energy converter used to change electrical energy into rotary mechanical energy.

Multinational corporation—A corporation that has operations in several different countries.

Net pay—The amount of a worker's pay after all deductions have been subtracted.

Net worth—Total company assets minus total liabilities.

Nitrogen oxide—Formed when air is used during the combustion process, this pollutant absorbs light and is responsible for the brownish color of smog.

Nondurable—Manufactured goods that are destroyed by use, or shortly after use.

Nonferrous—Metals that contain little or no iron.

Nonpoint source pollution—Used to describe pollution that cannot be traced back to a single source.

Occupational Safety and Health Administration (OSHA)—The federal agency that makes and enforces safety standards in the workplace.

One-touch set-up—Another term for single set-up.

Operation process chart—A graphic display of the operations and inspections performed on each part of a product.

Operation sheet—Details the work to be done at each work station in a manufacturing line.

Output—The actual result, or product, obtained from a system.

Oxyacetylene torch—The most common flame cutting tool; it can produce flames with temperatures higher than 6,000° F.

Ozone—An indirect product of combustion, formed as a result of chemical reactions between nitrogen oxides and hydrocarbons where sunlight causes the reaction to occur.

Ozone layer depletion—A layer in the stratosphere, important to all life because it screens out dangerous ultraviolet radiation, being depleted by certain pollutants.

Particulates—A form of air pollution consisting of tiny particles (usually carbon) that are emitted during combustion processes.

Partnership—Two or more people who share, or co-own, a business.

pH—A measurement of the acid/base content of a substance.

Pharmaceuticals—Medicinal drugs.

Photosynthesis—Production of organic substances, like sugar, from carbon dioxide and water by the action of light on chlorophyll in green plants.

Physical coating—A type of coating process where a thin layer of a coating material is applied to the surface of another material using a brushing, rolling, dipping, spraying, plating, or printing process.

Pilot run—A practice session during tooling up when the manufacturing system is tested to make sure all systems work as planned.

Planned (or built-in) obsolescence—A technique of designing products or product parts to wear out or break down after so many months or years.

Plastic deformation—A permanent change in the shape of a material that has been stretched, compressed, twisted, or sheared beyond its elastic limit, but has not fractured.

Pliers—Hand tools used to hold small parts.

Pneumatics—A fluid power system that uses air under pressure to do work.

Pollution—Outputs of the manufacturing processes`, and other processes, that cause physical changes to air, water, or land that are harmful to living things.

Polymeric—A classification of manufacturing materials that includes natural polymers like wood and rubber, and synthetic polymers like plastics.

Polymerize—A process that uses heat and pressure to produce plastic materials.

Precision measurement—A characteristic of mass production referring to the exactness of measurement to at least $1/1,000$ of an inch.

Primary manufacturing—Manufacturing processes that obtain raw materials, refine raw materials, and convert raw materials into standard forms of industrial materials.

Problem-solving—Using skills to gain an in-depth understanding of a problem and using appropriate techniques to solve the problem.

Process—Any kind of doing or action that is performed to provide an outcome.

Process layout—Plant layout where machines and tools used to perform similar processes are grouped together.

Product layout—Plant layout that creates a continuous flow from raw materials to finished product.

Product planning—Ensures that new products are added, old ones discontinued, and questionable ones changed (based on market research).

Product service—Important to the long-term success of a company, product service may include proper installation and long-term maintenance agreements.

Production control—Ensuring the optimum use of workers, materials, and machines to meet customer orders and delivery schedules.

Production expenses budget—The money spent to actually manufacture a product.

Productivity—A measure of manufacturing efficiency, productivity is found by dividing the number of products manufactured by some unit of time, usually worker hour.

Profit—The money left over after a product is sold and all the inputs are paid for (all expenses have been paid).

Profitable—A company that makes money on the products it makes and sells.

Profit/loss statements—A report of how much money the company made (profit) or lost (loss) during a certain time period. This statement is also called an income statement.

Prototype—A fully functional, full-size model of the product.

Proxy—A declaration signed by stockholders, letting the management vote and make decisions as they see fit.

Public relations—How a company is viewed by and deals with the public.

Pump—A device used to pressurize air or liquids; important for hydraulic and pneumatic power systems.

Punches—Tools used to punch out or shear materials.

Purchase order—Gives the vendor permission to send materials being bought by the purchasing department.

Purchase requisition—A request for vendors to supply bids and quotes on items the purchasing department will buy for a manufacturing company; identifies quality, quantity, and delivery time specifications.

Purchasing—Branch of the finance department responsible for buying the needed inputs.

QC circles—Groups of workers who meet on a regular basis to discuss and solve quality problems.

Quality control—The activities carried out to meet the quality objectives set for products.

Quote—A price that is not guaranteed by the vendor.

Radiant energy—Also called electromagnetic energy, radiant energy is visible and invisible light energy.

Raw materials—Metal, ceramic, or polymer (plant and animal) materials obtained from air, earth, or water before they are converted into industrial materials by primary manufacturing companies.

Recycling—Reprocessing scrap materials to make new materials.

Renderings—Comprehensive sketches that show the finished product with all details included.

Renewable energy sources—Sources of energy that can be replaced or renewed, given enough time.

Repetitive manufacturing—Another term for continuous manufacturing; the product is moved continuously along the production line.

Repetitive timing—A method of timing elements in which the timing device is started at the beginning and stopped at the end of each element.

Representative group—A group of people that represents the targeted consumer group.

Research and Development—The process of developing prototypes for new products; workers in the engineering department perform R&D.

Robot—A reprogrammable multifunctional manipulator designed to move material, parts, tools, or specialized devices through variable programmed motions for the performance of a variety of tasks. (Robot Institute of America).

Rolls—Tools used to form metal into desired shapes.

Sales forecast—Based on information from market research, sales forecasts are usually projected for a year and then broken into quarters, months, and weeks.

Sales projections budget—An estimate of the number of products the market researchers expect the company to sell.

Saw blades—Tools used to separate materials along straight or curved lines.

Scrap—An output of the manufacturing process that cannot easily or economically be reused.

Secondary manufacturing—Manufacturing processes that use forming, separating, and combining processes to convert standard industrial materials into finished products that can be purchased by consumers in local stores.

Secured landfills—Landfills that are properly lined and covered with a means to remove drainage.

Selling expenses budget—Includes advertising costs, transporting the product to the consumer, and commissions for sales workers.

Separating—Processes that cut down the size of materials by removing excess material.

Set-up—The term used to describe all the activities necessary to prepare and organize the tools, machines and materials for manufacturing a product.

Shearing—Materials separating processes that cut excess material or reduce the size of standard stock with blades, punches, dies, or rotary cutters with no loss of material.

Shear plane—The exact place where a chip is formed and separated from a material by a cutting tool during a chip removing materials separating processes.

Simulation—A broad term describing various forecasting techniques, such as role-playing, modeling, and gaming.

Single set-up—A tooling change that takes one minute or less.

Skilled workers—Get the production facility ready to manufacture the product by designing and making specialized tools, jigs and fixtures, and quality control devices.

Smog—The combination of smoke and fog that has resulted from the combustion of fossil fuels.

Soft technology—Technology that considers the impacts of technology on people, the environment and society as it considers productivity and profits. Soft technology is also called appropriate technology.

Software—The set of coded instructions written to control the operations of the computer.

Softwood—Classification of wood that comes from coniferous trees that bear cones, such as pines and firs.

Source separation—Consumers separate their wastes at home.

Specialization—A stage in the development of manufacturing during which manufacturers gained expertise in a particular trade.

Standardization—A characteristic of mass production, closely related to precision measurement, that produces standardized parts.

Standard of living—A term used to describe the quality of life; one variable is the availability of manufactured goods.

Standard stock—Common shapes, sizes, or weights that industrial materials are produced for convenient use by consumers. Examples include plywood sheets; lumber boards; steel coils, sheets, bars, or pipes; plastic sheets, pellets, or powder; and bolts of fabric.

Statisticians—Marketing workers who compile statistics from consumer surveys.

Stock—Certificate that represents ownership in a corporation.

Stockholder equity—The claim made against company assets by the actual owners of the company—the stockholders. Stockholder equity equals the value of stock issued by the company.

Stockholders—Individuals who invest in a company by buying stocks.

Stockless production—Another name for JIT manufacturing.

Stretching—Materials forming processes that use tensile force to pull materials into desired shapes.

Subsystem—A system that works with other subsystems to help a larger system function.

Sulfur oxides—Fuels and some trash contain impurities in the form of sulfur which when combusted is emitted as exhaust.

Superalloy—Alloys created in space that can not be combined on earth; they will have superior qualities.

Supervisors—Management workers who make sure workers in their departments carry out the policies established by the upper-level managers.

Surface impoundments—Large amounts of water that carry small amounts of waste are discharged into a sealed pit where the water evaporates and wastes settle and accumulate.

Survey—A marketing tool used to gather specific information needed to predict product sales. Surveys are usually conducted over the telephone.

Synchronization—A characteristic of mass production that plans for tools, machines, materials, workers, and actions to be in the right place at the right time.

Synthetic organic chemicals—The basis of all plastics, synthetic fibers, resins, drugs, pesticides, detergents, solvents, and many other products.

System—A way to organize information to make it easier to understand and remember.

Technician—A skilled and experienced design or production worker; examples include drafters, designers, and machinists.

Technological literacy—The ability to understand how technology works, to adapt to changes in work created by new technologies, and to understand how using new technologies will affect people, society, and the environment.

Technologist—The term is used today to mean technician.

Technology—The use of acquired knowledge to process resources to satisfy human needs and wants.

Technology transfer—The transfer of knowledge about tools, machines, materials, and processes used in communication, transportation, production, and energy systems.

Tensile strength—Property of a material to resist being pulled apart.

Thermal energy—Heat generated by the movement of molecules in materials.

Thermal refining—Processes that use heat to refine raw materials.

Thermoplastics—Plastics that can be reheated and reshaped.

Thermosets—Plastics that cannot be reheated and reshaped.

Thumbnail sketches—Small sketches or doodles the designer uses to record any ideas on paper; also called rough sketches.

Time-motion studies—A technique for finding the most efficient way to complete tasks.

Time study—Measuring the amount of time needed to do a job.

Tool—A device used to extend human capabilities in performing the work of processing (changing) materials or information.

Tooling—The special tools and devices that help production workers make product parts of consistent size, shape, and quality.

Torsion—A force that twists materials.

Toughness—A property that shows the ability of a material to be hard but not brittle.

Transfer station sorting—Consumer waste is collected and brought to a transfer station where it is sorted according to recyclable materials.

Trend—The direction or tendency of recent events in society.

Turbine—An energy converter used to change the mechanical energy of wind, water, or steam into rotary mechanical energy; wind mills and water wheels are examples.

Unemployment compensation insurance—Money deducted from a worker's pay and used to pay back the worker in the event of a future layoff.

Unit costs—The costs to manufacture each product or unit; variable costs are given in unit costs.

Unlimited energy sources—Sources of energy that are expected to be available forever.

Variable costs—Manufacturing expenses that increase or decrease with the quantity of products manufactured.

Vendor—A company that sells needed inputs to the manufacturing company; also called a supplier.

Verification—The stage in the design engineering process when the designer makes sure the product design actually works as intended by testing prototypes.

Viscosity—A property that describes how well liquid materials flow and mix together. Thick liquids have high viscosity and do not flow and mix well, while thin liquids have low viscosity and do flow and mix well.

Wage incentive—A work measurement wage incentive increases a worker's pay for meeting or beating the standard (average) time for an operation.

Waste—Post-consumer outputs that are thrown away rather than reused or recycled.

Watts—A measure of the total amount of electrical energy used by a machine or other electrical device. The formula for calculating watts is: WATTS = VOLTS × AMPS.

Work envelope—The area in which the robot can reach and work.

Working drawings—A set of drawings and plans that include all the size, shape, and manufacturing information needed by the production department; includes detail and assembly drawings.

Work measurement—The study of the efficiency of workers doing their job (time involved versus the cost to manufacture the product).

Workstation—Places in a production line where operations occur, such as machines and benches.

INDEX